Honda Accord Automotive Repair Manual

by Colin Brown, Larry Warren and John H Haynes

Member of the Guild of Motoring Writers

Models covered:
All Honda Accord models
1984 through 1989

(9A14 - 42011)
(1221)

ABCDE
FG.

2

Haynes Publishing Group
Sparkford Nr Yeovil
Somerset BA22 7JJ England

Haynes North America, Inc
861 Lawrence Drive
Newbury Park
California 91320 USA

Acknowledgements

Technical writers who contributed to this project include Mike Stubblefield, Ken Freund and Bob Henderson.

A book in the Haynes Automotive Repair Manual Series

Printed in the U.S.A.

ISBN 1 85010 615 0

Library of Congress Catalog Card Number 89-85322

98-256

Contents

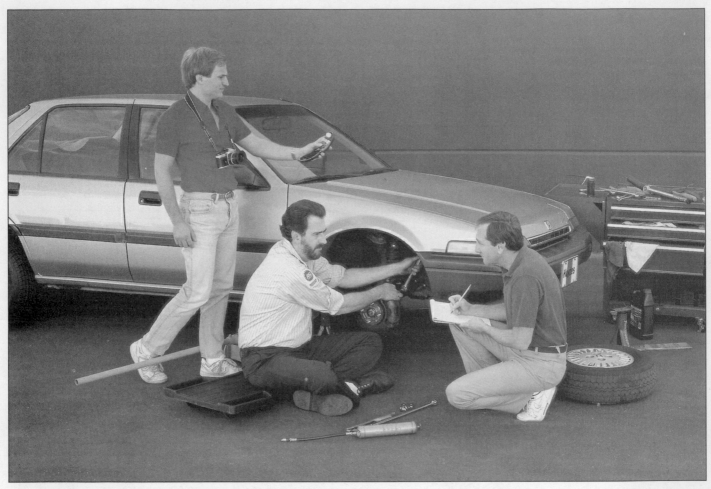

Haynes photographer, mechanic and author with Honda Accord DX

Introduction to the Honda Accord

Honda Accord models are available in two-door coupe and liftback and four-door sedan body styles.

The transversely mounted inline four-cylinder engines used in these models are equipped with either a carburetor or port-type fuel injection. Some models feature three valves per cylinder.

The engine drives the front wheels through either a five-speed manual or four-speed automatic transaxle via independent driveaxles.

Independent suspension, featuring coil spring/strut units, is used on all four wheels.

The power-assisted rack and pinion steering is mounted behind the engine.

The brakes are power assisted with discs at the front and drums or discs (on some later models) at the rear.

About this manual

Its purpose

The purpose of this manual is to help you get the best value from your vehicle. It can do so in several ways. It can help you decide what work must be done, even if you choose to have it done by a dealer service department or a repair shop; it provides information and procedures for routine maintenance and servicing; and it offers diagnostic and repair procedures to follow when trouble occurs.

We hope you use the manual to tackle the work yourself. For many simpler jobs, doing it yourself may be quicker than arranging an appointment to get the vehicle into a shop and making the trips to leave it and pick it up. More importantly, a lot of money can be saved by avoiding the expense the shop must pass on to you to cover its labor and overhead costs. An added benefit is the sense of satisfaction and accomplishment that you feel after doing the job yourself.

Using the manual

The manual is divided into Chapters. Each Chapter is divided into numbered Sections, which are headed in bold type between horizontal lines. Each Section consists of consecutively numbered paragraphs.

At the beginning of each numbered Section you will be referred to any illustrations which apply to the procedures in that Section. The reference numbers used in illustration captions pinpoint the pertinent Section and the Step within that Section. That is, illustration 3.2 means the illustration refers to Section 3 and Step (or paragraph) 2 within that Section.

Procedures, once described in the text, are not normally repeated. When it's necessary to refer to another Chapter, the reference will be given as Chapter and Section number. Cross references given without use of the word "Chapter" apply to Sections and/or paragraphs in the same Chapter. For example, "see Section 8" means in the same Chapter.

References to the left or right side of the vehicle assume you are sitting in the driver's seat, facing forward.

Even though we have prepared this manual with extreme care, neither the publisher nor the author can accept responsibility for any errors in, or omissions from, the information given.

NOTE

A **Note** provides information necessary to properly complete a procedure or information which will make the procedure easier to understand.

CAUTION

A **Caution** provides a special procedure or special steps which must be taken while completing the procedure where the Caution is found. Not heeding a Caution can result in damage to the assembly being worked on.

WARNING

A **Warning** provides a special procedure or special steps which must be taken while completing the procedure where the Warning is found. Not heeding a Warning can result in personal injury.

Vehicle identification numbers

Modifications are a continuing and unpublicized process in vehicle manufacturing. Since spare parts manuals and lists are compiled on a numerical basis, the individual vehicle numbers are essential to correctly identify the component required.

Number locations

A   The Vehicle Identification Number (VIN) (visible through the drivers side of the windshield from outside the vehicle)
B   VIN (firewall location)
C   Engine number (1984 and 1985 models)
D   Transaxle number
E   Engine number

Vehicle Identification Number (VIN)

This very important identification number is stamped on a plate attached to the left side cowling just inside the windshield on the driver's side of the vehicle as well as on the firewall **(see illustration)**. The VIN also appears on the Vehicle Certificate of Title and Registration. It contains information such as where and when the vehicle was manufactured, the model year and the body style.

Engine number

The engine number is stamped on the right side of the engine block just below the cylinder head and is also located on a tag on the left inner fender (later models) or the left front door pillar (earlier models).

Transaxle number

The transaxle number is stamped on the top of the transaxle housing and is visible in the engine compartment.

Buying parts

Replacement parts are available from many sources, which generally fall into one of two categories - authorized dealer parts departments and independent retail auto parts stores. Our advice concerning these parts is as follows:

Retail auto parts stores: Good auto parts stores will stock frequently needed components which wear out relatively fast, such as clutch components, exhaust systems, brake parts, tune-up parts, etc. These stores often supply new or reconditioned parts on an exchange basis, which can save a considerable amount of money. Discount auto parts stores are often very good places to buy materials and parts needed for general vehicle maintenance such as oil, grease, filters, spark plugs, belts, touch-up paint, bulbs, etc. They also usually sell tools and general accessories, have convenient hours, charge lower prices and can often be found not far from home.

Authorized dealer parts department: This is the best source for parts which are unique to the vehicle and not generally available elsewhere (such as major engine parts, transmission parts, trim pieces, etc.).

Warranty information: If the vehicle is still covered under warranty, be sure that any replacement parts purchased - regardless of the source - do not invalidate the warranty!

To be sure of obtaining the correct parts, have engine and chassis numbers available and, if possible, take the old parts along for positive identification.

Maintenance techniques, tools and working facilities

Maintenance techniques

There are a number of techniques involved in maintenance and repair that will be referred to throughout this manual. Application of these techniques will enable the home mechanic to be more efficient, better organized and capable of performing the various tasks properly, which will ensure that the repair job is thorough and complete.

Fasteners

Fasteners are nuts, bolts, studs and screws used to hold two or more parts together. There are a few things to keep in mind when working with fasteners. Almost all of them use a locking device of some type, either a lockwasher, locknut, locking tab or thread adhesive. All threaded fasteners should be clean and straight, with undamaged threads and undamaged corners on the hex head where the wrench fits. Develop the habit of replacing all damaged nuts and bolts with new ones. Special locknuts with nylon or fiber inserts can only be used once. If they are removed, they lose their locking ability and must be replaced with new ones.

Rusted nuts and bolts should be treated with a penetrating fluid to ease removal and prevent breakage. Some mechanics use turpentine in a spout-type oil can, which works quite well. After applying the rust penetrant, let it work for a few minutes before trying to loosen the nut or bolt. Badly rusted fasteners may have to be chiseled or sawed off or removed with a special nut breaker, available at tool stores.

If a bolt or stud breaks off in an assembly, it can be drilled and removed with a special tool commonly available for this purpose. Most automotive machine shops can perform this task, as well as other repair procedures, such as the repair of threaded holes that have been stripped out.

Flat washers and lockwashers, when removed from an assembly, should always be replaced exactly as removed. Replace any damaged washers with new ones. Never use a lockwasher on any soft metal surface (such as aluminum), thin sheet metal or plastic.

Fastener sizes

For a number of reasons, automobile manufacturers are making wider and wider use of metric fasteners. Therefore, it is important to be able to tell the difference between standard (sometimes called U.S. or SAE) and metric hardware, since they cannot be interchanged.

All bolts, whether standard or metric, are sized according to diameter, thread pitch and length. For example, a standard 1/2 - 13 x 1 bolt is 1/2 inch in diameter, has 13 threads per inch and is 1 inch long. An M12 - 1.75 x 25 metric bolt is 12 mm in diameter, has a thread pitch of 1.75 mm (the distance between threads) and is 25 mm long. The two bolts are nearly identical, and easily confused, but they are not interchangeable.

In addition to the differences in diameter, thread pitch and length, metric and standard bolts can also be distinguished by examining the bolt heads. To begin with, the distance across the flats on a standard bolt head is measured in inches, while the same dimension on a metric bolt is sized in millimeters (the same is true for nuts). As a result, a standard wrench should not be used on a metric bolt and a metric wrench should not be used on a standard bolt. Also, most standard bolts have slashes radiating out from the center of the head to denote the grade or strength of the bolt, which is an indication of the amount of torque that can be applied to it. The greater the number of slashes, the greater the strength of the bolt. Grades 0 through 5 are commonly used on automobiles. Metric bolts have a property class (grade) number, rather than a slash, molded into their heads to indicate bolt strength. In this case, the higher the number, the stronger the bolt. Property class numbers 8.8, 9.8 and 10.9 are commonly used on automobiles.

Strength markings can also be used to distinguish standard hex nuts from metric hex nuts. Many standard nuts have dots stamped into one side, while metric nuts are marked with a number. The greater the number of dots, or the higher the number, the greater the strength of the nut.

Metric studs are also marked on their ends according to property class (grade). Larger studs are numbered (the same as metric bolts), while smaller studs carry a geometric code to denote grade.

It should be noted that many fasteners, especially Grades 0 through 2, have no distinguishing marks on them. When such is the case, the only way to determine whether it is standard or metric is to measure the thread pitch or compare it to a known fastener of the same size.

Standard fasteners are often referred to as SAE, as opposed to metric. However, it should be noted that SAE technically refers to a non-metric fine thread fastener only. Coarse thread non-metric fasteners are referred to as USS sizes.

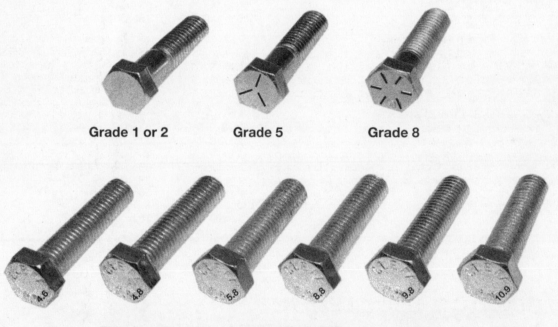

Grade 1 or 2   Grade 5   Grade 8

Bolt strength marking (standard/SAE/USS; bottom - metric)

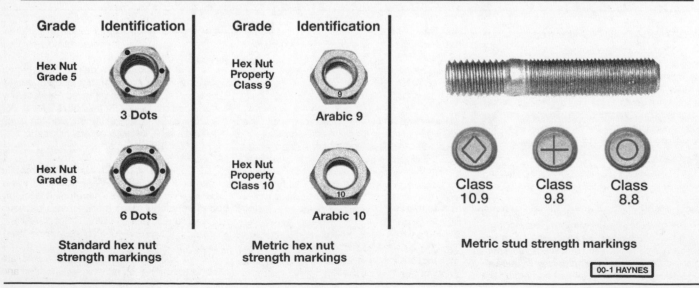

Grade	Identification	Grade	Identification
Hex Nut Grade 5	3 Dots	Hex Nut Property Class 9	Arabic 9
Hex Nut Grade 8	6 Dots	Hex Nut Property Class 10	Arabic 10

Class 10.9   Class 9.8   Class 8.8

Standard hex nut strength markings

Metric hex nut strength markings

Metric stud strength markings

Since fasteners of the same size (both standard and metric) may have different strength ratings, be sure to reinstall any bolts, studs or nuts removed from your vehicle in their original locations. Also, when replacing a fastener with a new one, make sure that the new one has a strength rating equal to or greater than the original.

Tightening sequences and procedures

Most threaded fasteners should be tightened to a specific torque value (torque is the twisting force applied to a threaded component such as a nut or bolt). Overtightening the fastener can weaken it and cause it to break, while undertightening can cause it to eventually come loose. Bolts, screws and studs, depending on the material they are made of and their thread diameters, have specific torque values, many of which are noted in the Specifications at the beginning of each Chapter. Be sure to follow the torque recommendations closely. For fasteners not assigned a specific torque, a general torque value chart is presented here as a guide. These torque values are for dry (unlubricated) fasteners threaded into steel or cast iron (not aluminum). As was previously mentioned, the size and grade of a fastener determine the amount of torque that can safely be applied to it. The figures listed here are approximate for Grade 2 and Grade 3 fasteners. Higher grades can tolerate higher torque values.

Fasteners laid out in a pattern, such as cylinder head bolts, oil pan bolts, differential cover bolts, etc., must be loosened or tightened in sequence to avoid warping the component. This sequence will normally be shown in the appropriate Chapter. If a specific pattern is not given, the following procedures can be used to prevent warping.

Metric thread sizes	Ft-lbs	Nm
M-6	6 to 9	9 to 12
M-8	14 to 21	19 to 28
M-10	28 to 40	38 to 54
M-12	50 to 71	68 to 96
M-14	80 to 140	109 to 154
Pipe thread sizes		
1/8	5 to 8	7 to 10
1/4	12 to 18	17 to 24
3/8	22 to 33	30 to 44
1/2	25 to 35	34 to 47
U.S. thread sizes		
1/4 - 20	6 to 9	9 to 12
5/16 - 18	12 to 18	17 to 24
5/16 - 24	14 to 20	19 to 27
3/8 - 16	22 to 32	30 to 43
3/8 - 24	27 to 38	37 to 51
7/16 - 14	40 to 55	55 to 74
7/16 - 20	40 to 60	55 to 81
1/2 - 13	55 to 80	75 to 108

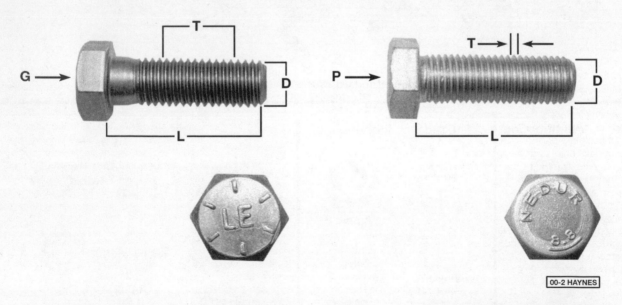

00-2 HAYNES

Standard (SAE and USS) bolt dimensions/grade marks

G   Grade marks (bolt strength)
L   Length (in inches)
T   Thread pitch (number of threads per inch)
D   Nominal diameter (in inches)

Metric bolt dimensions/grade marks

P   Property class (bolt strength)
L   Length (in millimeters)
T   Thread pitch (distance between threads in millimeters)
D   Diameter

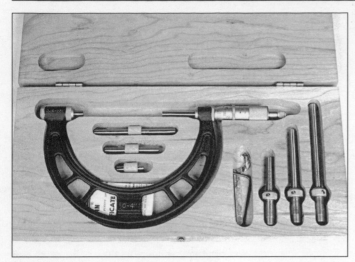

Micrometer set

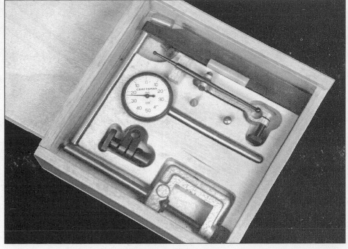

Dial indicator set

Initially, the bolts or nuts should be assembled finger-tight only. Next, they should be tightened one full turn each, in a criss-cross or diagonal pattern. After each one has been tightened one full turn, return to the first one and tighten them all one-half turn, following the same pattern. Finally, tighten each of them one-quarter turn at a time until each fastener has been tightened to the proper torque. To loosen and remove the fasteners, the procedure would be reversed.

Component disassembly

Component disassembly should be done with care and purpose to help ensure that the parts go back together properly. Always keep track of the sequence in which parts are removed. Make note of special characteristics or marks on parts that can be installed more than one way, such as a grooved thrust washer on a shaft. It is a good idea to lay the disassembled parts out on a clean surface in the order that they were removed. It may also be helpful to make sketches or take instant photos of components before removal.

When removing fasteners from a component, keep track of their locations. Sometimes threading a bolt back in a part, or putting the washers and nut back on a stud, can prevent mix-ups later. If nuts and bolts cannot be returned to their original locations, they should be kept in a compartmented box or a series of small boxes. A cupcake or muffin tin is ideal for this purpose, since each cavity can hold the bolts and nuts from a particular area (i.e. oil pan bolts, valve cover bolts, engine mount bolts, etc.). A pan of this type is especially helpful when working on assemblies with very small parts, such as the carburetor, alternator, valve train or interior dash and trim pieces. The cavities can be marked with paint or tape to identify the contents.

Whenever wiring looms, harnesses or connectors are separated, it is a good idea to identify the two halves with numbered pieces of masking tape so they can be easily reconnected.

Gasket sealing surfaces

Throughout any vehicle, gaskets are used to seal the mating surfaces between two parts and keep lubricants, fluids, vacuum or pressure contained in an assembly.

Many times these gaskets are coated with a liquid or paste-type gasket sealing compound before assembly. Age, heat and pressure can sometimes cause the two parts to stick together so tightly that they are very difficult to separate. Often, the assembly can be loosened by striking it with a soft-face hammer near the mating surfaces. A regular hammer can be used if a block of wood is placed between the hammer and the part. Do not hammer on cast parts or parts that could be easily damaged. With any particularly stubborn part, always recheck to make sure that every fastener has been removed.

Avoid using a screwdriver or bar to pry apart an assembly, as they can easily mar the gasket sealing surfaces of the parts, which must remain smooth. If prying is absolutely necessary, use an old broom handle, but keep in mind that extra clean up will be necessary if the wood splinters.

After the parts are separated, the old gasket must be carefully scraped off and the gasket surfaces cleaned. Stubborn gasket material can be soaked with rust penetrant or treated with a special chemical to soften it so it can be easily scraped off. A scraper can be fashioned from a piece of copper tubing by flattening and sharpening one end. Copper is recommended because it is usually softer than the surfaces to be scraped, which reduces the chance of gouging the part. Some gaskets can be removed with a wire brush, but regardless of the method used, the mating surfaces must be left clean and smooth. If for some reason the gasket surface is gouged, then a gasket sealer thick enough to fill scratches will have to be used during reassembly of the components. For most applications, a non-drying (or semi-drying) gasket sealer should be used.

Hose removal tips

Warning: *If the vehicle is equipped with air conditioning, do not disconnect any of the A/C hoses without first having the system depressurized by a dealer service department or a service station.*

Hose removal precautions closely parallel gasket removal precautions. Avoid scratching or gouging the surface that the hose mates against or the connection may leak. This is especially true for radiator hoses. Because of various chemical reactions, the rubber in hoses can bond itself to the metal spigot that the hose fits over. To remove a hose, first loosen the hose clamps that secure it to the spigot. Then, with slip-joint pliers, grab the hose at the clamp and rotate it around the spigot. Work it back and forth until it is completely free, then pull it off. Silicone or other lubricants will ease removal if they can be applied between the hose and the outside of the spigot. Apply the same lubricant to the inside of the hose and the outside of the spigot to simplify installation.

As a last resort (and if the hose is to be replaced with a new one anyway), the rubber can be slit with a knife and the hose peeled from the spigot. If this must be done, be careful that the metal connection is not damaged.

If a hose clamp is broken or damaged, do not reuse it. Wire-type clamps usually weaken with age, so it is a good idea to replace them with screw-type clamps whenever a hose is removed.

Tools

A selection of good tools is a basic requirement for anyone who plans to maintain and repair his or her own vehicle. For the owner who has few tools, the initial investment might seem high, but when compared to the spiraling costs of professional auto maintenance and repair, it is a wise one.

To help the owner decide which tools are needed to perform the tasks detailed in this manual, the following tool lists are offered: *Maintenance and minor repair,*

Dial caliper

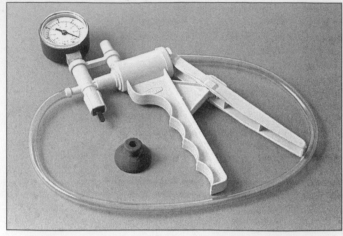

Hand-operated vacuum pump

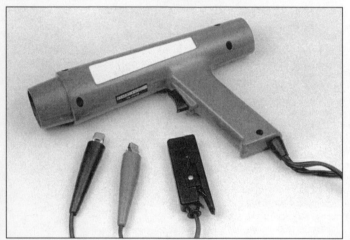

Timing light

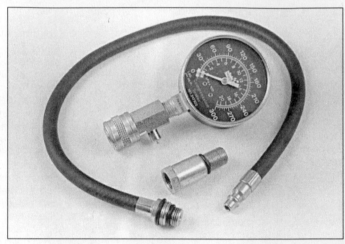

Compression gauge with spark plug hole adapter

Damper/steering wheel puller

General purpose puller

Hydraulic lifter removal tool

Repair/overhaul and *Special.*

The newcomer to practical mechanics should start off with the *maintenance and minor repair* tool kit, which is adequate for the simpler jobs performed on a vehicle. Then, as confidence and experience grow, the owner can tackle more difficult tasks, buying additional tools as they are needed.

Eventually the basic kit will be expanded into the *repair and overhaul* tool set. Over a period of time, the experienced do-it-yourselfer will assemble a tool set complete enough for most repair and overhaul procedures and will add tools from the special category when it is felt that the expense is justified by the frequency of use.

Maintenance and minor repair tool kit

The tools in this list should be considered the minimum required for performance of routine maintenance, servicing and minor repair work. We recommend the purchase of combination wrenches (box-end and open-

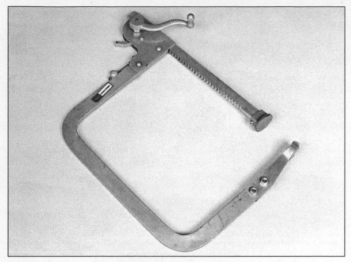

Valve spring compressor

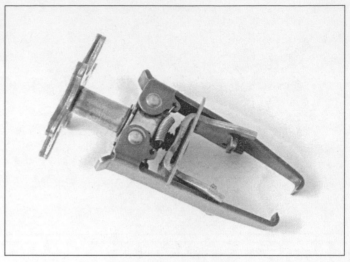

Valve spring compressor

Ridge reamer

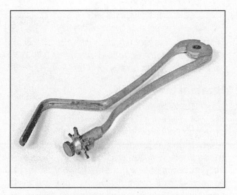

Piston ring groove cleaning tool

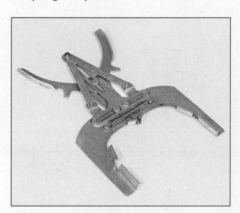

Ring removal/installation tool

end combined in one wrench). While more expensive than open end wrenches, they offer the advantages of both types of wrench.

> Combination wrench set (1/4-inch to
>   1 inch or 6 mm to 19 mm)
> Adjustable wrench, 8 inch
> Spark plug wrench with rubber insert
> Spark plug gap adjusting tool
> Feeler gauge set
> Brake bleeder wrench
> Standard screwdriver (5/16-inch x
>   6 inch)
> Phillips screwdriver (No. 2 x 6 inch)
> Combination pliers - 6 inch
> Hacksaw and assortment of blades
> Tire pressure gauge
> Grease gun
> Oil can
> Fine emery cloth
> Wire brush
> Battery post and cable cleaning tool
> Oil filter wrench
> Funnel (medium size)
> Safety goggles
> Jackstands (2)
> Drain pan

Note: *If basic tune-ups are going to be part of routine maintenance, it will be necessary to purchase a good quality stroboscopic timing*

light and combination tachometer/dwell meter. Although they are included in the list of special tools, it is mentioned here because they are absolutely necessary for tuning most vehicles properly.

Repair and overhaul tool set

These tools are essential for anyone who plans to perform major repairs and are in addition to those in the maintenance and minor repair tool kit. Included is a comprehensive set of sockets which, though expensive, are invaluable because of their versatility, especially when various extensions and drives are available. We recommend the 1/2-inch drive over the 3/8-inch drive. Although the larger drive is bulky and more expensive, it has the capacity of accepting a very wide range of large sockets. Ideally, however, the mechanic should have a 3/8-inch drive set and a 1/2-inch drive set.

> Socket set(s)
> Reversible ratchet
> Extension - 10 inch
> Universal joint
> Torque wrench (same size drive as
>   sockets)
> Ball peen hammer - 8 ounce
> Soft-face hammer (plastic/rubber)

Ring compressor

> Standard screwdriver (1/4-inch x 6 inch)
> Standard screwdriver (stubby -
>   5/16-inch)
> Phillips screwdriver (No. 3 x 8 inch)
> Phillips screwdriver (stubby - No. 2)
> Pliers - vise grip
> Pliers - lineman's
> Pliers - needle nose
> Pliers - snap-ring (internal and external)
> Cold chisel - 1/2-inch

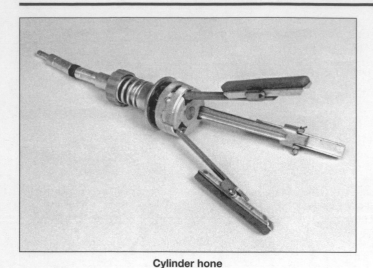

Cylinder hone

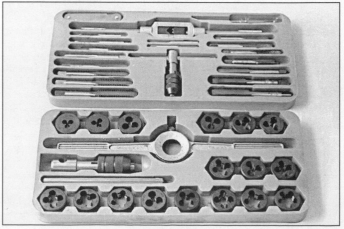

Brake hold-down spring tool

Scribe
Scraper (made from flattened copper tubing)
Centerpunch
Pin punches (1/16, 1/8, 3/16-inch)
Steel rule/straightedge - 12 inch
Allen wrench set (1/8 to 3/8-inch or 4 mm to 10 mm)
A selection of files

Wire brush (large)
Jackstands (second set)
Jack (scissor or hydraulic type)

Note: *Another tool which is often useful is an electric drill with a chuck capacity of 3/8-inch and a set of good quality drill bits.*

Special tools

The tools in this list include those which are not used regularly, are expensive to buy, or which need to be used in accordance with their manufacturer's instructions. Unless these tools will be used frequently, it is not very economical to purchase many of them. A consideration would be to split the cost and use between yourself and a friend or friends. In addition, most of these tools can be obtained from a tool rental shop on a temporary basis.

This list primarily contains only those tools and instruments widely available to the public, and not those special tools produced by the vehicle manufacturer for distribution to dealer service departments. Occasionally, references to the manufacturer's special tools are included in the text of this manual. Generally, an alternative method of doing the job without the special tool is offered. How-

ever, sometimes there is no alternative to their use. Where this is the case, and the tool cannot be purchased or borrowed, the work should be turned over to the dealer service department or an automotive repair shop.

Valve spring compressor
Piston ring groove cleaning tool
Piston ring compressor
Piston ring installation tool
Cylinder compression gauge
Cylinder ridge reamer
Cylinder surfacing hone
Cylinder bore gauge
Micrometers and/or dial calipers
Hydraulic lifter removal tool
Balljoint separator
Universal-type puller
Impact screwdriver
Dial indicator set
Stroboscopic timing light (inductive pick-up)
Hand operated vacuum/pressure pump
Tachometer/dwell meter
Universal electrical multimeter
Cable hoist
Brake spring removal and installation tools
Floor jack

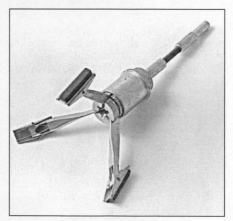

Brake cylinder hone

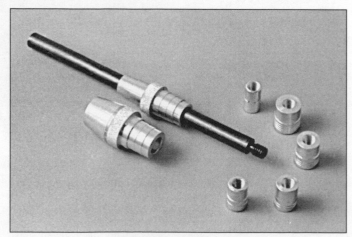

Clutch plate alignment tool

Tap and die set

Buying tools

For the do-it-yourselfer who is just starting to get involved in vehicle maintenance and repair, there are a number of options available when purchasing tools. If maintenance and minor repair is the extent of the work to be done, the purchase of individual tools is satisfactory. If, on the other hand, extensive work is planned, it would be a good idea to purchase a modest tool set from one of the large retail chain stores. A set can usually be bought at a substantial savings over the individual tool prices, and they often come with a tool box. As additional tools are needed, add-on sets, individual tools and a larger tool box can be purchased to expand the tool selection. Building a tool set gradually allows the cost of the tools to be spread over a longer period of time and gives the mechanic the freedom to choose only those tools that will actually be used.

Tool stores will often be the only source of some of the special tools that are needed, but regardless of where tools are bought, try to avoid cheap ones, especially when buying screwdrivers and sockets, because they won't last very long. The expense involved in replacing cheap tools will eventually be greater than the initial cost of quality tools.

Care and maintenance of tools

Good tools are expensive, so it makes sense to treat them with respect. Keep them clean and in usable condition and store them properly when not in use. Always wipe off any dirt, grease or metal chips before putting them away. Never leave tools lying around in the work area. Upon completion of a job, always check closely under the hood for tools that may have been left there so they won't get lost during a test drive.

Some tools, such as screwdrivers, pliers, wrenches and sockets, can be hung on a panel mounted on the garage or workshop wall, while others should be kept in a tool box or tray. Measuring instruments, gauges, meters, etc. must be carefully stored where they cannot be damaged by weather or impact from other tools.

When tools are used with care and stored properly, they will last a very long time. Even with the best of care, though, tools will wear out if used frequently. When a tool is damaged or worn out, replace it. Subsequent jobs will be safer and more enjoyable if you do.

How to repair damaged threads

Sometimes, the internal threads of a nut or bolt hole can become stripped, usually from overtightening. Stripping threads is an all-too-common occurrence, especially when working with aluminum parts, because aluminum is so soft that it easily strips out.

Usually, external or internal threads are only partially stripped. After they've been cleaned up with a tap or die, they'll still work. Sometimes, however, threads are badly damaged. When this happens, you've got three choices:

1) Drill and tap the hole to the next suitable oversize and install a larger diameter bolt, screw or stud.

2) Drill and tap the hole to accept a threaded plug, then drill and tap the plug to the original screw size. You can also buy a plug already threaded to the original size. Then you simply drill a hole to the specified size, then run the threaded plug into the hole with a bolt and jam nut. Once the plug is fully seated, remove the jam nut and bolt.

3) The third method uses a patented thread repair kit like Heli-Coil or Slimsert. These easy-to-use kits are designed to repair damaged threads in straight-through holes and blind holes. Both are available as kits which can handle a variety of sizes and thread patterns. Drill the hole, then tap it with the special included tap. Install the Heli-Coil and the hole is back to its original diameter and thread pitch.

Regardless of which method you use, be sure to proceed calmly and carefully. A little impatience or carelessness during one of these relatively simple procedures can ruin your whole day's work and cost you a bundle if you wreck an expensive part.

Working facilities

Not to be overlooked when discussing tools is the workshop. If anything more than routine maintenance is to be carried out, some sort of suitable work area is essential.

It is understood, and appreciated, that many home mechanics do not have a good workshop or garage available, and end up removing an engine or doing major repairs outside. It is recommended, however, that the overhaul or repair be completed under the cover of a roof.

A clean, flat workbench or table of comfortable working height is an absolute necessity. The workbench should be equipped with a vise that has a jaw opening of at least four inches.

As mentioned previously, some clean, dry storage space is also required for tools, as well as the lubricants, fluids, cleaning solvents, etc. which soon become necessary.

Sometimes waste oil and fluids, drained from the engine or cooling system during normal maintenance or repairs, present a disposal problem. To avoid pouring them on the ground or into a sewage system, pour the used fluids into large containers, seal them with caps and take them to an authorized disposal site or recycling center. Plastic jugs, such as old antifreeze containers, are ideal for this purpose.

Always keep a supply of old newspapers and clean rags available. Old towels are excellent for mopping up spills. Many mechanics use rolls of paper towels for most work because they are readily available and disposable. To help keep the area under the vehicle clean, a large cardboard box can be cut open and flattened to protect the garage or shop floor.

Whenever working over a painted surface, such as when leaning over a fender to service something under the hood, always cover it with an old blanket or bedspread to protect the finish. Vinyl covered pads, made especially for this purpose, are available at auto parts stores.

Booster battery (jump) starting

Booster battery (jump) starting

Observe the following precautions when using a booster battery to start a vehicle:

a) *Before connecting the booster battery, make sure the ignition switch is in the Off position.*

b) *Ensure that all electrical equipment (lights, heater, wipers etc.) are switched off.*

c) *Make sure that the booster battery is the same voltage as the discharged battery in the vehicle.*

d) *If the battery is being jump started from the battery in another vehicle, the two vehicles MUST NOT TOUCH each other.*

e) *Make sure the transaxle is in Neutral (manual transaxle) or Park (automatic transaxle).*

f) *Wear eye protection when jump starting a vehicle.*

Connect one jumper lead between the positive (+) terminals of the two batteries. Connect the other jumper lead first to the negative (-) terminal of the booster battery, then to a good engine ground on the vehicle to be started **(see illustration)**. Attach the lead at least 18 inches from the battery, if possible. Make sure that the jumper leads will not contact the fan, drivebelt of other moving parts of the engine.

Start the engine using the booster battery and allow the engine idle speed to stabilize. Disconnect the jumper leads in the reverse order of connection.

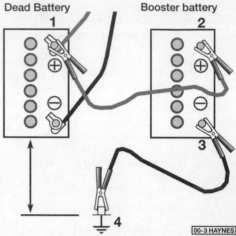

Make the booster battery cable connections in the numerical order shown (note that the negative cable of the booster battery is NOT attached to the negative terminal of the dead battery)

Jacking and towing

Jacking

Warning: *The jack supplied with the vehicle should only be used for raising the vehicle when changing a tire or placing jackstands under the frame. Never work under the vehicle or start the engine while the jack is being used as the only means of support.*

The vehicle must be on a level surface with the wheels blocked and the transaxle in Park (automatic) or Reverse (manual). Apply the parking brake if the front of the vehicle must be raised. Make sure no one is in the vehicle as it's being raised with the jack.

Remove the jack, lug nut wrench and spare tire (if needed) from the vehicle. On SE-i models, if a tire is being replaced, use a screwdriver to remove the center cap from the wheel cover. Loosen the lug nuts one-half turn, but leave them in place until the tire is raised off the ground.

Position the jack under the vehicle at the indicated jacking point. There's a front and rear jacking point on each side of the vehicle **(see illustrations)**.

Turn the jack handle clockwise until the tire clears the ground, then remove the lug nuts and wheel cover. Pull the tire off and replace it with the spare. Reposition the wheel cover. Replace the lug nuts with the beveled edges facing in and tighten them snugly. Don't attempt to tighten them completely until the vehicle is lowered or it could slip off the jack.

Turn the jack handle counterclockwise to lower the vehicle. Remove the jack and tighten the lug nuts in a criss-cross pattern. If possible, tighten the nuts with a torque wrench (see Chapter 1 for the torque figures). If you don't have access to a torque wrench, have the nuts checked by a service station or repair shop as soon as possible. On SE-i models, reinstall the center cap after checking to see if the retainer ring in the wheel cover moves freely. Point the "H" mark toward the valve stem and tap the cap into place.

Stow the tire, jack and wrench and unblock the wheels.

Towing

As a general rule, the vehicle should be towed with the front (drive) wheels off the ground. Be sure to release the parking brake. If the vehicle is being towed with the front wheels on the ground, place the transaxle in Neutral. Also, the ignition key must be in the I position, since the steering lock mechanism isn't strong enough to hold the front wheels straight while towing. Do not exceed 35 mph or tow for distances over 50 miles with the front wheels on the ground.

Equipment specifically designed for towing should be used. It should be attached to the main structural members of the vehicle, not the bumpers or brackets.

Safety is a major consideration when towing and all applicable state and local laws must be obeyed. A safety chain must be used at all times. Remember that power steering and brakes won't work with the engine off.

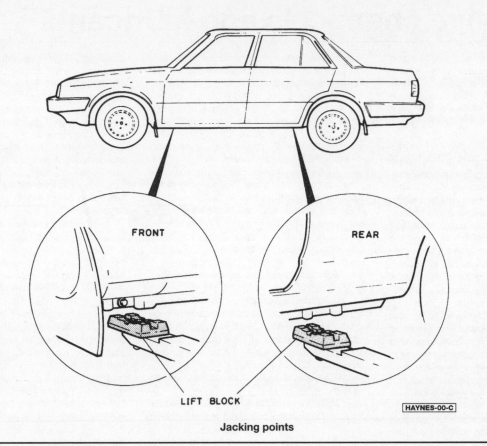

LIFT BLOCK

HAYNES-00-C

Jacking points

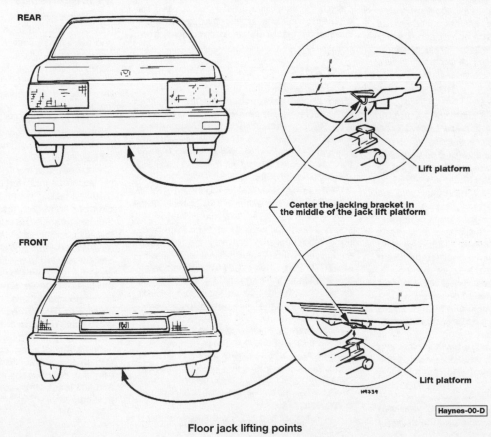

REAR

FRONT

Lift platform

Center the jacking bracket in
the middle of the jack lift platform

Lift platform

Haynes-00-D

Floor jack lifting points

Automotive chemicals and lubricants

A number of automotive chemicals and lubricants are available for use during vehicle maintenance and repair. They include a wide variety of products ranging from cleaning solvents and degreasers to lubricants and protective sprays for rubber, plastic and vinyl.

Cleaners

Carburetor cleaner and choke cleaner is a strong solvent for gum, varnish and carbon. Most carburetor cleaners leave a dry-type lubricant film which will not harden or gum up. Because of this film it is not recommended for use on electrical components.

Brake system cleaner is used to remove grease and brake fluid from the brake system, where clean surfaces are absolutely necessary. It leaves no residue and often eliminates brake squeal caused by contaminants.

Electrical cleaner removes oxidation, corrosion and carbon deposits from electrical contacts, restoring full current flow. It can also be used to clean spark plugs, carburetor jets, voltage regulators and other parts where an oil-free surface is desired.

Demoisturants remove water and moisture from electrical components such as alternators, voltage regulators, electrical connectors and fuse blocks. They are non-conductive, non-corrosive and non-flammable.

Degreasers are heavy-duty solvents used to remove grease from the outside of the engine and from chassis components. They can be sprayed or brushed on and, depending on the type, are rinsed off either with water or solvent.

Lubricants

Motor oil is the lubricant formulated for use in engines. It normally contains a wide variety of additives to prevent corrosion and reduce foaming and wear. Motor oil comes in various weights (viscosity ratings) from 0 to 50. The recommended weight of the oil depends on the season, temperature and the demands on the engine. Light oil is used in cold climates and under light load conditions. Heavy oil is used in hot climates and where high loads are encountered. Multi-viscosity oils are designed to have characteristics of both light and heavy oils and are available in a number of weights from 5W-20 to 20W-50.

Gear oil is designed to be used in differentials, manual transmissions and other areas where high-temperature lubrication is required.

Chassis and wheel bearing grease is a heavy grease used where increased loads and friction are encountered, such as for wheel bearings, balljoints, tie-rod ends and universal joints.

High-temperature wheel bearing grease is designed to withstand the extreme temperatures encountered by wheel bearings in disc brake equipped vehicles. It usually contains molybdenum disulfide (moly), which is a dry-type lubricant.

White grease is a heavy grease for metal-to-metal applications where water is a problem. White grease stays soft under both low and high temperatures (usually from -100 to +190-degrees F), and will not wash off or dilute in the presence of water.

Assembly lube is a special extreme pressure lubricant, usually containing moly, used to lubricate high-load parts (such as main and rod bearings and cam lobes) for initial start-up of a new engine. The assembly lube lubricates the parts without being squeezed out or washed away until the engine oiling system begins to function.

Silicone lubricants are used to protect rubber, plastic, vinyl and nylon parts.

Graphite lubricants are used where oils cannot be used due to contamination problems, such as in locks. The dry graphite will lubricate metal parts while remaining uncontaminated by dirt, water, oil or acids. It is electrically conductive and will not foul electrical contacts in locks such as the ignition switch.

Moly penetrants loosen and lubricate frozen, rusted and corroded fasteners and prevent future rusting or freezing.

Heat-sink grease is a special electrically non-conductive grease that is used for mounting electronic ignition modules where it is essential that heat is transferred away from the module.

Sealants

RTV sealant is one of the most widely used gasket compounds. Made from silicone, RTV is air curing, it seals, bonds, waterproofs, fills surface irregularities, remains flexible, doesn't shrink, is relatively easy to remove, and is used as a supplementary sealer with almost all low and medium temperature gaskets.

Anaerobic sealant is much like RTV in that it can be used either to seal gaskets or to form gaskets by itself. It remains flexible, is solvent resistant and fills surface imperfections. The difference between an anaerobic sealant and an RTV-type sealant is in the curing. RTV cures when exposed to air, while an anaerobic sealant cures only in the absence of air. This means that an anaerobic sealant cures only after the assembly of parts, sealing them together.

Thread and pipe sealant is used for sealing hydraulic and pneumatic fittings and vacuum lines. It is usually made from a Teflon compound, and comes in a spray, a paint-on liquid and as a wrap-around tape.

Chemicals

Anti-seize compound prevents seizing, galling, cold welding, rust and corrosion in fasteners. High-temperature ant-seize, usually made with copper and graphite lubricants, is used for exhaust system and exhaust manifold bolts.

Anaerobic locking compounds are used to keep fasteners from vibrating or working loose and cure only after installation, in the absence of air. Medium strength locking compound is used for small nuts, bolts and screws that may be removed later. High-strength locking compound is for large nuts, bolts and studs which aren't removed on a regular basis.

Oil additives range from viscosity index improvers to chemical treatments that claim to reduce internal engine friction. It should be noted that most oil manufacturers caution against using additives with their oils.

Gas additives perform several functions, depending on their chemical makeup. They usually contain solvents that help dissolve gum and varnish that build up on carburetor, fuel injection and intake parts. They also serve to break down carbon deposits that form on the inside surfaces of the combustion chambers. Some additives contain upper cylinder lubricants for valves and piston rings, and others contain chemicals to remove condensation from the gas tank.

Miscellaneous

Brake fluid is specially formulated hydraulic fluid that can withstand the heat and pressure encountered in brake systems. Care must be taken so this fluid does not come in contact with painted surfaces or plastics. An opened container should always be resealed to prevent contamination by water or dirt.

Weatherstrip adhesive is used to bond weatherstripping around doors, windows and trunk lids. It is sometimes used to attach trim pieces.

Undercoating is a petroleum-based, tar-like substance that is designed to protect metal surfaces on the underside of the vehicle from corrosion. It also acts as a sound-deadening agent by insulating the bottom of the vehicle.

Waxes and polishes are used to help protect painted and plated surfaces from the weather. Different types of paint may require the use of different types of wax and polish. Some polishes utilize a chemical or abrasive cleaner to help remove the top layer of oxidized (dull) paint on older vehicles. In recent years many non-wax polishes that contain a wide variety of chemicals such as polymers and silicones have been introduced. These non-wax polishes are usually easier to apply and last longer than conventional waxes and polishes.

Conversion factors

Length (distance)
Inches (in)	X	25.4	= Millimetres (mm)	X 0.0394	= Inches (in)
Feet (ft)	X	0.305	= Metres (m)	X 3.281	= Feet (ft)
Miles	X	1.609	= Kilometres (km)	X 0.621	= Miles

Volume (capacity)
Cubic inches (cu in; in³)	X	16.387	= Cubic centimetres (cc; cm³)	X 0.061	= Cubic inches (cu in; in³)
Imperial pints (Imp pt)	X	0.568	= Litres (l)	X 1.76	= Imperial pints (Imp pt)
Imperial quarts (Imp qt)	X	1.137	= Litres (l)	X 0.88	= Imperial quarts (Imp qt)
Imperial quarts (Imp qt)	X	1.201	= US quarts (US qt)	X 0.833	= Imperial quarts (Imp qt)
US quarts (US qt)	X	0.946	= Litres (l)	X 1.057	= US quarts (US qt)
Imperial gallons (Imp gal)	X	4.546	= Litres (l)	X 0.22	= Imperial gallons (Imp gal)
Imperial gallons (Imp gal)	X	1.201	= US gallons (US gal)	X 0.833	= Imperial gallons (Imp gal)
US gallons (US gal)	X	3.785	= Litres (l)	X 0.264	= US gallons (US gal)

Mass (weight)
Ounces (oz)	X	28.35	= Grams (g)	X 0.035	= Ounces (oz)
Pounds (lb)	X	0.454	= Kilograms (kg)	X 2.205	= Pounds (lb)

Force
Ounces-force (ozf; oz)	X	0.278	= Newtons (N)	X 3.6	= Ounces-force (ozf; oz)
Pounds-force (lbf; lb)	X	4.448	= Newtons (N)	X 0.225	= Pounds-force (lbf; lb)
Newtons (N)	X	0.1	= Kilograms-force (kgf; kg)	X 9.81	= Newtons (N)

Pressure
Pounds-force per square inch (psi; lbf/in²; lb/in²)	X	0.070	= Kilograms-force per square centimetre (kgf/cm²; kg/cm²)	X 14.223	= Pounds-force per square inch (psi; lbf/in²; lb/in²)
Pounds-force per square inch (psi; lbf/in²; lb/in²)	X	0.068	= Atmospheres (atm)	X 14.696	= Pounds-force per square inch (psi; lbf/in²; lb/ln²)
Pounds-force per square inch (psi; lbf/in²; lb/in²)	X	0.069	= Bars	X 14.5	= Pounds-force per square inch (psi; lbf/in²; lb/in²)
Pounds-force per square inch (psi; lbf/in²; lb/in²)	X	6.895	= Kilopascals (kPa)	X 0.145	= Pounds-force per square inch (psi; lbf/in²; lb/in²)
Kilopascals (kPa)	X	0.01	= Kilograms-force per square centimetre (kgf/cm²; kg/cm²)	X 98.1	= Kilopascals (kPa)

Torque (moment of force)
Pounds-force inches (lbf in; lb in)	X	1.152	= Kilograms-force centimetre (kgf cm; kg cm)	X 0.868	= Pounds-force inches (lbf in; lb in)
Pounds-force inches (lbf in; lb in)	X	0.113	= Newton metres (Nm)	X 8.85	= Pounds-force inches (lbf in; lb in)
Pounds-force inches (lbf in; lb in)	X	0.083	= Pounds-force feet (lbf ft; lb ft)	X 12	= Pounds-force inches (lbf in; lb in)
Pounds-force feet (lbf ft; lb ft)	X	0.138	= Kilograms-force metres (kgf m; kg m)	X 7.233	= Pounds-force feet (lbf ft; lb ft)
Pounds-force feet (lbf ft; lb ft)	X	1.356	= Newton metres (Nm)	X 0.738	= Pounds-force feet (lbf ft; lb ft)
Newton metres (Nm)	X	0.102	= Kilograms-force metres (kgf m; kg m)	X 9.804	= Newton metres (Nm)

Vacuum
Inches mercury (in. Hg)	X	3.377	= Kilopascals (kPa)	X 0.2961	= Inches mercury
Inches mercury (in. Hg)	X	25.4	= Millimeters mercury (mm Hg)	X 0.0394	= Inches mercury

Power
Horsepower (hp)	X	745.7	= Watts (W)	X 0.0013	= Horsepower (hp)

Velocity (speed)
Miles per hour (miles/hr; mph)	X	1.609	= Kilometres per hour (km/hr; kph)	X 0.621	= Miles per hour (miles/hr; mph)

Fuel consumption*
Miles per gallon, Imperial (mpg)	X	0.354	= Kilometres per litre (km/l)	X 2.825	= Miles per gallon, Imperial (mpg)
Miles per gallon, US (mpg)	X	0.425	= Kilometres per litre (km/l)	X 2.352	= Miles per gallon, US (mpg)

Temperature
Degrees Fahrenheit = (°C x 1.8) + 32

Degrees Celsius (Degrees Centigrade; °C) = (°F - 32) x 0.56

*It is common practice to convert from miles per gallon (mpg) to litres/100 kilometres (l/100km),
where mpg (Imperial) x l/100 km = 282 and mpg (US) x l/100 km = 235

Safety first!

Regardless of how enthusiastic you may be about getting on with the job at hand, take the time to ensure that your safety is not jeopardized. A moment's lack of attention can result in an accident, as can failure to observe certain simple safety precautions. The possibility of an accident will always exist, and the following points should not be considered a comprehensive list of all dangers. Rather, they are intended to make you aware of the risks and to encourage a safety conscious approach to all work you carry out on your vehicle.

Essential DOs and DON'Ts

DON'T rely on a jack when working under the vehicle. Always use approved jackstands to support the weight of the vehicle and place them under the recommended lift or support points.

DON'T attempt to loosen extremely tight fasteners (i.e. wheel lug nuts) while the vehicle is on a jack - it may fall.

DON'T start the engine without first making sure that the transmission is in Neutral (or Park where applicable) and the parking brake is set.

DON'T remove the radiator cap from a hot cooling system - let it cool or cover it with a cloth and release the pressure gradually.

DON'T attempt to drain the engine oil until you are sure it has cooled to the point that it will not burn you.

DON'T touch any part of the engine or exhaust system until it has cooled sufficiently to avoid burns.

DON'T siphon toxic liquids such as gasoline, antifreeze and brake fluid by mouth, or allow them to remain on your skin.

DON'T inhale brake lining dust - it is potentially hazardous (see *Asbestos* below).

DON'T allow spilled oil or grease to remain on the floor - wipe it up before someone slips on it.

DON'T use loose fitting wrenches or other tools which may slip and cause injury.

DON'T push on wrenches when loosening or tightening nuts or bolts. Always try to pull the wrench toward you. If the situation calls for pushing the wrench away, push with an open hand to avoid scraped knuckles if the wrench should slip.

DON'T attempt to lift a heavy component alone - get someone to help you.

DON'T rush or take unsafe shortcuts to finish a job.

DON'T allow children or animals in or around the vehicle while you are working on it.

DO wear eye protection when using power tools such as a drill, sander, bench grinder, etc. and when working under a vehicle.

DO keep loose clothing and long hair well out of the way of moving parts.

DO make sure that any hoist used has a safe working load rating adequate for the job.

DO get someone to check on you periodically when working alone on a vehicle.

DO carry out work in a logical sequence and make sure that everything is correctly assembled and tightened.

DO keep chemicals and fluids tightly capped and out of the reach of children and pets.

DO remember that your vehicle's safety affects that of yourself and others. If in doubt on any point, get professional advice.

Asbestos

Certain friction, insulating, sealing, and other products - such as brake linings, brake bands, clutch linings, torque converters, gaskets, etc. - may contain asbestos. Extreme care must be taken to avoid inhalation of dust from such products, since it is hazardous to health. If in doubt, assume that they do contain asbestos.

Fire

Remember at all times that gasoline is highly flammable. Never smoke or have any kind of open flame around when working on a vehicle. But the risk does not end there. A spark caused by an electrical short circuit, by two metal surfaces contacting each other, or even by static electricity built up in your body under certain conditions, can ignite gasoline vapors, which in a confined space are highly explosive. Do not, under any circumstances, use gasoline for cleaning parts. Use an approved safety solvent.

Always disconnect the battery ground (-) cable at the battery before working on any part of the fuel system or electrical system. Never risk spilling fuel on a hot engine or exhaust component. It is strongly recommended that a fire extinguisher suitable for use on fuel and electrical fires be kept handy in the garage or workshop at all times. Never try to extinguish a fuel or electrical fire with water.

Fumes

Certain fumes are highly toxic and can quickly cause unconsciousness and even death if inhaled to any extent. Gasoline vapor falls into this category, as do the vapors from some cleaning solvents. Any draining or pouring of such volatile fluids should be done in a well ventilated area.

When using cleaning fluids and solvents, read the instructions on the container carefully. Never use materials from unmarked containers.

Never run the engine in an enclosed space, such as a garage. Exhaust fumes contain carbon monoxide, which is extremely poisonous. If you need to run the engine, always do so in the open air, or at least have the rear of the vehicle outside the work area.

If you are fortunate enough to have the use of an inspection pit, never drain or pour gasoline and never run the engine while the vehicle is over the pit. The fumes, being heavier than air, will concentrate in the pit with possibly lethal results.

The battery

Never create a spark or allow a bare light bulb near a battery. They normally give off a certain amount of hydrogen gas, which is highly explosive.

Always disconnect the battery ground (-) cable at the battery before working on the fuel or electrical systems.

If possible, loosen the filler caps or cover when charging the battery from an external source (this does not apply to sealed or maintenance-free batteries). Do not charge at an excessive rate or the battery may burst.

Take care when adding water to a non maintenance-free battery and when carrying a battery. The electrolyte, even when diluted, is very corrosive and should not be allowed to contact clothing or skin.

Always wear eye protection when cleaning the battery to prevent the caustic deposits from entering your eyes.

Household current

When using an electric power tool, inspection light, etc., which operates on household current, always make sure that the tool is correctly connected to its plug and that, where necessary, it is properly grounded. Do not use such items in damp conditions and, again, do not create a spark or apply excessive heat in the vicinity of fuel or fuel vapor.

Secondary ignition system voltage

A severe electric shock can result from touching certain parts of the ignition system (such as the spark plug wires) when the engine is running or being cranked, particularly if components are damp or the insulation is defective. In the case of an electronic ignition system, the secondary system voltage is much higher and could prove fatal.

Troubleshooting

Contents

This section provides an easy reference guide to the more common problems which may occur during the operation of your vehicle. These problems and their possible causes are grouped under headings denoting various components or systems, such as Engine, Cooling system, etc. They also refer you to the chapter and/or section which deals with the problem.

Remember that successful troubleshooting is not a mysterious black art practiced only by professional mechanics. It is simply the result of the right knowledge combined with an intelligent, systematic approach to the problem. Always work by a process of elimination, starting with the simplest solution and working through to the most complex - and never overlook the obvious. Anyone can run the gas tank dry or leave the lights on overnight, so don't assume that you are exempt from such oversights.

Finally, always establish a clear idea of why a problem has occurred and take steps to ensure that it doesn't happen again. If the electrical system fails because of a poor connection, check the other connections in the system to make sure that they don't fail as well. If a particular fuse continues to blow, find out why - don't just replace one fuse after another. Remember, failure of a small component can often be indicative of potential failure or incorrect functioning of a more important component or system.

Engine

1   Engine will not rotate when attempting to start

1   Battery terminal connections loose or corroded (Chapter 1).
2   Battery discharged or faulty (Chapter 1).
3   Automatic transaxle not completely engaged in Park (Chapter 7) or clutch not completely depressed (Chapter 8).
4   Broken, loose or disconnected wiring in the starting circuit (Chapters 5 and 12).
5   Starter motor pinion jammed in flywheel ring gear (Chapter 5).
6   Starter solenoid faulty (Chapter 5).
7   Starter motor faulty (Chapter 5).
8   Ignition switch faulty (Chapter 12).
9   Starter pinion or flywheel teeth worn or broken (Chapter 5).

2   Engine rotates but will not start

1   Fuel tank empty.
2   Battery discharged (engine rotates slowly) (Chapter 5).
3   Battery terminal connections loose or corroded (Chapter 1).
4   Leaking fuel injector(s), faulty carburetor, fuel pump, pressure regulator, etc. (Chapter 4).
5   Fuel not reaching fuel rail or carburetor (Chapter 4).
6   Ignition components damp or damaged (Chapter 5).
7   Worn, faulty or incorrectly gapped spark plugs (Chapter 1).
8   Broken, loose or disconnected wiring in the starting circuit (Chapter 5).
9   Loose distributor is changing ignition timing (Chapter 5).
10 Broken, loose or disconnected wires at the ignition coil or faulty coil (Chapter 5).

3   Engine hard to start when cold

1   Battery discharged or low (Chapter 1).
2   Malfunctioning fuel system (Chapter 4).
3   Faulty cold start injector (Chapter 4).

4   Injector(s) leaking (Chapter 4).
5   Distributor rotor carbon tracked (Chapter 5).
6   Carburetor choke not operating properly (Chapter 1).

4   Engine hard to start when hot

1   Air filter clogged (Chapter 1).
2   Fuel not reaching the carburetor or fuel injection system (Chapter 4).
3   Corroded battery connections, especially ground (Chapter 1).

5   Starter motor noisy or excessively rough in engagement

1   Pinion or flywheel gear teeth worn or broken (Chapter 5).
2   Starter motor mounting bolts loose or missing (Chapter 5).

6   Engine starts but stops immediately

1   Loose or faulty electrical connections at distributor, coil or alternator (Chapter 5).
2   Insufficient fuel reaching the carburetor or fuel injector(s) (Chapters 1 and 4).
3   Vacuum leak at the gasket between the intake manifold/plenum and throttle body (Chapters 1 and 4).

7   Oil puddle under engine

1   Oil pan gasket and/or oil pan drain bolt washer leaking (Chapter 2).
2   Oil pressure sending unit leaking (Chapter 2).
3   Cylinder head cover leaking (Chapter 2).
4   Engine oil seals leaking (Chapter 2).

8   Engine lopes while idling or idles erratically

1   Vacuum leakage (Chapters 2 and 4).
2   Leaking EGR valve (Chapter 6).
3   Air filter clogged (Chapter 1).
4   Fuel pump not delivering sufficient fuel to the carburetor or fuel injection system (Chapter 4).
5   Leaking head gasket (Chapter 2).
6   Timing belt and/or pulleys worn (Chapter 2).
7   Camshaft lobes worn (Chapter 2).

9   Engine misses at idle speed

1   Spark plugs worn or not gapped properly (Chapter 1).
2   Faulty spark plug wires (Chapter 1).

3   Vacuum leaks (Chapter 1).
4   Incorrect ignition timing (Chapter 1).
5   Uneven or low compression (Chapter 2).

10   Engine misses throughout driving speed range

1   Fuel filter clogged and/or impurities in the fuel system (Chapter 1).
2   Low fuel output at the injector(s) or carburetor (Chapter 4).
3   Faulty or incorrectly gapped spark plugs (Chapter 1).
4   Incorrect ignition timing (Chapter 5).
5   Cracked distributor cap, disconnected distributor wires or damaged distributor components (Chapters 1 and 5).
6   Leaking spark plug wires (Chapters 1 or 5).
7   Faulty emission system components (Chapter 6).
8   Low or uneven cylinder compression pressures (Chapter 2).
9   Weak or faulty ignition system (Chapter 5).
10 Vacuum leak in fuel injection system, carburetor, intake manifold, air control valve or vacuum hoses (Chapter 4).

11   Engine stumbles on acceleration

1   Spark plugs fouled (Chapter 1).
2   Fuel injection system or carburetor needs adjustment or repair (Chapter 4).
3   Fuel filter clogged (Chapters 1 and 4).
4   Incorrect ignition timing (Chapter 5).
5   Intake manifold air leak (Chapters 2 and 4).

12   Engine surges while holding accelerator steady

1   Intake air leak (Chapter 4).
2   Fuel pump faulty (Chapter 4).
3   Loose fuel injector wire harness connectors (Chapter 4).

13   Engine stalls

1   Idle speed incorrect (Chapter 1).
2   Fuel filter clogged and/or water and impurities in the fuel system (Chapters 1 and 4).
3   Distributor components damp or damaged (Chapter 5).
4   Faulty emissions system components (Chapter 6).
5   Faulty or incorrectly gapped spark plugs (Chapter 1).
6   Faulty spark plug wires (Chapter 1).
7   Vacuum leak in the fuel injection system, carburetor, intake manifold or vacuum hoses (Chapters 2 and 4).
8   Valve clearances incorrectly set (Chapter 1).

14 Engine lacks power

1 Incorrect ignition timing (Chapter 5).
2 Excessive play in distributor shaft (Chapter 5).
3 Worn rotor, distributor cap or wires (Chapters 1 and 5).
4 Faulty or incorrectly gapped spark plugs (Chapter 1).
5 Fuel injection system or carburetor out of adjustment or excessively worn (Chapter 4).
6 Faulty coil (Chapter 5).
7 Brakes binding (Chapter 9).
8 Automatic transaxle fluid level incorrect (Chapter 1).
9 Clutch slipping (Chapter 8).
10 Fuel filter clogged and/or impurities in the fuel system (Chapters 1 and 4).
11 Emission control system not functioning properly (Chapter 6).
12 Low or uneven cylinder compression pressures (Chapter 2).

15 Engine backfires

1 Emission control system not functioning properly (Chapter 6).
2 Ignition timing incorrect (Chapter 5).
3 Faulty secondary ignition system (cracked spark plug insulator, faulty plug wires, distributor cap and/or rotor) (Chapters 1 and 5).
4 Fuel injection system or carburetor in need of adjustment or worn excessively (Chapter 4).
5 Vacuum leak at fuel injector(s), carburetor, intake manifold, air control valve or vacuum hoses (Chapters 2 and 4).
6 Valve clearances incorrectly set and/or valves sticking (Chapter 1).

16 Pinging or knocking engine sounds during acceleration or uphill

1 Incorrect grade of fuel.
2 Ignition timing incorrect (Chapter 5).
3 Fuel injection system in need of adjustment (Chapter 4).
4 Improper or damaged spark plugs or wires (Chapter 1).
5 Worn or damaged distributor components (Chapter 5).
6 Faulty emission system (Chapter 6).
7 Vacuum leak (Chapters 2 and 4).

17 Engine runs with oil pressure light on

1 Low oil level (Chapter 1).
2 Idle rpm below specification (Chapter 1).
3 Short in wiring circuit (Chapter 12).
4 Faulty oil pressure sender (Chapter 2).

5 Worn engine bearings and/or oil pump (Chapter 2).

18 Engine diesels (continues to run) after switching off

1 Idle speed too high (Chapter 1).
2 Excessive engine operating temperature (Chapter 3).

Engine electrical system

19 Battery will not hold a charge

1 Alternator drivebelt defective or not adjusted properly (Chapter 1).
2 Battery electrolyte level low (Chapter 1).
3 Battery terminals loose or corroded (Chapter 1).
4 Alternator no charging properly (Chapter 5).
5 Loose, broken or faulty wiring in the charging circuit (Chapter 5).
6 Short in vehicle wiring (Chapter 12).
7 Internally defective battery (Chapters 1 and 5).

20 Alternator light fails to go out

1 Faulty alternator or charging circuit (Chapter 5).
2 Alternator drivebelt defective or out of adjustment (Chapter 1).
3 Alternator voltage regulator inoperative (Chapter 5).

21 Alternator light fails to come on when key is turned on

1 Warning light bulb defective (Chapter 12).
2 Fault in the printed circuit, dash wiring or bulb holder (Chapter 12).

Fuel system

22 Excessive fuel consumption

1 Dirty or clogged air filter element (Chapter 1).
2 Incorrectly set ignition timing (Chapter 5).
3 Emissions system not functioning properly (Chapter 6).
4 Fuel injection or carburetor internal parts excessively worn or damaged (Chapter 4).
5 Low tire pressure or incorrect tire size (Chapter 1).

23 Fuel leakage and/or fuel odor

1 Leaking fuel feed or return line (Chapters 1 and 4).
2 Tank overfilled.
3 Evaporative canister filter clogged (Chapters 1 and 6).
4 Fuel injector internal parts excessively worn (Chapter 4).

Cooling system

24 Overheating

1 Insufficient coolant in system (Chapter 1).
2 Water pump drivebelt defective or out of adjustment (Chapter 1).
3 Radiator core blocked or grille restricted (Chapter 3).
4 Thermostat faulty (Chapter 3).
5 Electric coolant fan blades broken or cracked (Chapter 3).
6 Radiator cap not maintaining proper pressure (Chapter 3).
7 Ignition timing incorrect (Chapter 5).

25 Overcooling

1 Faulty thermostat (Chapter 3).
2 Inaccurate temperature gauge sending unit (Chapter 3)

26 External coolant leakage

1 Deteriorated/damaged hoses; loose clamps (Chapters 1 and 3).
2 Water pump seal defective (Chapter 3).
3 Leakage from radiator core or coolant reservoir bottle (Chapter 3).
4 Engine drain or water jacket core plugs leaking (Chapter 2).

27 Internal coolant leakage

1 Leaking cylinder head gasket (Chapter 2).
2 Cracked cylinder bore or cylinder head (Chapter 2).

28 Coolant loss

1 Too much coolant in system (Chapter 1).
2 Coolant boiling away because of overheating (Chapter 3).
3 Internal or external leakage (Chapter 3).
4 Faulty radiator cap (Chapter 3).

29 Poor coolant circulation

1 Inoperative water pump (Chapter 3).

2   Restriction in cooling system (Chapters 1 and 3).
3   Water pump drivebelt defective/out of adjustment (Chapter 1).
4   Thermostat sticking (Chapter 3).

Clutch

30 Pedal travels to floor - no pressure or very little resistance

1   Broken clutch cable (Chapter 8).
2   Broken release bearing or fork (Chapter 8).

31 Unable to select gears

1   Faulty transaxle (Chapter 7).
2   Faulty clutch disc (Chapter 8).
3   Fork and bearing not assembled properly (Chapter 8).
4   Faulty pressure plate (Chapter 8).
5   Pressure plate-to-flywheel bolts loose (Chapter 8).

32 Clutch slips (engine speed increases with no increase in vehicle speed)

1   Clutch plate worn (Chapter 8).
2   Clutch plate is oil soaked by leaking rear main seal (Chapter 8).
3   Clutch plate not seated. It may take 30 or 40 normal starts for a new one to seat.
4   Warped pressure plate or flywheel (Chapter 8).
5   Weak diaphragm spring (Chapter 8).
6   Clutch plate overheated. Allow to cool.

33 Grabbing (chattering) as clutch is engaged

1   Oil on clutch plate lining, burned or glazed facings (Chapter 8).
2   Worn or loose engine or transaxle mounts (Chapters 2 and 7).
3   Worn splines on clutch plate hub (Chapter 8).
4   Warped pressure plate or flywheel (Chapter 8).
5   Burned or smeared resin on flywheel or pressure plate (Chapter 8).

34 Transaxle rattling (clicking)

1   Release fork loose (Chapter 8).
2   Clutch plate damper spring failure (Chapter 8).
3   Low engine idle speed (Chapter 1).

35 Noise in clutch area

1   Fork shaft improperly installed (Chapter 8).
2   Faulty bearing (Chapter 8).

36 Clutch pedal stays on floor

1   Broken clutch cable (Chapter 8).
2   Broken release bearing or fork (Chapter 8).

37 High pedal effort

1   Clutch cable or linkage binding (Chapter 8).
2   Pressure plate faulty (Chapter 8).

Manual transaxle

38 Knocking noise at low speeds

1   Worn driveaxle constant velocity (CV) joints (Chapter 8).
2   Worn side gear shaft counterbore in differential case (Chapter 7A).*

39 Noise most pronounced when turning

Differential gear noise (Chapter 7A).*

40 Clunk on acceleration or deceleration

1   Loose engine or transaxle mounts (Chapters 2 and 7A).
2   Worn differential pinion shaft in case.*
3   Worn side gear shaft counterbore in differential case (Chapter 7A).*
4   Worn or damaged driveaxle inboard CV joints (Chapter 8).

41 Clicking noise in turns

Worn or damaged outboard CV joint (Chapter 8).

42 Vibration

1   Rough wheel bearing (Chapters 1 and 10).
2   Damaged driveaxle (Chapter 8).
3   Out of round tires (Chapter 1).
4   Tire out of balance (Chapters 1 and 10).
5   Worn CV joint (Chapter 8).

43 Noisy in neutral with engine running

1   Damaged input gear bearing (Chapter 7A).*
2   Damaged clutch release bearing (Chapter 8).

44 Noisy in one particular gear

1   Damaged or worn constant mesh gears (Chapter 7A).*
2   Damaged or worn synchronizers (Chapter 7A).*
3   Bent reverse fork (Chapter 7A).*
4   Damaged fourth speed gear or output gear (Chapter 7A).*
5   Worn or damaged reverse idler gear or idler bushing (Chapter 7A).*

45 Noisy in all gears

1   Insufficient lubricant (Chapter 7A).
2   Damaged or worn bearings (Chapter 7A).*
3   Worn or damaged input gear shaft and/or output gear shaft (Chapter 7A).*

46 Slips out of gear

1   Worn or improperly adjusted linkage (Chapter 7A).
2   Transaxle loose on engine (Chapter 7A).
3   Shift linkage does not work freely, binds (Chapter 7A).
4   Input gear bearing retainer broken or loose (Chapter 7A).*
5   Dirt between clutch cover and engine housing (Chapter 7A).
6   Worn shift fork (Chapter 7A).*

47 Leaks lubricant

1   Side gear shaft seals worn (Chapter 8).
2   Excessive amount of lubricant in transaxle (Chapters 1 and 7A).
3   Loose or broken input gear shaft bearing retainer (Chapter 7A).*
4   Input gear bearing retainer O-ring and/or lip seal damaged (Chapter 7A).*

Automatic transaxle

Note: *Due to the complexity of the automatic transaxle, it is difficult for the home mechanic to properly diagnose and service this component. For problems other than the following, the vehicle should be taken to a dealer or transmission shop.*

48 Fluid leakage

1   Automatic transaxle fluid is a deep red

color. Fluid leaks should not be confused with engine oil, which can easily be blown onto the transaxle by air flow.

2   To pinpoint a leak, first remove all built-up dirt and grime from the transaxle housing with degreasing agents and/or steam cleaning. Then drive the vehicle at low speeds so air flow will not blow the leak far from its source. Raise the vehicle and determine where the leak is coming from. Common areas of leakage are:

a) *Pan (Chapters 1 and 7)*
b) *Transaxle oil lines (Chapter 7)*
c) *Speed sensor (Chapter 7)*

49   Transaxle fluid brown or has a burned smell

Transaxle fluid burned (Chapter 1).

50   General shift mechanism problems

1   Chapter 7, Part B, deals with checking and adjusting the shift linkage on automatic transaxles. Common problems which may be attributed to poorly adjusted linkage are:

a) *Engine starting in gears other than Park or Neutral.*
b) *Indicator on shifter pointing to a gear other than the one actually being used.*
c) *Vehicle moves when in Park.*

2   Refer to Chapter 7B for the shift linkage adjustment procedure.

51   Transaxle will not downshift with accelerator pedal pressed to the floor

Throttle valve cable out of adjustment (Chapter 7B).

52   Engine will start in gears other than Park or Neutral

Neutral start switch malfunctioning (Chapter 7B).

53   Transaxle slips, shifts roughly, is noisy or has no drive in forward or reverse gears

There are many probable causes for the above problems, but the home mechanic should be concerned with only one possibility - fluid level. Before taking the vehicle to a repair shop, check the level and condition of the fluid as described in Chapter 1. Correct the fluid level as necessary or change the fluid and filter if needed. If the problem persists, have a professional diagnose the cause.

Driveaxles

54   Clicking noise in turns

Worn or damaged outboard CV joint (Chapter 8).

55   Shudder or vibration during acceleration

1   Excessive toe-in (Chapter 10).
2   Incorrect spring heights (Chapter 10).
3   Worn or damaged inboard or outboard CV joints (Chapter 8).
4   Sticking inboard CV joint assembly (Chapter 8).

56   Vibration at highway speeds

1   Out of balance front wheels and/or tires (Chapters 1 and 10).
2   Out of round front tires (Chapters 1 and 10).
3   Worn CV joint(s) (Chapter 8).

Brakes

Note: *Before assuming that a brake problem exists, make sure that:*

a) *The tires are in good condition and properly inflated (Chapter 1).*
b) *The front end alignment is correct (Chapter 10).*
c) *The vehicle is not loaded with weight in an unequal manner.*

57   Vehicle pulls to one side during braking

1   Incorrect tire pressures (Chapter 1).
2   Front end out of line (have the front end aligned).
3   Front, or rear, tires not matched to one another.
4   Restricted brake lines or hoses (Chapter 9).
5   Malfunctioning drum brake or caliper assembly (Chapter 9).
6   Loose suspension parts (Chapter 10).
7   Loose calipers (Chapter 9).
8   Excessive wear of brake shoe or pad material or disc/drum on one side.

58   Noise (high-pitched squeal when the brakes are applied)

Front and/or rear disc brake pads worn out. The noise comes from the wear sensor rubbing against the disc (does not apply to all vehicles). Replace pads with new ones immediately (Chapter 9).

59   Brake roughness (pedal pulsates)

1   Excessive lateral runout (Chapter 9).
2   Uneven pad wear (Chapter 9).
3   Defective rotor (Chapter 9).

60   Excessive brake pedal effort required to stop vehicle

1   Malfunctioning power brake booster (Chapter 9).
2   Partial system failure (Chapter 9).
3   Excessively worn pads or shoes (Chapter 9).
4   Piston in caliper or wheel cylinder stuck or sluggish (Chapter 9).
5   Brake pads or shoes contaminated with oil or grease (Chapter 9).
6   New pads or shoes installed and not yet seated. It will take a while for the new material to seat against the rotor or drum.

61   Excessive brake pedal travel

1   Partial brake system failure (Chapter 9).
2   Insufficient fluid in master cylinder (Chapters 1 and 9).
3   Air trapped in system (Chapters 1 and 9).

62   Dragging brakes

1   Incorrect adjustment of brake light switch (Chapter 9).
2   Master cylinder pistons not returning correctly (Chapter 9).
3   Restricted brakes lines or hoses (Chapters 1 and 9).
4   Incorrect parking brake adjustment (Chapter 9).

63   Grabbing or uneven braking action

1   Malfunction of proportioning valve (Chapter 9).
2   Malfunction of power brake booster unit (Chapter 9).
3   Binding brake pedal mechanism (Chapter 9).

64   Brake pedal feels spongy when depressed

1   Air in hydraulic lines (Chapter 9).
2   Master cylinder mounting bolts loose (Chapter 9).
3   Master cylinder defective (Chapter 9).

65 Brake pedal travels to the floor with little resistance

1 Little or no fluid in the master cylinder reservoir caused by leaking caliper piston(s) (Chapter 9).
2 Loose, damaged or disconnected brake lines (Chapter 9).

66 Parking brake does not hold

Parking brake linkage improperly adjusted (Chapters 1 and 9).

Suspension and steering systems

Note: *Before attempting to diagnose the suspension and steering systems, perform the following preliminary checks:*
a) *Tires for wrong pressure and uneven wear.*
b) *Steering universal joints from the column to the rack and pinion for loose connectors or wear.*
c) *Front and rear suspension and the rack and pinion assembly for loose or damaged parts.*
d) *Out-of-round or out-of-balance tires, bent rims and loose and/or rough wheel bearings.*

67 Vehicle pulls to one side

1 Mismatched or uneven tires (Chapter 10).
2 Broken or sagging springs (Chapter 10).
3 Wheel alignment (Chapter 10).
4 Front brake dragging (Chapter 9).

68 Abnormal or excessive tire wear

1 Wheel alignment (Chapter 10).
2 Sagging or broken springs (Chapter 10).
3 Tire out of balance (Chapter 10).
4 Worn strut damper (Chapter 10).
5 Overloaded vehicle.
6 Tires not rotated regularly.

69 Wheel makes a thumping noise

1 Blister or bump on tire (Chapter 10).
2 Improper strut damper action (Chapter 10).

70 Shimmy, shake or vibration

1 Tire or wheel out-of-balance or out-of-round (Chapter 10).
2 Loose or worn wheel bearings (Chapters 1, 8 and 10).
3 Worn tie-rod ends (Chapter 10).

4 Worn lower balljoints (Chapters 1 and 10).
5 Excessive wheel runout (Chapter 10).
6 Blister or bump on tire (Chapter 10).

71 Hard steering

1 Lack of lubrication at balljoints, tie-rod ends and rack and pinion assembly (Chapter 10).
2 Front wheel alignment (Chapter 10).
3 Low tire pressure(s) (Chapters 1 and 10).

72 Poor returnability of steering to center

1 Lack of lubrication at balljoints and tie-rod ends (Chapter 10).
2 Binding in balljoints (Chapter 10).
3 Binding in steering column (Chapter 10).
4 Lack of lubricant in rack and pinion assembly (Chapter 10).
5 Front wheel alignment (Chapter 10).

73 Abnormal noise at the front end

1 Lack of lubrication at balljoints and tie-rod ends (Chapters 1 and 10).
2 Damaged strut mounting (Chapter 10).
3 Worn control arm bushings or tie-rod ends (Chapter 10).
4 Loose stabilizer bar (Chapter 10).
5 Loose wheel nuts (Chapters 1 and 10).
6 Loose suspension bolts (Chapter 10).

74 Wander or poor steering stability

1 Mismatched or uneven tires (Chapter 10).
2 Lack of lubrication at balljoints and tie-rod ends (Chapters 1 and 10).
3 Worn strut assemblies (Chapter 10).
4 Loose stabilizer bar (Chapter 10).
5 Broken or sagging springs (Chapter 10).
6 Wheel alignment (Chapter 10).

75 Erratic steering when braking

1 Wheel bearings worn (Chapter 10).
2 Broken or sagging springs (Chapter 10).
3 Leaking wheel cylinder or caliper (Chapter 10).
4 Warped rotors or drums (Chapter 10).

76 Excessive pitching and/or rolling around corners or during braking

1 Loose stabilizer bar (Chapter 10).
2 Worn strut dampers or mountings (Chapter 10).
3 Broken or sagging springs (Chapter 10).
4 Overloaded vehicle.

77 Suspension bottoms

1 Overloaded vehicle.
2 Worn strut dampers (Chapter 10).
3 Incorrect, broken or sagging springs (Chapter 10).

78 Cupped tires

1 Front wheel or rear wheel alignment (Chapter 10).
2 Worn strut dampers (Chapter 10).
3 Wheel bearings worn (Chapter 10).
4 Excessive tire or wheel runout (Chapter 10).
5 Worn balljoints (Chapter 10).

79 Excessive tire wear on outside edge

1 Inflation pressures incorrect (Chapter 1).
2 Excessive speed in turns.
3 Front end alignment incorrect (excessive toe-in). Have professionally aligned.
4 Suspension arm bent or twisted (Chapter 10).

80 Excessive tire wear on inside edge

1 Inflation pressures incorrect (Chapter 1).
2 Front end alignment incorrect (toe-out). Have professionally aligned.
3 Loose or damaged steering components (Chapter 10).

81 Tire tread worn in one place

1 Tires out of balance.
2 Damaged or buckled wheel. Inspect and replace if necessary.
3 Defective tire (Chapter 1).

82 Excessive play or looseness in steering system

1 Wheel bearing(s) worn (Chapter 10).
2 Tie-rod end loose (Chapter 10).
3 Rack and pinion loose (Chapter 10).
4 Worn or loose steering intermediate shaft (Chapter 10).

83 Rattling or clicking noise in rack and pinion

1 Insufficient or improper lubricant in rack and pinion assembly (Chapter 10).
2 Rack and pinion attachment loose (Chapter 10).

Chapter 1
Tune-up and routine maintenance

Contents

1

Specifications

Recommended lubricants and fluids

Note: *Listed here are manufacturer recommendations at the time this manual was written. Manufacturers occasionally upgrade their fluid and lubricant specifications, so check with your auto parts store for current recommendations.*

Engine oil type	API grade SF or SF/CC multigrade and fuel efficient oil
Viscosity	See accompanying chart
Fuel	Unleaded gasoline, 87 octane or higher

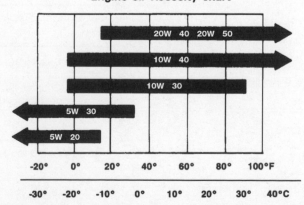

Engine oil viscosity chart

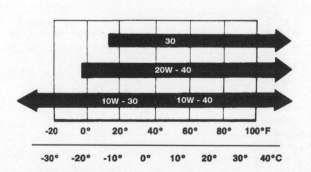

Manual transaxle lubricant viscosity chart

Recommended SAE viscosity grades for engine oils and manual transaxle lubricants

For best fuel economy and cold starting, select the lowest SAE viscosity grade oil for the expected temperature range

Recommended lubricants and fluids

Automatic transaxle fluid type .... **Dexron II** automatic transmission fluid
Manual transaxle
    Lubricant type .... API grade SE or SF engine oil
    Viscosity .... See accompanying chart
Brake fluid type... DOT 3 brake fluid
Power steering system fluid .... Honda power steering fluid

Capacities

Engine oil .... 3.7 qt (3.5 liter)
Automatic transaxle
    1984 and 1985 .... 3.0 qt (2.84 liter)
    1986 on .... 3.2 qt (3.0 liter)
Manual transaxle .... 2.4 qt (2.3 liter)
Coolant .... 5.5 qt (5.3 liter) (approximately)

Ignition system

Spark plug type and gap
    Carbureted engines .... ND W16EKR-S11 (or equivalent) @ 0.039 to 0.043 inch
    Fuel-injected engines .... ND W16EXR-U11 (or equivalent) @ 0.039 to 0.043 inch
Spark plug wire resistance .... Less than 25000 ohms
Ignition timing .... Refer to the vehicle emission control information label in the engine
compartment
Engine firing order 1-3-4-2

Cooling system

Thermostat rating
    Starts to open .... 190-degrees F (88-degrees C)
    Fully open .... 212-degrees F (100-degrees C)

Accessory drivebelt deflection

Power steering pump .... 3/4 to 7/8-inch (18 to 22 mm)
Alternator .... 1/4-inch (6 mm)
Air conditioning compressor.. 3/8 to 1/2-inch (10 to 12 mm)

Clutch

Clutch cable release arm freeplay .... 13/64 to 1/4-inch (5.2 to 6.4 mm)

Brakes

Disc brake pad lining thickness (minimum) .... 1/16-inch (1.6 mm)
Drum brake shoe lining thickness (minimum).......................... 3/32-inch (2 mm)
Parking brake adjustment
    1984 and 1985 .... 4 to 8 clicks
    1986 on .... 7 to 11 clicks

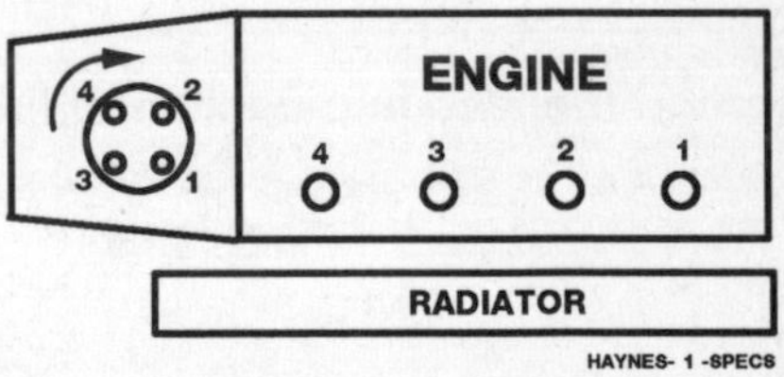

The cylinder locations are shown above - the firing order is 1-3-4-2

Suspension and steering

Steering wheel free play limit... 3/64-inch (1 mm)
Balljoint allowable movement
    1984 and 1985 .... 1/16-inch (1.6 mm)
    1986 on .... None

General

Valve clearances (engine cold)
    Intake valve .... 0.005 to 0.007 in (0.12 to 0.17 mm)
    Exhaust valve .... 0.010 to 0.012 in (0.25 to 0.30 mm)
    Auxiliary valve... 0.005 to 0.007 in (0.12 to 0.17 mm)
Throttle cable deflection limit .... 3/16 to 3/8 in (4 to 10 mm)

Torque specifications

	Ft-lbs
Automatic transaxle drain plug	29
Manual transaxle drain and filler plugs	30 to 40
Rear wheel bearing spindle nuts	
Initial torque	30
Final torque	3
Wheel lug nuts	80
Fuel filter (fuel injected models)	
Banjo bolt	16
Service bolt	9
Clamp bolt	9

1 Introduction

This chapter is designed to help the home mechanic maintain the Honda Accord for peak performance, economy, safety and long life.

On the following pages is a master maintenance schedule, followed by sections dealing specifically with each item on the schedule. Visual checks, adjustments, component replacement and other helpful items are included. Refer to the accompanying photos of the engine compartment and the underside of the vehicle for the location of various components.

Servicing your Accord in accordance with the mileage/time maintenance schedule and the following Sections will provide it with a planned maintenance program that should result in a long and reliable service life. This is a comprehensive plan, so maintaining some items but not others at the specified service intervals will not produce the same results.

As you service your Accord, you will discover that many of the procedures can - and should - be grouped together because of the nature of the particular procedure you're performing or because of the close proximity of two otherwise unrelated components to one another.

For example, if the vehicle is raised for chassis lubrication, you should inspect the exhaust, suspension, steering and fuel systems while you're under the vehicle. When you're rotating the tires, it makes good sense to check the brakes and wheel bearings since the wheels are already removed.

Finally, let's suppose you have to borrow or rent a torque wrench. Even if you only need to tighten the spark plugs, you might as well check the torque of as many critical fasteners as time allows.

The first step of this maintenance program is to prepare yourself before the actual work begins. Read through all sections pertinent to the procedures you're planning to do, then make a list of and gather together all the parts and tools you will need to do the job. If it looks as if you might run into problems during a particular segment of some procedure, seek advice from your local parts man or dealer service department.

1

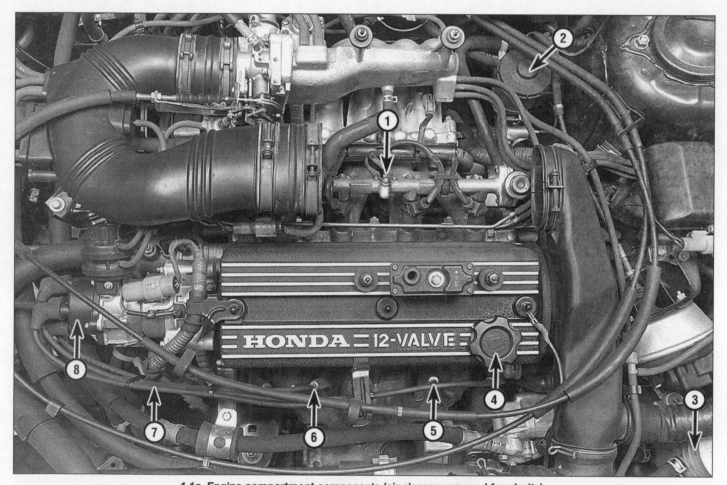

1.1a Engine compartment components (air cleaner removed for clarity)

1	Fuel injector rail	4	Oil filler cap
2	Brake fluid reservoir	5	Engine oil dipstick
3	Power steering fluid reservoir	6	Spark plug

7	Spark plug wire
8	Distributor cap

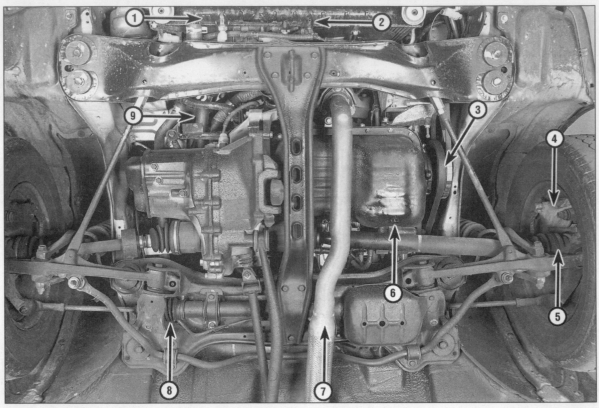

1.1b Engine compartment underside components

1	Radiator	4	Brake caliper	7	Exhaust pipe
2	Radiator drain plug	5	Driveaxle boot	8	Steering gear boot
3	Drivebelts	6	Engine oil drain plug	9	Radiator hose

1.1c Vehicle rear underside components

1	Fuel tank	3	Suspension shock strut/spring unit	5	Fuel filter
2	Muffler	4	Exhaust pipe	6	Fuel tank filler neck

2 Honda Accord Maintenance schedule

The maintenance intervals in this manual are provided with the assumption that you, not the dealer, will be doing the work. These are the minimum maintenance intervals recommended by the factory for Accords that are driven daily. If you wish to keep your vehicle in peak condition at all times, you may wish to perform some of these procedures even more often. Because frequent maintenance enhances the efficiency, performance and resale value of your car, we encourage you to do so. If you drive in dusty areas, tow a trailer, idle or drive at low speeds for extended periods or drive for short distances (less than four miles) in below freezing temperatures, shorter intervals are also recommended.

When your vehicle is new, it should be serviced by a factory authorized dealer service department to protect the factory warranty. In many cases, the initial maintenance check is done at no cost to the owner.

Every 250 miles or weekly, whichever comes first

Check the engine oil level (Section 4)
Check the engine coolant level (Section 4)
Check the windshield washer fluid level (Section 4)
Check the brake fluid level (Section 4)
Check the tires and tire pressures (Section 5)

Every 3000 miles or 3 months, whichever comes first

All items listed above plus:
Check the power steering fluid level (Section 6)
Check the automatic transaxle fluid level (Section 7)
Change the engine oil and oil filter (Section 8)

Every 7500 miles or 6 months, whichever comes first

All items listed above plus:
Inspect and replace, if necessary, the windshield wiper blades (Section 9)
Check and adjust, if necessary, the clutch release arm freeplay (Section 16)
Check and service the battery (Section 10)
Check and adjust, if necessary, the engine drivebelts (Section 11)
Inspect and replace, if necessary, all underhood hoses (Section 12)
Check the cooling system (Section 13)
Rotate the tires (Section 14)
Check the front disc brake pads (Section 15)

Every 15,000 miles or 12 months, whichever comes first

All items listed above plus:
Adjust the valve clearances (Section 20)
Inspect the brake system (Section 15)*
Replace the air filter (Section 17)

Inspect the fuel system (Section 21)
Check and replace, if necessary, the spark plugs (Section 18)
Inspect and replace, if necessary, the spark plug wires, distributor cap and rotor (Section 19)
Change the automatic transaxle fluid (1984 and 1985 models) (Section 30)**
Check the manual transaxle lubricant level (Section 22)*
Inspect the suspension and steering components (Section 23)*
Check the driveaxle boots (Section 24)

Every 30,000 miles or 24 months, whichever comes first

All items listed above plus:
Check the operation of the carburetor choke system (Section 25)
Check and replace, if necessary, the PCV valve (Section 26)
Service the cooling system (drain, flush and refill) (Section 27)
Inspect the exhaust system (Section 28)
Replace the brake fluid (Section 29)
Change the automatic transaxle fluid (1986 and later models) (Section 30)**
Change the manual transaxle lubricant (Section 31)

Every 60,000 miles or 24 months, whichever comes first

All items listed above plus:
Replace the fuel filter (Section 38)
Check and repack, if necessary, the rear wheel bearings (1984 and 1985 models) (Section 39)
Check and adjust, if necessary, the engine ignition timing (Section 32)
Check and adjust, if necessary, the engine idle speed (Section 35)
Inspect the evaporative emissions control system (Section 36)
Check the Exhaust Gas Recirculation (EGR) system (Section 37)
Check the operation of the thermostatic air cleaner (Section 33)
Check the operation of the throttle linkage (Section 34)
Inspect and replace, if necessary, the timing belt (Chapter 2A).

*This item is affected by "severe" operating conditions as described below. If your vehicle is operated under "severe" conditions, perform all maintenance indicated with a * at 3000 mile/3 month intervals.*

Severe conditions are indicated if you mainly operate your vehicle under one or more of the following conditions:

Operating in dusty areas
Towing a trailer
Idling for extended periods and/or low speed operation
Operating when outside temperatures remain below freezing and when most trips are less than four miles

** If operated under one or more of the following conditions, change the automatic transaxle fluid and filter every 7500 miles (1984 and 1985 models) or 15,000 miles (1986 through 1989 models):

In heavy city traffic where the outside temperature regularly reaches 90-degrees F (32-degrees C) or higher
In hilly or mountainous terrain

1

4.2 The engine oil dipstick (arrow) is located at the front side of the engine, behind the radiator

3   Tune-up general information

The term *tune-up* is used in this manual to represent a combination of individual operations rather than one specific procedure.

If, from the time the vehicle is new, the routine maintenance schedule is followed closely and frequent checks are made of fluid levels and high wear items, as suggested throughout this manual, the engine will be kept in relatively good running condition and the need for additional work will be minimized.

More likely than not, however, there will be times when the engine is running poorly due to lack of regular maintenance. This is even more likely if a used vehicle, which has not received regular and frequent maintenance checks, is purchased. In such cases, an engine tune-up will be needed outside of the regular routine maintenance intervals.

The first step in any tune-up or engine diagnosis to help correct a poor running engine would be a cylinder compression check. A check of the engine compression (Chapter 2 Part B) will give valuable information regarding the overall performance of

4.4 The oil level should be between the two holes in the dipstick - if it isn't, add enough oil to bring the level to or near the upper hole (it takes one quart to raise the level from the lower to the upper hole)

many internal components and should be used as a basis for tune-up and repair procedures. If, for instance, a compression check indicates serious internal engine wear, a conventional tune-up will not help the running condition of the engine and would be a waste of time and money. Because of its importance, compression checking should be performed by someone with the proper compression testing gauge and the knowledge to use it properly.

The following series of operations are those most often needed to bring a generally poor running engine back into a proper state of tune.

Minor tune-up

Clean, inspect and test the battery
Check all engine related fluids
Check and adjust the drivebelts
Replace the spark plugs
Inspect the distributor cap and rotor
Inspect the spark plug and coil wires
Check and adjust the idle speed
Check the air filter
Check the cooling system
Check all underhood hoses

Major tune-up

All items listed under minor tune-up, plus . . .

Check the EGR system
Check the ignition system
Check the charging system
Check the fuel system
Replace the air filter
Replace the distributor cap and rotor
Replace the spark plug wires

4   Fluid level checks

1   Fluids are an essential part of the lubrication, cooling, brake, clutch and other systems. Because these fluids gradually become depleted and/or contaminated during normal operation of the vehicle, they must be periodically replenished. See *Recommended lubri-*

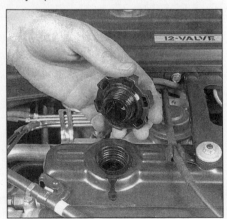

4.6 The threaded oil filler cap is located on the camshaft cover - to prevent dirt from contaminating the engine, always make sure the area around this opening is clean before unscrewing the cap

cants, fluids and capacities at the beginning of this Chapter before adding fluid to any of the following components. **Note:** *The vehicle must be on level ground before fluid levels can be checked.*

Engine oil

Refer to illustrations 4.2, 4.4 and 4.6

2   The engine oil level is checked with a dipstick located at the front side of the engine **(see illustration)**. The dipstick extends through a metal tube from which it protrudes down into the engine oil pan.

3   The oil level should be checked before the vehicle has been driven, or about 15 minutes after the engine has been shut off. If the oil is checked immediately after driving the vehicle, some of the oil will remain in the upper engine components, producing an inaccurate reading on the dipstick.

4   Pull the dipstick from the tube and wipe all the oil from the end with a clean rag or paper towel. Insert the clean dipstick all the way back into its metal tube and pull it out again. Observe the oil at the end of the dipstick. At its highest point, the level should be between the upper and lower holes **(see illustration)**.

5   It takes one quart of oil to raise the level from the lower hole to the upper hole on the dipstick. Do not allow the level to drop below the lower hole or oil starvation may cause engine damage. Conversely, overfilling the engine (adding oil above the upper hole) may cause oil fouled spark plugs, oil leaks or oil seal failures.

6   Remove the threaded cap from the camshaft cover to add oil **(see illustration)**. Use an oil can spout or funnel to prevent spills. After adding the oil, install the filler cap hand tight. Start the engine and look carefully for any small leaks around the oil filter or drain plug. Stop the engine and check the oil level again after it has had sufficient time to drain from the upper block and cylinder head galleys.

7   Checking the oil level is an important preventive maintenance step. A continually dropping oil level indicates oil leakage through damaged seals, from loose connections, or past worn rings or valve guides. If the oil looks milky in color or has water droplets in it, a cylinder head gasket may be blown. The engine should be checked immediately. The condition of the oil should also be checked. Each time you check the oil level, slide your thumb and index finger up the dipstick before wiping off the oil. If you see small dirt or metal particles clinging to the dipstick, the oil should be changed (see Section 8).

Engine coolant

Refer to illustration 4.9

8   All vehicles covered by this manual are equipped with a pressurized coolant recovery system. A white coolant reservoir located in the right front corner of the engine compartment is connected by a hose to the base of

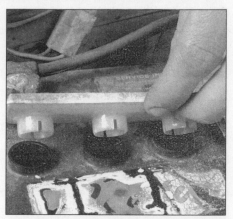

4.9 Make sure the coolant level in the reservoir is between the Max and Min lines (which can be seen below the battery using a flashlight) - if it's below the Min line, add a sufficient quantity of the specified mixture of antifreeze and water

4.14 The windshield washer fluid reservoir tank is located in the right front corner of the engine compartment - fluid can be added after flipping up the cap

4.15 If you have a conventional battery, keep the electrolyte level of all the cells in the battery between the Upper and Lower levels - use only distilled water to replenish a cell and never overfill it or electrolyte may squirt out of the battery during periods of heavy charging

the coolant filler cap. If the coolant heats up during engine operation, coolant can escape through a pressurized filler cap, then through a connecting hose into the reservoir. As the engine cools, the coolant is automatically drawn back into the cooling system to maintain the correct level.

9   The coolant level should be checked regularly. It must be between the Max and Min lines on the tank. The level will vary with the temperature of the engine. When the engine is cold, the coolant level should be at or slightly above the Min mark on the tank. Once the engine has warmed up, the level should be at or near the Max mark. If it isn't, allow the fluid in the tank to cool, then remove the cap from the reservoir **(see illustration)** and add coolant to bring the level up to the Max line. Use only ethylene/glycol type coolant and water in the mixture ratio recommended by your owner's manual. Do not use supplemental inhibitors or additives. If only a small amount of coolant is required to bring the system up to the proper level, water can be used. However, repeated additions of

water will dilute the recommended antifreeze and water solution. In order to maintain the proper ratio of antifreeze and water, it is advisable to top up the coolant level with the correct mixture. Refer to your owner's manual for the recommended ratio.

10   If the coolant level drops within a short time after replenishment, there may be a leak in the system. Inspect the radiator, hoses, engine coolant filler cap, drain plugs, air bleeder plugs and water pump. If no leak is evident, have the radiator cap pressure tested by your dealer. **Warning:** *Never remove the radiator cap or the coolant recovery reservoir cap when the engine is running or has just been shut down, because the cooling system is hot. Escaping steam and scalding liquid could cause serious injury.*

11   If it is necessary to open the radiator cap, wait until the system has cooled completely, then wrap a thick cloth around the cap and turn it to the first stop. If any steam escapes, wait until the system has cooled further, then remove the cap.

12   When checking the coolant level, always note its condition. It should be relatively clear. If it is brown or rust colored, the system should be drained, flushed and refilled. Even if the coolant appears to be normal, the corrosion inhibitors wear out with use, so it must be replaced at the specified intervals.

13   Do not allow antifreeze to come in contact with your skin or painted surfaces of the vehicle. Flush contacted areas immediately with plenty of water.

Windshield washer fluid

Refer to illustration 4.14

14   Fluid for the windshield washer system is stored in a plastic reservoir which is located at the right front corner of the engine compartment **(see illustration)**. In milder climates, plain water can be used to top up the reservoir, but the reservoir should be kept no more than 2/3 full to allow for expansion should the water freeze. In colder climates,

the use of a specially designed windshield washer fluid, available at your dealer and any auto parts store, will help lower the freezing point of the fluid. Mix the solution with water in accordance with the manufacturer's directions on the container. Do not use regular antifreeze. It will damage the vehicle's paint.

Battery electrolyte

Refer to illustration 4.15

15   Most vehicles covered by this manual are equipped with a battery which is permanently sealed (except for vent holes) and has no filler caps. Water doesn't have to be added to these batteries at any time. If a conventional battery is installed on your vehicle, check the electrolyte level of all six battery cells. It must be between the upper and lower levels **(see illustration)**. If the level is low, unsnap or unscrew the filler/vent cap and add distilled water. Install and securely retighten the cap. **Caution:** *Overfilling the cells may cause electrolyte to spill over during periods of heavy charging, causing corrosion or damage.*

Brake fluid

Refer to illustration 4.17

16   The brake master cylinder is mounted on the front of the power booster unit in the engine compartment.

17   To check the fluid level of the brake master cylinder reservoir, simply look at the MAX and MIN marks on the reservoir **(see illustration)**. The level should be between the two marks.

18   If the level is low, wipe the top of the reservoir cover with a clean rag to prevent contamination of the brake system before lifting the cap.

19   Add only the specified brake fluid to the brake reservoir (refer to *Recommended lubricants and fluids* at the front of this chapter or to your owner's manual). Mixing different types of brake fluid can damage the system.

4.17 The brake fluid level should be kept between the Max and Min marks on the translucent plastic reservoir - lift up the cap to add fluid

Fill the brake master cylinder reservoir only to about 3/4-inch below the Max line - this brings the fluid to the correct level when you put the cap back on. **Warning:** *Use caution when filling the reservoir - brake fluid can harm your eyes and damage painted surfaces. Do not use brake fluid that has been opened for more than one year or has been left open. Brake fluid absorbs moisture from the air. Excess moisture can cause a dangerous loss of braking.*

20 While the reservoir cap is removed, inspect the master cylinder reservoir for contamination. If deposits, dirt particles or water droplets are present, the system should be drained and refilled (see Chapter 9).

21 After filling the reservoir to the proper level, make sure the lid is properly seated to prevent fluid leakage and/or system pressure loss.

22 The brake fluid in the master cylinder will drop slightly as the brake pads at each wheel wear down during normal operation. If the master cylinder requires repeated replenishing to keep it at the proper level, this is an indication of leakage in the brake system, which should be corrected immediately. Check all brake lines and connections, along with the wheel cylinders and booster (see Section 15 for more information).

23 If, upon checking the master cylinder fluid level, you discover an empty or nearly empty reservoir, the brake system should be bled (see Chapter 9).

5   Tire and tire pressure checks

Refer to illustrations 5.2, 5.3, 5.4a, 5.4b and 5.8

1 Periodic inspection of the tires may spare you from the inconvenience of being stranded with a flat tire. It can also provide you with vital information regarding possible problems in the steering and suspension systems before major damage occurs.

2 Normal tread wear can be monitored with a simple, inexpensive device known as a tread depth indicator **(see illustration)**. When the tread depth reaches the specified minimum, replace the tire(s).

3 Note any abnormal tread wear **(see illustration)**. Tread pattern irregularities such as cupping, flat spots and more wear on one side than the other are indications of front end alignment and/or balance problems. If any of these conditions are noted, take the vehicle to a tire shop or service station to correct the problem.

4 Look closely for cuts, punctures and embedded nails or tacks. Sometimes a tire will hold its air pressure for a short time or leak down very slowly even after a nail has embedded itself into the tread. If a slow leak persists, check the valve core to make sure it is tight **(see illustration)**. Examine the tread for an object that may have embedded itself into the tire or for a "plug" that may have begun to leak (radial tire punctures are repaired with a plug

5.2 A tire tread depth indicator should be used to monitor tire wear - they are available at auto parts stores and service stations and cost very little

that is installed in a puncture). If a puncture is suspected, it can be easily verified by spraying a solution of soapy water onto the puncture area **(see illustration)**. The soapy solution will bubble if there is a leak. Unless the puncture is inordinately large, a tire shop or gas station can usually repair the punctured tire.

5 Carefully inspect the inboard sidewall of each tire for evidence of brake fluid leakage. If you see any, inspect the brakes immediately.

6 Correct tire air pressure adds miles to the lifespan of the tires, improves mileage and enhances overall ride quality. Tire pres-

UNDERINFLATION

**INCORRECT TOE-IN
OR EXTREME CAMBER**

CUPPING

Cupping may be caused by:
- Underinflation and/or mechanical irregularities such as out-of-balance condition of wheel and/or tire, and bent or damaged wheel.
- Loose or worn steering tie-rod or steering idler arm.
- Loose, damaged or worn front suspension parts.

OVERINFLATION

**FEATHERING DUE
TO MISALIGNMENT**

**5.3 This chart will help you determine the condition of your tires, the probable cause(s)
of abnormal wear and the corrective action necessary**

5.4a If a tire loses air on a steady basis, check the valve core first to make sure it's snug (special inexpensive wrenches are commonly available at auto parts stores)

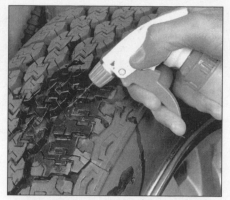

5.4b If the valve core is tight, raise the corner of the vehicle with the low tire and spray a soapy water solution onto the tread as the tire is turned slowly - slow leaks will cause small bubbles to appear

5.8 To extend the life of the tires, check the air pressure at least once a week with an accurate gauge (don't forget the spare!)

6.2 The power steering fluid reservoir is translucent so the fluid level can be checked without removing the cap - keep the level between the two lines (arrows)

sure cannot be accurately estimated by looking at a tire, particularly if it is a radial. A tire pressure gauge is therefore essential. Keep an accurate gauge in the glovebox. The pressure gauges fitted to the nozzles of air hoses at gas stations are often inaccurate.

7 Always check tire pressure when the tires are cold. "Cold," in this case, means the vehicle has not been driven over a mile in the three hours preceding a tire pressure check. A pressure rise of four to eight pounds is not uncommon once the tires are warm.

8 Unscrew the valve cap protruding from the wheel or hubcap and push the gauge firmly onto the valve **(see illustration)**. Note the reading on the gauge and compare this figure to the recommended tire pressure shown on the tire placard on the left door jamb. Be sure to reinstall the valve cap to keep dirt and moisture out of the valve stem mechanism. Check all four tires and, if necessary, add enough air to bring them up to the recommended pressure levels.

9 Don't forget to keep the spare tire inflated to the specified pressure (consult your owner's manual). Note that the air pressure specified for the compact spare is significantly higher than the pressure of the regular tires.

6 Power steering fluid level check

Refer to illustration 6.2

1 Unlike manual steering, the power steering system relies on fluid which may, over a period of time, require replenishing.

2 The fluid reservoir for the power steering pump is located on the inner fender panel near the left front of the engine compartment **(see illustration)**.

3 For the check, the front wheels should be pointed straight ahead and the engine should be off.

4 The reservoir is translucent plastic and the fluid level can be checked visually **(see illustration 6.2)**.

5 If additional fluid is required, pour the specified type directly into the reservoir, using a funnel to prevent spills.

6 If the reservoir requires frequent fluid additions, all power steering hoses, hose connections, the power steering pump and the rack and pinion assembly should be carefully checked for leaks.

7 Automatic transaxle fluid level check

Refer to illustrations 7.3 and 7.5

1 The level of the automatic transaxle fluid should be carefully maintained. Low fluid level can lead to slipping or loss of drive, while overfilling can cause foaming, loss of fluid and transaxle damage.

2 The transaxle fluid level should only be checked when the engine is off.

3 Remove the dipstick **(see illustration)**. Check the level of the fluid on the dipstick and note its condition.

4 Wipe the fluid from the dipstick with a clean rag and reinsert it, but don't screw it in.

5 Pull the dipstick out again and note the fluid level **(see illustration)**. The level should be between the Full and Add marks on the dipstick. If the level is low, add the specified automatic transmission fluid through the dipstick opening with a funnel.

6 Add just enough of the specified fluid to

fill the transaxle to the proper level. It takes about one pint to raise the level from the Add mark to the Full mark, so add the fluid a little at a time and keep checking the level until it is correct.

7 The condition of the fluid should also be checked along with the level. If the fluid at the end of the dipstick is black or a dark reddish-brown color, or if it emits a burned smell, the fluid should be changed (see Section 30). If you are in doubt about the condition of the fluid, purchase some new fluid and compare the two for color and smell.

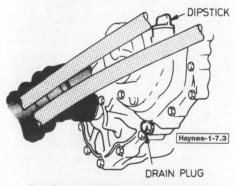

7.3 The automatic transaxle dipstick screws into the transaxle case

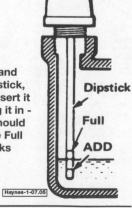

7.5 Unscrew and remove the dipstick, wipe it off and insert it without screwing it in - the fluid level should be between the Full and Add marks

1

8 Engine oil and oil filter change

Refer to illustrations 8.2, 8.7, 8.12 and 8.14

1 Frequent oil changes are the best preventive maintenance the home mechanic can give the engine, because aging oil becomes diluted and contaminated, which leads to premature engine wear.

2 Make sure you have all the necessary tools before you begin this procedure **(see illustration)**. You should also have plenty of rags or newspapers handy for mopping up any spills.

3 Access to the underside of the vehicle is greatly improved if the vehicle can be lifted on a hoist, driven onto ramps or supported by jackstands. **Warning:** *Do not work under a vehicle which is supported only by a bumper, hydraulic or scissors-type jack.*

4 If this is your first oil change, get under the vehicle and familiarize yourself with the locations of the oil drain plug and the oil filter. The engine and exhaust components will be warm during the actual work, so try to anticipate any potential problems before the engine and accessories are hot.

5 Park the vehicle on a level spot. Start the engine and allow it to reach its normal operating temperature. Warm oil and sludge will flow out more easily. Turn off the engine when it's warmed up. Remove the filler cap from the camshaft cover.

6 Raise the vehicle and support it securely on jackstands. **Warning:** *To avoid personal injury, never get beneath the vehicle when it is supported by only by a jack. The jack provided with your vehicle is designed solely for raising the vehicle to remove and replace the wheels. Always use jackstands to support the vehicle when it becomes necessary to place your body underneath the vehicle.*

7 Being careful not to touch the hot exhaust components, place the drain pan under the drain plug in the bottom of the pan and remove the plug **(see illustration)**. You may want to wear gloves while unscrewing the plug the final few turns if the engine is hot.

8 Allow the old oil to drain into the pan. It may be necessary to move the pan farther under the engine as the oil flow slows to a trickle. Inspect the old oil for the presence of metal shavings and chips.

9 After all the oil has drained, wipe off the drain plug with a clean rag. Even minute metal particles clinging to the plug would immediately contaminate the new oil.

10 Clean the area around the drain plug opening, reinstall the plug and tighten it securely, but do not strip the threads.

11 Move the drain pan into position under the oil filter.

12 Loosen the oil filter **(see illustration)** by turning it counterclockwise with the filter wrench. Any standard filter wrench will work. Sometimes the oil filter is screwed on so tightly that it cannot be loosened. If this situation occurs, punch a metal bar or long screwdriver directly through the side of the canister and use it as a T-bar to turn the filter. Be prepared for oil to spurt out of the canister as it is punctured. Once the filter is loose, use your hands to unscrew it from the block. Just as the filter is detached from the block, immediately tilt the open end up to prevent the oil inside the filter from spilling out. **Warning:** *The engine exhaust manifold may still be hot, so be careful.*

13 With a clean rag, wipe off the mounting surface on the block. If a residue of old oil is allowed to remain, it will smoke when the block is heated up. It will also prevent the new filter from seating properly. Also make sure that the none of the old gasket remains stuck to the mounting surface. It can be removed with a scraper if necessary.

14 Compare the old filter with the new one to make sure they are the same type. Smear some clean engine oil on the rubber gasket of the new filter and screw it into place **(see illustration)**. Because overtightening the filter will damage the gasket, do not use a filter wrench to tighten the filter. Tighten it *by hand* until the gasket contacts the seating surface. Then seat the filter by giving it an additional 3/4-turn.

15 Remove all tools, rags, etc. from under

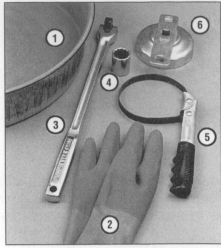

8.2 These tools are required when changing the engine oil and filter

1 **Drain pan** - It should be fairly shallow in depth, but wide in order to prevent spills

2 **Rubber gloves** - When removing the drain plug and filter, you will get oil on your hands (the gloves will prevent burns)

3 **Breaker bar** - Sometimes the oil drain plug is tight and a long breaker bar is needed to loosen it

4 **Socket** - This is used with the breaker bar or a ratchet (must be the correct size to fit the drain plug)

5 **Filter wrench** - This is a metal band-type wrench, which requires clearance around the filter to be effective

6 **Filter wrench** - This type fits on the bottom of the filter and can be turned with a ratchet or breaker bar (different size wrenches are available for different types of filters)

the vehicle, being careful not to spill the oil in the drain pan, then lower the vehicle.

16 Add new oil to the engine through the oil filler cap in the camshaft cover. Use a spout or funnel to prevent oil from spilling onto the

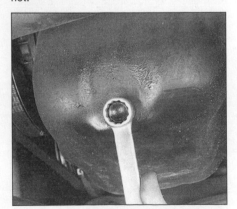

8.7 Use the proper size box end wrench or six-point socket to remove the oil drain plug without rounding off its corners

8.12 The oil filter is usually on very tight and will require a special wrench for removal - DO NOT use the wrench to tighten the new filter (view is from beneath the driver's side of the vehicle)

8.14 Lubricate the oil filter gasket with clean engine oil before installing the filter on the engine

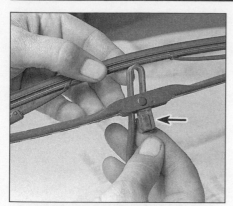

9.9 On 1986 through 1989 models, press in on the lock tab (arrow) and push the blade assembly out of the hook at the end to remove it

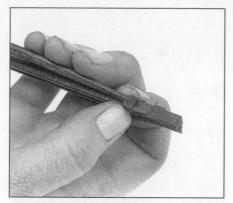

9.10 Squeeze the blade element tabs, pull the element out of the metal frame and remove it

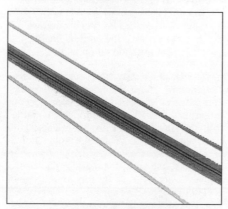

9.11 Install the metal retainers in the new wiper element before inserting it into the frame

10.1 Tools and materials required for battery maintenance

1   *Face shield/safety goggles* - When removing corrosion with a brush, the acidic particles can easily fly up into your eyes
2   *Baking soda* - A solution of baking soda and water can be used to neutralize corrosion
3   *Petroleum jelly* - A layer of this on the battery posts will help prevent corrosion
4   *Battery post/cable cleaner* - This wire brush cleaning tool will remove all traces of corrosion from the battery posts and cable clamps
5   *Treated felt washers* - Placing one of these on each post, directly under the cable clamps, will help prevent corrosion
6   *Puller* - Sometimes the cable clamps are very difficult to pull off the posts, even after the nut has been completely loosened. This tool pulls the clamp straight up and off the post without damage
7   *Battery post/cable cleaner* - Here is another cleaning tool which is a slightly different version of number 4 above, but it does the same thing
8   *Rubber gloves* - Another safety item to consider when servicing the battery; remember there's acid inside the battery!

top of the engine. Pour three quarts of fresh oil into the engine. Wait a few minutes to allow the oil to drain into the pan, then check the level on the oil dipstick (see Section 4 if necessary). If the oil level is at or near the upper hole on the dipstick, install the filler cap hand tight, start the engine and allow the new oil to circulate.

17   Allow the engine to run for about a minute. While the engine is running, look under the vehicle and check for leaks at the oil pan drain plug and around the oil filter. If either is leaking, stop the engine and tighten the plug or filter slightly.

18   Wait a few minutes to allow the oil to trickle down into the pan, then recheck the level on the dipstick and, if necessary, add enough oil to bring the level to the upper hole.

19   During the first few trips after an oil change, make it a point to check frequently for leaks and proper oil level.

20   The old oil drained from the engine cannot be reused in its present state and should be discarded. Oil reclamation centers, auto repair shops and gas stations will normally accept the oil, which can be refined and used again. After the oil has cooled, it can be drained into a suitable container (capped plastic jugs, topped bottles, milk cartons, etc.) for transport to one of these disposal sites.

9   Windshield wiper blade inspection and replacement

Refer to illustrations 9.9, 9.10 and 9.11

1   The windshield wiper and blade assembly should be inspected periodically for damage, loose components and cracked or worn blade elements.

2   Road film can build up on the wiper blades and affect their efficiency, so they should be washed regularly with a mild detergent solution.

3   The action of the wiping mechanism can loosen bolts, nuts and fasteners, so they should be checked and tightened, as necessary, at the same time the wiper blades are

checked.

4   If the wiper blade elements are cracked, worn or warped, or no longer clean adequately, they should be replaced with new ones.

5   Lift the arm assembly away from the glass for clearance.

1984 and 1985 models

6   Remove the screws and detach the wiper assembly from the arm.

7   Unhook the retainer at the end from the metal frame and slide the element out.

8   Insert the new element into the frame fully until the retainer locks it in place.

1986 and later models

9   Press in on the lock tab and push the blade assembly down the wiper arm, out of the hook at the end **(see illustration)**.

10   Squeeze the blade element tabs tightly and pull the element out of the metal frame **(see illustration)**.

11   Remove the metal retainers from the element and install them in the new element **(see illustration)**.

12   Insert the element into the frame and push it until the element tabs lock.

13   Place the metal arm assembly in the hook on the wiper arm and press it into place until the lock tab snaps into place.

10   Battery check and maintenance

Refer to illustrations 10.1, 10.6a, 10.6b, 10.7a and 10.7b

1   A routine preventive maintenance program for the battery in your vehicle is the only way to ensure quick and reliable starts. But before performing any battery maintenance, make sure that you have the proper equipment necessary to work safely around the battery **(see illustration)**.

2   There are also several precautions that should be taken whenever battery maintenance is performed. Before servicing the battery, always turn the engine and all acces-

1

10.6a Battery terminal corrosion usually appears as light, fluffy powder

10.6b Removing a cable from the battery post with a wrench - sometimes if corrosion has caused deterioration of the nut hex a pair of special battery pliers is required for this procedure (always remove the negative cable first and hook it up last!)

10.7a Regardless of the type of the tool used to clean the battery post, a clean, shiny surface should be the result

10.7b When cleaning the cable clamps, all corrosion must be removed (the inside of the clamp is tapered to match the taper on the post, so don't remove too much material)

sories off and disconnect the cable from the negative terminal of the battery.

3   The battery produces hydrogen gas, which is both flammable and explosive. Never create a spark, smoke or light a match around the battery. Always charge the battery in a ventilated area.

4   Electrolyte contains poisonous and corrosive sulfuric acid. Do not allow it to get in your eyes, on your skin on your clothes. Never ingest it. Wear protective safety glasses when working near the battery. Keep children away from the battery.

5   Note the external condition of the battery. If the positive terminal and cable clamp on your vehicle's battery is equipped with a rubber protector, make sure that it's not torn or damaged. It should completely cover the terminal. Look for any corroded or loose connections, cracks in the case or cover or loose hold-down clamps. Also check the entire length of each cable for cracks and frayed conductors.

6   If corrosion, which looks like white, fluffy deposits **(see illustration)** is evident, particularly around the terminals, the battery should be removed for cleaning. Loosen the cable clamp nuts with a wrench, being careful to remove the negative cable first, and slide the off the terminals **(see illustration)**. Then disconnect the hold-down clamp nuts, remove the clamp and lift the battery from the engine compartment.

7   Clean the cable clamps thoroughly with a battery brush or a terminal cleaner and a solution of warm water and baking soda **(see illustration)**. Wash the terminals and the top of the battery case with the same solution but make sure that the solution doesn't get into the battery. When cleaning the cables, terminals and battery top, wear safety goggles and rubber gloves to prevent any solution from coming in contact with your eyes or hands. Wear old clothes too - even diluted, sulfuric acid splashed onto clothes will burn holes in them. If the terminals have been extensively corroded, clean them up with a terminal cleaner **(see illustration)**. Thoroughly wash all cleaned areas with plain water.

8   Before reinstalling the battery in the engine compartment, inspect the plastic bat-

tery carrier. If it's dirty or covered with corrosion, remove it and clean it in the same solution of warm water and baking soda. Inspect the metal brackets which support the carrier to make sure that they are not covered with corrosion. If they are, wash them off. If corrosion is extensive, sand the brackets down to bare metal and spray them with a zinc-based primer (available in spray cans at auto paint and body supply stores).

9   Reinstall the battery carrier and the battery back into the engine compartment. Make sure that no parts or wires are laying on the carrier during installation of the battery.

10   Install a pair of specially treated felt washers around the terminals (available at auto parts stores), then coat the terminals and the cable clamps with petroleum jelly or grease to prevent further corrosion. Install the cable clamps and tighten the nuts, being careful to install the negative cable last.

11   Install the hold-down clamp and nuts. Tighten the nuts only enough to hold the battery firmly in place. Overtightening these nuts can crack the battery case.

12   Further information on the battery, charging and jump starting can be found in Chapter 5 and at the front of this manual.

11   Drivebelt check, adjustment and replacement

Refer to illustrations 11.2, 11.3a, 11.3b, 11.4, 11.6, 11.7 and 11.10

Check

1   The alternator and air conditioning compressor drivebelts are either V-belts or V-ribbed belts. Sometimes referred to as "fan" belts, the drivebelts are located at the left end of the engine. The good condition and proper adjustment of the alternator belt is critical to the operation of the engine. Because of their composition and the high stresses to which they are subjected, drivebelts stretch and

deteriorate as they get older. They must therefore be periodically inspected.

2   The number of belts used on a particular vehicle depends on the accessories installed. One belt transmits power from the crankshaft to the alternator and water pump **(see illustration)**. If your vehicle is equipped with power steering or air conditioning, the power steering pump and/or A/C compressor is driven by another belt or belts.

3   With the engine off, open the hood and locate the drivebelts at the left end of the engine. With a flashlight, check each belt: On V-belts, check for cracks and separation of the belt plies **(see illustration)**. On V-ribbed belts, check for separation of the adhesive rubber on both sides of the core, core separation from the belt side, a severed core, separation of the ribs from the adhesive rubber, cracking or separation of the ribs, and torn or worn ribs or cracks in the inner ridges of the ribs **(see illustration)**. On both belt types, check for fraying and glazing, which gives the belt a shiny appearance. Both sides of the belt should be inspected, which means you will have to twist the belt to check the underside. Use your fingers to feel the belt where you can't see it. If any of the above conditions are evident, replace the belt (go to Step 8).

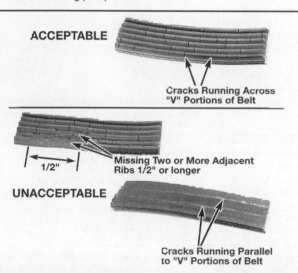

11.2 Typical drivebelt layout

1   Alternator and water pump belt
2   Power steering pump belt

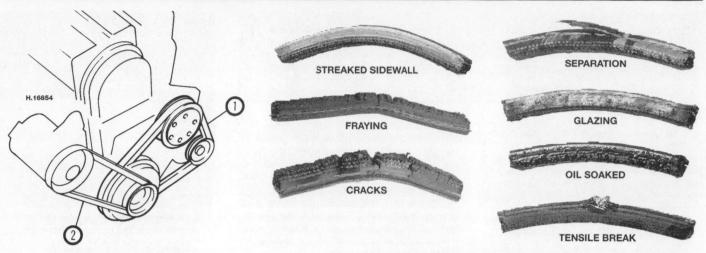

STREAKED SIDEWALL

FRAYING

CRACKS

SEPARATION

GLAZING

OIL SOAKED

TENSILE BREAK

**11.3a Here are some of the more common problems associated with V-belts -
check the belts very carefully to prevent an untimely breakdown**

ACCEPTABLE

Cracks Running Across
"V" Portions of Belt

1/2"

Missing Two or More Adjacent
Ribs 1/2" or longer

UNACCEPTABLE

Cracks Running Parallel
to "V" Portions of Belt

**11.3b Check V-ribbed belts for signs of wear like these -
if the belt looks worn, replace it**

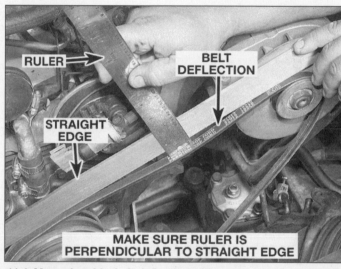

RULER

BELT
DEFLECTION

STRAIGHT
EDGE

**MAKE SURE RULER IS
PERPENDICULAR TO STRAIGHT EDGE**

11.4 Measuring drivebelt deflection with a straightedge and ruler

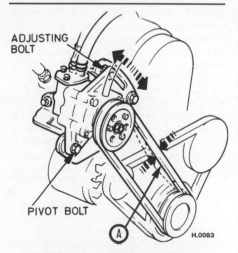

ADJUSTING
BOLT

PIVOT BOLT

H.0083

**11.6 Typical power steering pump
drivebelt adjustment details**

A   Drivebelt deflection

**11.7 Loosen the nut on the other side of
the pivot bolt (A), loosen the locknut (B),
then adjust the belt tension with the
adjusting bolt (C) - after adjustment,
be sure to tighten the locknuts**

4   The tightness of each belt is checked by pushing on it at a distance halfway between the pulleys **(see illustration)**. Apply about 10 pounds of force with your thumb and see how much the belt moves down (deflects). Refer to the Specifications for the amount of deflection allowed in each belt.

Adjustment

5   If adjustment is necessary, it is done by moving the belt-driven accessory on the bracket.

6   For some components, there will be an adjusting bolt and a pivot bolt **(see illustration)**. Both must be loosened slightly to enable you to move the component. After the two bolts have been loosened, move the component away from the engine (to tighten the belt) or toward the engine (to loosen the belt). After adjustment, tighten the bolts securely.

7   On some components, loosen the pivot bolt and locknut on the adjusting bolt. Turn the adjusting bolt to tension the belt **(see illustration)**.

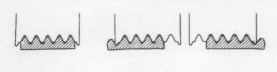

CORRECT   WRONG   WRONG

11.10 When installing a V-ribbed belt, make sure it is centered on the pulley - it must not overlap either edge of the pulley

Replacement

8   To replace a belt, follow the above procedures for drivebelt adjustment but slip the belt off the crankshaft pulley and remove it. If you are replacing the alternator belt, you will have to remove the air conditioning compressor belt first because of the way they are arranged on the crankshaft pulley. Because of this and because belts tend to wear out more or less together, it is a good idea to replace both belts at the same time. Mark each belt and its appropriate pulley groove so the replacement belts can be installed in their proper positions.

9   Take the old belts to the parts store in order to make a direct comparison for length, width and design.

10   After replacing a V-ribbed drivebelt, make sure it fits properly in the ribbed grooves in the pulleys **(see illustration)**. It is essential that the belt be properly centered.

11   Adjust the belt(s) in accordance with the procedure outlined above.

12   Underhood hose check and replacement

Caution: *Replacement of air conditioning hoses must be left to a dealer service department or air conditioning shop that has the equipment to depressurize the system safely. Never remove air conditioning components or hoses until the system has been depressurized.*

General

1   High temperatures in the engine compartment can cause the deterioration of the rubber and plastic hoses used for engine, accessory and emission systems operation. Periodic inspection should be made for cracks, loose clamps, material hardening and leaks.

2   Information specific to the cooling system hoses can be found in Section 13.

3   Some, but not all, hoses are secured to the fittings with clamps. Where clamps are used, check to be sure they haven't lost their tension, allowing the hose to leak. If clamps aren't used, make sure the hose has not expanded and/or hardened where it slips over the fitting, allowing it to leak.

Vacuum hoses

4   It's quite common for vacuum hoses, especially those in the emissions system, to be color coded or identified by colored stripes molded into them. Various systems require hoses with different wall thicknesses, collapse resistance and temperature resis-

tance. When replacing hoses, be sure the new ones are made of the same material.

5   Often the only effective way to check a hose is to remove it completely from the vehicle. If more than one hose is removed, be sure to label the hoses and fittings to ensure correct installation.

6   When checking vacuum hoses, be sure to include any plastic T-fittings in the check. Inspect the fittings for cracks and the hose where it fits over the fitting for distortion, which could cause leakage.

7   A small piece of vacuum hose (1/4-inch inside diameter) can be used as a stethoscope to detect vacuum leaks. Hold one end of the hose to your ear and probe around vacuum hoses and fittings, listening for the "hissing" sound characteristic of a vacuum leak. **Warning:** *When probing with the vacuum hose stethoscope, be very careful not to come into contact with moving engine components such as the drivebelts, cooling fan, etc.*

Fuel hose

Warning: *There are certain precautions which must be taken when inspecting or servicing fuel system components. Work in a well ventilated area and do not allow open flames (cigarettes, appliance pilot lights, etc.) or bare light bulbs near the work area. Mop up any spills immediately and do not store fuel soaked rags where they could ignite. On vehicles equipped with fuel injection, the fuel system is under pressure, so if any fuel lines are to be disconnected, the pressure in the system must be relieved first (see Chapter 4 for more information).*

8   Check all rubber fuel lines for deterioration and chafing. Check especially for cracks in areas where the hose bends and just before fittings, such as where a hose attaches to the fuel filter.

9   High quality fuel line, usually identified by the word *Fluroelastomer* printed on the hose, should be used for fuel line replacement. Never, under any circumstances, use unreinforced vacuum line, clear plastic tubing or water hose for fuel lines.

10   Spring-type clamps are commonly used on fuel lines. These clamps often lose their tension over a period of time, and can be "sprung" during removal. Replace all spring-type clamps with screw clamps whenever a hose is replaced.

Metal lines

11   Sections of metal line are often used for fuel line between the fuel pump and fuel injection unit. Check carefully to be sure the line has not been bent or crimped and that cracks have not started in the line.

12   If a section of metal fuel line must be

Check for a chafed area that could fail prematurely.

Check for a soft area indicating the hose has deteriorated inside.

Overtightening the clamp on a hardened hose will damage the hose and cause a leak.

Check each hose for swelling and oil-soaked ends. Cracks and breaks can be located by squeezing the hose.

13.4 Hoses, like drivebelts, have a habit of failing at the worst possible time - to prevent the inconvenience of a blown radiator or heater hose, inspect them carefully as shown here

replaced, only seamless steel tubing should be used, since copper and aluminum tubing don't have the strength necessary to withstand normal engine vibration.

13   Check the metal brake lines where they enter the master cylinder and brake proportioning unit (if used) for cracks in the lines or loose fittings. Any sign of brake fluid leakage calls for an immediate thorough inspection of the brake system.

13   Cooling system check

Refer to illustration 13.4

1   Many major engine failures can be attributed to a faulty cooling system. If the vehicle is equipped with an automatic transmission, the cooling system also cools the transmission fluid and thus plays an important role in prolonging transmission life.

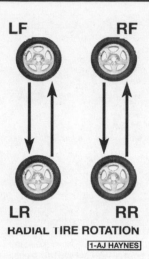

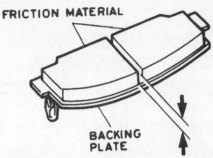

H.0085

14.2 The recommended tire rotation pattern for these models

15.6 You will find an inspection hole like this in each caliper - placing a steel ruler across the hole should enable you to determine the thickness of remaining pad material

15.9 If a more precise measurement of pad thickness is necessary, remove the pads and measure the remaining friction material - spraying the pad with brake cleaner will help you determine where the friction material ends and the steel backing plate begins

2   The cooling system should be checked with the engine cold. Do this before the vehicle is driven for the day or after the engine has been shut off for at least three hours.

3   Remove the radiator cap by turning it to the left until it reaches a stop. If you hear a hissing sound (indicating there is still pressure in the system), wait until it stops. Now press down on the cap with the palm of your hand and continue turning to the left until the cap can be removed. Thoroughly clean the cap, inside and out, with clean water. Also clean the filler neck on the radiator. All traces of corrosion should be removed. The coolant inside the radiator should be relatively transparent. If it's rust colored, the system should be drained and refilled (Section 27). If the coolant level isn't up to the top, add additional antifreeze/coolant mixture (see Section 4).

4   Carefully check the large upper and lower radiator hoses along with the smaller diameter heater hoses which run from the engine to the firewall. Inspect each hose along its entire length, replacing any hose which is cracked, swollen or shows signs of deterioration. Cracks may become more apparent if the hose is squeezed **(see illustration)**. Regardless of condition, it's a good idea to replace hoses with new ones every two years.

5   Make sure that all hose connections are tight. A leak in the cooling system will usually show up as white or rust colored deposits on the areas adjoining the leak. If wire-type clamps are used at the ends of the hoses, it may be a good idea to replace them with more secure screw-type clamps.

6   Use compressed air or a soft brush to remove bugs, leaves, etc. from the front of the radiator or air conditioning condenser. Be careful not to damage the delicate cooling fins or cut yourself on them.

7   Every other inspection, or at the first indication of cooling system problems, have the cap and system pressure tested. If you don't have a pressure tester, most gas stations and repair shops will do this for a minimal charge.

14 Tire rotation

Refer to illustration 14.2

1   The tires should be rotated at the specified intervals and whenever uneven wear is noticed. Since the vehicle will be raised and the tires removed anyway, check the brakes (Section 15) at this time.

2   Radial tires must be rotated in a specific pattern **(see illustration)**.

3   Refer to the information in *Jacking and towing* at the front of this manual for the proper procedures to follow when raising the vehicle and changing a tire. If the brakes are to be checked, do not apply the parking brake as stated. Make sure the tires are blocked to prevent the vehicle from rolling.

4   Preferably, the entire vehicle should be raised at the same time. This can be done on a hoist or by jacking up each corner and then lowering the vehicle onto jackstands placed under the frame rails. Always use four jackstands and make sure the vehicle is firmly supported.

5   After rotation, check and adjust the tire pressures as necessary and be sure to check the lug nut tightness.

6   For further information on the wheels and tires, refer to Chapter 10.

15 Brake check

Refer to illustrations 15.6, 15.9, 15.14 and 15.16

Note: *For detailed photographs of the brake system, refer to Chapter 9.*

1   In addition to the specified intervals, the brakes should be inspected every time the wheels are removed or whenever a defect is suspected. Any of the following symptoms could indicate a potential brake system defect: The vehicle pulls to one side when the brake pedal is depressed; the brakes make squealing or dragging noises when applied; brake travel is excessive; the pedal pulsates;

brake fluid leaks, usually onto the inside of the tire or wheel.

2   The disc brake pads have built-in wear indicators which should make a high pitched squealing or scraping noise when they are worn to the replacement point. When you hear this noise, replace the pads immediately or expensive damage to the rotors can result.

3   Loosen the wheel lug nuts.

4   Raise the vehicle and place it securely on jackstands.

5   Remove the wheels (see *Jacking and towing* at the front of this book, or your owner's manual, if necessary).

Disc brakes

6   There are two pads - an outer and an inner - in each caliper. The pads are visible through an inspection hole in each caliper **(see illustration)**.

7   Check the pad thickness by looking at each end of the caliper and through the inspection hole in the caliper body. If the lining material is less than the specified thickness, replace the pads. **Note:** *Keep in mind that the lining material is riveted or bonded to a metal backing plate and the metal portion is not included in this measurement.*

8   If it is difficult to determine the exact thickness of the remaining pad material by the above method, or if you are at all concerned about the condition of the pads, remove the caliper(s), then remove the pads from the calipers for further inspection (see Chapter 9).

9   Once the pads are removed from the calipers, clean them with brake cleaner and remeasure them with a small steel pocket ruler or a vernier caliper **(see illustration)**.

10   Measure the disc rotor thickness with a micrometer to make sure that it still has service life remaining. If any disc is thinner than the specified minimum thickness, replace it (see Chapter 9). Even if the rotor has service life remaining, check its condition. Look for scoring, gouging and burned spots. If these conditions exist, remove the rotor and have it resurfaced (see Chapter 9).

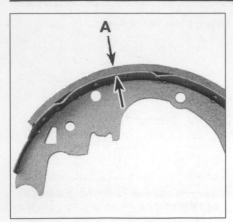

15.14 The rear brake shoe lining thickness (A) is measured from the outer surface of the lining to the metal shoe

15.16 Use a small screwdriver to carefully peel back the rubber boots (arrow) on both sides of the wheel cylinder - if there's any brake fluid behind the boots, the wheel cylinders must be replaced (trailing brake shoe pulled down for clarity)

16.2 Move the clutch release arm up and down and measure the freeplay (view is from beneath the driver's side of the vehicle)

11   Before installing the wheels, check all brake lines and hoses for damage, wear, deformation, cracks, corrosion, leakage, bends and twists, particularly in the vicinity of the rubber hoses at the calipers. Check the clamps for tightness and the connections for leakage. Make sure all hoses and lines are clear of sharp edges, moving parts and the exhaust system. If any of the above conditions are noted, repair, reroute or replace the lines and/or fittings as necessary (see Chapter 9).

Rear drum brakes

12   Refer to Chapter 9 and remove the rear brake drums.
13   **Warning:** *Brake dust produced by lining wear and deposited on brake components contains asbestos, which is hazardous to your health. DO NOT blow it out with compressed air and DO NOT inhale it! DO NOT use gasoline or solvents to remove the dust. Brake system cleaner should be used to flush the dust into a drain pan. After the brake components are wiped clean with a damp rag, dispose of the contaminated rag(s) and solvent in a covered and labelled container. Try to use non-asbestos replacement parts whenever possible.*
14   Note the thickness of the lining material on the rear brake shoes **(see illustration)** and look for signs of contamination by brake fluid and grease. If the lining material is within 1/16-inch of the recessed rivets or metal shoes, replace the brake shoes with new ones. The shoes should also be replaced if they are cracked, glazed (shiny lining surfaces) or contaminated with brake fluid or grease. See Chapter 9 for the replacement procedure.
15   Check the shoe return and hold-down springs and the adjusting mechanism to make sure they're installed correctly and in good condition. Deteriorated or distorted springs, if not replaced, could allow the linings to drag and wear prematurely.
16   Check the wheel cylinders for leakage by carefully peeling back the rubber boots **(see illustration)**. If brake fluid is noted

behind the boots, the wheel cylinders must be replaced (see Chapter 9).
17   Check the drums for cracks, score marks, deep scratches and hard spots, which will appear as small discolored areas. If imperfections cannot be removed with emery cloth, the drums must be resurfaced by an automotive machine shop (see Chapter 9 for more detailed information).
18   Refer to Chapter 9 and install the brake drums.
19   Install the wheels and snug the wheel lug nuts finger tight.
20   Remove the jackstands and lower the vehicle.
21   Tighten the wheel lug nuts to the specified torque.

Brake booster check

22   Sit in the driver's seat and perform the following sequence of tests.
23   With the engine stopped, depress the brake pedal several times- the travel distance should not change.
24   With the brake fully depressed, start the engine - the pedal should move down a little when the engine starts.
25   Depress the brake, stop the engine and hold the pedal in for about 30 seconds - the pedal should neither sink nor rise.
26   Restart the engine, run it for about a minute and turn it off. Then firmly depress the brake several times - the pedal travel should decrease with each application.
27   If your brakes do not operate as described above when the preceding tests are performed, the brake booster is either in need of repair or has failed. Refer to Chapter 9 for the removal procedure.

Parking brake

28   Slowly pull up on the parking brake and count the number of clicks you hear until the handle is up as far as it will go. The adjustment is correct if you hear the specified number of clicks. If you hear more or fewer clicks,

16.3 Turn the knurled knob (arrow) (it is easier to reach from the engine compartment) to adjust the clutch release arm freeplay

it's time to adjust the parking brake (see Chapter 9).
29   An alternative method of checking the parking brake is to park the vehicle on a steep hill with the parking brake set and the transmission in Neutral. If the parking brake cannot prevent the vehicle from rolling, it is in need of adjustment (see Chapter 9).

16   Clutch release arm freeplay check and adjustment

Refer to illustrations 16.2 and 16.3
1   Raise the vehicle and support it securely on jackstands.
2   Move the clutch release arm up and down and measure the freeplay **(see illustration)**.
3   If the freeplay is not as specified, turn the knurled knob at the top of the bracket to adjust the freeplay **(see illustration)**. Turn the knob counterclockwise to increase the freeplay and clockwise to decrease it. Operate the clutch several times and recheck the freeplay, adjusting as necessary.

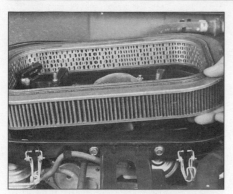

17.3 On carburetor-equipped models, remove the air cleaner cover and lift out the filter element

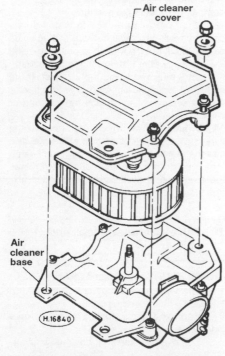

17.4 On earlier fuel-injected models, remove the bolts and lift off the cover for access to the filter element - later models use clips to secure the cover

17.9 Remove the screws, lift the housing away and pull out the PCV filter (arrow)

17 Air and PCV filter replacement

Refer to illustrations 17.3, 17.4 and 17.9

1 At the specified intervals, the air filter and (if equipped) PCV filter should be replaced with new ones. The engine air cleaner also supplies filtered air to the PCV system.

2 The filter is located on top of the carburetor or fuel injection unit or in a housing next to the engine.

3 On carburetor-equipped models, remove the wing nut(s) on top of the filter housing, release the clips on the side of the filter housing and lift off the air cleaner cover for access to the filter element **(see illustration)**.

4 On fuel injection-equipped models, remove the nuts and lift off the air cleaner cover (early models) or disengage the clips and pull the cover back (later models) for access to the element **(see illustration)**.

5 While the air cleaner cover is off, be careful not to drop anything down into the carburetor, fuel injection unit or air cleaner assembly.

6 Lift the air filter element out of the housing and wipe out the inside of the air cleaner housing with a clean rag.

7 Place the new filter in the air cleaner housing. Make sure it seats properly in the bottom of the housing.

8 The PCV filter is located in a housing on the side of the air cleaner housing on some

models. **Note:** *On some models, the PCV filter is mounted on the camshaft cover. See Chapter 6 for the replacement procedure.*

9 Remove the housing screws and lift out the old filter **(see illustration)**.

10 Install the new PCV filter.

11 Install the air cleaner cover and any hoses which were disconnected.

18 Spark plug check and replacement

Refer to illustrations 18.1, 18.4a, 18.4b, 18.6, and 18.10

1 Spark plug replacement requires a spark plug socket which fits onto a ratchet wrench. This socket is lined with a rubber grommet to protect the porcelain insulator of the spark plug and to hold the plug while you insert it into the spark plug hole. You will also need a wire-type feeler gauge to check and adjust the spark plug gap and a torque wrench to tighten the new plugs to the specified torque **(see illustration)**.

2 If you are replacing the plugs, purchase the new plugs, adjust them to the proper gap and then replace each plug one at a time. **Note:** *When buying new spark plugs, it's essential that you obtain the correct plugs for your specific vehicle. This information can be found on the Vehicle Emissions Control Information (VECI) label located on the underside of the hood or in the owner's manual. If these two sources specify different plugs, purchase the spark plug type specified on the VECI label because that information is provided specifically for your engine.*

3 Inspect each of the new plugs for defects. If there are any signs of cracks in the porcelain insulator of a plug, don't use it.

4 Check the electrode gaps of the new plugs. Check the gap by inserting the wire gauge of the proper thickness between the electrodes at the tip of the plug **(see illustration)**. The gap between the electrodes should be identical to that specified on the VECI

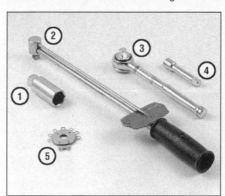

18.1 Tools required for changing spark plugs

1 **Spark plug socket** - This will have special padding inside to protect the spark plug porcelain insulator

2 **Torque wrench** - Although not mandatory, use of this tool is the best way to ensure that the plugs are tightened properly

3 **Ratchet** - Standard hand tool to fit the spark plug socket

4 **Extension** - Depending on the model and accessories, installed on your vehicle you may need special extensions and universal joints to reach one or more of the plugs

5 **Spark plug gap gauge** - This gauge for checking the gap comes in a variety of styles. Make sure the gap for your engine is included

18.4a Spark plug manufacturers recommend using a wiretype gauge when checking the gap - if the wire does not slide between the electrodes with a slight drag, adjustment is required

label. If the gap is incorrect, use the notched adjuster on the feeler gauge body to bend the curved side electrode slightly **(see illustration)**.

5   If the side electrode is not exactly over the center electrode, use the notched adjuster to align them. **Caution:** *If the gap of a new plug must be adjusted, bend only the base of the ground electrode do not touch the tip.*

Removal

6   To prevent the possibility of mixing up spark plug wires, work on one spark plug at a time. Remove the wire and boot from one spark plug. Grasp the boot - not the cable - as shown, give it a half twisting motion and pull straight out **(see illustration)**.

7   If compressed air is available, blow any dirt or foreign material away from the spark plug area before proceeding (a common bicycle pump will also work).

8   Remove the spark plug.

9   Whether you are replacing the plugs at this time or intend to reuse the old plugs, compare each old spark plug with those shown in the accompanying color photos to determine the overall running condition of the engine.

Installation

10   It's often difficult to insert spark plugs into their holes without cross-threading them. To avoid this possibility, fit a short piece of 3/16-inch ID rubber hose over the end of the spark plug **(see illustration)**. The flexible hose acts as a universal joint to help align the plug with the plug hole. Should the plug begin to cross-thread, the hose will slip on the spark plug, preventing thread damage. Tighten the plug securely.

11   Attach the plug wire to the new spark plug, again using a twisting motion on the boot until it is firmly seated on the end of the spark plug.

12   Follow the above procedure for the remaining spark plugs, replacing them one at a time to prevent mixing up the spark plug wires.

19   Spark plug wire, distributor cap and rotor check and replacement

Refer to illustrations 19.11 and 19.12

1   The spark plug wires should be checked whenever new spark plugs are installed.

2   Begin this procedure by making a visual check of the spark plug wires while the engine is running. In a darkened garage (make sure there is ventilation) start the engine and observe each plug wire. Be careful not to come into contact with any moving engine parts. If there is a break in the wire, you will see arcing or a small spark at the damaged area. If arcing is noticed, make a note to obtain new wires, then allow the engine to cool and check the distributor cap and rotor.

18.4b   To change the gap, bend the side electrode only, as indicated by the arrows, and be very careful not to crack or chip the porcelain insulator surrounding the center electrode

3   The spark plug wires should be inspected one at a time to prevent mixing up the order, which is essential for proper engine operation. Each original plug wire should be numbered to help identify its location. If the number is illegible, a piece of tape can be marked with the correct number and wrapped around the plug wire.

4   Disconnect the plug wire from the spark plug. A removal tool can be used for this purpose or you can grasp the rubber boot, twist the boot half a turn and pull the boot free. Do not pull on the wire itself.

5   Check inside the boot for corrosion, which will look like a white crusty powder.

6   Push the wire and boot back onto the end of the spark plug. It should fit tightly onto the end of the plug. If it doesn't, remove the wire and use pliers to carefully crimp the metal connector inside the wire boot until the fit is snug.

7   Using a clean rag, wipe the entire length of the wire to remove built-up dirt and grease. Once the wire is clean, check for burns, cracks and other damage. Do not bend the wire sharply, because the conductor might break.

8   Disconnect the wire from the distributor. Again, pull only on the rubber boot. Check for

corrosion and a tight fit. Replace the wire in the distributor.

9   Inspect the remaining spark plug wires, making sure that each one is securely fastened at the distributor and spark plug when the check is complete.

10   If new spark plug wires are required, purchase a set for your specific engine model. Pre-cut wire sets with the boots already installed are available. Remove and replace the wires one at a time to avoid mix-ups in the firing order.

11   Detach the distributor cap by removing the two cap retaining bolts. Look inside it for cracks, carbon tracks and worn, burned or loose contacts **(see illustration)**.

12   Pull the rotor off the distributor shaft and examine it for cracks and carbon tracks **(see illustration)**. Replace the cap and rotor if any damage or defects are noted.

13   It is common practice to install a new cap and rotor whenever new spark plug wires are installed, but if you wish to continue using the old cap, check the resistance between the spark plug wires and the cap first. If the indicated resistance is more than the specified maximum value, replace the cap and/or wires.

14   When installing a new cap, remove the wires from the old cap one at a time and attach them to the new cap in the exact same location- do not simultaneously remove all the wires from the old cap or firing order mix-ups may occur.

20   Valve clearance check and adjustment

Refer to illustrations 20.5 and 20.6

1   The valve clearances are checked and adjusted with the engine cold.

2   Remove the air cleaner assembly (see Chapter 4).

3   Remove the camshaft cover (see Chapter 2A).

4   Using the procedure in Chapter 2A, position the number one piston (the one closest to the drivebelt end of the engine) at Top Dead Center (TDC).

5   With the engine in this position, the

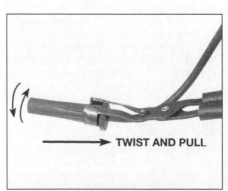

18.6   When removing the spark plug wires, pull only on the boot and use a twisting/pulling motion

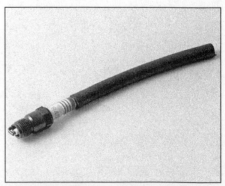

18.10   A length of 3/16-inch ID rubber hose will save time and prevent damaged threads when installing the spark plugs

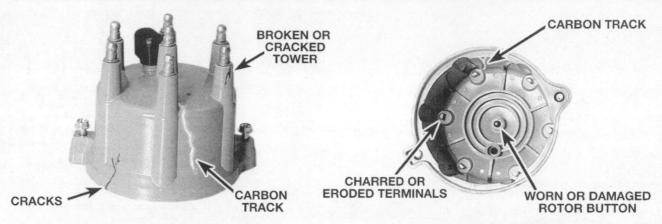

19.11 Shown here are some of the common defects to look for when inspecting the distributor cap (if in doubt about its condition, install a new one)

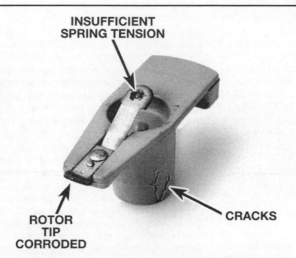

19.12 The ignition rotor should be checked for wear and corrosion as indicated here (if in doubt about its condition, buy a new one)

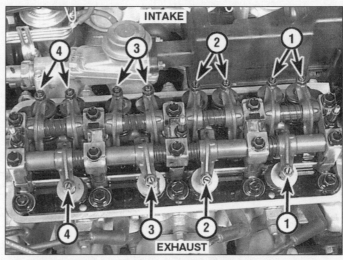

20.5 Valve adjustment screw locations and numbering - twelve-valve (two intake valves per cylinder) engine shown

number one cylinder valve adjustment can be checked and adjusted (see illustration).

6 Start with the intake valve clearance. **Note:** *Some models have two intake valves per cylinder; on these models, the adjustment procedure and clearance are the same for both valves.* Insert a feeler gauge of the specified thickness between the intake valve stem

and the adjusting screw. Withdraw it; you should feel a slight drag. If there's no drag or a heavy drag, loosen the adjuster nut and back off the adjuster screw (see illustration). Carefully tighten the adjuster screw until you can feel a slight drag on the feeler gauge as you withdraw it.

7 Hold the adjuster screw with a screw-

20.6 To adjust valve clearance, loosen the adjuster nut with a wrench and back off the adjuster screw with a screwdriver; carefully tighten the adjuster screw until you feel a slight drag when withdrawing the feeler gauge, then tighten the adjuster nut while still holding the adjuster screw with a screwdriver (adjusting an exhaust valve is shown)

driver (to keep it from turning) and tighten the locknut. Recheck the clearance to make sure it hasn't changed.

8 Adjust the number one exhaust valve using the same procedure you used for the intake valve(s). Be sure to use a feeler gauge of the specified thickness. If your vehicle is equipped with auxiliary valves (smaller valves, adjacent to the exhaust valves, which are actuated by extensions on each exhaust valve rocker arm), also adjust the number one auxiliary valve using the same procedure. Note that the auxiliary valves have a different clearance than exhaust valves.

9 Using the procedure in Chapter 2A, position the number three piston at TDC. Check and adjust the number three cylinder valve clearances.

10 Position the number four piston at TDC. Check and adjust the number four cylinder valves.

11 Position the number two piston at TDC. Check and adjust the number two cylinder valves.

12 Install the camshaft cover and the air cleaner assembly.

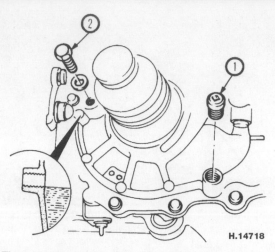

22.1 The manual transaxle drain (1) and fill (2) plugs are located on the right side of the transaxle case

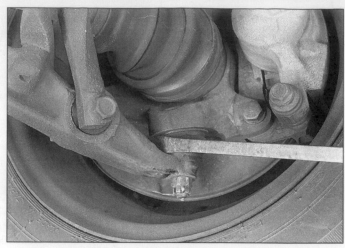

23.8 Pry between the balljoint and lower suspension arm to check for movement indicating balljoint wear

21   Fuel system check

Warning: *Certain precautions should be observed when inspecting or servicing the fuel system components. Work in a well ventilated area and do not allow open flames (cigarettes, appliance pilot lights, etc.) near the work area. Mop up spills immediately and do not store fuel soaked rags where they could ignite. It is a good idea to keep a dry chemical (Class B) fire extinguisher near the work area any time the fuel system is being serviced.*

1   If you smell gasoline while driving or after the vehicle has been sitting in the sun, inspect the fuel system immediately.

2   Remove the gas filler cap and inspect it for damage and corrosion. The gasket should have an unbroken sealing imprint. If the gasket is damaged or corroded, remove it and install a new one.

3   Inspect the fuel feed and return lines for cracks. Make sure all fuel line connections are tight. **Warning:** *It is necessary to relieve the fuel system pressure on fuel-injection equipped models before servicing fuel system components. The correct procedures for fuel system pressure relief are outlined in Chapter 4.*

4   Since some components of the fuel system - the fuel tank and part of the fuel feed and return lines, for example - are underneath the vehicle, they can be inspected more easily with the vehicle raised on a hoist. If that's not possible, raise the vehicle and secure it on jackstands.

5   With the vehicle raised and safely supported, inspect the gas tank and filler neck for punctures, cracks and other damage. The connection between the filler neck and the tank is particularly critical. Sometimes a rubber filler neck will leak because of loose clamps or deteriorated rubber. These are problems a home mechanic can usually rectify. **Warning:** *Do not, under any circumstances, try to repair a fuel tank (except rubber components). A welding torch or any*

open flame can easily cause fuel vapors inside the tank to explode.

6   Carefully check all rubber hoses and metal lines leading away from the fuel tank. Check for loose connections, deteriorated hoses, crimped lines and other damage. Carefully inspect the lines from the tank to the fuel injection system or carburetor. Repair or replace damaged sections as necessary.

22   Manual transaxle lubricant level check

Refer to illustration 22.1

1   The manual transaxle does not have a dipstick. To check the fluid level, raise the vehicle and support it securely on jackstands. The fill plug is on the right side of the transaxle housing **(see illustration)**. Remove it. If the lubricant level is correct, it should be up to the lower edge of the hole.

2   If the transaxle needs more lubricant (if the level is not up to the hole), use a syringe to add more. Stop filling the transaxle when the lubricant begins to run out the hole.

3   Install the plug and tighten it securely. Drive the vehicle a short distance, then check for leaks.

23   Steering and suspension check

Refer to illustrations 23.8 and 23.9
Note: *For detailed illustrations of the steering and suspension components, refer to Chapter 10.*

With the wheels on the ground

1   With the vehicle stopped and the front wheels pointed straight ahead, rock the steering wheel gently back and forth. If free play is excessive , a front wheel bearing, main shaft yoke, intermediate shaft yoke, lower arm balljoint or steering system joint is worn or the steering gear is out of adjustment

or broken. Refer to Chapter 10 for the appropriate repair procedure.

2   Other symptoms, such as excessive vehicle body movement over rough roads, swaying (leaning) around corners and binding as the steering wheel is turned, may indicate faulty steering and/or suspension components.

3   Check the shock absorbers by pushing down and releasing the vehicle several times at each corner. If the vehicle does not come back to a level position within one or two bounces, the shocks/struts are worn and must be replaced. When bouncing the vehicle up and down, listen for squeaks and noises from the suspension components. Additional information on suspension components can be found in Chapter 10.

4   Note whether the vehicle looks canted to one side or corner. If is, try to level it by rocking it down. If this doesn't work, look for bad springs or worn or loose suspension parts.

Under the vehicle

5   Raise the vehicle with a floor jack and support it securely on jackstands. See *Jacking and towing* at the front of this book for the proper jacking points.

6   Check the tires for irregular wear patterns (see Section 5) and proper inflation.

7   Inspect the universal joint between the steering shaft and the steering gear housing. Check the steering gear housing for grease leakage or oozing. Make sure that the dust seals and boots are not damaged and that the boot clamps are not loose. Check the steering linkage for looseness or damage. Check the tie-rod ends for excessive play. Look for loose bolts, broken or disconnected parts and deteriorated rubber bushings on all suspension and steering components. While an assistant turns the steering wheel from side to side, check the steering components for free movement, chafing and binding. If the steering components do not seem to be reacting with the movement of the steering wheel, try to determine where the slack is locate.

8   Check the balljoints for wear by prying

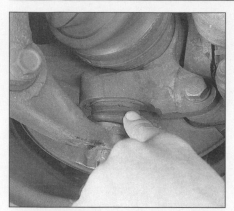

23.9 Push on the balljoint boot to check for tears and grease leaks

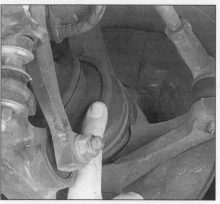

24.2 Flex the driveaxle boots by hand to check for tears, cracks and leaking grease

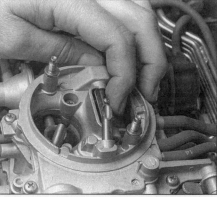

25.3 The carburetor choke plate is visible after removing the top cover of the air cleaner (air cleaner assembly shown removed for clarity)

between each balljoint and lower suspension arm **(see illustration)** to ensure the balljoint has no play. If any balljoint does have play, replace it. Refer to Chapter 10 for the front balljoint replacement procedure.

9   Inspect the balljoint boots for tears and leaking grease **(see illustration)**. Replace the boots with new ones if they are damaged (see Chapter 10).

24   Driveaxle boot check

Refer to illustration 24.2

1   The driveaxle boots are very important because they prevent dirt, water and foreign material from entering and damaging the constant velocity (CV) joints. Oil and grease can cause the boot material to deteriorate prematurely, so it's a good idea to wash the boots with soap and water.

2   Inspect the boots for tears and cracks as well as loose clamps **(see illustration)**. If there is any evidence of cracks or leaking grease, they must be replaced as described in Chapter 8.

25   Carburetor choke check

Refer to illustration 25.3

1   The choke operates only when the engine is cold, so this check should be performed before the engine has been started for the day.

2   Take off the top cover of the air cleaner assembly. It's held in place by two nuts at the center and clips on the front and rear side. If any vacuum hoses must be disconnected, make sure you tag the hoses for reinstallation in their original positions. Place the top cover and nuts aside, out of the way of moving engine components.

3   Look at the center of the air cleaner housing. You will notice a flat plate at the carburetor opening **(see illustration)**.

4   Press the accelerator pedal to the floor. The plate should close completely. Start the engine while you watch the plate at the carburetor. Don't position your face near the carburetor, as the engine could backfire,

causing serious burns. When the engine starts, the choke plate should open slightly.

5   Allow the engine to continue running at an idle speed. As the engine warms up to operating temperature, the plate should slowly open, allowing more air to enter through the top of the carburetor.

6   After a few minutes, the choke plate should be fully open to the vertical position. Tap the accelerator to make sure the fast idle cam disengages.

7   You'll notice that the engine speed corresponds with the plate opening. With the plate fully closed, the engine should run at a fast idle speed. As the plate opens and the throttle is moved to disengage the fast idle cam, the engine speed will decrease.

26   Positive Crankcase Ventilation (PCV) valve check and replacement

Refer to illustration 26.6

Note: *for a detailed discussion of the PCV system, refer to Chapter 6*

1   The PCV valve is located in the camshaft cover, in the crankcase breather chamber or in the hose which connects the crankcase breather chamber to the intake manifold. The PCV valve requires different checking procedures, depending on location.

Check

Valve mounted in the camshaft cover

2   With the engine idling at normal operating temperature, pull the valve (with hose attached) from the rubber grommet in the camshaft cover.

3   Place your finger over the valve opening. If there's no vacuum at the valve, check for a plugged valve or a plugged or deteriorated hose. Replace the valve or hose if necessary.

4   Turn the engine off and shake the PCV valve, listening for a rattle. If the valve doesn't rattle, replace it with a new one.

5   Press the valve back into the grommet in the camshaft cover.

Valve mounted in the crankcase breather or breather hose

6   With the engine idling at normal operating temperature, squeeze the PCV hose located at the top of the engine gently shut with a pair of pliers, using a rag to protect the hose surface **(see illustration)**. Pinch the hose as gently as possible to avoid damaging the hose.

7   If the PCV valve is operating properly, it will make a clicking sound when the hose is pinched shut. If it doesn't, replace the valve.

8   Check the hoses between the intake manifold and breather chamber for plugging, deterioration and other damage. Replace hoses as necessary.

Replacement

9   Detach the hose or hoses and remove the valve, noting its installed position and direction.

10   When purchasing a replacement PCV valve, make sure it's for your particular vehicle and engine size. Compare the old valve with a new one to make sure they're the same.

11   Installation is the reverse of removal.

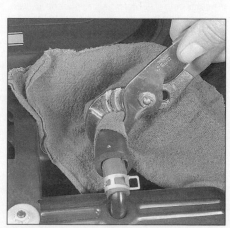

26.6 Squeeze the PCV hose gently with a pair of pliers - use a rag to protect the hose surface

1

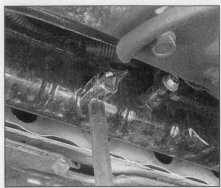

27.4 On most models you will have to remove a cover for access to the radiator drain fitting located at the bottom of the radiator - before opening the valve, push a short section of 3/8-inch inner diameter plastic hose onto the plastic fitting to direct the coolant into the container

27 Cooling system servicing (draining, flushing and refilling)

Refer to illustrations 27.4 and 27.13
Warning: *Antifreeze is a corrosive and poisonous solution, so be careful not to spill any of the coolant mixture on the vehicle's paint or your skin. If this happens, rinse immediately with plenty of clean water. Consult local authorities regarding proper disposal procedures for antifreeze before draining the cooling system. In many areas, reclamation centers have been established to collect used oil and coolant mixtures.*

1   Periodically, the cooling system should be drained, flushed and refilled to replenish the antifreeze mixture and prevent formation of rust and corrosion, which can impair the performance of the cooling system and cause engine damage. When the cooling system is serviced, all hoses and the radiator cap should be checked and replaced if necessary.

Draining

2   Apply the parking brake and block the wheels. If the vehicle has just been driven, wait several hours to allow the engine to cool down before beginning this procedure.
3   Once the engine is completely cool, remove the radiator cap.
4   Move a large container under the radiator drain fitting to catch the coolant. Attach a 3/8-inch inner diameter hose to the drain fitting to direct the coolant into the container (some models are already equipped with a hose), then open the drain fitting (a pair of pliers may be required to turn it) **(see illustration)**.
5   After the coolant stops flowing out of the radiator, move the container under the engine block drain plug on the front side of the engine. Loosen the plug and allow the coolant in the block to drain.
6   While the coolant is draining, check the condition of the radiator hoses, heater hoses and clamps (refer to Section 13 if necessary).

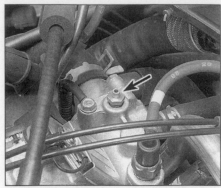

27.13 The coolant bleeder screw (arrow) is located on the thermostat housing - the screw must be opened during the filling process to bleed air out of the system

7   Replace any damaged clamps or hoses (refer to Chapter 3 for detailed replacement procedures).

Flushing

8   Once the system is completely drained, flush the radiator with fresh water from a garden hose until water runs clear at the drain. The flushing action of the water will remove sediments from the radiator but will not remove rust and scale from the engine and cooling tube surfaces.
9   These deposits can be removed by the chemical action of a cleaner. Follow the procedure outlined in the manufacturer's instructions. If the radiator is severely corroded, damaged or leaking, it should be removed (see Chapter 3) and taken to a radiator repair shop.
10   Remove the overflow hose from the coolant recovery reservoir. Drain the reservoir and flush it with clean water, then reconnect the hose.

Refilling

11   Close and tighten the radiator drain. Install and tighten the block drain plug.
12   Place the heater temperature control in the maximum heat position.
13   Loosen the coolant bleeder screw in the thermostat housing **(see illustration)**.
14   Slowly add new coolant (a 50/50 mixture of water and antifreeze) to the radiator until bubble-free coolant flows from the bleeder screw. Tighten the screw and continue adding coolant to the radiator until it's full. Add coolant to the reservoir until the level is at the upper mark.
15   Leave the radiator cap off and run the engine in a well-ventilated area until the thermostat opens (coolant will begin flowing through the radiator and the upper radiator hose will become hot).
16   Turn the engine off and let it cool. Add more coolant mixture to bring the level back up to the lip on the radiator filler neck.
17   Squeeze the upper radiator hose to expel air, then add more coolant mixture if necessary. Replace the radiator cap.
18   Start the engine, allow it to reach normal operating temperature and check for leaks.

28 Exhaust system check

1   With the engine cold (at least three hours after the vehicle has been driven), check the complete exhaust system from its starting point at the engine to the end of the tailpipe. This should be done on a hoist where unrestricted access is available.
2   Check the pipes and connections for evidence of leaks, severe corrosion or damage. Make sure that all brackets and hangers are in good condition and tight.
3   At the same time, inspect the underside of the body for holes, corrosion, open seams, etc. which may allow exhaust gases to enter the passenger compartment. Seal all body openings with silicone sealer or body putty.
4   Rattles and other noises can often be traced to the exhaust system, especially the mounts and hangers. Try to move the pipes, muffler and catalytic converter. If the components can come in contact with the body or suspension parts, secure the exhaust system with new mounts.
5   Check the running condition of the engine by inspecting inside the end of the tailpipe. The exhaust deposits here are an indication of engine state-of-tune. If the pipe is black and sooty or coated with white deposits, the engine is in need of a tune-up, including a thorough fuel system inspection and adjustment.

29 Brake fluid replacement

1   Because brake fluid absorbs moisture which could ultimately cause corrosion of the brake components, and air which could make the braking system less effective, the fluid should be replaced at the specified intervals. This job can be accomplished for a nominal fee by a properly equipped brake shop using a pressure bleeder. The task can also be done by the home mechanic with the help of an assistant. To bleed the air and old fluid and replace it with fresh fluid from sealed containers, refer to the brake bleeding procedure in Chapter 9.
2   If there is any possibility that incorrect fluid has been used in the system, drain all the fluid and flush the system with methylated spirits. Replace all piston seals and cups, as they will be affected and could possibly fail under pressure.

30 Automatic transaxle fluid change

1   At the specified time intervals, the automatic transaxle fluid should be drained and replaced.
2   Before beginning work, purchase the specified transmission fluid (see *Recommended fluids and lubricants* at the front of this chapter).
3   Other tools necessary for this job include jackstands to support the vehicle in a raised position, an appropriately-sized

wrench, a drain pan capable of holding at least eight pints, newspapers and clean rags.

4   The fluid should be drained immediately after the vehicle has been driven. Hot fluid is more effective than cold fluid at removing built up sediment. **Caution:** *Fluid temperature can exceed 350° in a hot transaxle. Wear protective gloves.*

5   After the vehicle has been driven to warm up the fluid, raise it and place it on jackstands for access to the transaxle and differential drain plugs.

6   Move the necessary equipment under the vehicle, being careful not to touch any of the hot exhaust components.

7   Place the drain pan under the drain plug in the transaxle **(see illustration 7.3)** and remove the drain plug with the wrench. Be sure the drain pan is in position, as fluid will come out with some force. Once the fluid is drained, clean the drain plug and reinstall it securely.

8   Lower the vehicle.

9   With the engine off, unscrew and remove the dipstick, then add new fluid to the transaxle through the dipstick hole (*see Recommended fluids and lubricants* for the recommended fluid type and capacity). Use a funnel to prevent spills. It is best to add a little fluid at a time, continually checking the level with the dipstick (see Section 7). Allow the fluid time to drain into the pan.

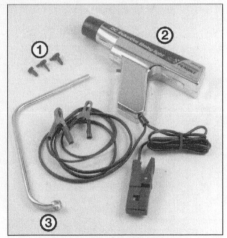

32.1 Tools needed to check and adjust the ignition timing

1   *Vacuum plugs - Vacuum hoses will, in most cases, have to be disconnected and plugged. Molded plugs in various shapes and sizes are available for this*

2   *Inductive pick-up timing light - Flashes a bright concentrated beam of light when the number one spark plug fires. Connect the leads according to the instructions supplied with the light*

3   *Distributor wrench - On some models, the hold-down bolt for the distributor is difficult to reach and turn with conventional wrenches or sockets. A special wrench like this must be used*

10   Start the engine and shift the selector into all positions from P through 2, then shift into P and apply the parking brake.

11   Turn off the engine and check the fluid level. Add fluid to bring the level between the Add and Full marks.

31   Manual transaxle lubricant change

Refer to illustration 31.3

1   Remove the drain plug and drain the fluid **(see illustration)**.

2   Reinstall the drain plug securely.

3   Add new fluid until it begins to run out of the filler hole (see Section 22). See Recommended lubricants and fluids for the specified lubricant type.

32   Ignition timing check and adjustment

Refer to illustrations 32.1, 32.5 and 32.7

Note: *It is imperative that the procedures included on the Vehicle Emissions Control Information (VECI) label be followed when adjusting the ignition timing. The label will include all information concerning preliminary steps to be performed before adjusting the timing, as well as the timing specifications.*

1   With the ignition off, locate the VECI label under the hood and read through and perform all preliminary instructions concerning ignition timing. Several special tools will be needed for this procedure **(see illustration)**.

2   On 1986 and later models, detach the

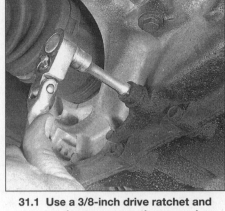

31.1 Use a 3/8-inch drive ratchet and extension to remove the manual transaxle drain plug

hoses from the distributor vacuum advance unit and plug the hoses.

3   With the ignition off, connect the inductive pick-up lead of the timing light to the number one spark plug (the one closest to the drivebelt end of the engine).

4   Connect the battery leads of the timing light according to the manufacturer's instructions (they are normally attached to the vehicle's battery terminals).

5   Remove the rubber plug in the bellhousing below the distributor and locate the timing marks and pointer inside **(see illustration)**.

6   Start the engine and point the timing light at the timing marks.

7   The appropriate line on the flywheel (refer to the VECI label) will appear stationary and be aligned with the pointer if the timing is correct. If an adjustment is required, loosen the adjusting bolt and rotate the distributor slightly until the timing is correct **(see illustration)**.

8   Tighten the adjusting bolt and recheck the timing.

9   Turn off the engine and remove the timing light.

10   Reconnect the vacuum advance hoses.

FLYWHEEL

32.5 After removing the rubber plug from the bellhousing, the pointer and timing marks on the flywheel are visible

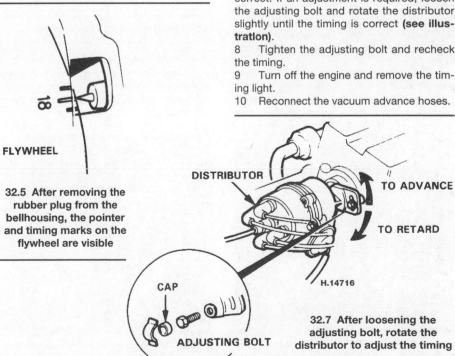

32.7 After loosening the adjusting bolt, rotate the distributor to adjust the timing

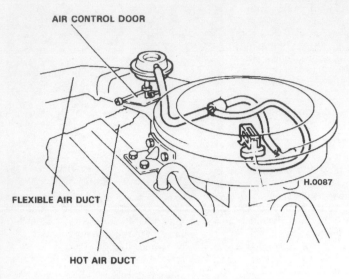

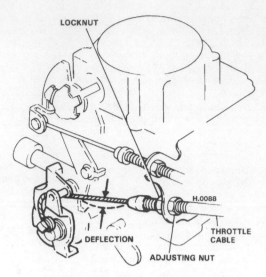

33.3 Thermostatic air cleaner details

34.3 Throttle cable adjustment details

33 Thermostatic air cleaner check (carburetor-equipped models)

Refer to illustrations 33.3

1   Some engines are equipped with a thermostatically controlled air cleaner which draws air to the carburetor from different locations, depending on engine temperature.
2   This is a visual check. If access is limited, a small mirror may have to be used.
3   Locate the air control door inside the air cleaner assembly. It's inside the long snorkel of the metal air cleaner housing (see illustration).
4   If there is a flexible air duct attached to the end of the snorkel, leading to an area behind the grille, disconnect it at the snorkel. This will enable you to look through the end of the snorkel and see the air control door inside.
5   The check should be done when the engine is cold. Start the engine and look through the snorkel at the air control door, which should move to a closed position. With

the door closed, air cannot enter through the end of the snorkel, but instead enters the air cleaner through the hot air duct attached to the exhaust manifold and the heat stove passage.
6   As the engine warms up to operating temperature, the air control door should open to allow air through the snorkel end. Depending on outside temperature, this may take 10-to-15 minutes. To speed up this check you can reconnect the snorkel air duct, drive the vehicle, then check to see if the air control door is completely open.
7   If the thermo-controlled air cleaner isn't operating properly see Chapter 6 for more information.

34 Throttle linkage inspection

Refer to illustration 34.3

1   Inspect the throttle linkage for damage and missing parts and for binding and interference when the accelerator pedal is depressed.

2   Lubricate the various linkage pivot points with engine oil.
3   Push on the throttle cable with your fingers to check the deflection. It should deflect about 3/16 to 3/8-inch. If the deflection is incorrect, loosen the locknut and turn the adjusting nut as necessary to adjust the tension (see illustration).
4   Tighten the locknut.

35 Idle speed check and adjustment

1   Engine idle speed is the speed at which the engine operates when no accelerator pedal pressure is applied, as when stopped at a traffic light. This speed is critical to the performance of the engine itself, as well as many subsystems.
2   Start the engine and allow it to warm up to normal operating temperature (the cooling fan should come on at least twice).
3   Stop the engine. Hook up a hand-held

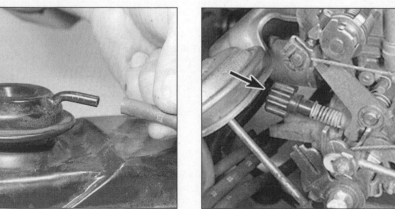

35.5 Detach the hose from the thermostatic air cleaner valve motor and plug the hose

35.6 On carbureted models, adjust the idle speed with the throttle stop screw (arrow)

35.8a On 1986 and 1987 models, disconnect and plug the hose that connects the idle control solenoid valve to the intake manifold

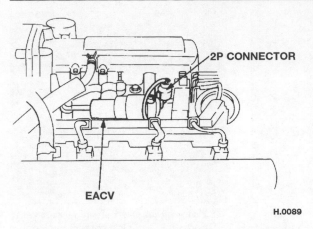

2P CONNECTOR

EACV

H.0089

35.8b On 1988 and later models, disconnect the 2P connector from the Electronic Air Control Valve (EACV)

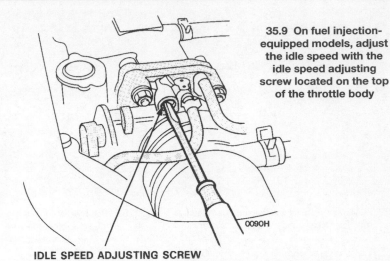

35.9 On fuel injection-equipped models, adjust the idle speed with the idle speed adjusting screw located on the top of the throttle body

0090H

IDLE SPEED ADJUSTING SCREW

tachometer in accordance with the manufacturer's instructions.

4   Set the parking brake firmly and block the wheels to prevent the vehicle from rolling. Place the transaxle in Neutral (manual transaxle) or Park (automatic transaxle). Start the engine and allow it to idle.

Carburetor-equipped models

Refer to illustrations 35.5 and 35.6

5   Disconnect the hose from the thermostatic air cleaner valve motor and plug the hose **(see illustration)**.

6   Start the engine, note the idle speed rpm on the tachometer and compare it to that specified on the VECI label. If the idle speed is too low or too high, adjust it by turning the throttle stop screw **(see illustration)**.

7   Turn off the engine, disconnect the tachometer and connect the thermostatic air cleaner hose.

Fuel injection-equipped models

Refer to illustrations 35.8a, 35.8b and 35.9

8   On 1986 and 1987 models, disconnect

and plug the vacuum hose which connects the idle control solenoid valve (located at the rear of the engine compartment on either the right or left side) to the intake manifold **(see illustration)**. On 1988 and later models disconnect the 2 connector from the Electronic Air Control Valve (EACV) **(see illustration)**.

9   Start the engine, note the idle speed rpm on the tachometer and compare it to that specified on the VECI label. If the idle speed is too low or too high, adjust it by turning the adjusting screw located on top of the throttle body **(see illustration)**.

10   Turn off the engine and disconnect the tachometer.

11   After adjustment, reconnect the idle control solenoid valve hose (1986 and 1987 models) or EACV connector (1988 and later models).

36 Evaporative emissions control system check

Refer to illustration 36.2

1   The function of the Fuel Evaporative

Emission Control (EVAP) System is to store fuel vapors from the fuel tank in a charcoal canister until they can be routed to the intake manifold where they mix with incoming air before being burned in the cylinder combustion chambers.

2   The most common symptom of a faulty evaporative emissions system is a strong fuel odor in the engine compartment. If a fuel odor is detected, inspect the charcoal canister, located on the left side of the engine compartment, and the hoses attached to it **(see illustration)**.

3   The evaporative emissions control system is explained in more detail in Chapter 6.

37 Exhaust Gas Recirculation (EGR) system check

Refer to illustration 37.2

1   The EGR valve is usually located on the intake manifold, adjacent to the carburetor or throttle body. Most of the time when a problem develops in this emissions system, it's due to a stuck or corroded EGR valve.

2   With the engine cold to prevent burns, push on the EGR valve diaphragm. Using moderate pressure, you should be able to press the diaphragm up-and-down within the housing **(see illustration)**.

3   If the diaphragm doesn't move or moves only with much effort, replace the EGR valve with a new one. If in doubt about the condition of the valve, compare the free movement of your EGR valve with a new valve.

4   Refer to Chapter 6 for more information on the EGR system.

38 Fuel filter replacement

Refer to illustrations 38.5, 38.6, 38.7, 38.8, 38.9 and 38.13

1   This job should be done with the engine cold (after sitting at least three hours). Place an approved gasoline container under the fuel filter.

36.2 Inspect the charcoal canister (arrow) and hoses attached to it for damage

37.2 To check the EGR valve, reach under it and push up on the diaphragm with a finger - you should be able to push the diaphragm up-and-down within the housing

1

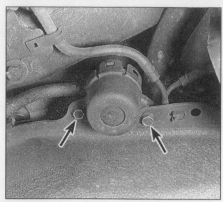

38.5 Remove the bolts (arrows) and lower the fuel filter and holder assembly

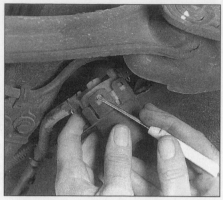

38.6 Pry the locking clips off the tabs while pushing the filter up out of the holder

38.7 Compress the fuel line clamps with pliers, then slide the clamps back on the hoses and disconnect the hoses from the filter

Carburetor-equipped models

2   These models are equipped with two filters: the main filter located under the vehicle adjacent to fuel tank and an auxiliary filter in the engine compartment.

Main filter

3   Raise the vehicle and support it securely on jackstands.
4   Use small locking pliers to clamp the fuel lines attached to the filter shut.
5   Remove the bolts and lower the fuel filter and holder assembly for access (see illustration).
6   Pry back the locking clips and push the

filter up out of the holder (see illustration).
7   Use pliers to slide the fuel line clamps back and disconnect the fuel hoses from the filter (see illustration).
8   Install the new filter by reversing the removal procedure. Make sure the arrow on the filter faces the front of the vehicle (see illustration).

Auxiliary filter

9   Use small locking pliers to clamp the fuel lines attached to the filter shut. Slide the fuel line clamps back using pliers, grasp the fuel lines and disconnect them from the filter using a twisting motion (see illustration).
10   Installation is the reverse of removal.

Fuel injection-equipped models

11   These models have one fuel filter, located in the engine compartment.
12   Place a shop towel or rag around the filter and depressurize the fuel system as described in Chapter 4.
13   Remove the banjo and service bolts, disconnect the fittings, remove the clamp and lift the filter from the engine compartment (see illustration).

14   Installation is the reverse of removal. use new banjo and service bolt washers. Tighten the bolts to the specified torque.

39   Rear wheel bearing check, repack and adjustment (1984 and 1985 models)

Refer to illustrations 39.1, 39.5, 39.15, 39.19 and 39.22
1   In most cases the rear wheel bearings will not need servicing until the brake shoes are changed. However, the bearings should be checked whenever the rear of the vehicle is raised for any reason. Several items, including a torque wrench and special grease, are required for this procedure (see illustration).
2   With the vehicle securely supported on jackstands, spin each wheel and check for noise, rolling resistance and free play.
3   Grasp the top of each tire with one hand and the bottom with the other. Move the wheel in-and-out on the spindle. If there's any noticeable movement, the bearings should be checked and then repacked with grease or replaced if necessary.

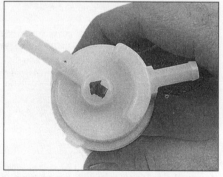

38.8 Make sure the arrow on the filter faces toward the front of the vehicle

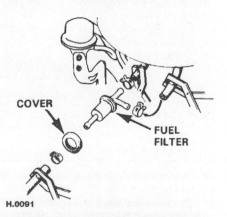

38.9 Auxiliary fuel filter (carburetor-equipped models) installation details

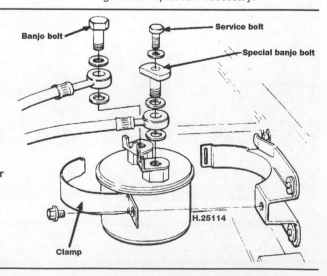

38.13 Fuel injection filter installation details

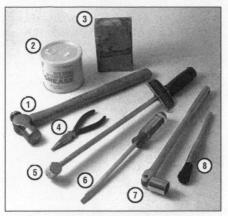

39.1 Tools and materials needed for rear wheel bearing maintenance

1   **Hammer** - *A common hammer will do just fine*
2   **Grease** - *High-temperature grease which is formulated specially for wheel bearings should be used*
3   **Wood block** - *If you have a scrap piece of 2x4, it can be used to drive the new seal into the hub*
4   **Needle-nose pliers** - *Used to straighten and remove the cotter pin in the spindle*
5   **Torque wrench** - *This is very important in this procedure; if the bearing is too tight, the wheel won't turn freely - if it is too loose, the wheel will "wobble' on the spindle. Either way, it could mean extensive damage*
6   **Screwdriver** - *Used to remove the seal from the hub (a long screwdriver would be preferred)*
7   **Socket/breaker bar** - *Needed to loosen the nut on the spindle if it is extremely tight*
8   **Brush** - *Together with some clean solvent, this will be used to remove old grease from the hub and spindle*

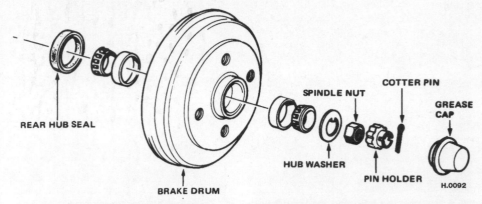

39.5 Rear hub and bearing components - exploded view

4   Remove the wheel.
5   Pry the grease cap out of the hub using a screwdriver or hammer and chisel **(see illustration)**.
6   Straighten the bent ends of the cotter pin, then pull the cotter pin out of the pin holder **(see illustration 39.5)**. Discard the cotter pin and use a new one during reassembly.
7   Remove the pin holder, spindle nut and washer from the end of the spindle.
8   Pull the hub assembly out slightly, then push it back into its original position. This should force the outer bearing off the spindle enough so it can be removed.
9   Pull the hub off the spindle.
10   Use a screwdriver to pry the seal out of the rear of the hub. As this is done, note how the seal is installed.
11   Remove the inner wheel bearing from the hub.
12   Use solvent to remove all traces of the old grease from the bearings, hub and spindle. A small brush may prove helpful; however make sure no bristles from the brush

39.15 Apply grease to the inner and outer bearing seats, shoulder and seal seat

embed themselves inside the bearing rollers. Allow the parts to air dry.
13   Carefully inspect the bearings for cracks, heat discoloration, worn rollers, etc. Check the bearing races inside the hub for wear and damage. If the bearing races are defective, the hubs should be taken to a machine shop with the facilities to remove the old races and press new ones in. Note that the bearings and races come as matched sets and old bearings should never be installed on new races.
14   Use high-temperature wheel bearing grease to pack the bearings. Work the grease completely into the bearings, forcing it between the rollers, cone and cage from the back side.
15   Apply a thin coat of grease to the spindle at the outer bearing seat, inner bearing seat, shoulder and seal seat **(see illustration)**.
16   Put a small quantity of grease inboard of each bearing race inside the hub. Using your finger, form a dam at these points to provide extra grease availability and to keep thinned grease from flowing out of the bearing.
17   Place the grease-packed inner bearing into the rear of the hub and put a little more grease outboard of the bearing.
18   Place a new seal over the inner bearing and tap the seal evenly into place with a hammer and block of wood until it's flush with the hub.

39.19 Press the grease-packed outer bearing securely into the hub

19   Carefully place the hub assembly onto the spindle and push the grease-packed outer bearing into the hub **(see illustration)**.
20   Install the washer and spindle nut. Tighten the nut to the specified initial torque.
21   Spin the hub in a forward direction to seat the bearings and remove any grease or burrs which could cause excessive bearing play later.
22   Loosen the spindle nut until it's just loose, no more.
23   Tighten the nut to the specified final torque.
24   Install the pin holder and a new cotter pin through the hole in the spindle and the slot in the pin holder. If the pin holder slots don't line up with the hole in the spindle, loosen the spindle nut slightly until they do. From the hand-tight position, the nut should not be loosened more than one-half flat to install the cotter pin.
25   Bend the ends of the cotter pin until they're flat against the nut. Cut off any extra length which could interfere with the grease cap.
26   Install the grease cap, tapping it into place with a hammer.
27   Install the tire/wheel assembly on the hub and tighten the lug nuts.
28   Grasp the top and bottom of the tire and check the bearings in the manner described earlier in this Section.
29   Lower the vehicle.

1

Notes

Chapter 2 Part A
Engines

Contents

Specifications

General

Displacement
 1984 and 1985 .... 1800 cc (112 c.i.)
 1986 on .... 2000 cc (119 c.i.)
Cylinder numbers (drivebelt end to transaxle end) 1-2-3-4
Firing order 1-3-4-2

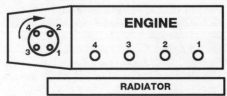

The cylinder locations are shown above -
the firing order is 1-3-4-2

Camshaft

End play
 Standard .... 0.002 to 0.006 in
  (0.05 to 0.15 mm)
 Service limit .... 0.02 in (0.5 mm)
Lobe height
 Fuel injected engines
  1984 and 1985
   Intake A .... 1.5297 in (38.855 mm)
   Intake B .... 1.5200 in (38.608 mm)
   Exhaust .... 1.5274 in (38.796 mm)
  1986 on
   Intake A .... 1.5296 in (38.853 mm)
   Intake B .... 1.5198 in (38.604 mm)
   Exhaust .... 1.5274 in (38.796 mm)
 Carbureted engines with manual transaxle
  1984 and 1985
   Intake A .... 1.492 in (37.899 mm)
   Intake B .... 1.497 in (38.028 mm)
   Exhaust .... 1.487 in (37.776 mm)
   Auxiliary .... 1.446 in (36.738 mm)
  1986 on
   Intake .... 1.5148 in (38.477 mm)
   Exhaust .... 1.5218 in (38.653 mm)

Camshaft (continued)

Carbureted engines with automatic transaxle
  1984 and 1985
    Intake A... 1.484 in (37.705 mm)
    Intake B... 1.502 in (38.157 mm)
    Exhaust... 1.487 in (37.776 mm)
    Auxiliary... 1.446 in (36.738 mm)
  1986 on
    Intake .... 1.5174 in (38.541 mm)
    Exhaust... 1.5200 in (38.607 mm)
Camshaft journal-to-bearing (oil) clearance
  Journals no. 1, 3 and 5
    Standard... 0.002 to 0.004 in (0.05 to 0.09 mm)
    Service limit... 0.006 in (0.15 mm)
  Journals no. 2 and 4
    Standard... 0.005 to 0.007 in (0.13 to 0.17 mm)
    Service limit... 0.009 in (0.23 mm)
Camshaft runout
  Standard... 0.001 in (0.03 mm)
  Service limit... 0.002 in (0.06 mm)
Rocker arm shaft-to-rocker arm oil clearance........... 0.003 in (0.08 mm)

Oil pump

Inner rotor tip clearance .... 0.006 in (0.15 mm)
Outer rotor-to-housing clearance........................... 0.004 to 0.007 in (0.10 to 0.18 mm)

Torque specifications

Ft-lbs

Air suction tube nuts.. 51
Camshaft sprocket bolt.. 27
Camshaft cover crown nuts...................................... 7
Crankshaft damper bolt
  1984 through 1988 83
  1989 108
Cylinder head bolts
  Step 1 22
  Step 2 49
Driveplate bolts (automatic transaxle) 54
EGR tube nut(s) 43
EGR tube flange nuts (fuel injected models) 7
Exhaust manifold-to-cylinder head bolts.................. 22
Exhaust manifold-to-header pipe self-locking nuts ... 40
Exhaust manifold bracket bolts................................ 20
Flywheel bolts (manual transaxle)............................ 76
Intake manifold bracket bolts................................... 16
Intake manifold part A-to-part B nuts....................... 17
Intake manifold-to-cylinder head bolts..................... 16
Oil pan bolts... 9
Oil pick-up tube bolts 9
Oil pump-to-engine block bolts/nuts........................ 9
Oil pump cover-to-pump screws............................... 5
Oil filter housing bolts 9
Rocker shaft pedestal bolts...................................... 16
Rocker shaft end cap bolts 9
Timing belt adjustment bolt 31

1　General information

This Part of Chapter 2 is devoted to in-vehicle repair procedures for the engine. All information concerning engine removal and installation and engine block and cylinder head overhaul can be found in Part B of this Chapter.

The following repair procedures are based on the assumption that the engine is installed in the vehicle. If the engine has been removed from the vehicle and mounted on a stand, many of the steps outlined in this Part of Chapter 2 will not apply.

The Specifications included in this Part of Chapter 2 apply only to the procedures contained in this Part. Part B of Chapter 2 contains the Specifications necessary for cylinder head and engine block rebuilding.

2　Repair operations possible with the engine in the vehicle

Many major repair operations can be accomplished without removing the engine from the vehicle.

Clean the engine compartment and the exterior of the engine with some type of degreaser before any work is done. It will make the job easier and help keep dirt out of the internal areas of the engine.

Depending on the components involved, it may be helpful to remove the hood to improve access to the engine as repairs are performed (refer to Chapter 11 if necessary). Cover the fenders to prevent damage to the paint. Special pads are available, but an old bedspread or blanket will also work.

If vacuum, exhaust, oil or coolant leaks develop, indicating a need for gasket or seal replacement, the repairs can generally be made with the engine in the vehicle. The intake and exhaust manifold gaskets, camshaft timing cover gasket, oil pan gasket, crankshaft oil seals and cylinder head gasket are all accessible with the engine in place.

Exterior engine components, such as the intake and exhaust manifolds, the oil pan, the oil pump, the water pump, the starter motor, the alternator, the distributor and the fuel system components can be removed for repair with the engine in place.

Since the cylinder head can be removed without pulling the engine, camshaft and valve component servicing can also be accomplished with the engine in the vehicle. Replacement of the timing belt and sprockets is also possible with the engine in the vehicle.

In extreme cases caused by a lack of necessary equipment, repair or replacement of piston rings, pistons, connecting rods and rod bearings is possible with the engine in the vehicle. However, this practice is not recommended because of the cleaning and preparation work that must be done to the components involved.

3 Top Dead Center (TDC) for number one piston - locating

Refer to illustrations 3.6, 3.7, 3.8 and 3.9
Note: *The following procedure is based on the assumption that the distributor is correctly installed. If you are trying to locate TDC to install the distributor correctly, piston position must be determined by feeling for compression at the number one spark plug hole, then aligning the ignition timing marks as described in step 8.*

1 Top Dead Center (TDC) is the highest point in the cylinder that each piston reaches as it travels up-and-down when the crankshaft turns. Each piston reaches TDC on the compression stroke and again on the exhaust stroke, but TDC generally refers to piston position on the compression stroke.
2 Positioning the piston(s) at TDC is an essential part of many procedures such as rocker arm removal, camshaft and timing belt/sprocket removal and distributor removal.

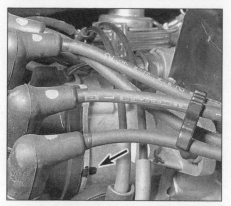

3.6 Make a mark (arrow) on the distributor body adjacent to the number one spark plug wire terminal

3 Before beginning this procedure, be sure to place the transmission in Neutral and apply the parking brake or block the rear wheels. Also, disable the ignition system by detaching the coil wire from the center terminal of the distributor cap and grounding it on the block with a jumper wire. Remove the spark plugs (see Chapter 1).
4 In order to bring any piston to TDC, the crankshaft must be turned using one of the methods outlined below. When looking at the drivebelt end of the engine, normal crankshaft rotation is counterclockwise.

a) *The preferred method is to turn the crankshaft with a socket and ratchet attached to the bolt threaded into the front of the crankshaft.*
b) *A remote starter switch, which may save some time, can also be used. Follow the instructions included with the switch. Once the piston is close to TDC, use a socket and ratchet as described in the previous paragraph.*
c) *If an assistant is available to turn the ignition switch to the Start position in short bursts, you can get the piston close to TDC without a remote starter switch. Make sure your assistant is out of the vehicle, away from the ignition switch, then use a socket and ratchet as described in Paragraph a) to complete the procedure.*

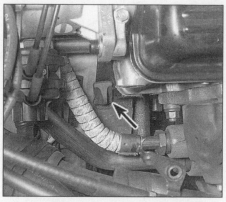

3.7 The timing mark opening is located below the distributor - remove the plug (arrow)

5 Note the position of the terminal for the number one spark plug wire on the distributor cap. If the terminal isn't marked, follow the plug wire from the number one cylinder spark plug to the cap.
6 Use a felt-tip pen or chalk to make a mark on the distributor body directly adjacent to the terminal **(see illustration)**.
7 Detach the cap from the distributor (see Chapter 1 if necessary), set it aside and remove the plug from the timing mark opening **(see illustration)**.
8 Turn the crankshaft (see Paragraph 4 above) until the T mark on the flywheel/driveplate is aligned with the pointer on the engine block (visible through the timing mark opening) **(see illustrations)**.
9 Look at the distributor rotor - it should be pointing directly at the mark you made on the distributor body. If it is, go to step 12.
10 If the rotor is 180 degrees off, the number one piston is at TDC on the exhaust stroke.
11 To get the piston to TDC on the compression stroke, turn the crankshaft one complete turn (360 degrees) counterclockwise. The rotor should now be pointing at the mark on the distributor. When the rotor is pointing at the number one spark plug wire terminal in the distributor cap and the ignition timing marks are aligned, the number one piston is at TDC on the compression stroke.

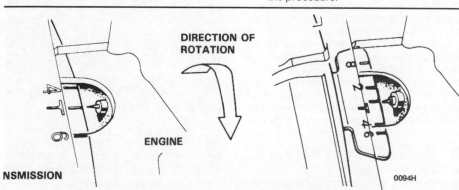

3.8 Typical timing marks - manual transaxle (left) and automatic transaxle (right) set at Top Dead Center

3.9 With the timing marks aligned, the rotor should be aligned with the mark you made on the distributor body (arrows)

2A

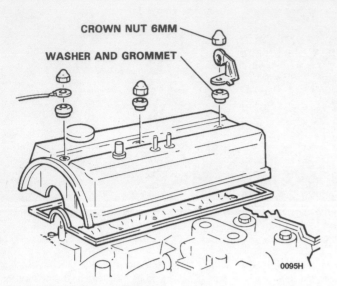

4.4a Exploded view of typical camshaft cover components - carbureted models

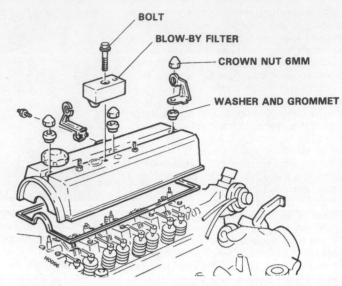

4.4b Exploded view of typical camshaft cover components - fuel-injected models

12   After the number one piston has been positioned at TDC on the compression stroke, TDC for any of the remaining pistons can be located by turning the crankshaft and following the firing order. Mark the remaining spark plug wire terminal locations on the distributor body just like you did for the number one terminal, then number the marks to correspond with the cylinder numbers. As you turn the crankshaft, the rotor will also turn. When it's pointing directly at one of the marks on the distributor, the piston for that particular cylinder is at TDC on the compression stroke.

4   Camshaft cover - removal and installation

Refer to illustrations 4.4a and 4.4b
1   Disconnect the negative cable from the battery.
2   Remove the air cleaner assembly (see Chapter 4).
3   Detach the crankcase ventilation tubes from the camshaft cover.
4   Remove the blow-by filter (fuel injected models) and any wiring and/or brackets from the camshaft cover **(see illustrations)**.
5   Remove the upper timing belt cover (see Section 7).
6   Remove the crown nuts, washers and grommets. Lift the camshaft cover from the engine.
7   Thoroughly clean the cover and gasket mating surfaces, removing any traces of old gasket material.
8   Using a new gasket, reinstall the cover and tighten the crown nuts to the specified torque.
9   Reinstall the remaining parts in the reverse order of removal.
10   Run the engine and check for oil leaks.

5   Intake manifold - removal and installation

Refer to illustrations 5.4, 5.5 and 5.6
1   Remove the air cleaner assembly and, on fuel injected models, relieve the fuel pressure (see Chapter 4).
2   Disconnect the negative cable from the battery.
3   Drain the cooling system (see Chapter 1).
4   Label, then disconnect all wires, control cables and hoses connecting the intake manifold to the vehicle **(see illustration)**.
5   On carbureted models, remove the two bolts that secure the manifold to the brackets and all the intake manifold-to-cylinder head nuts **(see illustration)**. Lift the manifold from the engine.
6   Fuel injected models have a two-piece manifold **(see illustration)**. Remove the manifold bracket-to-manifold bolts, unscrew the nuts and lift off part B of the manifold. Remove the intake manifold-to-cylinder head nuts and lift off part A of the manifold.
7   Thoroughly clean the gasket mating surfaces on the manifold (or manifold parts) and the cylinder head, removing all traces of old gasket material. If you will be replacing the manifold, transfer all detachable parts **(see illustration 5.5 or 5.6)** to the new manifold.
8   Using a new gasket, reinstall the manifold (or, on fuel injected models, part A of the manifold). Tighten the nuts from the center outward in several steps to the specified torque. On fuel injected models, reinstall part B of the manifold, using a new gasket and tightening the nuts from the center outward to the specified torque.
9   Reinstall the remaining parts in the reverse order of removal. Tighten the intake manifold bracket bolts to the specified torque.

10   Refill the radiator.
11   Run the engine, checking for leaks and proper operation.

6   Exhaust manifold - removal and installation

Refer to illustrations 6.3a and 6.3b
Warning: *The engine must be completely cool before beginning this procedure.*
1   Disconnect the negative cable from the battery.
2   Unplug the oxygen sensor wire harness. If you're installing a new manifold, remove the sensor (see Chapter 6).
3   Remove the three bolts that secure the exhaust manifold shroud to the manifold. Then remove the shroud, EGR tub and air suction tube (if equipped) from the manifold **(see illustrations)**.
4   Apply penetrating oil to the exhaust manifold mounting nuts/bolts.

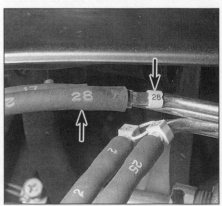

5.4 Check each wire, cable or hose connection to see if it's numbered (arrows); if not, number it yourself with tape and a marker prior to disassembly

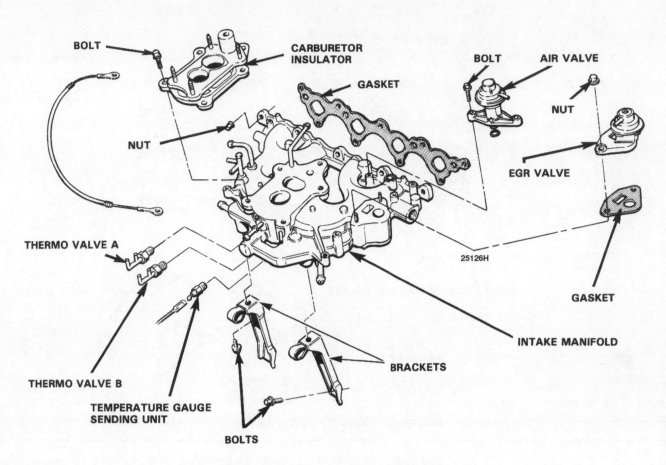

5.5 Exploded view of intake manifold - carbureted models

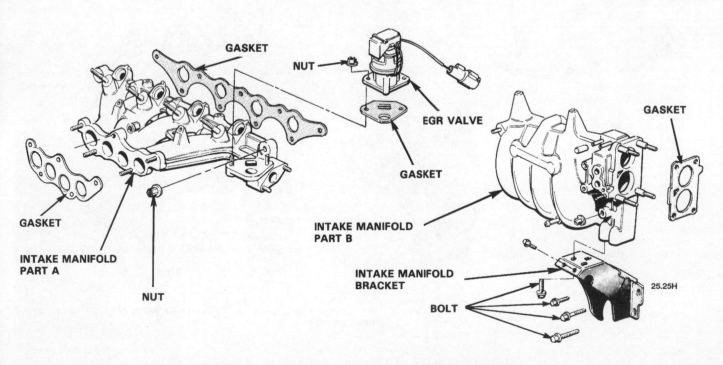

5.6 Exploded view of intake manifold - fuel injected models

2A

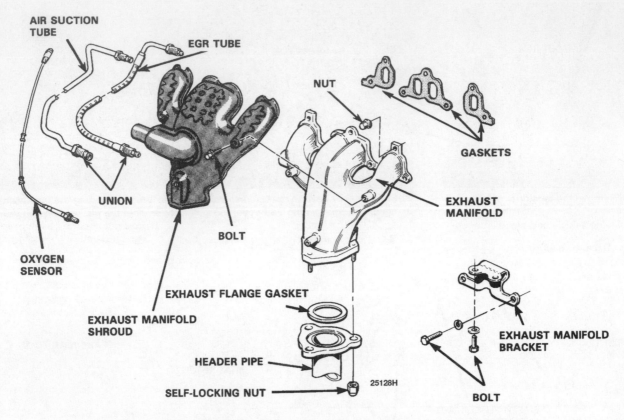

6.3a Exploded view of typical exhaust manifold components - carbureted models

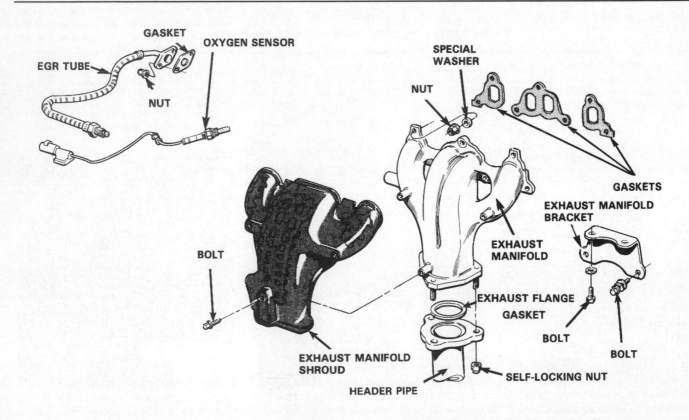

6.3b Exploded view of typical exhaust manifold components - fuel injected models

7.9a Remove the tensioner seal, . . .

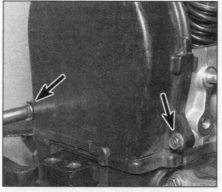

7.9b . . . then remove the bolts (arrows) and the upper timing belt cover

7.9c When removing the upper timing belt cover, note the gasket beneath the cover - it does not need to be removed or replaced unless it's damaged

5   Raise the vehicle and place it securely on jackstands.
6   From underneath the vehicle, apply penetrating oil to the two exhaust manifold-to-bracket bolts and the three self locking nuts on the header pipe flange.
7   Remove the self-locking nuts and separate the header pipe from the exhaust manifold.
8   Remove the exhaust manifold-to-bracket bolts.
9   Lower the vehicle.
10   Remove the nuts and detach the manifold and gaskets.
11   Use a scraper to remove all traces of old gasket material and carbon deposits from the manifold and cylinder head mating surfaces. If the gasket was leaking, have the manifold checked for warpage at an automotive machine shop and resurfaced if necessary.
12   Position new gaskets on the cylinder head.
13   Install the manifold and thread the mounting nuts into place.
14   Working from the center out, tighten the nuts to the specified torque in three or four equal steps.
15   Reinstall the remaining parts in the reverse order of removal. Be sure to use new self-locking nuts, a new exhaust flange gasket and a new EGR tube flange gasket (fuel injected models). Tighten all fasteners to the specified torque.

16   Run the engine and check for exhaust leaks.

7   Timing belt and sprockets - removal, inspection and installation

Removal

Refer to illustrations 7.9a, 7.9b, 7.9c, 7.13, 7.14, 7.15, 7.16, 7.17a, 7.17b and 7.17c, 7.18a and 7.18b

1   Disconnect the negative cable from the battery.
2   Block the rear wheels and set the parking brake.
3   Loosen the lug nuts on the left front wheel and raise the front of the vehicle. Support the front of the vehicle securely on jackstands.
4   Remove the left front wheel for easier access to the end of the crankshaft.
5   Support the engine with a floor jack. Place a block of wood between the jack pad and the oil pan to avoid damaging the pan.
6   Remove the left engine mount (see Section 17).
7   Remove the spark plugs and drivebelts (see Chapter 1).
8   Position the number one piston at Top Dead Center (see Section 3).
9   Remove the tensioner seal and the

upper timing belt cover **(see illustrations)**. Note the gasket beneath the cover **(see illustration)**. It does not need to be removed or replaced unless it's damaged.
10   Remove the alternator and bracket (see Chapter 5).
11   Unbolt the power steering pump without disconnecting the hoses and set it aside (see Chapter 10).
12   On air conditioned vehicles, detach the wiring and unbolt the air conditioning compressor, setting it aside without disconnecting the refrigerant hoses (see Chapter 3).
13   To keep the crankshaft pulley from turning, have an assistant hold a large screwdriver firmly against the ring gear teeth **(see illustration)** and loosen the pulley-to-crankshaft bolt with a socket and breaker bar. Slip the pulley off the crankshaft.
14   Remove the water pump pulley **(see illustration)**.
15   Remove the lower timing belt cover **(see illustration)**.
16   If you intend to reuse the timing belt, paint match marks to align the sprockets with the belt and an arrow to indicate the direction

7.13 Have an assistant hold a large screwdriver against the ring gear teeth inside the timing mark hole

7.14 Remove the pump pulley retaining bolts (arrows) then slip off the pulley

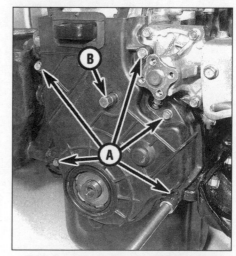

7.15 To remove the lower timing belt cover, unscrew the mounting bolts (A) - use the timing belt tensioner bolt (B) to adjust the timing belt tension

2A

7.16 If you intend to reuse the belt, paint an arrow on the belt to indicate direction of rotation and match marks (arrow) to align the sprockets with the belt

7.17a Remove the outer belt guide - note that the curved outer edge faces away from the belt (belt removed for clarity)

7.17b It's not necessary to remove the crankshaft sprocket unless you intend to replace the oil seal

7.17c After removing the sprocket, slide off the inner belt guide; note that the curved edge faces away from the timing belt

7.18a Remove the camshaft sprocket bolt (arrow) - when reinstalling the sprocket, the dot (arrow) or UP mark should be at the top (twelve o'clock position)

7.18b After you have removed the camshaft sprocket, remove the Woodruff key (arrow) from the camshaft

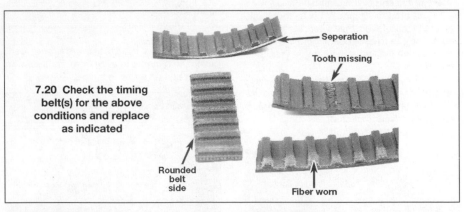

7.20 Check the timing belt(s) for the above conditions and replace as indicated

Seperation

Tooth missing

Rounded belt side

Fiber worn

7.19 Check the belt adjustment idler pulley for rough rotation and bearing play

of rotation **(see illustration)**.

17   Loosen the timing belt tensioner bolt **(see illustration 7.15)**, remove the outer belt guide **(see illustration)** and slip the belt off. Note the way the belt guide is facing for proper reinstallation. If you are replacing the crankshaft oil seal, slip the sprocket and inner belt guide off the crankshaft **(see illustrations)**.

18   If you are replacing the camshaft or camshaft oil seal, slip a lever or large screwdriver through the camshaft sprocket to keep it from rotating and remove the bolt and sprocket **(see illustration)**. Also remove the Woodruff key **(see illustration)**.

Inspection

Refer to illustrations 7.19, 7.20

19   Rotate the belt adjustment idler pulley by hand and move it side-to-side, checking for bearing play and rough rotation **(see illustration)**. Replace it if roughness or play is detected.

20   Inspect the timing belt for wear (especially on the thrust side of the teeth), cracks, splits, fraying and oil contamination **(see illustrations)**. Replace the belt if any of these conditions is present.

7.22 There are two index grooves on the right face of the camshaft sprocket- each must be parallel to the cylinder head gasket surface (arrow)

8.2 Insert a seal removal tool or screwdriver between the crankshaft and front oil seal to pry the seal out of the bore

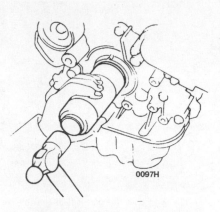

8.4 Lubricate the seal lip and carefully tap the new crankshaft seal into place with a large socket or piece of pipe and a hammer

9.2 Insert a small screwdriver between the seal lip and camshaft (arrow) to remove the seal

2A

Installation

Refer to illustration 7.22

21 If you removed the sprockets, reinstall them. Don't forget the Woodruff key for the camshaft sprocket and the inner belt guide for the crankshaft sprocket (you may leave the outer guide off for now). Tighten the camshaft sprocket bolt to the specified torque.

22 Before installing the timing belt, ensure the camshaft sprocket is installed with the dot or "UP" mark at the top **(see illustration 7.18a)** and the two index marks in line with the cylinder head **(see illustration)**.

23 Temporarily reinstall the crankshaft pulley bolt and turn the crankshaft (if it was disturbed) until the timing marks on the flywheel/driveplate and the pointer on the bellhousing are aligned (see Section 3).

24 Install the timing belt with slight tension between the sprockets on the forward-facing side. With the belt tensioner bolt loose, slowly rotate the crankshaft counter-clockwise for a distance of three teeth on the camshaft sprocket. This puts tension on the belt.

25 Tighten the belt tensioner bolt.

9.4 Use a hammer and a section of pipe or a large socket to tap the new seal into place

26 Carefully turn the crankshaft through two revolutions and recheck the timing marks and camshaft sprocket index marks for proper alignment. If the crankshaft binds or seems to hit something, do not force it, as the valves may be hitting the pistons. If this happens, valve timing is incorrect. Remove the belt and go back to Step 22.

27 Remove the crankshaft pulley bolt.

28 Reinstall the remaining parts in the reverse order of removal. Tighten the crankshaft pulley bolt to the specified torque.

29 Run the engine and check for proper operation.

8 Front crankshaft oil seal - replacement

Refer to illustrations 8.2 and 8.4

1 Remove the timing belt and crankshaft sprocket (see Section 7).

2 Note how far the seal is seated in the bore, then carefully pry it out of the bore with a screwdriver or seal removal tool **(see illustration)**. Don't scratch the housing bore or damage the crankshaft in the process (if the crankshaft is damaged, the new seal will end up leaking).

3 Clean the bore in the housing and coat the outer edge of the new seal with engine oil or multi-purpose grease. Apply moly-base grease to the seal lip.

4 Using a socket with an outside diameter slightly smaller than the outside diameter of the seal, carefully drive the new seal into place with a hammer **(see illustration)**. Make sure it's installed squarely and driven in to the same depth as the original. If a socket isn't available, a short section of large diameter pipe will also work. Check the seal after installation to make sure the garter spring didn't pop out of place.

5 Reinstall the crankshaft sprocket and timing belt (see Section 7).

6 Run the engine and check for oil leaks at the front seal.

9 Camshaft oil seal - replacement

Refer to illustrations 9.2 and 9.4

1 Remove the timing belt and camshaft sprocket (see Section 7).

2 Note how far the seal is seated in the bore, then carefully pry it out with a small screwdriver **(see illustration)**. Don't scratch the bore or damage the camshaft in the process (if the camshaft is damaged, the new seal will end up leaking).

3 Clean the bore and coat the outer edge of the new seal with engine oil or multi-purpose grease. Apply moly-base grease to the seal lip.

4 Using a socket with an outside diameter slightly smaller than the outside diameter of the seal, carefully drive the new seal into place with a hammer **(see illustration)**. Make sure it's installed squarely and driven in to the same depth as the original. If a socket isn't available, a short section of pipe will also work.

5 Reinstall the camshaft sprocket and timing belt (see Section 7).

6 Run the engine and check for oil leaks at the camshaft seal.

10 Camshaft and rocker arms - removal, inspection and installation

Removal

Refer to illustrations 10.3, 10.4a, 10.4b and 10.5

1 Remove the camshaft cover (see Section 4) and the timing belt and camshaft sprocket (see Section 7).

2 Remove the distributor (see Chapter 5).

3 Loosen the valve adjustment locknuts and back off the adjustment screws until they no longer hold the valves open (see Chapter 1). Measure the camshaft end play with a dial indicator **(see illustration)**. If it is greater than the specified maximum, the camshaft and/or the cylinder head is excessively worn and will have to be replaced.

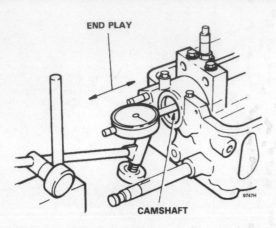

END PLAY

CAMSHAFT

9747H

10.3 To check camshaft end play, mount a dial indicator as shown and slide the camshaft back and forth (arrows)

10.4a Loosen the rocker pedestal bolts (arrows), . . .

4   Loosen each rocker pedestal bolt **(see illustration)**, two turns at a time, using a diagonal pattern. Once all bolts are loose, lift the rocker assembly off the engine as a unit **(see illustration)**. Leaving the bolts in their holes will hold the rocker assembly together.

5   Lift the camshaft from the cylinder head **(see illustration)** and clean it thoroughly.

Inspection

Refer to illustrations 10.6, 10.7, 10.8a, 10.8b, 10.8c, 10.9a, 10.9b, 10.9c and 10.10

6   Visually examine the camshaft lobes **(see illustration)** and bearing journals for wear, pitting, score marks, galling and evidence of overheating (blue, discolored areas). Also look for flaking away of the hardened surface layer of each lobe.

7   Using a micrometer, measure the height of each camshaft lobe **(see illustration)**. If any measurements are less than specified, replace the camshaft.

8   Check the oil clearance for each camshaft journal as follows:

  a) *Clean the bearing caps and camshaft journals with lacquer thinner or acetone and a clean cloth.*

  b) *Carefully lay the camshaft in place in the head. Don't use any lubrication.* **Note:** *Do not rotate the camshaft during this procedure.*

  c) *Lay a strip of Plastigage on each journal **(see illustration)**.*

  d) *Set the rocker arm assembly in place and install the pedestal bolts finger-tight.*

  e) *Tighten the bolts to the specified torque in two-turn increments, following the sequence shown **(see illustration)**.*

  f) *Remove the bolts as described in Step 4 and lift off the rocker arm assembly.*

  g) *Compare the width of the crushed Plastigage on each journal (at it's widest point) to the scale on the Plastigage envelope **(see illustration)**.*

10.4b . . . then lift off the rocker assembly - leaving the pedestal bolts in place will hold the assembly together while it is removed from the cylinder head

10.5 Once the rocker arm assembly is removed, the camshaft can be lifted out

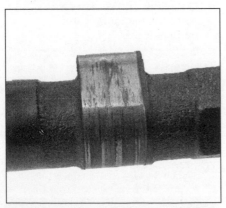

10.6 Check the camshaft lobes for pitting, wear and score marks - if scoring is excessive, as is the case here, replace the camshaft

10.7 Measuring camshaft lobe heights

10.8a Lay a strip of Plastigage on each camshaft journal

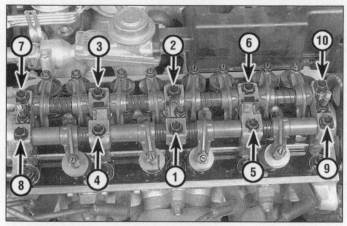

10.8b Rocker pedestal bolt tightening sequence

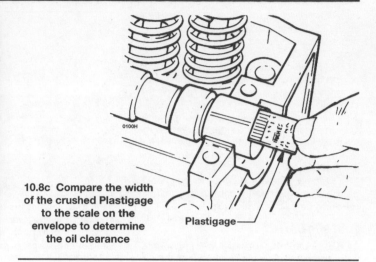

10.8c Compare the width of the crushed Plastigage to the scale on the envelope to determine the oil clearance

Plastigage

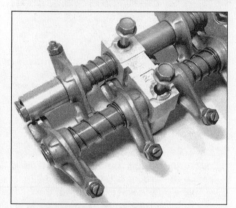

10.9a Rocker assemblies slide off the shaft after removal of the pedestal bolts

h) If the clearance is greater than specified, the camshaft and/or cylinder head is excessively worn and will have to be replaced.
i) Scrape off the Plastigage with your fingernail or the edge of a credit card - don't nick or scratch the journals or bearing caps.

9   Slip the bolts out of the rocker arm assembly and slide the components off the shafts. Store all the components in order so they may be reinstalled in the same positions (see illustrations).
10   Visually inspect the rocker arms (see illustration) and shafts for wear. Check the rocker arm-to-camshaft contact faces and

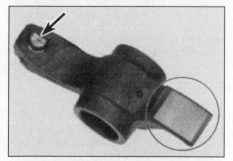

10.10 Check the camshaft contact face and the ends of the adjusting screws for wear and damage

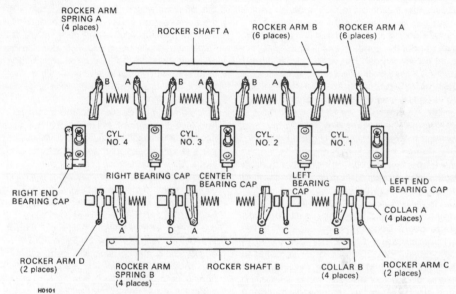

10.9b Exploded view of the rocker arm assembly - carbureted engines

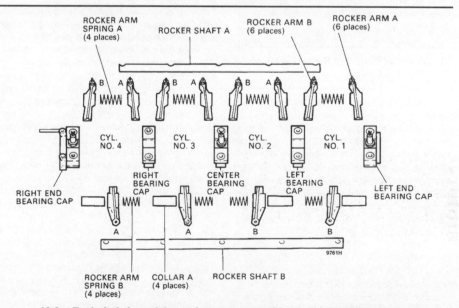

10.9c Exploded view of the rocker arm assembly - fuel injected engines

the shaft bores. Also note the condition of the adjustment screws and locknuts, the bearing cap wear surfaces and the springs and bushings.

11 Measure the rocker shaft diameters with a micrometer where they show the most wear (thinnest measurement) and record the dimensions.

12 Measure the rocker arm bore inside diameters and record the dimensions. Subtract rocker arm shaft diameter from rocker arm bore inside diameter to determine oil clearance.

13 Compare the oil clearance to the specification and replace any components which are worn beyond specification.

Installation

14 Lubricate the rocker arm components, camshaft lobes, journals and seal contact surfaces with engine assembly lube or moly-based grease. Assemble the rocker arm components on the shafts and install the pedestal bolts to hold the components in place.

15 Lay the camshaft in the cylinder head with its keyway facing upward (twelve o'clock position).

16 Install a new camshaft oil seal (see Section 9).

17 Install the rocker arm assembly and screw in the pedestal bolts finger tight.

18 Tighten the rocker shaft bolts two turns at a time following the tightening sequence shown in illustration 10.8b until the specified torque is reached.

19 Install the Woodruff key in the end of the camshaft and slip the timing belt sprocket into position. Tighten the sprocket bolt to the specified torque. Slip a pry bar or large screwdriver through a hole in the sprocket to keep it from turning. Ensure the alignment hole is at the top and the index marks on each side are parallel to the cylinder head **(see illustration 7.22)**.

20 Reinstall the timing belt and the remaining components in the reverse order of removal.

11 Valve springs, retainers and seals - replacement

Refer to illustrations 11.4, 11.9 and 11.7

Note: *Broken valve springs and defective valve stem seals can be replaced without removing the cylinder head. Two special tools and a compressed air source are normally required to perform this operation, so read through this Section carefully and rent or buy the tools before beginning the job. If compressed air isn't available, a length of nylon rope can be used to keep the valves from falling into the cylinder during this procedure.*

1 Refer to Section 4 and remove the camshaft cover from the cylinder head.

2 Remove the spark plug from the cylinder which has the defective component. If all of the valve stem seals are being replaced, all of the spark plugs should be removed.

3 Turn the crankshaft until the piston in

11.4 This is what the air hose adapter that threads into the spark plug hole looks like - they're commonly available from auto parts stores

the affected cylinder is at top dead center on the compression stroke (refer to Section 3 for instructions). If you're replacing all of the valve stem seals, begin with cylinder number one and work on the valves for one cylinder at a time. Move from cylinder-to-cylinder following the firing order sequence (see the Specifications).

4 Thread an adapter into the spark plug hole **(see illustration)** and connect an air hose from a compressed air source to it. Most auto parts stores can supply the air hose adapter. **Note:** *Many cylinder compression gauges utilize a screw-in fitting that may work with your air hose quick-disconnect fitting.*

5 Remove the rocker arm assembly (see Section 10)

6 Apply compressed air to the cylinder. **Warning:** *The piston may be forced down by compressed air, causing the crankshaft to turn suddenly. If the wrench used when positioning the number one piston at TDC is still attached to the bolt in the crankshaft nose, it could cause damage or injury when the crankshaft moves.*

7 The valves should be held in place by the air pressure. If the valve faces or seats are in poor condition, leaks may prevent air pressure from retaining the valves - refer to the alternative procedure below.

8 If you don't have access to compressed air, an alternative method can be used. Position the piston at a point just before TDC on the compression stroke, then feed a long piece of nylon rope through the spark plug hole until it fills the combustion chamber. Be sure to leave the end of the rope hanging out of the engine so it can be removed easily. Use a large ratchet and socket to rotate the crankshaft in the normal direction of rotation (counterclockwise) until **slight** resistance is felt.

9 Stuff shop rags into the cylinder head holes above and below the valves to prevent parts and tools from falling into the engine, then use a valve spring compressor to compress the spring. Remove the keepers with small needle-nose pliers or a magnet **(see illustration). Note:** *A couple of different types of tools are available for compressing*

11.9 Valve spring compressor (2) releasing the valve keepers (1)

11.17 Apply a small dab of grease to each keeper before installation to hold it in place on the valve stem until the spring is released

the valve springs with the head in place. One type grips the lower spring coils and presses on the retainer as the knob is turned, while the other type utilizes the rocker arm shaft for leverage. Both types work very well, although the lever type is usually less expensive.

10 Remove the spring retainer and valve spring(s), then remove the guide seal. **Note:** *If air pressure fails to hold the valve in the closed position during this operation, the valve face and/or seat is probably damaged. If so, the cylinder head will have to be removed for additional repair operations.*

11 Wrap a rubber band or tape around the top of the valve stem so the valve won't fall into the combustion chamber, then release the air pressure. **Note:** *If a rope was used instead of air pressure, turn the crankshaft slightly in the direction opposite normal rotation.*

12 Inspect the valve stem for damage. Rotate the valve in the guide and check the end for eccentric movement, which would indicate that the valve is bent.

13 Move the valve up-and-down in the guide and make sure it doesn't bind. If the valve stem binds, either the valve is bent or the guide is damaged. In either case, the head will have to be removed for repair.

14 Reapply air pressure to the cylinder to retain the valve in the closed position, then remove the tape or rubber band from the valve stem. If a rope was used instead of air pressure, rotate the crankshaft in the normal direction of rotation until slight resistance is felt.

15   Lubricate the valve stem with engine oil and install a new guide seal. **Note:** *Intake and exhaust seals are not interchangeable. Intake seals have a white spring and exhaust seals have a black spring.*

16   Install the spring in position over the valve. **Note:** *Place the end of the valve springs with closely wound coils or paint marks toward the cylinder head.*

17   Install the valve spring retainer. Compress the valve spring and carefully position the keepers in the groove. Apply a small dab of grease to the inside of each keeper to hold it in place if necessary **(see illustration)**.

18   Remove the pressure from the spring tool and make sure the keepers are seated.

19   Disconnect the air hose and remove the adapter from the spark plug hole. If a rope was used in place of air pressure, pull it out of the cylinder.

20   Refer to Section 10 and install the rocker arm assembly.

21   Install the spark plug(s) and hook up the wire(s).

22   Refer to Section 4 and install the camshaft cover.

23   Start and run the engine, then check for oil leaks and unusual sounds coming from the camshaft cover area.

12   Cylinder head - removal and installation

Note: *The engine must be completely cool before beginning this procedure.*

Removal

Refer to illustrations 12.10, 12.11, 12.12a and 12.12b

1   Disconnect the negative cable from the battery.

2   Drain the coolant from the engine block and radiator (see Chapter 1).

3   Drain the engine oil and remove the oil filter (see Chapter 1).

4   On fuel injected models, relieve fuel pressure (see Chapter 4).

5   Remove the intake manifold (see Section 5).

6   Remove the exhaust manifold (see Section 6).

7   Remove the timing belt and camshaft sprocket (see Section 7).

8   Remove the camshafts and rocker arm assembly (see Section 11).

9   Check the cylinder head. Label and remove any remaining items, such as coolant fittings, tubes, cables, hoses or wires. At this point the head should be ready for removal.

10   Using a socket and breaker bar, loosen the cylinder head bolts in 1/4-turn increments until they can be removed by hand. Reverse the recommended tightening sequence **(see illustration)** to avoid warping or cracking the head.

11   Lift the cylinder head off the engine block **(see illustration)**. If it's stuck, very carefully pry up at the ends, beyond the gasket surface.

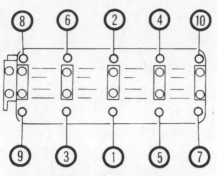

12.10 Cylinder head bolt tightening sequence - when loosening the bolts, reverse this sequence

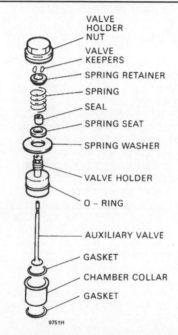

12.12a Auxiliary valve components - exploded view

12   Remove all external components from the head to allow for thorough cleaning and inspection. Some engines are equipped with auxiliary valves. These may be removed from the cylinder head after unscrewing the valve holder nut with a deep socket **(see illustration)**. The valve can be disassembled for seal replacement **(see illustration)**. If any components are worn, the entire assembly should be replaced. Always use a new gasket and O-ring when installing an auxiliary valve.

13   See Chapter 2B for cylinder head servicing procedures.

Installation

Refer to illustrations 12.14, 12.18 and 12.20

14   Remove the oil control jet **(see illustration)** and clean its orifices.

15   Use a gasket scraper to remove all traces of carbon and old gasket material from the cylinder head and block mating surfaces, then clean the mating surfaces with lacquer thinner or acetone. If there's oil on the mating

12.11 Lift the cylinder head straight up until it clears the locating dowels

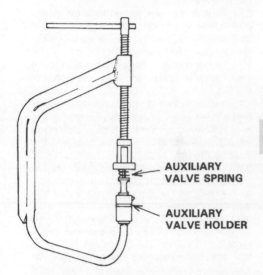

12.12b A valve spring compressor can be used to compress the spring and remove the keepers so the auxiliary valve assembly can be dismantled - spring compressors of this type can be rented

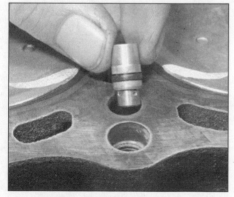

12.14 Remove the oil control jet

surfaces when the head is installed, the gasket may not seal correctly and leaks could develop. When working on the block, stuff the cylinders with clean shop rags to keep out debris. Use a vacuum cleaner to remove material that falls into the cylinders.

2A

16   Check the block and head mating surfaces for nicks, deep scratches and other damage. If damage is slight, it can be removed with a file; if it's excessive, machining may be the only alternative.

17   Use a tap of the correct size to chase the threads in the head bolt holes, then clean the holes with compressed air - make sure that nothing remains in the holes. **Warning:** *Wear eye protection when using compressed air for cleaning.*

18   Mount each bolt in a vise and run a die down the threads to remove corrosion and restore the threads **(see illustration)**. Dirt, corrosion, sealant and damaged threads will affect torque readings.

19   Reinstall the oil control jet. Be sure to use a new O-ring.

20   Position the new gasket over the dowel pins in the block **(see illustration)**.

21   Carefully set the head on the block without disturbing the gasket.

22   Before installing the head bolts, apply a small amount of clean engine oil to the threads.

23   Install the bolts in their original locations and tighten them finger tight. Following the recommended sequence **(see illustration 12.10)**, tighten the bolts in two steps to the specified torque.

24   The remaining installation steps are the reverse of removal.

25   Check and adjust the valves as necessary (see Chapter 1).

26   Refill the cooling system, install a new oil filter and add oil to the engine (see Chapter 1).

27   Run the engine and check for leaks. Set the ignition timing (see Chapter 1) and road test the vehicle.

13 Oil pan - removal and installation

Refer to illustrations 13.7a, 13.7b, 13.13a, 13.13b, 13.15a and 13.15b

1   Disconnect the negative cable from the battery.

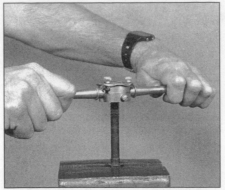

12.18 A die can be used to remove corrosion from the head bolt threads prior to installation

2   Set the parking brake and block the rear wheels.

3   Raise the front of the vehicle and support it securely on jackstands.

4   Remove the splash shields under the engine, if equipped.

5   Drain the engine oil and remove the oil filter (see Chapter 1). Remove the oil dipstick.

6   Disconnect the front exhaust pipe from the engine and remove the clamp behind the engine to allow the pipe to hang down.

7   Attach a hoist and lifting sling to the engine (see Chapter 2, Part B,
Section 5) and raise the engine just enough to take the weight off the lower engine mount. Unbolt the lower engine mount (see Section 17), then remove the crossmember under the oil pan **(see illustrations)**.

8   Remove the engine-to-transaxle dust shield.

9   Remove the bolts and detach the oil pan. If it's stuck, pry it loose very carefully with a small screwdriver or putty knife. Don't damage the mating surfaces of the pan and block or oil leaks could develop. If necessary, remove the oil pickup tube assembly **(see illustration)**.

10   Use a scraper to remove all traces of old gasket material and sealant from the block

12.20 Fit the new gasket over the dowel pins (arrows)

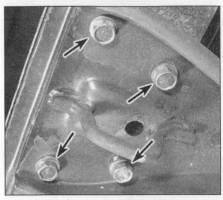

13.7a Remove the front bolts (arrows) from the center crossmember . . .

and oil pan. Clean the mating surfaces with lacquer thinner or acetone.

11   Make sure the threaded bolt holes in the block are clean.

12   Check the oil pan flange for distortion, particularly around the bolt holes. If necessary, place the pan on a block of wood and use a hammer to flatten and restore the gasket surface.

13   Inspect the oil pump pick-up tube assembly for cracks and a blocked strainer. If the pick-up was removed, install it now, using a new O-ring **(see illustration)**. Tighten the bolts to the specified torque.

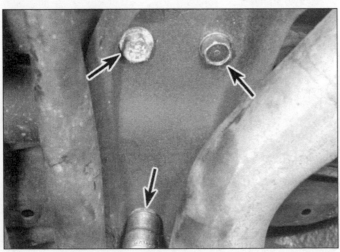

13.7b . . . then remove the rear bolts (arrows)

13.9 Three bolts (shown removed) secure the oil pick-up tube assembly to the engine

13.13 Use a new O-ring (arrow) on the oil pick-up tube

13.14 Apply sealer to the corners (arrows)

13.15a Be sure the oil pan gasket fits over the locating pins (arrow)

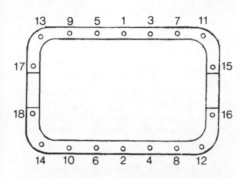

13.15b Oil pan bolt tightening sequence

14   Apply RTV sealant to the four oil pan corners **(see illustration)**. **Note:** *The oil pan must be installed within three minutes once the sealer has been applied.*

15   Carefully position a new gasket **(see illustration)** and the oil pan on the engine block. Install the bolts. Following the tightening sequence **(see illustration)**, tighten them to the specified torque in three or four steps.

16   The remainder of installation is the reverse of removal. Be sure to add oil and install a new oil filter.

17   Run the engine and check for oil pressure and leaks.

2A

14   Oil pump - removal, inspection and installation

Refer to illustrations 14.2a, 14.2b, 14.3, 14.4a, 14.4b, 14.4c, 14.5a, 14.5b, 14.7a and 14.7b

1   Remove the timing belt (see Section 7).

2   Unbolt the oil pump from the block **(see illustration)** and lift it out of the engine compartment. Be sure to remove the gasket and O-ring **(see illustration)**.

3   Remove the pump housing screws and lift off the cover **(see illustration)**.

4   Lift out the outer rotor **(see illustrations)**, clean all parts in solvent, then inspect them for wear and damage.

5   Measure the outer rotor-to-housing and inner rotor tip clearance with feeler gauges **(see illustrations)**. Compare the results to the specifications.

14.2a Remove the oil pump retaining bolts

14.2b Remove the oil pump-to-block gasket and O-ring (arrows)

14.3 Remove the pump housing screws and lift off the cover

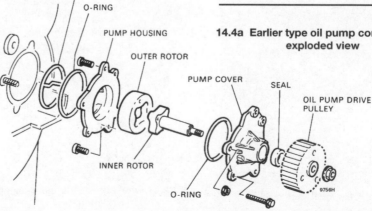

GASKET

O-RING

PUMP HOUSING

OUTER ROTOR

PUMP COVER

SEAL

OIL PUMP DRIVE PULLEY

INNER ROTOR

O-RING

9756H

14.4a Earlier type oil pump components - exploded view

6   Replace the pump if the clearances are excessive or signs of wear or damage are visible.

7   Install a new O-ring between the cover and pump housing **(see illustration)**. Install the outer rotor in the pump cover with the mark facing outward **(see illustration)**. Pack the pump cavity with petroleum jelly, apply thread locking compound to the screws and install the pump cover. Tighten the pump cover screws to the specified torque.

8   Position a new O-ring and gasket on the pump and install it on the engine block. Install the nuts and bolts and tighten them to the specified torque.

9   Reinstall the timing belt and related components.

10   Check the oil level and add oil, if necessary. Start the engine and check for oil pressure and leaks.

11   Recheck the oil level.

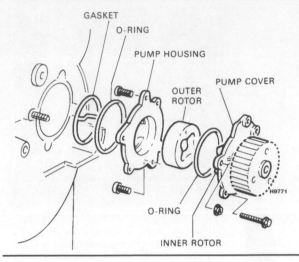

14.4b Later type oil pump components - exploded view

15 Flywheel/driveplate - removal and installation

Refer to illustrations 15.3a, 15.3b and 15.8

1   Raise the vehicle and support it securely on jackstands, then refer to Chapter 7 and remove the transaxle. If it's leaking, now would be a very good time to replace the front pump seal/O-ring (automatic transaxle only).

2   Remove the pressure plate and clutch disc (see Chapter 8) (manual transaxle equipped vehicles). Now is a good time to check/replace the clutch components and pilot bearing.

3   Remove the bolts that secure the flywheel/driveplate to the crankshaft **(see illus-**

tration). Remove the washer from the driveplate. If the crankshaft turns, wedge a large screwdriver into the ring gear to jam the flywheel.

4   Remove the flywheel/driveplate from the crankshaft. Since the flywheel is fairly heavy, be sure to support it while removing the last bolt.

5   Clean the flywheel to remove grease and oil. Inspect the surface for cracks, rivet

14.5a Measure the outer rotor-to housing clearance

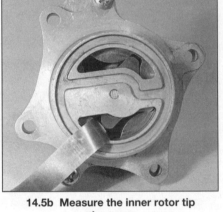

14.5b Measure the inner rotor tip clearance

14.7a Replace the cover O-ring

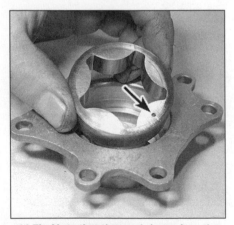

14.7b Note that the mark (arrow) on the outer rotor must face out

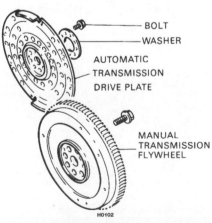

15.3a Flywheel/driveplate components - exploded view

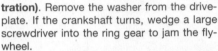

15.3b Most models use twelve-point mounting bolts - a twelve-point socket is required

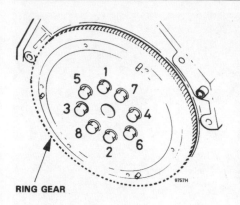

15.8 Flywheel/driveplate bolt tightening sequence

16.3 Pry out the rear main oil seal very carefully - don't damage the surface of the crankshaft or the new seal will leak

16.5 If the special tools are not available, you may be able to tap around the outer edge of the new oil seal with a mallet and a blunt punch to seat the seal squarely in the bore

grooves, burned areas and score marks. Light scoring can be removed with emery cloth. Check for cracked and broken ring gear teeth. Lay the flywheel on a flat surface and use a straightedge to check for warpage.

6   Clean and inspect the mating surfaces of the flywheel/driveplate and the crankshaft. If the crankshaft rear seal is leaking, replace it before reinstalling the flywheel/driveplate.

7   Position the flywheel/driveplate against the crankshaft. Note that most engines have an alignment dowel to ensure correct installation. Before installing the bolts, apply thread locking compound to the threads. Be sure to install the spacer washer with the driveplate.

8   After installing the flywheel/driveplate bolts finger tight, wedge a screwdriver into the ring gear teeth to keep the flywheel/driveplate from turning. Tighten the bolts to the specified torque, working in several stages and following the tightening sequence **(see illustration)**.

9   The remainder of installation is the reverse of the removal procedure.

16 Rear crankshaft oil seal - replacement

Refer to illustrations 16.3 and 16.5

1   Remove the transaxle (see Chapter 7).

2   Remove the flywheel/driveplate (see Section 15).

3   The old seal can be removed by gently prying it out with a screwdriver **(see illustration)**. Be sure to note how far it's recessed into the bore before removing it; the new seal will have to be driven in an equal amount. **Caution:** *Be very careful not to scratch or otherwise damage the crankshaft or the bore in the housing as oil leaks could develop.*

4   Clean the crankshaft and seal bore with lacquer thinner or acetone and a clean cloth. Check the seal contact surface very carefully for scratches and nicks that could damage the new seal lip and cause oil leaks. If the crankshaft is damaged, try to clean up the damage with crocus cloth. If this won't clean up the damage the only alternative is a new or different crankshaft.

5   Lubricate the lips of the seal with moly-based grease. Also fill the spring groove with grease to help keep the spring from popping out. Press the seal into place, using special tools 07948-SB00101 and 07749-0010000 or equivalent. If the special tools are unavailable, you may be able to tap the seal into position with a blunt punch and a mallet **(see illustration)**. If you must use this method, be very careful not to damage the seal or crankshaft.

6   Reinstall the flywheel/driveplate and transaxle, run the engine and check for oil leaks.

17 Engine mounts and torque strut - check and replacement

Refer to illustrations 17.9, 17.11a, 17.11b, 17.14 and 17.17

1   The engine is attached to the chassis by four weight-bearing mounts and a torque strut. The engine mounts and strut seldom require attention, but if they are broken or deteriorated mounts should be replaced immediately or the added strain placed on the driveline components may cause damage or wear.

Check

2   During the check, the engine must be raised slightly to remove the weight from the mounts.

3   Raise the vehicle and support it securely on jackstands, then position a jack under the engine oil pan. Place a large block of wood between the jack head and the oil pan, then carefully raise the engine just enough to take the weight off the mounts. **Warning:** *DO NOT place any part of your body under the engine when it's supported only by a jack!*

4   Check the mounts to see if the rubber is cracked, hardened or separated from the metal plates. Sometimes the rubber will split right down the center.

5   Check for relative movement between the mount plates and the engine or frame (use a large screwdriver or pry bar to attempt

to move the mounts). If movement is noted, lower the engine and tighten the mount fasteners.

6   Rubber preservative should be applied to the mounts to slow deterioration.

Replacement

7   Disconnect the negative battery cable from the battery, then raise the vehicle and support it securely on jackstands (if not already done).

8   Support the engine with a floor jack under the oil pan. Place a block of wood between the jack head and the oil pan to protect the pan from damage. **Warning:** *Do not place any part of your body under the engine when its supported only by a jack.* **Note:** *When installing any of the mounts or the torque strut, use thread locking compound on the attaching nuts and/or bolts.*

Lower mount

9   Remove the nuts and bolts **(see illustration)** and slip the lower mount out of the vehicle.

10   Installation is the reverse of removal. Be sure to tighten the nuts and bolts securely.

17.9 The lower mount (viewed from below) is attached to the longitudinal crossmember - remove the nuts and bolts (arrows) and slip it out

2A

17.11a The front mount is located between the engine and radiator on the forward transverse crossmember - remove the nut (A), lift the engine until the bracket is above the stud, then remove the bolts (B) and pull out the mount

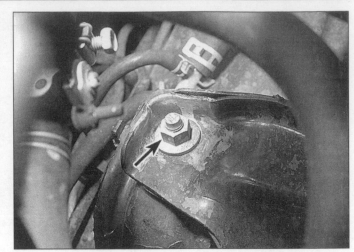

17.11b The rear mount is located below the intake manifold - remove the nut (arrow) and lift the engine enough to raise the bracket clear of the stud, then remove the two bolts that secure the mount to the crossmember and pull out the mount

Front and rear mounts

11   Remove the engine mount-to-bracket nut and raise the engine until the stud protruding from the mount comes out of the hole in the bracket **(see illustrations)**.

12   Unbolt the mount from the bracket and lift it from the vehicle.

13   Bolt the mount to the crossmember, lower the engine until it rests on the mount and install the nut. Be sure the nut and bolts are tightened securely.

Left mount

14   For clearance to remove the left mount **(see illustration)**, you may need to loosen the fasteners on the other mounts, raise the engine slightly and shift it to the right.

15   Remove the through bolt and pull the mount out of its mounting bracket.

16   Installation is the reverse of removal. Tighten the bolts securely.

Torque strut

17   Unbolt the torque strut from the engine bracket **(see illustration)**.

18   If you are removing the engine, swing the rod upward, pivoting at the firewall.

19   To remove the torque strut, unbolt it at the firewall and lift it from the bracket.

20   Installation is the reverse of removal. Be sure to tighten the bolts securely.

17.14 The left mount is located adjacent to the timing belt cover - remove the through bolt (arrow - barely visible in this photo) Note: Some mounts have vertical through bolts, others have horizontal ones

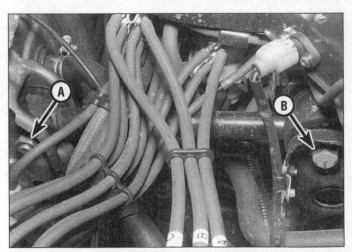

17.17 The torque strut is located between the engine and the firewall - remove the through bolt from the engine bracket (A) - if you are removing the engine, pivot the strut up at the firewall - if you are removing the strut, also remove the through bolt at the firewall bracket (B)

Chapter 2 Part B
General engine overhaul procedures

Contents

Specifications

General

Displacement
1984 and 1985	112 c.i. (1800 cc)
1986 on	121 c.i. (2000 cc)

Compression (at 300 rpm, wide open throttle)
Nominal
Carbureted engines	171 psi
Fuel-injected engines	178 psi

Minimum
Carbureted engines	142 psi
Fuel-injected engines	149 psi
Maximum variation between cylinders	28 psi

Oil pressure (at normal operating temperature)
At idle	14 psi minimum
At 3000 rpm	54 to 65 psi

Crankshaft and bearings

Crankshaft end play	
Standard	0.004 to 0.014 in (0.10 to 0.35 mm)
Service limit	0.018 in (0.45 mm)
Main bearing journal diameter	1.9685 to 1.9694 in (50.000 to 50.024 mm)
Main bearing journal taper/out-of-round	
Standard	0.0002 in (0.005 mm)
Service limit	0.0004 in (0.010 mm)
Main bearing-to-journal oil clearance	
Numbers 1, 2, 4, and 5	0.0010 to 0.0022 in (0.026 to 0.055 mm)
Number 3	0.0013 to 0.0024 in (0.032 to 0.061 mm)
Service limit (all main bearings)	0.003 in (0.07 mm)
Connecting rod journal diameter	1.7707 to 1.7717 in (44.976 to 45.000 mm)
Connecting rod journal taper/out-of-round	
Standard	0.0002 in (0.005 mm)
Service limit	0.0004 in (0.010 mm)
Connecting rod bearing-to-journal oil clearance	
Standard	0.0008 to 0.0015 in (0.020 to 0.038 mm)
Service limit	0.003 in (0.07 mm)
Connecting rod end play	
Standard	0.006 to 0.012 in (0.15 to 0.30 mm)
Service limit	0.016 in (0.40 mm)

Cylinder block

Surface warpage limit	0.003 in (0.08 mm)
Bore diameter	
1984 and 1985	
A (no marking)	
Standard	3.1500 to 3.1504 in (80.01 to 80.02 mm)
Service limit	3.1516 in (80.05 mm)
B	
Standard	3.1496 to 3.1500 in (80.0 to 80.01 mm)
Service limit	3.1512 in (80.04 mm)
1986 on	
A (no marking)	
Standard	3.2562 to 3.2566 in (82.71 to 82.72 mm)
Service limit	3.2578 in (80.01 to 80.02 mm)
B	
Standard	3.2559 to 3.2563 in (82.70 to 82.71 mm)
Service limit	3.2574 in (82.74 mm)
Piston-to-bore clearance	
Standard	0.0008 to 0.0016 in (0.020 to 0.040 mm)
Service limit	0.003 in (0.08 mm)
Bore taper/out-of-round limit	0.002 in (0.05 mm)

Pistons

Diameter (measured 0.83 in [21 mm] above bottom of skirt)	
1984 and 1985	
A (no marking)	
Standard	3.1488 to 3.1492 in (79.98 to 79.99 mm)
Service limit	3.1484 in (79.97)
B	
Standard	3.1484 to 3.1488 in (79.97 to 79.98 mm)
Service limit	3.1480 in (79.96)
1986 on	
A (no marking)	
Standard	3.2574 to 3.2551 in (82.67 to 82.68 mm)
Service limit	3.2563 in (82.71 mm)
B	
Standard	3.2543 to 3.2574 in (82.66 to 82.67 mm)
Service limit	3.2559 in (82.70)
Piston ring side clearance	
1984 and 1985	
Standard	0.0008 to 0.0018 in (0.020 to 0.045 mm)
Service limit	0.005 in (0.13 mm)
1986 on	
Standard	0.0012 to 0.0024 in (0.03 to 0.06 mm)
Service limit	0.005 in (0.13 mm)

Ring end gap
    1984 and 1985
        Top and second ring
            Standard .... 0.006 to 0.014 in (0.15 to 0.35 mm)
            Service limit .... 0.023 in (0.60 mm)
        Oil ring
            Standard .... 0.008 to 0.035 in (0.20 to 0.9 mm)
            Service limit .... 0.040 in (1.0 mm)
    1986
        Top ring
            Standard .... 0.008 to 0.014 in (0.20 to 0.35 mm)
            Service limit .... 0.023 in (0.60 mm)
        Second ring
            Standard .... 0.010 to 0.015 in (0.25 to 0.37 mm)
            Service limit .... 0.023 in (0.60 mm)
        Oil ring
            Standard .... 0.008 to 0.028 in (0.20 to 0.70 mm)
            Service limit .... 0.030 in (0.80 mm)
    1987
        Top ring
            Standard .... 0.008 to 0.014 in (0.20 to 0.35 mm)
            Service limit .... 0.023 in (0.60 mm)
        Second ring
            Standard .... 0.012 to 0.017 in (0.30 to 0.42 mm)
            Service limit .... 0.023 in (0.60 mm)
        Oil ring
            Standard .... 0.008 to 0.035 in (0.20 to 0.9 mm)
            Service limit .... 0.040 in (1.0 mm)
    1988 and 1989
        Top ring
            Standard .... 0.008 to 0.014 in (0.20 to 0.35 mm)
            Service limit .... 0.023 in (0.60 mm)
        Second ring
            Standard .... 0.012 to 0.018 in (0.30 to 0.45 mm)
            Service limit .... 0.023 in (0.60 mm)
        Oil ring
            Standard .... 0.008 to 0.028 in (0.20 to 0.7 mm)
            Service limit .... 0.040 in (1.0 mm)

Valves and springs

Valve stem O.D.
    Auxiliary valve (1984 and 1985)
        Standard .... 0.2587 to 0.2593 in (6.572 to 6.587 mm)
        Service limit .... 0.257 in (6.54 mm)
    Intake valve
        Standard .... 0.2591 to 0.2594 in (6.58 to 6.59 mm)
        Service limit .... 0.258 in (6.55 mm)
    Exhaust valve
        Standard .... 0.2732 to 0.2736 in (6.94 to 6.95 mm)
        Service limit .... 0.272 in (6.91 mm)
Stem-to-guide clearance
    Auxiliary valve (1984 and 1985)
        Standard .... 0.001 to 0.002 in (0.023 to 0.058 mm)
        Service limit .... 0.003 in (0.08 mm)
    Intake valve
        Standard .... 0.001 to 0.002 in (0.02 to 0.05 mm)
        Service limit .... 0.003 in (0.08 mm)
    Exhaust valve
        Standard .... 0.002 to 0.004 in (0.06 to 0.09 mm)
        Service limit .... 0.005 in (0.12 mm)
Spring installed height
    Auxiliary valve (1984 and 1985) .... 0.984 in (24.99 mm)
    Intake valve
        1984 and 1985 .... 1.488 in (37.5 mm)
        1986 on .... 1.660 in (42.2 mm)
    Exhaust valve
        1984 and 1985 .... 1.488 in (37.5 mm)
        1986 on .... 1.460 in (77.3 mm)
Spring squareness (service limit) .... 0.068 in (1.75 mm)

2B

Valves and springs (continued)

Spring free length
  1984 and 1985
    Auxiliary valve
      Standard .... 1.25 in (31.73 mm)
      Service limit .... 1.22 in (31.0 mm)
    Intake valve (outer)
      Standard .... 1.846 in (46.88 mm)
      Service limit .... 1.816 in (46.13 mm)
    Exhaust valve (outer)
      Standard .... 2.010 in (51.05 mm)
      Service limit .... 1.95 in (49.5 mm)
    Inner valve springs (exhaust and intake)
      Standard .... 1.57 in (39.8 mm)
      Service limit .... 1.53 in (38.8 mm)
  1986 and 1987
    Intake valve
      Standard .... 1.94 in (49.2 mm)
      Service limit .... 1.90 in (48.2 mm)
    Exhaust valve (outer)
      Standard .... 1.96 in (49.8 mm)
      Service limit .... 1.92 in (48.8 mm)
    Exhaust valve (inner)
      Standard .... 1.57 in (39.8 mm)
      Service limit .... 1.53 in (38.8 mm)
  1988 and 1989
    Intake valve
      Standard .... 1.91 in (48.54 mm)
      Service limit .... 1.87 in (47.59 mm)
    Exhaust valve (outer)
      Standard .... 1.93 in (49.05 mm)
      Service limit .... 1.89 in (48.07 mm)
    Exhaust valve (inner)
      Standard .... 1.67 in (42.41 mm)
      Service limit .... 1.63 in (41.40 mm)
Valve margin
  Intake valve
    Standard .... 0.053 to 0.065 in (1.35 to 1.65 mm)
    Service limit .... 0.057 in (1.45 mm)
  Exhaust valve
    1984 and 1985 .... 0.069 to 0.077 in (1.75 to 1.95 mm)
    1986 on
      Standard .... 0.065 to 0.077 in (1.65 to 1.95 mm)
      Service limit .... 0.057 in (1.45 mm)

Torque specifications*

	Ft-lbs	Nm
Connecting rod bolts	23	31
Main bearing cap bolts	48	65

* **Note:** *Refer to Part A for additional torque specifications*

---

1   General information

Included in this portion of Chapter 2 are the general overhaul procedures for the cylinder head and internal engine components.

The information ranges from advice concerning preparation for an overhaul and the purchase of replacement parts to detailed, step-by-step procedures covering removal and installation of internal engine components and the inspection of parts.

The following Sections have been written based on the assumption that the engine has been removed from the vehicle. For information concerning in-vehicle engine repair, as well as removal and installation of the external components necessary for the overhaul, see Part A of this Chapter and Section 7 of this Part.

The Specifications included in this Part are only those necessary for the inspection and overhaul procedures which follow. Refer to Part A for additional Specifications.

2   Engine overhaul - general information

Refer to illustrations 2.4a and 2.4b

It's not always easy to determine when, or if, an engine should be completely overhauled, as a number of factors must be considered.

High mileage is not necessarily an indication that an overhaul is needed, while low mileage doesn't preclude the need for an overhaul. Frequency of servicing is probably the most important consideration. An engine that's had regular and frequent oil and filter changes, as well as other required maintenance, will most likely give many thousands of miles of reliable service. Conversely, a neglected engine may require an overhaul very early in its life.

Excessive oil consumption is an indication that piston rings, valve seals and/or valve guides are in need of attention. Make sure that oil leaks aren't responsible before deciding that the rings and/or guides are bad. Perform a cylinder compression check to determine the extent of the work required (see Section 3).

Check the oil pressure with a gauge installed in place of the oil pressure sending unit **(see illustrations)** and compare it to the Specifications. If it's extremely low, the bearings and/or oil pump are probably worn out.

Loss of power, rough running, knocking or metallic engine noises, excessive valve train noise and high fuel consumption rates may also point to the need for an overhaul, especially if they're all present at the same time. If a complete tune-up doesn't remedy the situation, major mechanical work is the only solution.

An engine overhaul involves restoring the internal parts to the specifications of a new engine. During an overhaul, the piston rings are replaced and the cylinder walls are reconditioned (rebored and/or honed). If a rebore is done by an automotive machine shop, new oversize pistons will also be installed. The main bearings, connecting rod bearings and camshaft bearings are generally replaced with new ones and, if necessary, the crankshaft may be reground to restore the journals. Generally, the valves are serviced as well, since they're usually in less than-perfect condition at this point. While the engine is being overhauled, other components, such as the distributor, starter and alternator, can be rebuilt as well. The end result should be a like new engine that will give many trouble free miles. **Note:** *Critical cooling system components such as the hoses, drivebelts, thermostat and water pump MUST be replaced with new parts when an engine is overhauled. The radiator should be checked carefully to ensure that it isn't clogged or leaking (see Chapter 3). Also, we don't recommend overhauling the oil pump - always install a new one when an engine is rebuilt.*

Before beginning the engine overhaul, read through the entire procedure to familiarize yourself with the scope and requirements of the job. Overhauling an engine isn't difficult, but it is time consuming. Plan on the vehicle being tied up for a minimum of two weeks, especially if parts must be taken to an automotive machine shop for repair or reconditioning. Check on availability of parts and make sure that any necessary special tools and equipment are obtained in advance. Most work can be done with typical hand tools, although a number of precision measuring tools are required for inspecting parts to determine if they must be replaced. Often an automotive machine shop will handle the inspection of parts and offer advice concerning reconditioning and replacement. **Note:** *Always wait until the engine has been completely disassembled and all components, especially the engine block, have been inspected before deciding what service and repair operations must be performed by an automotive machine shop. Since the block's condition will be the major factor to consider when determining whether to overhaul the original engine or buy a rebuilt one, never purchase parts or have machine work done*

2.4a The oil pressure sending unit is located in the top of the oil filter housing (housing shown removed for clarity) - remove the sending unit to install a test gauge

on other components until the block has been thoroughly inspected. As a general rule, time is the primary cost of an overhaul, so it doesn't pay to install worn or substandard parts.

As a final note, to ensure maximum life and minimum trouble from a rebuilt engine, everything must be assembled with care in a spotlessly clean environment.

3   Cylinder compression check

Refer to illustration 3.6

1   A compression check will tell you what mechanical condition the upper end (pistons, rings, valves, head gaskets) of your engine is in. Specifically, it can tell you if the compression is down due to leakage caused by worn piston rings, defective valves and seats or a blown head gasket. **Note:** *The engine must be at normal operating temperature and the battery must be fully charged for this check. Also, if the engine is equipped with a carburetor, the choke valve must be all the way open to get an accurate compression reading (if the engine's warm, the choke should be open).*

2   Begin by cleaning the area around the spark plugs before you remove them (compressed air should be used, if available, otherwise a small brush or even a bicycle tire pump will work). The idea is to prevent dirt from getting into the cylinders as the compression check is being done.

3   Remove all of the spark plugs from the engine (Chapter 1).

4   Block the throttle wide open.

5   Detach the coil wire from the center of the distributor cap and ground it on the engine block. Use a jumper wire with alligator clips on each end to ensure a good ground. On EFI equipped vehicles, the fuel pump circuit should also be disabled (see Chapter 4).

6   Install the compression gauge in the number one spark plug hole **(see illustration)**.

7   Crank the engine over at least seven compression strokes and watch the gauge.

2.4b With the test gauge connected to the sending unit port, run the engine and note the readings

The compression should build up quickly in a healthy engine. Low compression on the first stroke, followed by gradually increasing pressure on successive strokes, indicates worn piston rings. A low compression reading on the first stroke, which doesn't build up during successive strokes, indicates leaking valves or a blown head gasket (a cracked head could also be the cause). Deposits on the undersides of the valve heads can also cause low compression. Record the highest gauge reading obtained.

8   Repeat the procedure for the remaining cylinders and compare the results to the Specifications.

9   Add some engine oil (about three squirts from a plunger-type oil can) to each cylinder, through the spark plug hole, and repeat the test.

10   If the compression increases after the oil is added, the piston rings are definitely worn. If the compression doesn't increase significantly, the leakage is occurring at the valves or head gasket. Leakage past the valves may be caused by burned valve seats and/or faces or warped, cracked or bent valves.

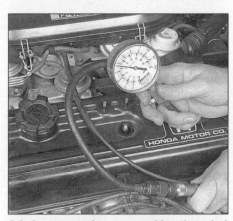

3.6 A compression gauge with a threaded fitting for the spark plug hole is preferred over the type that requires hand pressure to maintain the seal - be sure to open the throttle as far as possible during the compression check!

2B

11   If two adjacent cylinders have equally low compression, there's a strong possibility that the head gasket between them is blown. The appearance of coolant in the combustion chambers or the crankcase would verify this condition.

12   If one cylinder is about 20 percent lower than the others, and the engine has a slightly rough idle, a worn lobe on the camshaft could be the cause.

13   If the compression is unusually high, the combustion chambers are probably coated with carbon deposits. If that's the case, the cylinder head should be removed and decarbonized.

14   If compression is way down or varies greatly between cylinders, it would be a good idea to have a leak-down test performed by an automotive repair shop. This test will pinpoint exactly where the leakage is occurring and how severe it is.

---

4   Engine removal - methods and precautions

If you've decided that an engine must be removed for overhaul or major repair work, several preliminary steps should be taken.

Locating a suitable place to work is extremely important. Adequate work space, along with storage space for the vehicle, will be needed. If a shop or garage isn't available, at the very least a flat, level, clean work surface made of concrete or asphalt is required.

Cleaning the engine compartment and engine before beginning the removal procedure will help keep tools clean and organized.

An engine hoist or A-frame will also be necessary. Make sure the equipment is rated in excess of the combined weight of the engine and accessories. Safety is of primary importance, considering the potential hazards involved in lifting the engine out of the vehicle.

If the engine is being removed by a novice, a helper should be available. Advice and aid from someone more experienced would also be helpful. There are many instances when one person cannot simultaneously perform all of the operations required when lifting the engine out of the vehicle.

Plan the operation ahead of time. Arrange for or obtain all of the tools and equipment you'll need prior to beginning the job. Some of the equipment necessary to perform engine removal and installation safely and with relative ease are (in addition to an engine hoist) a heavy duty floor jack, complete sets of wrenches and sockets as described in the front of this manual, wooden blocks and plenty of rags and cleaning solvent for mopping up spilled oil, coolant and gasoline. If the hoist must be rented, make sure that you arrange for it in advance and perform all of the operations possible without it beforehand. This will save you money and time.

Plan for the vehicle to be out of use for quite a while. A machine shop will be required to perform some of the work which the do-it yourselfer can't accomplish without special equipment. These shops often have a busy schedule, so it would be a good idea to consult them before removing the engine in order to accurately estimate the amount of time required to rebuild or repair components that may need work.

Always be extremely careful when removing and installing the engine. Serious injury can result from careless actions. Plan ahead, take your time and a job of this nature, although major, can be accomplished successfully.

---

5   Engine - removal and installation

Refer to illustrations 5.6, 5.14, 5.17 and 5.21
Note: *Read through the entire Section before beginning this procedure. The engine and transaxle are removed as a unit and then separated outside the vehicle.*

Removal

1   On fuel-injected models, relieve the fuel system pressure (see Chapter 4).

2   Disconnect the negative cable from the battery.

3   Place protective covers on the fenders and cowl and remove the hood (see Chapter 11).

4   Remove the air cleaner assembly (see Chapter 4).

5   Raise the vehicle and support it securely on jackstands. Drain the cooling system and engine oil and remove the drivebelts (see Chapter 1).

6   Clearly label, then disconnect all vacuum lines, coolant and emissions hoses, wiring harness connectors, ground straps and fuel lines. Masking tape and/or a touch up paint applicator work well for marking items **(see illustration)**. Take instant photos or sketch the locations of components and brackets.

7   Remove the cooling fan(s), shroud(s) and radiator (see Chapter 3).

8   Release the residual fuel pressure in the tank by removing the gas cap, then undo the fuel lines connecting the engine to the chassis (see Chapter 4). Plug or cap all open fittings.

9   Disconnect the throttle linkage (and TV linkage and speed control cable, when equipped) from the engine (see Chapter 4).

10   On power steering equipped vehicles, unbolt the power steering pump. If clearance allows, tie the pump aside without disconnecting the hoses. If necessary, remove the pump (see Chapter 10).

11   On A/C equipped vehicles, unbolt the compressor and set it aside (see Chapter 3). Do not disconnect the refrigerant hoses.

12   Detach the exhaust pipe from the manifold (see Chapter 2A).

13   Remove the driveaxles (see Chapter 8), wire harness, shift linkage and speedometer cable from the transaxle (see Chapter 7).

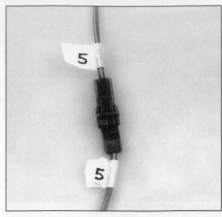

5.6 Label both ends of each wire (as well as each vacuum hose, coolant hose and fuel hose) before disconnecting it

14   Attach a lifting sling to the brackets on the engine. Position a hoist and connect the sling to it. Take up the slack until there is slight tension on the hoist **(see illustration)**.

15   Recheck to be sure nothing except the mounts are still connecting the engine/transaxle to the vehicle. Disconnect anything still remaining.

16   Support the transaxle with a floor jack. Place a block of wood on the jack head to prevent damage to the transaxle. Remove the through-bolts and nuts from the engine mounts and torque strut (see Chapter 2A). Unbolt the transaxle mount bracket (if equipped) from the transaxle (see Chapter 7). **Warning:** *DO NOT place any part of your body under the engine/transaxle when it's supported only by a hoist or other lifting device.*

17   Slowly lift the engine/transaxle out of the vehicle **(see illustration)**. It may be necessary to pry the mounts away from the frame brackets.

18   Move the engine/transaxle away from the vehicle and carefully lower the hoist until the transaxle is supported in a level position.

19   Remove the engine block-to-transaxle brace.

20   On automatic transaxle equipped models, detach the torque converter dust shield from the lower bellhousing. Remove the torque converter-to-driveplate fasteners (see Chapter 7) and push the converter back slightly into the bellhousing.

21   Remove the engine-to-transaxle bolts and separate the engine from the transaxle **(see illustration)**. The torque converter should remain in the transaxle.

22   Place the engine on the floor or remove the flywheel/driveplate and mount the engine on an engine stand.

Installation

23   Check the engine/transaxle mounts. If they're worn or damaged, replace them.

24   On manual transaxle equipped models, inspect the clutch components (see Chapter 8) and on automatic models inspect the con-

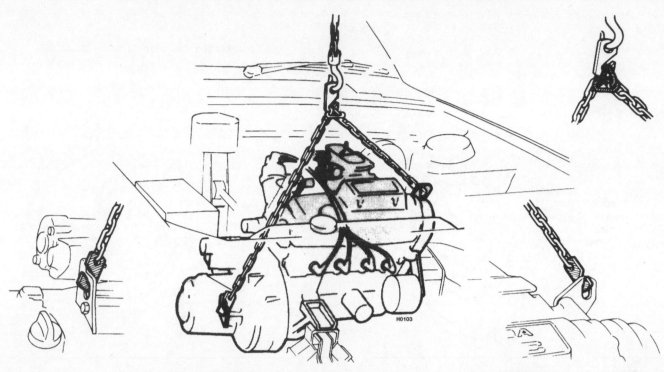

5.14 Attach the sling to the brackets on the engine and attach a hoist to the sling

verter seal and bushing.

25   On manual transaxle equipped vehicles, apply a dab of high temperature grease to the pilot bearing.

26   On automatic transaxle equipped models, apply a dab of grease to the nose of the converter and to the seal lips.

27   Carefully guide the transaxle into place, following the procedure outlined in Chapter 7. **Caution:** *Do not use the bolts to force the engine and transaxle into alignment. It may crack or damage major components.*

28   Install the engine-to-transaxle bolts and tighten them securely.

29   Attach the hoist to the engine and carefully lower the engine/transaxle assembly into the engine compartment.

30   Install the mount bolts and tighten them securely.

31   Reinstall the remaining components and fasteners in the reverse order of removal.

32   Add coolant, oil, power steering and transmission fluids as needed (see Chapter 1).

33   Run the engine and check for proper operation and leaks. Shut off the engine and recheck the fluid levels.

6   Engine rebuilding alternatives

The do-it-yourselfer is faced with a number of options when performing an engine overhaul. The decision to replace the engine block, piston/connecting rod assemblies and crankshaft depends on a number of factors, with the number one consideration being the condition of the block. Other considerations are cost, access to machine shop facilities, parts availability, time required to complete the project and the extent of prior mechanical experience on the part of the do-it-yourselfer.

Some of the rebuilding alternatives include:

Individual parts - If the inspection procedures reveal that the engine block and most engine components are in reusable condition, purchasing individual parts may be the most economical alternative. The block, crankshaft and piston/connecting rod assemblies should all be inspected carefully. Even if the block shows little wear, the cylinder bores should be surface honed.

Short block - A short block consists of an engine block with a crankshaft and piston/connecting rod assemblies already installed. All new bearings are incorporated and all clearances will be correct. The existing camshaft, valve train components, cylinder head and external parts can be bolted to the short block with little or no machine shop work necessary.

Long block - A long block consists of a short block plus an oil pump, oil pan, cylinder head, camshaft cover, camshaft and valve train components, timing sprockets and timing belt. All components are installed with new bearings, seals and gaskets incorporated throughout. The installation of manifolds and external parts is all that's necessary.

Give careful thought to which alternative is best for you and discuss the situation with local automotive machine shops, auto parts dealers and experienced rebuilders before ordering or purchasing replacement parts.

5.17 Slowly lift the engine/transaxle assembly from the vehicle

5.21 Remove the bolts and separate the engine and transaxle

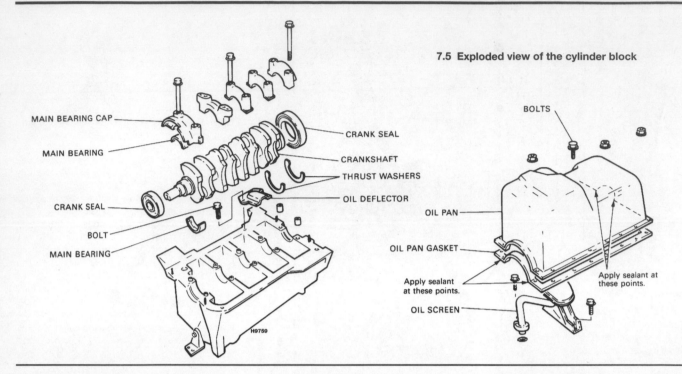

7.5 Exploded view of the cylinder block

7   Engine overhaul - disassembly sequence

Refer to illustration 7.5

1   It's much easier to disassemble and work on the engine if it's mounted on a portable engine stand. A stand can often be rented quite cheaply from an equipment rental yard. Before the engine is mounted on a stand, the flywheel/driveplate and rear oil seal should be removed from the engine.

2   If a stand isn't available, it's possible to disassemble the engine with it blocked up on the floor. Be extra careful not to tip or drop the engine when working without a stand.

3   If you're going to obtain a rebuilt engine, all external components must come off first, to be transferred to the replacement engine, just as they will if you're doing a complete engine overhaul yourself. These include:

Alternator and brackets
Emissions control components
Distributor, spark plug wires and spark plugs
Thermostat and housing cover
Water pump
Carburetor or EFI components
Intake/exhaust manifolds
Oil filter
Engine mounts
Clutch and flywheel/driveplate

Note: *When removing the external components from the engine, pay close attention to details that may be helpful or important during installation. Note the installed position of gaskets, seals, spacers, pins, brackets, washers, bolts and other small items.*

4   If you're obtaining a short block, which consists of the engine block, crankshaft, pistons and connecting rods all assembled, then the cylinder head, oil pan and oil pump will have to be removed as well. See *Engine rebuilding alternatives* for additional information regarding the different possibilities to be considered.

5   If you're planning a complete overhaul, the engine must be disassembled and the internal components removed in the following order **(see illustration)**.

Camshaft cover(s)
Intake and exhaust manifolds
Timing belt covers
Timing belt and sprockets
Cylinder head
Oil pan
Oil pump
Piston/connecting rod assemblies
Crankshaft and main bearings

6   Before beginning the disassembly and overhaul procedures, make sure the following items are available. Also, refer *to Engine overhaul -reassembly* sequence for a list of tools and materials needed for engine reassembly.

Common hand tools
Small cardboard boxes or plastic bags for storing parts
Gasket scraper
Ridge reamer
Vibration damper puller
Micrometers
Telescoping gauges
Dial indicator set
Valve spring compressor
Cylinder surfacing hone
Piston ring groove cleaning tool
Electric drill motor
Tap and die set
Wire brushes
Oil gallery brushes
Cleaning solvent

8   Cylinder head - disassembly

Refer to illustrations 8.2, 8.3 and 8.4

Note: *New and rebuilt cylinder heads are commonly available for most engines at dealerships and auto parts stores. Due to the fact that some specialized tools are necessary for the disassembly and inspection procedures, and replacement parts may not be readily available, it may be more practical and economical for the home mechanic to purchase a replacement head rather than taking the time to disassemble, inspect and recondition the original.*

1   Cylinder head disassembly involves removal of the intake and exhaust valves and related components. If they're still in place, remove the auxiliary valves (if equipped), rocker arms and camshaft from the cylinder head. Refer to Chapter 2A for further information. Label the parts or store the separately so they can be reinstalled in their original locations.

2   Before the valves are removed, arrange to label and store them, along with their related components, so they can be kept separate and reinstalled in the same valve guides they are removed from **(see illustration)**.

3   Compress the springs on the first valve with a spring compressor and remove the keepers **(see illustration)**. Carefully release the valve spring compressor and remove the retainer, the spring and the spring seat (if used).

4   Pull the valve out of the head, then remove the oil seal from the guide. If the valve binds in the guide (won't pull through), push it back into the head and deburr the area around the keeper groove with a fine file or whetstone **(see illustration)**.

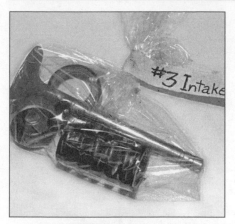

8.2 A small plastic bag, with an appropriate label, can be used to store the valve train components so they can be kept together and reinstalled in the correct location

5   Repeat the procedure for the remaining valves. Remember to keep all the parts for each valve together so they can be reinstalled in the same locations.
6   Once the valves and related components have been removed and stored in an organized manner, the head should be thoroughly cleaned and inspected. If a complete engine overhaul is being done, finish the engine disassembly procedures before beginning the cylinder head cleaning and inspection process.

9   Cylinder head - cleaning and inspection

Refer to illustrations 9.11, 9.13, 9.14, 9.15, 9.16 and 9.17
1   Thorough cleaning of the cylinder head(s) and related valve train components, followed by a detailed inspection, will enable you to decide how much valve service work

8.3 Use a valve spring compressor to compress the spring, then remove the keepers from the valve stem

must be done during the engine overhaul. **Note:** *If the engine was severely overheated, the cylinder head is probably warped (see Step 12).*

Cleaning

2   Scrape all traces of old gasket material and sealing compound off the head gasket, intake manifold and exhaust manifold sealing surfaces. Be very careful not to gouge the cylinder head. Special gasket removal solvents that soften gaskets and make removal much easier are available at auto parts stores.
3   Remove all built up scale from the coolant passages.
4   Run a stiff wire brush through the various holes to remove deposits that may have formed in them.
5   Run an appropriate size tap into each of the threaded holes to remove corrosion and thread sealant that may be present. If compressed air is available, use it to clear the holes of debris produced by this operation.

Warning: *Wear eye protection when using compressed air!*
6   Clean the cylinder head with solvent and dry it thoroughly. Compressed air will speed the drying process and ensure all holes and recessed areas are clean. **Note:** *Decarbonizing chemicals are available and may prove very useful when cleaning cylinder heads and valve train components. They are very caustic and should be used with caution. Be sure to follow the instructions on the container.*
7   Clean the rocker arms with solvent and dry them thoroughly (don't mix them up during the cleaning process). Compressed air will speed the drying process and can be used to clean out the oil passages.
8   Clean all the valve springs, spring seats, keepers and retainers with solvent and dry them thoroughly. Clean the components from one valve at a time to avoid mixing up the parts.
9   Scrape off any heavy deposits that may have formed on the valves, then use a motorized wire brush to remove deposits from the valve heads and stems. **Warning:** *Wear eye protection. Again, make sure the valves don't get mixed up.*

Inspection

Note: *Be sure to perform all of the following inspection procedures before concluding that machine shop work is required. Make a list of the items that need attention.*

Cylinder head
10   Inspect the head very carefully for cracks, evidence of coolant leakage and other damage. If cracks are found, check with an automotive machine shop concerning repair. If repair isn't possible, a new cylinder head should be obtained.
11   Using a precision straightedge and feeler gauge, check the head gasket mating surface for warpage **(see illustration)**. If the warpage exceeds the specified limit, it can be resurfaced at an automotive machine shop.

2B

8.4 If the valve won't pull through the guide, deburr the edge of the stem end and the area around the keeper grooves with a file or whetstone

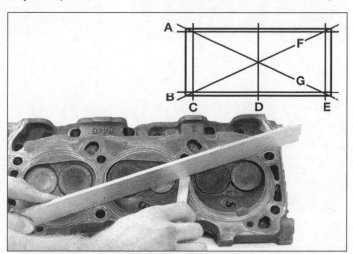

9.11 Check the cylinder head gasket surface for warpage by trying to slip a feeler gauge under the straightedge (see the Specifications for the maximum warpage allowed and use a feeler gauge of that thickness)

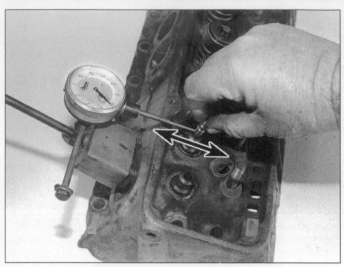

9.13 A dial indicator can be used to determine the valve stem-to-guide clearance (move the valve stem as indicated by the arrows)

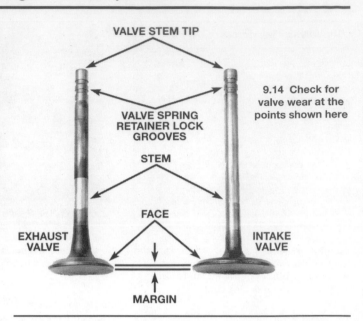

VALVE STEM TIP

9.14 Check for valve wear at the points shown here

VALVE SPRING RETAINER LOCK GROOVES

STEM

FACE

EXHAUST VALVE

INTAKE VALVE

MARGIN

12   Examine the valve seats in each of the combustion chambers. If they're pitted, cracked or burned, the head will require valve service that's beyond the scope of the home mechanic.

13   Check the valve stem-to-guide clearance by measuring the lateral movement of the valve stem with a dial indicator attached securely to the head **(see illustration)**. The valve must be in the guide and approximately 1/16-inch off the seat. The total valve stem movement indicated by the gauge needle must be divided by two to obtain the actual clearance. After this is done, if there's still some doubt regarding the condition of the valve guides they should be checked by an automotive machine shop (the cost should be minimal).

Valves

14   Carefully inspect each valve face for uneven wear, deformation, cracks, pits and burned areas **(see illustration)**. Check the valve stem for scuffing and galling and the neck for cracks. Rotate the valve and

check for any obvious indication that it's bent. Look for pits and excessive wear on the end of the stem. The presence of any of these conditions indicates the need for valve service by an automotive machine shop.

15   Measure the margin width on each valve **(see illustration)**. Any valve with a margin narrower than specified will have to be replaced with a new one.

Valve components

16   Check each valve spring for wear (on the ends) and pits. Measure the free length and compare it to the Specifications **(see illustration)**. Any springs that are shorter than specified have sagged and should not be reused. The tension of all springs should be checked with a special fixture before deciding that they're suitable for use in a rebuilt engine (take the springs to an automotive machine shop for this check).

17   Stand each spring on a flat surface and check it for squareness **(see illustration)**. If any of the springs are distorted or sagged, replace all of them with new parts.

18   Check the spring retainers and keepers for obvious wear and cracks. Any questionable parts should be replaced with new ones, as extensive damage will occur if they fail during engine operation.

Rocker arm components

19   Check the rocker arm faces (the areas that contact the camshaft and valve stems) for pits, wear, galling, score marks and rough spots. Check the rocker arm-to-shaft contact areas and adjuster screws as well. Look for cracks in each rocker arm.

20   Check the rocker shaft bolt holes in the cylinder head for damaged threads and secure installation.

21   Any damaged or excessively worn parts must be replaced with new ones.

22   If the inspection process indicates that the valve components are in generally poor condition and worn beyond the limits specified, which is usually the case in an engine that's being overhauled, reassemble the valves in the cylinder head and refer to Section 10 for valve servicing recommendations.

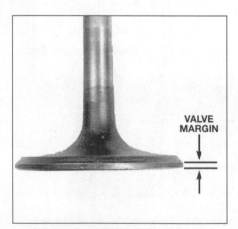

VALVE MARGIN

9.15 The margin width on each valve must be as specified (if no margin exists, the valve cannot be reused)

9.16 Measure the free length of each valve spring with a dial or vernier caliper

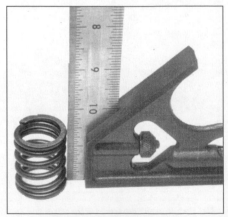

9.17 Check each valve spring for squareness

10 Valves - servicing

1 Because of the complex nature of the job and the special tools and equipment needed, servicing of the valves, the valve seats and the valve guides, commonly known as a valve job, should be done by a professional.

2 The home mechanic can remove and disassemble the head, do the initial cleaning and inspection, then reassemble and deliver it to a dealer service department or an automotive machine shop for the actual service work. Doing the inspection will enable you to see what condition the head and valvetrain components are in and will ensure that you know what work and new parts are required when dealing with an automotive machine shop.

3 The dealer service department, or automotive machine shop, will remove the valves and springs, recondition or replace the valves and valve seats, recondition the valve guides, check and replace the valve springs, spring retainers and keepers (as necessary), replace the valve seals with new ones, reassemble the valve components and make sure the installed spring height is correct. The cylinder head gasket surface will also be resurfaced if it's warped.

4 After the valve job has been performed by a professional, the head will be in like new condition. When the head is returned, be sure to clean it again before installation on the engine to remove any metal particles and abrasive grit that may still be present from the valve service or head resurfacing operations. Use compressed air, if available, to blow out all the oil holes and passages.

11 Cylinder head - reassembly

Refer to illustrations 11.3a, 11.3b, 11.5a, 11.5b, 11.5c and 11.8

1 Regardless of whether or not the head was sent to an automotive repair shop for valve servicing, make sure it's clean before beginning reassembly.

2 If the head was sent out for valve servicing, the valves and related components will already be in place. Begin the reassembly procedure with Step 8.

3 Drop the spring seats over the valve guides **(see illustration)**, install new seals on each of the valve guides. Note that the intake and exhaust seals are not interchangeable. Intake seals have white springs and exhaust seals have black spring. Using a hammer and a deep socket or seal installation tool, gently tap each seal into place until it's completely seated on the guide **(see illustration)**. Don't twist or cock the seals during installation or they won't seal properly on the valve stems.

4 Beginning at one end of the head, lubricate and install the first valve. Apply moly-base grease or clean engine oil to the valve stem.

5 Set the valve springs and retainers in

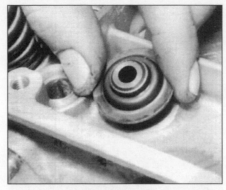

11.3a Drop the spring seats over the valve guides

place **(see illustrations)** (not that the intake and exhaust retainers are different and should not be interchanged). Exhaust valves have an inner and an outer spring.

6 Compress the springs with a valve spring compressor and carefully install the keepers in the upper groove, then slowly

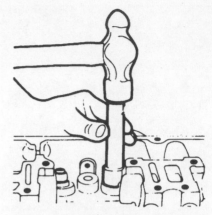

11.3b Gently tap the valve seals into place with a seal installation tool or a deep socket and hammer

release the compressor and make sure the keepers seat properly. Apply a small dab of grease to each keeper to hold it in place if necessary.

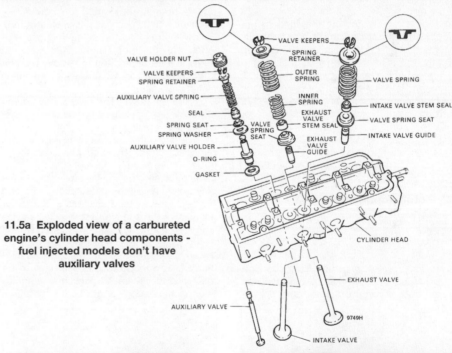

11.5a Exploded view of a carbureted engine's cylinder head components - fuel injected models don't have auxiliary valves

11.5b Make sure each outer valve spring (right) is installed with the narrow pitch end (arrow) against the cylinder head

11.5c Install the valve retainer over the springs and valve stem

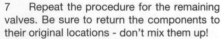

11.8 Double-check the height with the valve springs installed (do this for each valve)

12.1 A ridge reamer is required to remove the ridge from the top of the cylinder - do this before removing the pistons!

12.3 Check the connecting rod end play with a feeler gauge as shown here

7   Repeat the procedure for the remaining valves. Be sure to return the components to their original locations - don't mix them up!
8   Check the installed valve spring height with a ruler graduated in 1/32-inch increments or a dial caliper. If the head was sent out for service work, the installed height should be correct (but don't automatically assume that it is). The measurement is taken from the top of each spring seat or shim(s) to the bottom of the retainer **(see illustration)**. If the height is greater than specified, shims can be added under the springs to correct it. **Caution:** *Don't, under any circumstances, shim the springs to the point where the installed height is less than specified.*
9   Lubricate and then install the camshaft and rocker arm assembly (see Chapter 2A).

12   Pistons/connecting rods - removal

Refer to illustrations 12.1, 12.3, 12..4a, 12.4b and 12.6
Note: *Prior to removing the piston/connecting rod assemblies, remove the cylinder head and oil pan by referring to the appropriate*

Sections in Chapter 2A.
1   Use your fingernail to feel if a ridge has formed at the upper limit of ring travel (about 1/4-inch down from the top of each cylinder). If carbon deposits or cylinder wear have produced ridges, they must be completely removed with a special tool **(see illustration)**. Follow the manufacturer's instructions provided with the tool. Failure to remove the ridges before attempting to remove the piston/connecting rod assemblies may result in piston breakage.
2   After the cylinder ridges have been removed, turn the engine upside-down so the crankshaft is facing up.
3   Before the connecting rods are removed, check the end play with feeler gauges. Slide them between the first connecting rod and the crankshaft throw until the play is removed **(see illustration)**. The end play is equal to the thickness of the feeler gauge(s). If the end play exceeds the service limit, new connecting rods will be required. If new rods (or a new crankshaft) are installed, the end play may fall under the specified minimum (if it does, the rods will have to be machined to restore it - consult an automotive machine shop for advice if necessary).

Repeat the procedure for the remaining connecting rods.
4   Check the connecting rods and caps for identification marks. If they aren't plainly marked, use a small center punch to make the appropriate number of indentations **(see illustration)** on each rod and cap (1, 2, 3, etc., depending on the cylinder they're associated with).
5   Loosen each of the connecting rod cap nuts 1/2-turn at a time until they can be removed by hand. Remove the number one connecting rod cap and bearing insert. Don't drop the bearing insert out of the cap.
6   Slip a short length of plastic or rubber hose over each connecting rod cap bolt to protect the crankshaft journal and cylinder wall as the piston is removed **(see illustration)**.
7   Remove the bearing insert and push the connecting rod/piston assembly out through the top of the engine. Use a wooden hammer handle to push on the upper bearing surface in the connecting rod. If resistance is felt, double-check to make sure that all of the ridge was removed from the cylinder.
8   Repeat the procedure for the remaining cylinders.

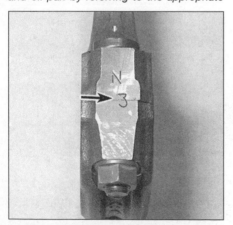

12.4a DO NOT confuse the stamped numbers on the parting surface, such as this 3 (arrow) with cylinder numbers - this number indicates big-end bore size

12.4b To avoid confusion during reassembly, the connecting rods and caps should be marked with a center punch to indicate which cylinder they're installed in

12.6 To prevent damage to the crankshaft journals and cylinder walls, slip sections of hose over the rod bolts before removing the pistons

13.1 Checking crankshaft end play with a dial indicator

13.3 If you use feeler gauges to check crankshaft end play, check it at the middle (number 3) main bearing journal

13.4a The main bearing caps should have numbers and arrows - this number indicates it is the second cap from the drivebelt end and the arrow points toward the drivebelt end

9   After removal, reassemble the connecting rod caps and bearing inserts in their respective connecting rods and install the cap nuts finger tight. Leaving the old bearing inserts in place until reassembly will help prevent the connecting rod bearing surfaces from being accidentally nicked or gouged.

10   Don't separate the pistons from the connecting rods (see Section 17 for additional information).

13   Crankshaft - removal

Refer to illustrations 13.1, 13.3 13.4a and 13.b

Note: *The crankshaft can be removed only after the engine has been removed from the vehicle. It's assumed that the flywheel or driveplate, crankshaft damper, timing belt, oil pan, oil pump and piston/connecting rod assemblies have already been removed.*

1   Before the crankshaft is removed, check the end play. Mount a dial indicator with the stem in line with the crankshaft and just touching the end of the crank shaft **(see illustration)**.

2   Push the crankshaft all the way to the rear and zero the dial indicator. Next, pry the crankshaft to the front as far as possible and check the reading on the dial indicator. The distance that it moves is the end play. If it's greater than specified, check the crankshaft thrust surfaces for wear. If no wear is evident, new main bearings should correct the end play.

3   If a dial indicator isn't available, feeler gauges can be used. Gently pry or push the crankshaft all the way to the front of the engine. Slip feeler gauges between the crankshaft and the front face of the thrust washer to determine the clearance **(see illustration)**.

4   Check the main bearing caps to see if they're marked to indicate their locations. They should be numbered consecutively from the front of the engine to the rear. If they aren't, mark them with number stamping dies or a center punch. Main bearing caps generally have a cast-in arrow, which points to the front of the engine **(see illustration)**. Loosen the main bearing cap bolts 1/4-turn at a time each, in the sequence shown **(see illustration)** until they can be removed by hand.

5   Gently tap the caps with a soft-face hammer, then separate them from the engine block. If necessary, use the bolts as levers to remove the caps. Try not to drop the bearing inserts if they come out with the caps.

6   Carefully lift the crankshaft out of the engine. It may be a good idea to have an assistant available, since the crankshaft is quite heavy. With the bearing inserts in place in the engine block and main bearing caps, return the caps to their respective locations on the engine block and tighten the bolts finger tight.

14   Engine block - cleaning

Refer to illustrations 14.1, 14.2a, 14.2b, 14.2c, 14.9 and 14. 11

Caution: *The core plugs (also known as freeze or soft plugs) may be difficult or impossible to retrieve if they're driven into the block coolant passages.*

1   Drill a small hole in the center of each core plug and pull it out with an auto body type dent puller **(see illustration)**.

2B

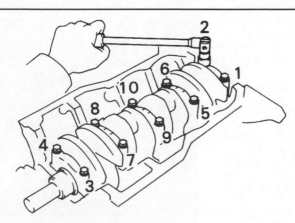

13.4b Loosen the main bearing cap bolts in this sequence

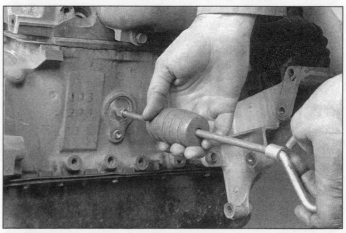

14.1 The core plugs should be removed with a puller - if they're driven into the block they may be impossible to retrieve

14.2a Unbolt and remove the oil filter housing

14.2b Unscrew the cap and remove the relief valve spring and piston from the oil filter housing

14.2c Remove the oil deflector from the bottom of the engine block

2   Remove all exterior components **(see illustration)** to allow thorough cleaning.

3   Using a gasket scraper, remove all traces of gasket material from the engine block Be very careful not to nick or gouge the gasket sealing surfaces.

4   Remove the main bearing caps and separate the bearings inserts from the caps and the engine block. Tag the bearings, indicating cylinder they were removed from and whether they war or the block, then set them aside.

5   Remove all of the threaded oil gallery plugs from the plugs are usually very tight - they may have to be drilled out and the holes retapped. Use new plugs when the engine is reassembled.

6   If the engine is extremely dirty it should be taken to an automotive machine shop to be steam cleaned or hot tanked.

7   After the block is returned, clean all oil holes and oil galleries one more time. Brushes, specifically designed for this purpose available at most auto parts stores. Flush the passages with warm water until the water runs clear, dry the block thoroughly and wipe all machined surfaces with a light, rust preventive oil. If you have access to compressed air, use it to speed the drying process and to blow out all the oil holes and galleries. **Warning:** *Wear eye protection when using compressed air!*

8   If the block isn't extremely dirty or sludged up, you can do an adequate cleaning job with hot soapy water and a stiff brush. Take plenty of time and do a thorough job. Regardless of the cleaning method used, be sure to clean all oil holes and galleries very thoroughly, dry the block completely and coat all machined surfaces with light oil.

9   The threaded holes in the block must be clean to ensure accurate torque readings during reassembly. Run the proper size tap into each of the holes to remove rust, corrosion, thread sealant or sludge and restore damaged threads (see Illustration). If possible, use compressed air to clear the holes of debris produced by this operation. Now is a good time to clean the threads on the head bolts and the main bearing cap bolts as well.

10   Reinstall the main bearing caps and

tighten the bolts finger tight.

11   After coating the sealing surfaces of the new core plugs with Permatex no. 2 sealant (or equivalent), install them in the engine block **(see illustration)**. Make sure they're driven in straight and seated properly or leakage could result. Special tools are available for this purpose, but a large socket, with an outside diameter that will just slip into the core plug, a 1/2-inch drive extension and a hammer will work just as well.

12   Apply non-hardening sealant (such as Permatex no. 2 or Teflon pipe sealant) to the new oil gallery plugs and thread them into the holes in the block. Make sure they're tightened securely.

13   If the engine isn't going to be reassembled right away, cover it with a large plastic trash bag to keep it clean.

15   Engine block - inspection

Refer to illustrations 15.4a, 15.4b, 15.4c, 15.13, 15.14a and 15. 14b

1   Before the block is inspected, it should be cleaned as described in Section 14.

2   Visually check the block for cracks, rust and corrosion. Look for tripped threads in the threaded holes. It's also a good idea to have the block checked for hidden cracks by an automotive machine shop that has the special equipment to do this type of work. If defects are found, have the block repaired, if possible, or replaced.

3   Check the cylinder bores for scuffing and scoring.

4   Measure the diameter of each cylinder at the top (just under the ridge area), center and bottom of the cylinder bore, parallel to the crankshaft axis **(see illustrations)**.

5   Next, measure each cylinder's diameter at the same three locations across the crankshaft axis. Compare the results to the Specifications.

6   If the required precision measuring tools aren't available, the piston-to-cylinder clearances can be obtained, though. not quite as accurately, using feeler gauge stock. Feeler gauge stock comes in 1 2-inch lengths and

14.9 All threaded holes in the block - particularly the main bearing cap and cylinder head bolt holes - should be cleaned and restored with a tap (be sure to remove debris from the holes after this is done)

various thicknesses and is generally available at auto parts stores. Purchase thicknesses equal to the specified maximum and minimum piston clearances.

7   To check the clearance, select a feeler gauge and slip it into the cylinder along with the matching piston. The piston must be

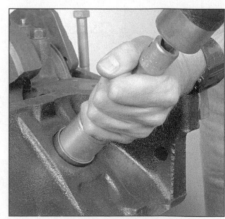

14.11 A large socket and an extension can be used to drive the new core plugs into the bores

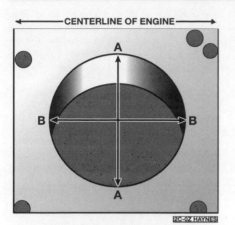

15.4a Measure the diameter of each cylinder just under the ridge area (A), at the center (B) and at the bottom

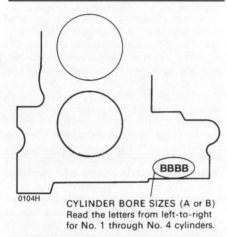

15.13 The cylinder bore size markings are stamped into the block above the water pump mounting point

positioned exactly as it normally would be. The feeler gauge must be between the piston and cylinder on one of the thrust faces (90 degrees to the piston pin bore).

8   The, piston should slip through the cylinder (with the feeler gauge in place) with moderate pressure.

9   If it fails through or slides through easily, the clearance is excessive and a new piston

15.14a Check the block deck for warpage with a precision straightedge and feeler gauges

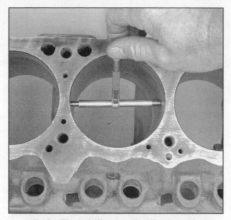

15.4b The ability to "feel" when the telescoping gauge is at the correct point will be developed over time, so work slowly and repeat the check until you're satisfied that the bore measurement is accurate

will be required. If the piston binds at the lower end of the cylinder and is loose toward the top, the cylinder is tapered. If tight spots are encountered as the piston/feeler gauge is rotated in the cylinder, the cylinder is out-of-round.

10   Repeat the procedure for the remaining pistons and cylinders.

11   If the cylinder walls are badly scuffed or scored, or if they're out of-round or tapered beyond the limits given in the Specifications, have 'the engine block rebored and honed at an automotive machine shop. If a rebore is done, oversize pistons and rings will be required.

12   If the cylinders are in reasonably good condition and not worn to the outside of the limits, and if the piston-to-cylinder clearances can be maintained properly, then they don't have to be rebored. Honing is all that's necessary (see Section 16).

13   Standard bore pistons fitted at the factory come in two sizes, designated A or B. The top of the pistons and the block (see illustration) are stamped to indicate which size was installed. Note: If no letter is stamped, it means size A was used. This marking information applies only to engines which have not been rebored.

15.14b Lay the straightedge across the block, diagonally and from end-to-end when making the check

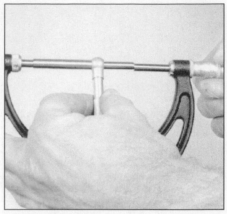

15.4c The gauge is then measured with a micrometer to determine the bore size

14   Using a precision straightedge and feeler gauge, check the block deck (the surface that mates with the cylinder head) for warpage (see illustrations). If it's warped beyond the specified limit, have it resurfaced by an automotive machine shop.

16   Cylinder honing

Refer to illustrations 16.3s and 16.3b

1   Prior to engine reassembly, the cylinder bores must be honed so the new piston rings will seat correctly and provide the best possible combustion chamber seal. **Note:** *If you don't have the tools or don't want to tackle the honing operation, most automotive machine shops will do it for a reasonable fee.*

2   Before honing the cylinders, install the main bearing caps and tighten the bolts to the specified torque.

3   Two types of cylinder hones are commonly available - the flex hone or "bottle brush" type and the more traditional surfacing hone with spring-loaded stones. Both will do the job, but for the less experienced mechanic the "bottle brush" hone will probably be easier to use. You'll also need some kerosene or honing oil, rags and an electric drill motor. Proceed as follows:

a) *Mount the hone in the drill motor, compress the stones and slip it into the first cylinder. Be sure to wear safety goggles or a face shield!*

b) *Lubricate the cylinder with plenty of honing oil, turn on the drill and move the hone up-and-down in the cylinder at a pace that will produce a fine crosshatch pattern on the cylinder walls. Ideally, the crosshatch lines should intersect at approximately a 60 degree angle (see Illustrations). Be sure to use plenty of lubricant and don't take off any more material than is absolutely necessary to produce the desired finish. Note: Piston ring manufacturers may specify a smaller crosshatch angle than the traditional 60 degree read and follow any instructions included with the new rings.*

2B

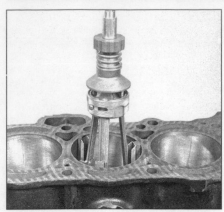

16.3a Lubricate the cylinder with plenty of oil and move the hone up and down in the cylinder at a pace which will produce a fine crosshatch pattern

c) *Don't withdraw the hone from the cylinder while it's running. Instead, shut off the drill and continue moving the hone up-and-down in the cylinder until it comes to a complete stop, then compress the stones and withdraw the hone. If you're using a "bottle brush" type hone, stop the drill motor, then turn the chuck in the normal direction of rotation while withdrawing the hone from the cylinder.*

d) *Wipe the oil out of the cylinder and repeat the procedure for the remaining cylinders.*

4   After the honing job is complete, chamfer the top edges of the cylinder bores with a small file so the rings won't catch when the pistons are installed. **Be very careful not to nick the cylinder walls with the end of the file.**

5   The entire engine block must be washed again very thoroughly with warm, soapy water to remove all traces of the abrasive grit produced during the honing operation. **Note:** *The bores can, be considered clean when a lint-free white cloth - dampened with clean engine oil used to wipe them out doesn't pick up anymore honing residue, which will show up as gray areas on the cloth. Be sure to run a brush through all oil holes and galleries and*

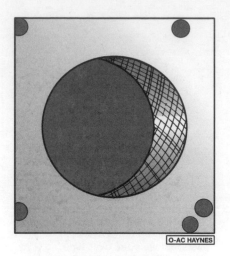

16.3b The crosshatch lines should intersect at approximately a 60-degree angle

flush them with running water.

6   After rinsing, dry the block and apply a coat of light rust preventive oil to all machined surfaces. Wrap the block in a plastic trash bag to keep it clean and set it aside until reassembly.

17 Pistons/connecting rods - inspection

Refer to illustrations 17.4a, 17.4b, 17. 10 and 17. 11

1   Before the inspection process can be carried out, the piston/connecting rod assemblies must be cleaned and the original piston rings removed from the pistons. **Note:** *Always use new piston rings when the engine is reassembled.*

2   Using a piston ring installation tool, carefully remove the rings from the pistons. Be careful not to nick or gouge the pistons in the process.

3   Scrape all traces of carbon from the top of the piston. A handheld wire brush or a piece of fine emery cloth can be used once

the majority of the deposits have been scraped away. Do not, under any circumstances, use a wire brush mounted in a drill motor to remove deposits from the pistons. The piston material is soft and may be eroded away by the wire brush.

4   Use a piston ring groove cleaning tool to remove carbon deposits from the ring grooves. If a tool isn't available, a piece broken off the old ring will do the job. Be very careful to remove only the carbon deposits - don't remove any metal and do not nick or scratch the sides of the ring grooves (see Illustrations).

5   Once the deposits have been removed, clean the piston/rod assemblies with solvent and dry them with compressed air (if available). Make sure the oil return holes in the back sides of the ring grooves are clear.

6   If the pistons and cylinder walls aren't damaged or worn excessively, and if the engine block is not rebored, new pistons won't be necessary. Normal piston wear appears as even vertical wear on the piston thrust surfaces and slight looseness of the top ring in its groove. New piston rings, however, should always be used when an engine is rebuilt.

7   Carefully inspect each piston for cracks around the skirt, at the pin bosses and- at the ring lands.

8   Look for scoring and scuffing on the thrust faces of the skirt, holes in the piston crown and burned areas at the edge of the crown. If the skirt is scored or scuffed, the engine may have been suffering from overheating and/or abnormal combustion, which caused excessively high operating temperatures. The cooling and lubrication systems should be checked thoroughly. A hole in the piston crown is an indication that abnormal combustion (preignition) was occurring. Burned areas at the edge of the piston crown are u usually evidence of spark knock (detonation). If any of the above problems exist, the causes must be corrected or the damage will occur again. The causes may include intake air leaks, incorrect fuel/air mixture, incorrect ignition timing and EGR system malfunctions.

9   Corrosion of the piston, in the form of small pits, indicates that coolant is leaking into the combustion chamber and/or the crankcase. Again, the cause must be corrected or the problem may persist in the rebuilt, engine.

10   Measure the piston ring side clearance by laying a new piston ring in each ring groove and slipping a feeler gauge in beside it **(see illustration)** Check the clearance at three or four locations around each groove. Be sure to use the correct ring for each groove - they are different. If the side clearance is greater than specified, new pistons will have to be used.

11   Check the piston-to-bore clearance by measuring the bore (see Section 15) and the piston diameter. Make sure the pistons and bores are correctly matched. Measure the piston across the skirt, at a 90-degree angle

17.4a The piston ring grooves can be cleaned with a special tool, as shown here, . . .

17.4b . . . or a section of a broken ring

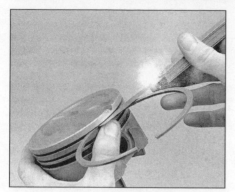

17.10 Check the ring side clearance with a feeler gauge at several points around the groove

17.11 Measure piston diameter at a 90 degree angle to the piston pin, at a point 21 mm (0.83-inch) above the bottom of the skirt

to and in line with the piston pin, 21 mm, (0.83 in) above the bottom of the skirt (see illustration). Subtract the piston diameter from the bore diameter to obtain the clearance. If it's greater than specified, the block will have to be rebored and new pistons and rings installed.

12 Check the piston-to-rod clearance by twisting the piston and rod in opposite directions. Any noticeable play indicates excessive wear, which must be corrected. The piston/connecting rod assemblies should be taken to an automotive machine shop to have the pistons and rods resized and new pins installed.

13 If the pistons must be removed from the connecting rods for any reason, they should be taken to an automotive machine shop. While they are there have the connecting rods checked for bend and twist, since automotive machine shops have special equipment for this purpose. **Note:** *Unless new pistons and/or connecting rods must be installed, do not disassemble the pistons and connecting rods.*

14 Check the connecting rods for cracks and other damage. Temporarily remove the rod caps, lift out the old bearing inserts, wipe the rod and cap bearing surfaces clean and inspect them for nicks, gouges and scratches. After checking the rods, replace the old bearings, slip the caps into place and

tighten the nuts finger tight. **Note:** *If the engine is being rebuilt because of a connecting rod knock, be sure to install new rods.*

18 Crankshaft - Inspection

Refer to illustration 18.6

1 Clean the crankshaft with solvent and dry it with compressed air (if available). Be sure to clean the oil holes with a stiff brush and flush them with solvent.

2 Check the main and connecting rod bearing journals for uneven wear, scoring, pits and cracks.

3 Rub a penny across each journal several times. If a journal picks up copper from the penny, it's too rough and must be reground.

4 Remove all burrs from the crankshaft oil holes with a stone, file or scraper.

5 Check the rest of the crankshaft for cracks and other damage. It should be magnafluxed to reveal hidden cracks -an automotive machine shop, will handle the procedure.

6 Using a micrometer, measure the diameter of the main and connecting rod journals and compare the results to the Specifications **(see illustration)**. By measuring the diameter at a number of points around each journal's circumference, you'll be able to determine whether or not the journal is out-of-round. Take the measurement at each end of the journal, near the crank throws, to determine if the journal is tapered.

7 If the crankshaft journals are damaged, tapered, out-of-round or worn beyond the limits given in the Specifications, have the crankshaft reground by an automotive machine shop. Be sure to use the correct size beating inserts if the crankshaft is reconditioned.

8 Check the oil seal journals at each and of the crankshaft for wear and damage. If the seal has worn a groove in the journal, or if it's nicked or scratched, the new seal may leak when the engine is reassembled. In some cases, an automotive machine shop may be able to repair the journal by pressing on a thin sleeve. If repair isn't feasible, a new or different crankshaft should be installed.

9 Refer to Section 19 and examine the main and rod bearing inserts.

19 Main and connecting rod bearings - inspection and selection

2B

Inspection

Refer to illustration 19. 1

1 Even though the main and connecting rod bearings should be replaced with new ones during the engine overhaul, the old bearings should be retained for close examination, as they may reveal valuable information about the condition of the engine **(see illustration)**.

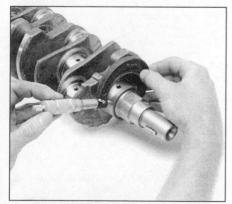

18.6 Measure the diameter of each crankshaft journal at several points to detect taper and out-of-round conditions

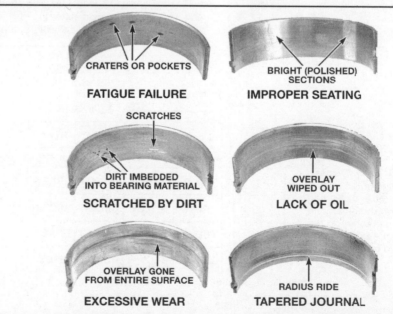

CRATERS OR POCKETS
FATIGUE FAILURE

BRIGHT (POLISHED) SECTIONS
IMPROPER SEATING

SCRATCHES
DIRT IMBEDDED INTO BEARING MATERIAL
SCRATCHED BY DIRT

OVERLAY WIPED OUT
LACK OF OIL

OVERLAY GONE FROM ENTIRE SURFACE
EXCESSIVE WEAR

RADIUS RIDE
TAPERED JOURNAL

19.1 When inspecting the main and connecting rod bearings, look for these problems

2   Bearing failure occurs because of lack of lubrication, the presence of dirt or other foreign particles, overloading the engine and corrosion Regardless of the cause of bearing failure, it must be corrected before the engine is reassembled to prevent it from happening again.

3   When examining the bearings, remove them from the engine block, the main bearing caps, the connecting rods and the rod caps and lay them out on a clean surface in the same general position as their location in the engine. This will enable you to match any bearing problems with the corresponding crankshaft journal.

4   Dirt and other foreign particles get into the engine in a variety of ways. It may be left in the engine during assembly, or it may pass through filters or the PCV system. It may get into the oil, and from there into the bearings. Metal chips from machining operations and normal engine wear are often present. Abrasives are sometimes left in engine components after reconditioning, especially when parts are not thoroughly cleaned using the proper cleaning methods. Whatever the source, these foreign objects often end up embedded in the soft bearing material and are easily recognized. Large particles will not embed in the bearing and will score or gouge the bearing and journal. The best prevention for this cause of bearing failure is to clean all parts thoroughly and keep everything spotlessly clean during engine assembly. Frequent and regular engine oil and filter changes are also recommended.

5   Lack of lubrication (or lubrication breakdown) has a number of interrelated causes. Excessive heat (which thins the oil), overloading (which squeezes the oil from the bearing face) and oil leakage or throw off (from excessive bearing clearances, worn oil pump or high engine speeds) all contribute to lubrication breakdown. Blocked oil passages, which usually are the result of misaligned oil holes in a bearing shell, will also oil starve a bearing and destroy it. When lack of lubrica-

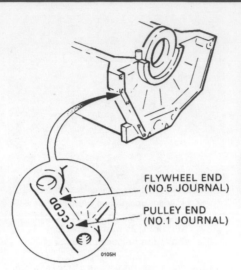

FLYWHEEL END (NO.5 JOURNAL)

PULLEY END (NO.1 JOURNAL)

0105H

19.10a Some engines have letters stamped into the bellhousing mating surface . . .

tion is the cause of bearing failure, the bearing material is wiped or extruded from the steel backing of the bearing. Temperatures may increase to the point where the steel backing turns blue from overheating.

6   Driving habits can have a definite effect on bearing life. Full throttle, low speed operation (lugging the engine) puts very high loads on bearings, which tends to squeeze out the oil film. These loads cause the bearings to flex, which produces fine cracks in the bearing face (fatigue failure). Eventually the bearing material will loosen in pieces and tear away from the steel backing. Short trip driving leads to corrosion of bearings because insufficient engine heat is produced to drive off the condensed water and corrosive gases. These products collect in the engine oil, forming acid and sludge. As the oil is carried to the engine bearings, the acid attacks and corrodes the bearing material.

7   Incorrect bearing installation during

19.10b . . . and others have Roman numerals to indicate main bearing bore size

Main Journal Code Locations (Numbers)

0106H

19.11 The main bearing journal grade numbers are stamped adjacent to their respective journals

engine assembly will lead to bearing failure as well. Tight fitting bearings leave insufficient bearing oil clearance and will result in oil starvation, Dirt or foreign particles trapped behind a bearing insert result in high spots on the bearing which lead to failure.

Selection

Refer to illustrations 19. 10e, 19. 10b, 19.11, 19.12, 19.14, 19.15 and 19.16

8   If the original bearings are worn or damaged, or if the oil clearances are incorrect (Section 22 or 23), the following procedures

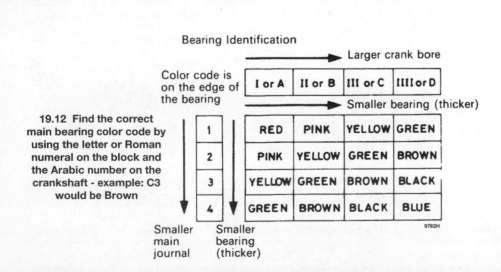

Bearing Identification

Color code is on the edge of the bearing

Larger crank bore →

Smaller bearing (thicker) →

	I or A	II or B	III or C	IIII or D
1	RED	PINK	YELLOW	GREEN
2	PINK	YELLOW	GREEN	BROWN
3	YELLOW	GREEN	BROWN	BLACK
4	GREEN	BROWN	BLACK	BLUE

Smaller main journal

Smaller bearing (thicker)

9762H

19.12 Find the correct main bearing color code by using the letter or Roman numeral on the block and the Arabic number on the crankshaft - example: C3 would be Brown

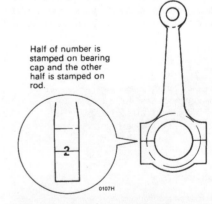

Half of number is stamped on bearing cap and the other half is stamped on rod.

0107H

19.14 The number stamped on the parting surface of the connecting rod and cap indicates the big-end bearing bore size - it does NOT indicate the cylinder number it came from

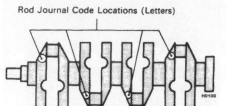

Rod Journal Code Locations (Letters)

19.15 The connecting rod bearing journal code letters are stamped adjacent to their respective journals

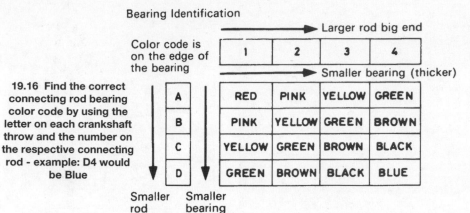

Bearing Identification

Color code is on the edge of the bearing

19.16 Find the correct connecting rod bearing color code by using the letter on each crankshaft throw and the number on the respective connecting rod - example: D4 would be Blue

Larger rod big end

Smaller bearing (thicker)

	1	2	3	4
A	RED	PINK	YELLOW	GREEN
B	PINK	YELLOW	GREEN	BROWN
C	YELLOW	GREEN	BROWN	BLACK
D	GREEN	BROWN	BLACK	BLUE

Smaller rod journal

Smaller bearing (thicker)

should be used to select the correct new bearings for engine reassembly. However, if the crankshaft has been reground, new undersize bearings must be installed - **the following procedure should not be used if undersize bearings are required!** The automotive machine shop that reconditions the crankshaft will provide or help you select the correct size bearings. Regardless of how the bearing sizes are determined, use the oil clearance, measured with Plastigage, as a guide to ensure the bearings are the right size.

Main bearings

9   If you need to use a STANDARD size main bearing, install one that has the same color code as the original bearing. The color code is on the edge of the bearing.

10   If the color code on the original main bearing has been obscured, locate the main journal grade marks stamped into the bell-housing mating surface on the engine block (See Illustrations).

11   Locate the main journal grade numbers on the crankshaft as well **(see illustration)**.

12   Use the accompanying chart to determine the correct bearings for each journal **(see illustration)**.

Connecting rod bearings

13   If you need to use a STANDARD size rod bearing, install one that has the same color code as the original.

14   If the color code has been obscured, locate the number stamped on the parting surface of the connecting rod and cap **(see illustration)**. This code indicates the connecting rod big-end bearing bore size.

15   Locate the letters stamped on the crankshaft **(see illustration)**. These denote the size of their respective connecting rod journals.

16   Use the accompanying chart **(see Illustration)** to determine the correct bearings for each journal.

All bearings

17   Remember, the oil clearance is the final judge when selecting new bearing sizes. If you have any questions or are unsure which bearings to use, get help from a Honda dealer parts or service department.

20   Engine overhaul - reassembly sequence

1   Before beginning engine reassembly, make sure you have all the necessary new parts, gaskets and seals as well as the following items on hand:

  Common hand tools
  A 1/12-inch drive torque wrench
  Piston ring installation tool
  Piston ring compressor
  Vibration damper
  Installation tool
  Short lengths of rubber or plastic hose to fit over connecting rod bolts
  Plastigage
  Feeler gauges
  A fine-tooth file
  New engine oil
  Engine assembly lube or moly-base grease
  Gasket sealant
  Thread locking compound

2   In order to save time and avoid problems, engine reassembly must be done in the following general order:

  Crankshaft and main bearings
  Piston rings
  Piston/connecting rod assemblies
  Oil pump
  Oil pan
  Cylinder head
  Camshaft and rocker arms
  Timing belt and sprockets
  Timing covers
  Intake and exhaust manifolds
  Camshaft cover
  Flywheel/driveplate

21   Piston rings - Installation

Refer to illustrations 21.3, 21.4, 21.5, 21.9a, 21.9b and 21.12

1   Before installing the new piston rings, the ring end gaps must be checked. It's assumed that the piston ring side clearance has been checked and verified correct (see Section 17).

2   Lay out the piston/connecting rod assemblies and the now ring sets so the ring sets will be matched with the same piston and cylinder during the end gap measurement and engine assembly.

3   Insert the top (number one) ring into the first cylinder and square it up with the cylinder walls by pushing it in with the top of the piston **(see Illustration)**. The ring should be near the bottom of the cylinder, at the lower limit of ring travel.

4   To measure the end gap, slip feeler gauges between the ends of the ring until a gauge equal to the gap width is found **(see Illustration)**. The feeler gauge should slide

2B

21.3 When checking piston ring end gap, the ring must be square in the cylinder bore (this is done by pushing the ring down with the top of a piston as shown)

21.4 With the ring square in the cylinder, measure the end gap with a feeler gauge

21.5 If the end gap is too small, clamp a file in a vise and file the ring ends (from the outside in only) to enlarge the gap slightly

21.9a Installing the spacer/expander in the oil control ring groove

21.9b DO NOT use a piston ring installation tool when installing the oil ring side rails

between the ring ends with a slight amount of drag. Compare the measurement to the Specifications. If the gap is larger or smaller then specified, double-check to make sure you have the correct rings before proceeding.

5   If the gap is too small, it must be enlarged or the ring ends may come in contact with each other during engine operation, which can cause serious damage to the engine. The end gap can be increased by filing the ring ends very carefully with a fine file, Mount the file in a vise equipped with soft jaws, slip the ring over the file face He with the ends contacting the file face and slowly move the ring to remove material from the ends. When performing this operation, file only from the outside in **(see Illustration)**.

6   Excess end gap isn't critical unless it's greater than 0.040-inch. Again, double-check to make sure you have the correct rings for your engine.

7   Repeat the procedure for each ring that will be installed in the first cylinder and for each ring in the remaining cylinders. Remember to keep rings, pistons and cylinders matched up.

8   Once the ring end gaps have been checked/corrected, the rings can be installed on the pistons.

9   The oil control ring, (lowest one on the piston) is usually installed first. It's usually composed of three separate components. Slip the spacer/expander into the groove **(see Illustration)**. If an anti-rotation tang is used, make sure it's inserted into the drilled hole in the ring groove. Next, install the lower side rail. Don't use a piston ring installation tool on the oil ring side rails, as they. may be damaged. Instead, place one end of the side rail into the groove between the spacer/expander and the ring land, hold it firmly in place and slide a finger around the piston while pushing the rail into the groove **(see Illustration)**. Next, install the upper side rail in the same manner.

10   After the three oil ring components have been installed, check to make sure that both the upper and lower side rails can be turned

smoothly in the ring groove.

11   The number two (middle) ring is installed next. It's usually stamped with a mark which must face up, toward the top of the piston. **Note:** *Always follow the instructions printed on the ring package or box - manufacturers may require different approaches. Do not mix up the top and middle rings, as they have different cross sections.*

12   Use a piston ring installation tool and make sure the identification mark is facing the top of the piston, then slip the ring into the middle groove on the piston **(see Illustration)**. Don't expand the ring any more than necessary to slide it over the piston.

13   Install the number one (top) ring in the same manner. Make sure the mark is facing up. Be careful not to confuse the number one and number two rings.

14   Repeat the procedure for the remaining pistons and rings.

22 Crankshaft - installation and main bearing oil clearance check

Refer to illustrations 22.6a, 22.6b, 22.11, 22.15, 22.21, 22.22a, 22.22b and 22.33

1   Crankshaft installation is the first step in engine reassembly. It' assumed at this point that the engine block and crankshaft have been cleaned, inspected and repaired or reconditioned.

2   Position the engine with the bottom facing up.

3   Remove the main bearing cap bolts and lift out the caps. Lay them out in the proper order to ensure correct installation.

4   If they're still in place, remove the original bearing inserts from the block and the main bearing caps. Wipe the bearing surfaces of the block and caps with a clean, lint-free cloth. They must be kept spotlessly clean.

Main bearing oil clearance check

5   Clean the back sides of the now main bearing inserts and lay one in each main

bearing saddle in the block. If one of the bearing inserts from each set has a large groove in it, make sure the grooved insert is installed in the block. Lay the other bearing from each set in the corresponding main bearing cap. Make sure the tab on the bearing insert fits its into the recess in the block or cap **Caution:** *The oil holes in the block must line up with the oil holes in the bearing insert. Do not hammer the bearing into place and don't nick or gouge the bearing faces. No lubrication should be used at this time.*

6   The thrust washer must be installed on the third main bearing cap and crankshaft journal **(see Illustrations)**.

7   Clean the faces of the bearings in the block and the crankshaft main bearing journals with a clean, lint-free cloth.

8   Check or clean the oil holes in the crankshaft, as any dirt here can go only one way - straight through the new bearings.

9   Once you're certain the crankshaft is clean, carefully lay it in position in the main bearings.

10   Before the crankshaft can be permanently installed, the main bearing oil clearance must be checked.

11   Cut several pieces of the appropriate size Plastigage (they must be slightly shorter than the width of the main bearings) and

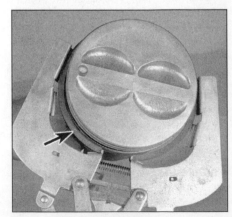

21.12 Install the compression rings with a ring expander

22.6a Place the lower washer into position on the number three crankshaft journal with the oil grooves facing OUT, then rotate the washer into position in the engine block's main bearing saddle

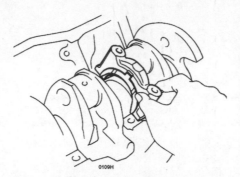

22.6b Install the thrust washer in the number three main bearing cap with the oil grooves facing OUT

22.11 Lay the Plastigage strips (arrow) on the main bearing journals, parallel to the crankshaft centerline

22.15 Compare the width of the crushed Plastigage to the scale on the container to determine the main bearing oil clearance (always take the measurement at the widest point of the Plastigage); be sure to use the correct scale - standard and metric scales are included

2B

place one piece on each crankshaft main bearing journal, parallel with the journal axis **(see illustration)**.

12   Clean the faces of the bearings in the caps and install the caps in their respective positions (don't mix them up) with the arrows pointing toward the front of the engine. Don't disturb the Plastigage.

13   Starting with the center main and working out toward the ends, tighten the main bearing cap bolts, in three steps, to the specified torque. Don't rotate the crankshaft at any time during this operation.

14   Remove the bolts and carefully liftoff the main bearing caps. Keep them in order. Don't disturb the Plastigage or rotate the crankshaft. If any of the main bearing caps are difficult to remove, tap them gently from side-to-side with a soft-face hammer to loosen them.

15   Compare the width of the crushed Plastigage on each journal to the scale printed on the Plastigage envelope to obtain the main bearing oil clearance (see Illustration). Check the Specifications to make sure it's correct.

16   If the clearance is not as specified, the bearing inserts may be the wrong size (which means different ones will be required). Before deciding, that different inserts are needed,

make sure that no dirt or oil was between the bearing inserts and the Caps or block when the clearance was measured. If the Plastigage was wider at one end than the other, the journal may be tapered (refer to Section 18).

17   Carefully scrape all traces of the Plastigage material off the main bearing journals and/or the bearing faces. Use your fingernail or the edge of a credit card - don't nick or scratch the bearing faces.

Final crankshaft installation

18   Carefully lift the crankshaft out of the engine.

19   Clean the bearing faces in the block, then apply a thin, uniform layer of moly-base grease or engine assembly lube to each of the bearing surfaces. Be sure to coat the grooved sides of the thrust washers, also.

20   Apply a light film of grease to the lips of both the front and rear crankshaft oil seals. Fill the seal spring grooves with grease. This helps keep the spring in place during installation. .

21   Slip the front and rear crankshaft oil seals onto their respective ends of the crankshaft with the spring side facing toward the crankshaft **(see illustration)**. Position them flush with the ends of the crankshaft.

22   Apply a thin coat of non-hardening sealer to the seams where the front and rear main bearing caps meet the engine block **(see illustrations)**.

22.21 Slip the front and rear seals onto the ends of the crankshaft, then position them flush with the ends

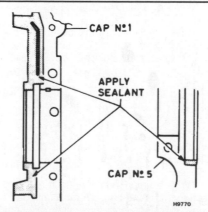

22.22a Apply non-hardening sealant to the shaded areas before installing the front and rear main bearing caps

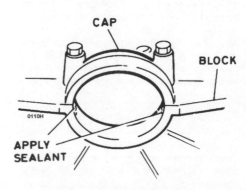

22.22b Apply non-hardening sealant to the parting surfaces of the bearing caps and block

22.33 Tap around the outer edge of the front and rear crankshaft seals with a hammer and a punch to seat them squarely in the bores

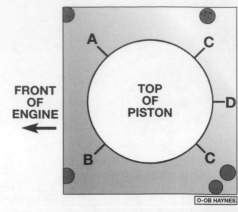

23.5 Ring end gap positions - align the oil ring spacer gap at A, the oil ring side rails at D (one inch either side of the pin centerline), and the compression rings at B and C, one inch either side of the pin centerline

23   Make sure the crankshaft journals are clean, then lay the crankshaft back in place in the block.,

24   Clean the faces of the bearings in the caps, then apply lubricant to them.

25   Install the caps in their respective positions with the arrows pointing toward the front of the engine. **Note:** *Be sure to install the thrust washers* **(see Illustration).**

26   Install the bolts.

27   Tighten all except the thrust bearing cap bolts to the specified torque (work from the center out and approach the final torque in three steps).

28   Tighten the thrust bearing cap bolts to 10-to-12 ft-lbs.

29   Tap the ends of the crankshaft forward and backward with a lead or brass hammer to line up the main bearing and crankshaft thrust surfaces.

30   Retighten all main bearing cap bolts to the specified torque, starting with the center main and working out toward the ends.

31   Rotate the crankshaft a number of times by hand to check for any obvious binding.

32   Check the crankshaft end play with a feeler gauge or a dial indicator as described in Section 13. The end play should be correct if the crankshaft thrust faces aren't worn or damaged and new thrust washers have been installed.

33   Check that the front and rear crankshaft seals are fully seated in their bores. Tap gently around the outer edge of the seals with a hammer and blunt punch (see Illustration).

23   Pistons/connecting rods - installation and rod bearing oil clearance check

Refer to illustrations 23.5, 23.9, 23.11, 23.13 and 23.17

1   Before installing the piston/connecting rod assemblies, the cylinder walls must be perfectly clean, the top edge of each cylinder must be chamfered, and the crankshaft must

be in place.

2   Remove the cap from the end of the number one connecting rod (refer to the marks made during removal). Remove the original bearing inserts and wipe the bearing surfaces of the connecting rod and cap with a clean, lint-free cloth. They must be kept spotlessly clean.

Connecting rod bearing oil clearance check

3   Clean the back side of the new upper bearing insert, then lay it in place in the connecting rod. Make sure the tab on the bearing fits into the recess in the rod. Don't hammer the bearing insert into place and be very careful not to nick or gouge the bearing face. Don't lubricate the bearing at this time.

4   Clean the back side of the other bearing insert and install it in the rod cap. Again, make sure the tab on the bearing fits into the recess in the cap, and don't apply any lubricant. It's critically important that the mating surfaces of the bearing and connecting rod are perfectly clean and oil free when they're assembled.

5   Position the piston ring gaps at the correct locations around the piston **(see Illustration).**

6   Slip a section of plastic or rubber hose over each connecting rod cap bolt.

7   Lubricate the piston and rings with clean engine oil and attach a piston ring compressor to the piston. Leave the skirt protruding about 1/4-inch to guide the piston into the cylinder. The rings must be compressed until they're flush with the piston.

8   Rotate the crankshaft until the number one connecting rod journal is at BDC (bottom dead canter) and apply a coat of engine oil to the cylinder walls.

9   With the marks on the piston and connecting rod **(see illustration)** facing the proper direction, gently insert the piston/connecting rod assembly into the number one cylinder bore and rest the bottom edge of the ring compressor on the engine block.

10   Tap the top edge of the ring compressor to make sure it's contacting the block around its entire circumference.

11   Gently tap on the top of the piston with the end of a wooden or plastic hammer handle **(see Illustration)** while guiding the end of the connecting rod into place on the crankshaft journal. The piston rings may try to pop out of the ring compressor just before entering the cylinder bore, so keep some downward pressure on the ring compressor. Work slowly, and if any resistance is felt as the piston enters the cylinder, stop immediately. Find out what's hanging up and fix it before proceeding. Do not, for any reason, force the piston into the cylinder - you might break a ring and/or the piston.

12   Once the piston/connecting rod assembly is installed, the connecting rod bearing oil clearance must be checked before the rod cap is permanently bolted in place.

13   Cut apiece of the appropriate size Plastigage slightly shorter than the width of the connecting rod bearing and lay it in place on the number one connecting rod journal, parallel with the journal axis (see Illustration).

14   Clean the connecting rod cap bearing face, remove the protective hoses from the connecting rod bolts and install the rod cap. Make sure the mating mark on the cap is on the same side as the mark on the connecting rod.

15   Install the nuts and tighten them to the specified torque, working up to it in three steps. **Note:** *Use a thin-wall socket to avoid erroneous torque readings that can result if the socket is wedged between the rod cap and nut. If the socket tends to wedge itself between the nut and the cap, lift up on it slightly until it no longer contacts the cap. Do not rotate the crankshaft at any time during this operation.*

16   Remove the nuts and data: detach the rod cap, being very careful not to disturb the Plastigage.

17   Compare the width of the crushed Plastigage to the scale printed on the Plastigage

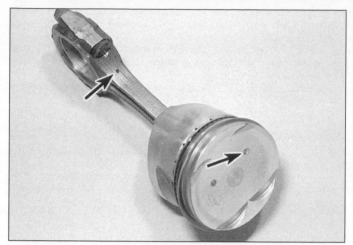

23.9 When installing pistons, the small holes on the pistons and connecting rods (arrows) should face the intake manifold side; if there are arrows on top of the piston, they should face the drivebelt end of the engine

23.11 The piston can be tapped (gently) into the cylinder bore with the end of a wooden or plastic hammer handle

envelope to obtain the oil clearance **(see illustration)**. Compare it to the Specifications to make sure the clearance is correct.

18   If the clearance is not as specified, the bearing inserts maybe the wrong size (which means different ones will be required). Before deciding that different inserts are needed, make sure that no dirt or oil was between the bearing inserts and the connecting rod or cap when the clearance was measured. Also, recheck the journal diameter. If the Plastigage was wider at one end than the other, the journal may be tapered (refer to Section 18).

Final connecting rod installation

19   Carefully scrape all traces of the Plastigage material off the rod journal and/or bearing face. Be very careful not to scratch the bearing - use your fingernail or the edge of a credit card.

20   Make sure the bearing faces are perfectly clean, then apply a uniform layer of clean moly-base grease or engine assembly lube to both, of them. You'll have to push the piston into the cylinder to expose the face of the bearing insert in the connecting rod - be sure to slip the protective hoses over the rod bolts first.

21   Slide the connecting rod back into place on the journal, remove the protective hoses from the rod cap bolts, install the rod cap and tighten the nuts to the specified torque, Again, work up to the torque in three steps.

22   Repeat the entire procedure for the remaining pistons/connecting rods.

23   The important points to remember are . . .

a) *Keep the backsides of the bearing inserts and the insides of the connecting rods and caps perfectly clean When assembling them.*

b) *Make sure you have the correct piston/rod assembly for each cylinder.*

c) *The marks on the piston and connecting rod must face the proper direction* **(see illustration 23.9)**.

d) *Lubricate the cylinder walls with clean oil.*

e) *Lubricate the bearing faces when installing the rod caps after the I oil clearance has been checked.*

f) *Be sure the match marks on the connecting rod and cap line up.*

24   After all the piston/connecting rod assemblies have been properly installed, rotate the crankshaft a number of times by hand to check for any obvious binding.

25   As a final step, the connecting rod end play must be checked. Refer to Section 12 for this procedure.

26   Compare the measured end play to the Specifications to make sure it's correct. If it was correct before disassembly and the original crankshaft and rods were reinstalled, it should still be right. If new rods or a new crankshaft were installed, the end play may be inadequate. If so, the rods will have to be removed and taken to an automotive machine shop for resizing.

23.13 Lay the Plastigage strips on each rod bearing journal, parallel to the crankshaft centerline

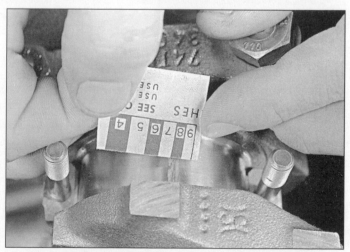

23.17 Measuring the width of the crushed Plastigage to determine the rod bearing oil clearance (be sure to use the correct scale - standard and metric scales are included)

24   Initial start-up and break-in after overhaul

Warning: *Have a fire extinguisher handy when starting the engine for the first time.*

1   Once the engine has been installed in the vehicle, double-check the engine oil and coolant levels.

2   With the spark plugs out of the engine and the ignition system disabled (see Section 3), crank the engine until oil pressure registers on the gauge or the light goes out.

3   Install the spark plugs, hook up the plug wires and restore the ignition system functions (Section 3).

4   Start the engine. It may take a few moments for the fuel system to build up pressure, but the engine should start without a great deal of effort. **Note:** *If backfiring occurs through the carburetor or throttle body, recheck the valve timing and ignition timing.*

5   After the engine starts, it should be allowed to warm up to normal operating temperature. While the engine is warming up, make a thorough check for fuel, oil and coolant leaks.

6   Shut the engine off and recheck the engine oil and coolant levels.

7   Drive the vehicle to an area with minimum traffic, accelerate at full throttle from 30 to 50 mph, then allow the vehicle to slow to 30 mph with the throttle closed. Repeat the procedure 10 or 12 times. This will load the piston rings and cause them to seat properly against the cylinder walls., Check again for oil and coolant leaks.

8   Drive the vehicle gently for the first 500 miles (no sustained high speeds) and keep a constant check on the oil level. It is not unusual for an engine to use oil during the break-in period.

9   At approximately 500 to 600 miles, change the oil and filter.

10   For the next few hundred miles, drive the vehicle normally. Do not pamper it or abuse it.

11   After 2000 miles, change the oil and filter again and consider the engine broken in.

Chapter 3
Cooling, heating and air conditioning systems

3

Contents

Specifications

General

Coolant capacity	See Chapter 1
Drivebelt deflection	See Chapter 1
Radiator pressure cap rating	11 to 15 psi
Thermostat rating	See Chapter 1

Torque specifications

	Ft-lbs
Water pump pulley bolts	9
Thermostat housing bolts	9
Water pump attaching bolts	9

1   General information

Refer to illustrations 1.2 and 1.3

Engine cooling system

All vehicles covered by this manual employ a pressurized engine cooling system with thermostatically controlled coolant circulation. An impeller type water pump mounted on the drivebelt end of the block pumps coolant through the engine. The coolant flows around each cylinder and toward the rear of the engine. Cast-in coolant passages direct coolant around the intake and exhaust ports, near the spark plug areas and in close proximity to the exhaust valve guides.

A wax pellet type thermostat is located in a housing near the drivebelt end of the engine. During warm up, the closed thermostat prevents coolant from circulating through the radiator. As the engine nears normal operating temperature, the thermostat opens and allows hot coolant to travel through the radiator, where it's cooled before returning to the engine **(see illustration)**.

The cooling system is sealed by a pressure type radiator cap, which raises the boiling point of the coolant and increases the cooling efficiency of the radiator. If the system pressure exceeds the cap pressure relief value, the excess pressure in the system forces the spring-loaded valve inside the cap off its seat and allows the coolant to escape through the overflow tube into a coolant reservoir. When the system cools the excess coolant is automatically drawn from the reservoir back into the radiator **(see illustration)**.

The coolant reservoir does double duty as both the point at which fresh coolant is added to the cooling system to maintain the proper fluid level and as a holding tank for overheated coolant.

This type of cooling system is known as a closed design because coolant that escapes past the pressure cap is saved and reused.

Heating system

The heating system consists of a blower fan and heater core located in the heater box, the hoses connecting the heater core to the engine cooling system and the heater/air conditioning control head on the dashboard. Hot engine coolant is circulated through the heater core. When the heater mode is activated, a flap door opens to expose the heater box to the passenger compartment. A fan switch on the control head activates the blower motor, which forces air through the core, heating the air.

Air conditioning system

The air conditioning system consists of a condenser mounted in front of the radiator, an evaporator mounted adjacent to the heater core, a compressor mounted on the

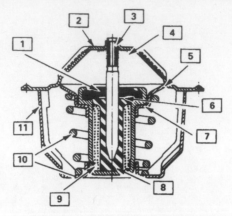

1.2 Pellet type thermostat - cutaway view

1	Flange seal	7	Valve
2	Flange	8	Rubber
3	Piston		diaphragm
4	Nut	9	Wax pellet
5	Valve seat	10	Coil spring
6	Teflon seal	11	Frame

engine, a filter-drier (accumulator) which contains a high pressure relief valve and the plumbing connecting all of the above components.

A blower fan forces the warmer air of the passenger compartment through the evaporator core (sort of a radiator-in-reverse), transferring the heat from the air to the refrigerant. The liquid refrigerant boils off into low pressure vapor, taking the heat with it when it leaves the evaporator.

2   Antifreeze - general information

Warning: *Do not allow antifreeze to come in contact with your skin or painted surfaces of the vehicle. Rinse off spills immediately with plenty of water. Antifreeze, if consumed, can be fatal to children and pets, so wipe up garage floor and drip pan coolant spills immediately. Keep antifreeze containers covered and repair leaks in your cooling system as soon as they are noticed.*

The cooling system should be filled with a water/ethylene glycol based antifreeze solution, which will prevent freezing down to at least -20 degrees F, or lower if local climate requires it. It also provides protection against corrosion and increases the coolant boiling point.

The cooling system should be drained, flushed and refilled at the specified intervals (see Chapter 1). Old or contaminated antifreeze solutions are likely to cause damage and encourage the formation of rust and scale in the system. Use distilled water with the antifreeze.

Before adding antifreeze, check all hose connections, because antifreeze tends to search out and leak through very minute openings. Engines don't normally consume coolant, so if the level goes down, find the cause and correct it.

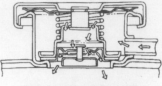

VACUUM RELIEF

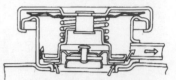

PRESSURE RELIEF

1.3 Pressure-type radiator cap

3.10a Remove the two bolts (arrows) that secure the thermostat housing cover to the thermostat housing - note that some models have an air cleaner support bracket between the bolts and the housing cover

The exact mixture of antifreeze-to-water which you should use depends on the relative weather conditions. The mixture should contain at least 50 percent antifreeze, but should never contain more than 70 percent antifreeze. Consult the mixture ratio chart on the antifreeze container before adding coolant. Hydrometers are available at most auto parts stores to test the coolant. Use antifreeze which meets the vehicle manufacturer's specifications.

3   Thermostat - check and replacement

Warning: *Do not remove the radiator cap, drain the coolant or replace the thermostat until the engine has cooled completely.*

Check

1   Before assuming the thermostat is to blame for a cooling system problem, check the coolant level, drivebelt tension (Chapter 1) and temperature gauge (or light) operation.

2   If the engine seems to be taking a long

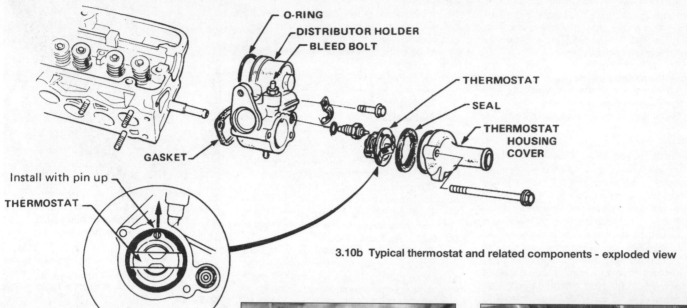

Install with pin up

THERMOSTAT

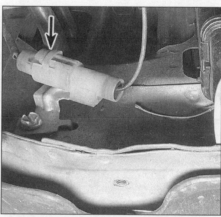

3.10b Typical thermostat and related components - exploded view

time to warm up (based on heater output or temperature gauge operation), the thermostat is probably stuck open. Replace the thermostat with a new one.

3 If the engine runs hot, use your hand to check the temperature of the upper radiator hose. If the hose isn't hot, but the engine is, the thermostat is probably stuck closed, preventing the coolant inside the engine from escaping to the radiator. Replace the thermostat. **Caution:** *Don't drive the vehicle without a thermostat. The computer may stay in open loop and emissions and fuel economy will suffer.*

4 If the upper radiator hose is hot, it means that the coolant is flowing and the thermostat is open. Consult the Troubleshooting Section at the front of this manual for cooling system diagnosis.

Replacement

Refer to illustrations 3.10a, 3.10b and 3.13

5 Disconnect the negative battery cable from the battery.

6 Drain the cooling system (see Chapter 1). If the coolant is relatively new or in good condition (see Chapter 1), save it and reuse it.

7 Follow the upper radiator hose to the engine to locate the thermostat housing.

8 Compress the hose clamp with pliers, then slide the clamp away from the thermostat housing. Detach the hose from the fitting. If it's stuck, grasp it near the end with a pair of Channelock pliers and twist it to break the seal, then pull it off. If the hose is old or deteriorated, cut it off and install a new one.

9 If the outer surface of the large fitting that mates with the hose is deteriorated (corroded, pitted, etc.) it may be damaged further by hose removal. If it is, the thermostat housing cover will have to be replaced.

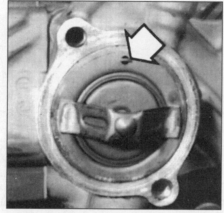

3.13 Install the thermostat with the air bleed (arrow) at the top and the spring-side toward the engine

10 Remove the bolts and detach the housing cover **(see illustrations)**. If the cover is stuck, tap it with a soft-face hammer to jar it loose. Be prepared for some coolant to spill as the gasket seal is broken.

11 Note how it's installed (which end is facing out), then remove the thermostat.

12 Stuff a rag into the engine opening, then remove all traces of old gasket material and sealant from the housing and cover with a gasket scraper. Remove the rag from the opening and clean the gasket mating surfaces with lacquer thinner or acetone.

13 Install the new thermostat in the housing. Make sure the correct end faces out - the spring end is normally directed into the engine **(see illustration)**. Make sure the air bleed is at the top.

14 Apply a thin, uniform layer of RTV sealant to both sides of the new seal and position it on the housing.

15 Install the cover and bolts. Tighten the bolts to the specified torque.

16 Reattach the hose to the fitting. Use a new hose clamp and tighten it securely.

4.3 The fan motor electrical connector is located adjacent to the fan motor - push down on the lock tab (arrow) and unplug it

17 Refill the cooling system (Chapter 1).

18 Start the engine and allow it to reach normal operating temperature, then check for leaks and proper thermostat operation (as described in Steps 2 through 4).

4 Engine cooling fan - check and replacement

Warning: *To avoid possible injury or damage, DO NOT operate the engine with a damaged fan. Do not attempt to repair fan blades - replace a damaged fan with a new one.*

Removal and installation

Refer to illustrations 4.3, 4.4a, 4.4b and 4.4c

1 Disconnect the negative battery cable from the battery.

2 Remove the fan wire harness from the clips.

3 Push down on the connector lock tab and unplug the fan wire harness **(see illustration)**.

4   Remove the throttle body air duct (if equipped) for access, then unbolt the fan bracket and shroud assembly **(see illustrations)**. Carefully lift the fan shroud assembly out of the engine compartment.

5   To detach the fan from the motor, remove the motor shaft clip.

6   To remove the bracket from the fan motor, remove the mounting nuts.

7   Installation is the reverse of removal.

Check

Refer to illustration 4.9

8   To test the motor, unplug the electrical connector at the motor and use jumper wires to connect the fan directly to the battery. If the fan still doesn't work, replace the motor.

9   If the motor tested OK, the fault lies in the coolant temperature switch or the wiring which connects the components. To test the switch, remove the connector plug **(see illustration)** and connect a jumper wire between the terminals in the plug. With the ignition on (but the engine off for safety) the fan should

come on.

10   If the fan does not come on, carefully check all wiring and connections. If no obvious problems are found, further diagnosis should be done by a dealer service department or repair shop.

---

5   Radiator - removal and installation

Refer to illustration 5.6, 5.8a, 5.8b and 5.13
Warning: *Wait until the engine is completely cool before beginning this procedure.*

1   Disconnect the negative battery cable from the battery.

2   Drain the cooling system (see Chapter 1). If the coolant is relatively new or in good condition, save it and reuse it.

3   Compress the hose clamps with pliers and slide them away from the radiator, then detach the radiator hoses from the fittings. If they're stuck, grasp each hose near the end with a pair of Channelock pliers and twist it to

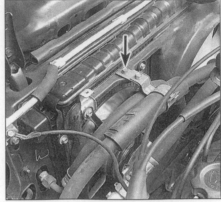

4.4a Remove the bolt (arrow) that secures the hose bracket (if equipped) to the fan shroud

break the seal, then pull it off - be careful not to distort the radiator fittings! If the hoses are old or deteriorated, cut them off and install new ones.

4.4b Working from below, remove the lower fan mounting bolts (arrows)

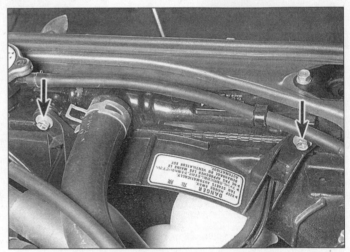

4.4c Remove the upper fan mounting bolts (arrows)

4.9 To test the coolant temperature switch, remove the connector plug (arrow) and use a jumper wire to connect the two terminals inside the connector plug - to remove the switch, drain the cooling system and unscrew the switch

5.6 Working from below, loosen the hose clamps (arrows) and separate the cooler line hoses from the radiator fittings

5.8a On models with front-mounted hood hinges, remove the radiator mounting bracket bolts (arrows) on each side of the radiator

5.8b On models with rear-mounted hood hinges, remove the bolts (arrows) from each side of the panel above the radiator

and repair leaks in your cooling system as soon as they are noticed.

1   The coolant reservoir is mounted adjacent to the radiator at the right front corner of the engine compartment.
2   Follow the overflow hose from the radiator neck to the top of the coolant reservoir. Remove the cap with the hose still attached **(see illustration)**. Detach the filler hose, if equipped **(see illustration)**.
3   The reservoir fits into a groove in the body. Lift it straight up to remove it.
4   Temporarily pour the coolant into a clean container. Wash out and inspect the reservoir for cracks and other damage. Replace it if it is damaged.
5   Installation is the reverse of removal. Refill the coolant reservoir. If the original coolant is in good condition (see Chapter 1), it can be reused.

4   Disconnect the reservoir hose from the radiator filler neck.
5   Remove the bolts that attach the fan bracket and shroud assembly to the radiator and lean the shroud toward the engine (see Section 4).
6   If the vehicle is equipped with an automatic transaxle, disconnect the cooler lines from the radiator **(see illustration)**. Use a drip pan to catch spilled fluid.
7   Plug the lines and fittings.
8   Remove the radiator mounting bolts **(see illustration)**.
9   Carefully lift out the radiator. Don't spill coolant on the vehicle or scratch the paint.
10   With the radiator removed, it can be inspected for leaks and damage. If it needs repair, have a radiator shop or dealer service department perform the work as special techniques are required.
11   Bugs and dirt can be removed from the radiator with compressed air and a soft brush. Don't bend the cooling fins as this is done.
12   Check the radiator mounts for deterioration and make sure there's nothing in them when the radiator is installed.

13   Installation is the reverse of the removal procedure. Be sure the rubber mounts are in place **(see illustration)**.
14   After installation, fill the cooling system with the proper mixture of antifreeze and water. Refer to Chapter 1 if necessary.
15   Start the engine and check for leaks. Allow the engine to reach normal operating temperature, indicated by the upper radiator hose becoming hot. Recheck the coolant level and add more if required.
16   If you're working on an automatic transaxle equipped vehicle, check and add fluid as needed.

6   Coolant reservoir - removal and installation

Refer to illustrations 6.2a and 6.2b
Warning: *Do not allow antifreeze to come in contact with your skin or painted surfaces of the vehicle. Rinse off spills immediately with plenty of water. Antifreeze, if consumed, can be fatal to children and pets, so wipe up garage floor and drip pan coolant spills immediately. Keep antifreeze containers covered*

7   Water pump - check

1   A failure in the water pump can cause serious engine damage due to overheating.
2   There are three ways to check the operation of the water pump while it's installed on the engine. If the pump is defective, it should be replaced with a new or rebuilt unit.
3   With the engine running at normal operating temperature, squeeze the upper radiator hose. If the water pump is working properly, a pressure surge should be felt as the hose is released. **Warning:** *Keep your hands away from the fan blades!*
4   Water pumps are equipped with weep or vent holes. If a failure occurs in the pump seal, coolant will leak from the hole. In most cases you'll need a flashlight and small mirror to find the hole on the water pump from underneath to check for leaks.
5   If the water pump shaft bearings fail there may be a howling sound at the front of the engine while it's running. Shaft wear can be felt if the water pump pulley is rocked up and down. Don't mistake drivebelt slippage, which causes a squealing sound, for water pump bearing failure.

3

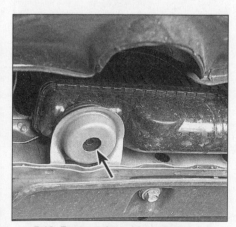

5.13 Be sure the rubber mount on each side is properly seated in the bracket (arrow)

6.2a Remove the cap with hose attached (arrow)

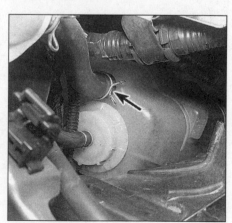

6.2b Compress the hose clamp with pliers, then pull off the filler hose (arrow)

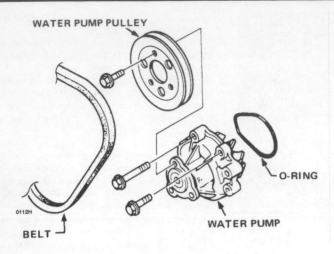

8.5 Water pump components - exploded view

8.10 Position the new O-ring in the water pump groove

8   Water pump - replacement

Refer to illustrations 8.5 and 8.10

Warning: *Wait until the engine is completely cool before beginning this procedure.*

1   Disconnect the negative battery cable from the battery.

2   Drain the cooling system (see Chapter 1). If the coolant is relatively new or in good condition, save it and reuse it.

3   Remove the drivebelt (see Chapter 1) and the pulley at the end of the water pump shaft.

4   Remove any accessory brackets from the water pump.

5   Remove the bolts and detach the water pump from the engine **(see illustration)**. Note the locations of the various lengths and different types of bolts as they're removed to ensure correct installation.

6   Clean the bolt threads and the threaded holes in the engine to remove corrosion and sealant.

7   Compare the new pump to the old one to make sure they're identical.

8   Remove all traces of old gasket sealer from the engine.

9   Clean the engine and new water pump mating surfaces with lacquer thinner or acetone.

10   Apply a thin layer of RTV sealant to the O-ring groove in the new pump, then carefully install a new O-ring in the pump **(see illustration)**.

11   Carefully attach the pump to the engine.

12   Install the bolts finger tight (if they also hold an accessory bracket in place, be sure to reposition the bracket at this time). Tighten them to the specified torque in 1/4-turn increments. Don't overtighten them or the pump may be distorted.

13   Reinstall all parts removed for access to the pump.

14   Refill and bleed the cooling system and check the drivebelt tension (see Chapter 1). Run the engine and check for leaks.

9   Coolant temperature sending unit - check and replacement

Refer to illustrations 9.1a and 9.1b

Warning: *Wait until the engine is completely cool before beginning this procedure.*

1   The coolant temperature indicator system is composed of a temperature gauge mounted in the instrument panel and a coolant temperature sending unit mounted on the engine **(see illustrations)**. Some vehicles have more than one sending unit, but only one is used for the indicator system.

Warning: *This vehicle is equipped with an electric cooling fan- stay clear of the fan blades, which can come on at any time.*

2   If an overheating indication occurs, check the coolant level in the system and then make sure the wiring between the gauge and the sending unit is secure and all fuses are intact.

3   Test the circuit by grounding the wire to the sending unit while the ignition is on

9.1a On carbureted models, the coolant temperature sending unit is mounted in the under side of the intake manifold (view is from below the vehicle)

9.1b On fuel-injected models, the coolant temperature sending unit is mounted in the thermostat housing (arrow)

10.4a To remove the blower unit, detach the flexible tube and wiring connector (arrows), . . .

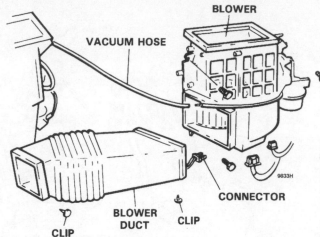

VACUUM HOSE

BLOWER

CONNECTOR

BLOWER DUCT

CLIP

CLIP

9833H

10.4b . . . remove the clips and disconnect the blower duct and vacuum hose, then remove the blower unit retaining screws

(engine not running for safety). If the gauge deflects full scale, replace the sending unit.

4   If the sending unit must be replaced, simply unscrew it from the engine and install the replacement. Use sealant on the threads.

Make sure the engine is cool before removing the defective sending unit. There will be some coolant loss as the unit is removed, so be prepared to catch it. Check the level after the replacement has been installed.

10 Blower unit - removal and installation

Refer to illustrations 10.4a, 10.4b and 10.5

1   Disconnect the negative cable from the battery.

2   Remove the glove compartment and right lower dash panel (see Chapter 11).

3   The blower unit is located in the passenger compartment above the right front footwell.

4   Disconnect the flexible tube and wiring connector from the blower unit, then remove blower duct, vacuum hose and the blower unit retaining screws **(see illustrations)**. Lower the unit from under the dash.

5   If the motor is being replaced, transfer the fan to the new motor prior to installation **(see illustration)**.

6   Installation is the reverse of removal. Check for proper operation.

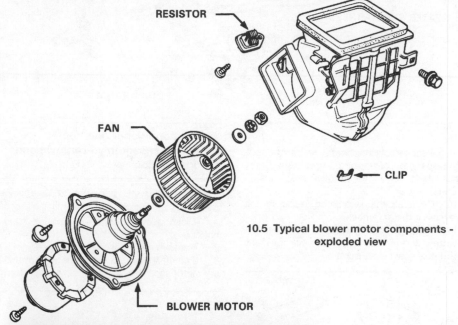

RESISTOR

FAN

BLOWER MOTOR

CLIP

10.5 Typical blower motor components - exploded view

11 Heater core - removal and installation

Refer to illustrations 11.3 and 11.6

1   Disconnect the negative cable from the battery.

2   Drain the cooling system (see Chapter 1).

3   Working in the engine compartment, disconnect the heater hoses from the heater control valve **(see illustration)**.

4   Remove the instrument panel and the center console (see Chapter 11).

5   Remove the heater controls (see Section 12) and disconnect the heater hoses under the dash, where they connect to the heater core.

6   Label and detach the air ducts, wiring and controls still attached to the heating unit **(see illustration)**.

7   Unbolt the heating unit and detach it from the vehicle.

8   Remove the screws and clips and separate the two halves of the housing. Take out the old heater core and install the new unit.

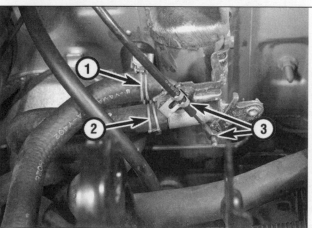

11.3 Loosen the hose clamps (arrows) and disconnect the heater hoses from the heater control valve - when removing the air conditioning and heater control assembly, unsnap the heater control valve cable clamp and disengage the cable from the arm (arrow)

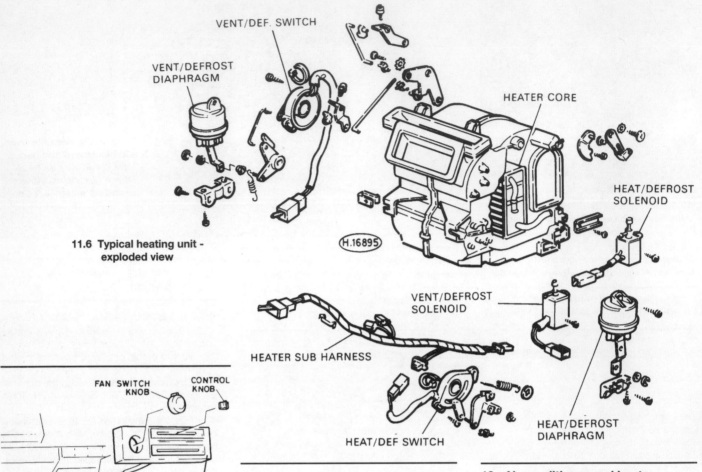

11.6 Typical heating unit - exploded view

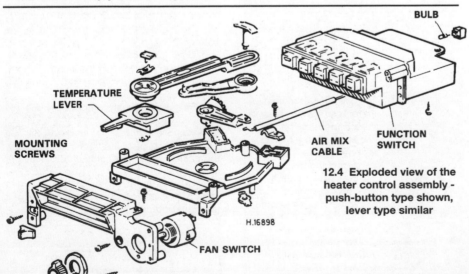

12.3 Pull off the knobs, then use a small screwdriver to pry off the faceplate

9   Reassemble the heater unit and check the operation of the air control flaps. If any parts bind, correct the problem before installation.

10   Reinstall the remaining parts in the reverse order of removal.

11   Refill the cooling system, reconnect the battery and run the engine. Check for leaks and proper system operation.

12   Air conditioner and heater control assembly - removal and installation

Refer to illustrations 12.3, 12.4, 12.5a, 12.5b and 12.8

1   Disconnect the negative cable from the battery.

2   Remove the radio (see Chapter 12).

3   Pull off the knobs (see illustration) and pry off the faceplate with a small screwdriver.

12.4 Exploded view of the heater control assembly - push-button type shown, lever type similar

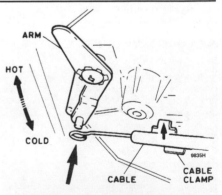

12.5a The air-mix cable (if equipped) is usually mounted on the left side of the heater housing - unsnap the cable from the clamp and disengage the end from the arm

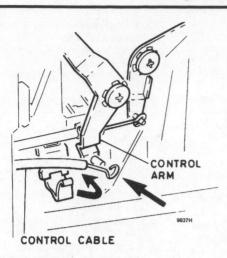

12.5b The heater function cable (if equipped) is usually mounted on the right side of the heater housing - it's disconnected the same way as the air-mix cable

12.8 Move the levers right and left and check for stiffness and binding through the full range of travel

4   Remove the mounting screws located on the front of the control assembly **(see illustration)**.

5   Pull the control out slightly. On some models it will be necessary to disconnect the cables at the operating ends before this is possible (see the accompanying illustrations and illustration 11.3). Before disconnecting the cables, mark the relationship of each cable to its cable clamp with white paint. This will ensure installation in the same position.

6   Detach the cables and wiring from the control assembly and lift the assembly from the dash.

7   To install the unit, reverse the above procedure.

8   To adjust the cables, align the marks you made earlier. Fasten the clips and check for stiffness or binding through the full range of operation **(see illustration)**.

9   Run the engine and check for proper functioning of the heater (and air conditioning, if equipped).

13   Air conditioning and heating system - check and maintenance

Air conditioning system

Refer to illustrations 13.1, 13.5, 13.6 and 13.9

Warning: *The air conditioning system is under high pressure. Do not loosen any hose fittings or remove any components until after the system has been discharged by a dealer service department or an automotive air conditioning shop. Always wear eye protection when adding refrigerant or disconnecting air conditioning system fittings.*

1   The following maintenance checks should be performed on a regular basis to ensure that the air conditioner continues to operate at peak efficiency.

a) *Inspect the condition of the compressor drivebelt. If it is worn or deteriorated, replace it (see Chapter 1).*

b) *Check the drivebelt tension and, if necessary, adjust it (see Chapter 1).*

c) *Inspect the system hoses. Look for cracks, bubbles, hardening and deterioration. Inspect the hoses and all fittings for oil bubbles or seepage. If there is any evidence of wear, damage or leakage, replace the hose(s).*

d) *Inspect the condenser fins for leaves, bugs and any other foreign material that may have embedded itself in the fins. Use a "fin comb" or compressed air to remove debris from the condenser.*

e) *Make sure the system has the correct refrigerant charge.*

f) *If you hear water sloshing around in the dash area or have water dripping on the carpet, slip the evaporator housing condensation drain tube off **(see illustration)** and insert a piece of wire into both the evaporator housing and the tube to clear any blockage.*

2   It's a good idea to operate the system for about ten minutes at least once a month.

This is particularly important during the winter months because long term non-use can cause hardening, and subsequent failure, of the seals. Note that running the defroster operates the system.

3   Because of the complexity of the air conditioning system and the special equipment necessary to service it, in-depth troubleshooting and repairs are beyond the scope of this manual. However, simple component replacement procedures are provided in this Chapter.

4   The most common cause of poor cooling is simply a low system refrigerant charge. If a noticeable drop in system cooling ability occurs, one on the following quick checks will help you determine whether the refrigerant level is low.

5   With the air conditioning operating, inspect the sight glass (see the accompanying illustration or illustration 14.3). If the refrigerant looks foamy, it's low. Charge the system (see below).

13.1 The evaporator housing condensation drain tube (arrow) is located under the dash near the center of the vehicle

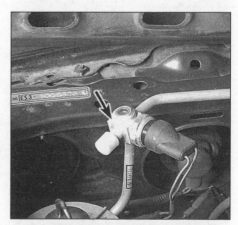

13.5 The sight glass on most models (arrow) is located in the left front corner of the engine compartment - on some models it's mounted in the top of the receiver-drier (see illustration 14.3)

13.6 Always connect the charging kit to the low pressure line - it's the larger diameter of the two lines

Adding refrigerant

6   Buy an automotive "charging kit" at an automotive parts store. A charging kit includes a 14-ounce can of refrigerant, a can tap valve and a short section of hose which can be attached between the tap valve and the system low side service valve. **Warning:** *Do not connect the "high side" of the system!* **(see illustration)**. Because one can of refrigerant may not be sufficient to bring the system charge up to its proper level, it's a good idea to buy a few additional cans. Make sure the first can you add to the system contains red refrigerant dye. If the system is leaking, the red dye will leak out with the refrigerant and help you pinpoint the location of the leak. **Warning:** *Wear eye protection while performing this Step.*

7   Hook up the charging kit in accordance with the manufacturer's instructions.

8   Warm up the engine and operate the system.

9   Place a thermometer in the center dashboard vent **(see illustration)** and add refrigerant until the indicated temperature is around 40 to 45 degrees F.

Heating systems

Refer to illustration 13.11

10   If the air coming out of the heater vents isn't hot, the problem could stem from any of the following causes:

a)   *The thermostat is stuck open, preventing the engine coolant from warming up enough to carry heat to the heater core. Replace the thermostat (see Section 3).*

b)   *A heater hose is blocked, preventing the flow of coolant through the heater core. Feel both heater hoses at the firewall. They should be hot. If one of them is cold, there is an obstruction in one of the hoses or in the heater core, or the heater control valve is shut. Detach the hoses and back flush the heater core with a water hose. If the heater core is clear but circulation is impeded, remove the two hoses and flush them out with a water hose.*

c)   *If flushing fails to remove the blockage from the heater core, the core must be replaced.*

11   If the blower motor speed does not correspond to the setting selected on the blower switch, the problem could be a bad fuse, circuit, switch, blower motor resistor or motor.

a)   *Before checking for an inoperative blower motor or circuit, always check the fuse first.*

b)   *Using a test light or voltmeter, check the voltage at the motor.*

c)   *Pull the heating/air conditioning control assembly (see Section 12) far enough from the dash to verify - with a test light or voltmeter- that current is reaching the blower switch on the control assembly. If the switch is not getting current, troubleshoot the circuit between the battery and the switch (see wiring diagrams at the end of this manual).*

d)   *Locate the blower motor resistor below the glove box* **(see illustration)**. *Check the resistor to make sure that it is getting current from the blower switch.*

1) *If the resistor is not getting current, check the wire.*
2) *If the wire is good, replace the switch (see Section 12).*

e)   *Using a test light or voltmeter, verify that the blower motor is getting current. If the blower motor is not getting current, replace the resistor.*

12   If there isn't any air coming out of the vents:

a)   *Turn the ignition ON and activate the fan control. Place your ear at the heating/air conditioning register (vent) and listen. Most motors are audible. Can you hear the motor running?*

b)   *If you can't (and have already verified that the blower switch and the blower motor resistor are good), the blower motor itself is probably bad (see Section 10).* **Note:** *You can determine the motor's condition by hooking up a fused jumper wire directly between battery voltage and the blower motor.*

13   If the carpet under the heater core is damp, or if antifreeze vapor or steam is coming through the vents, the heater core is leaking. Remove it (see Section 11) and install a new unit (most radiator shops will not repair a leaking heater core).

14   Air conditioning receiver/drier - removal and installation

Refer to illustrations 14.3 and 14.4
Warning: *For this operation, the system must be discharged by an air conditioning technician. Do not attempt to do this by yourself. The refrigerant is under high pressure and can cause serious injury and respiratory irritation.*

1   Have the refrigerant discharged by an air conditioning technician.

2   Disconnect the battery, (see Chapter 5) and detach the left front fender liner.

3   Disconnect the refrigerant lines **(see illustration)** from the receiver/drier and cap

13.9 Place a thermometer in the center dash vent to monitor the temperature of the air entering the passenger compartment

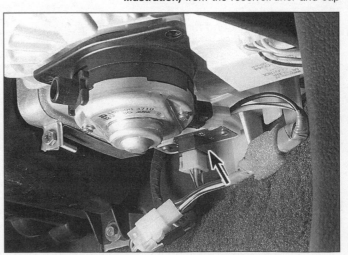

13.11 The blower resistor (arrow) is located under the right side of the dash behind the blower motor

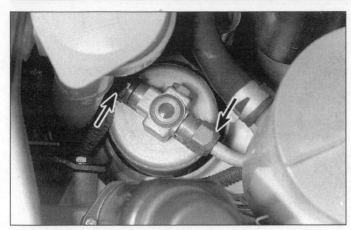

14.3 Using a flare-nut wrench, disconnect the refrigerant lines (arrows) - note that this receiver/drier has the sight glass mounted in the top

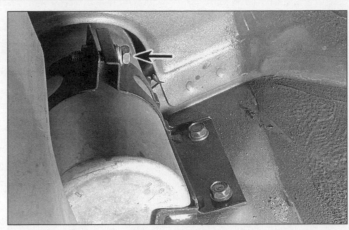

14.4 Working inside the left front wheel housing, loosen the pinch bolt (arrow), then, from the engine compartment, lift the unit out of the mounting bracket

the open fittings to prevent dirt and moisture entry.

4   Loosen the pinch bolt and slip the receiver/drier out of the bracket **(see illustration)**.

5   Installation is the reverse of removal.

6   Have the system evacuated, charged and leak tested by the shop that discharged it. If the receiver was replaced, have them add about 20 cc (0.7 oz.) refrigeration oil.

15   Air conditioning compressor - removal and installation

Refer to illustration 15.7

Warning: *The air conditioning system is under high pressure. DO NOT disassemble any part of the system (hoses, compressor, line fittings, etc.) until after the system has been depressurized by a dealer service department or service station.*

1   Have the A/C system discharged (see **Warning** above).

2   Disconnect the negative battery cable from the battery and raise the front of the vehicle, supporting it securely on jackstands.

3   Working from below the left front corner of the engine compartment, disconnect the compressor clutch wiring harness.

4   Remove the drivebelt (see Chapter 1).

5   Disconnect the refrigerant lines from the compressor. Plug the open fittings to prevent entry of dirt and moisture.

6   Remove the power steering pump (see Chapter 10) and any other components that may obstruct access to the compressor.

7   Unbolt the compressor from the mounting brackets **(see illustration)** and remove it from the vehicle.

8   If a new compressor is being installed, follow the directions with the compressor regarding the draining of excess oil prior to installation.

9   The clutch may have to be transferred from the original to the new compressor.

10   Installation is the reverse of removal. Replace all O-rings with new ones specifi-

cally made for A/C system use and lubricate them with refrigerant oil.

11   Have the system evacuated, recharged and leak tested by the shop that discharged it.

16   Air conditioning condenser - removal and installation

Refer to illustrations 16.4a, 16.4b, 16.5a and 16.5b

Warning: *For this operation, the system must be discharged by an air conditioning technician. Do not attempt to do this by yourself. The refrigerant is under high pressure and can cause serious injury and respiratory irritation.*

1   Have the refrigerant discharged by an air conditioning technician.

2   Remove the radiator as described in Section 5.

3   Disconnect the negative cable from the battery.

4   Remove the grille (and hood on models with front-mounted hood hinges) for access (see Chapter 11) and disconnect the lower and upper fittings **(see illustrations)**. Cap the

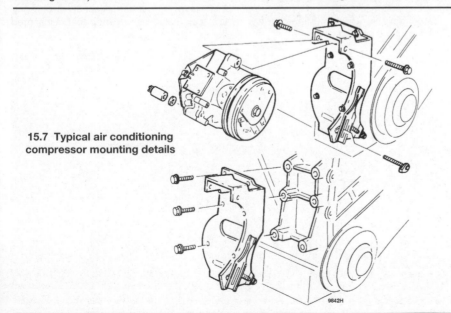

15.7 Typical air conditioning compressor mounting details

9842H

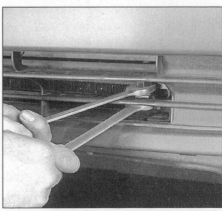

16.4a The lower fitting can be reached below the bumper - when loosening it, use two wrenches to avoid twisting the tube

3

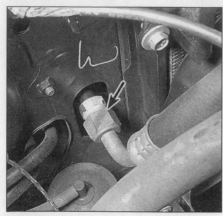

16.4b The upper fitting (arrow) can be reached from the engine compartment, adjacent to the left side of the radiator - again, use two wrenches to loosen it

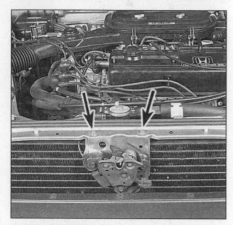

16.5b To detach the condenser on rear-hinged hoods, remove the bolts (arrows) and detach the hood latch - on front-hinged hoods, remove the hood

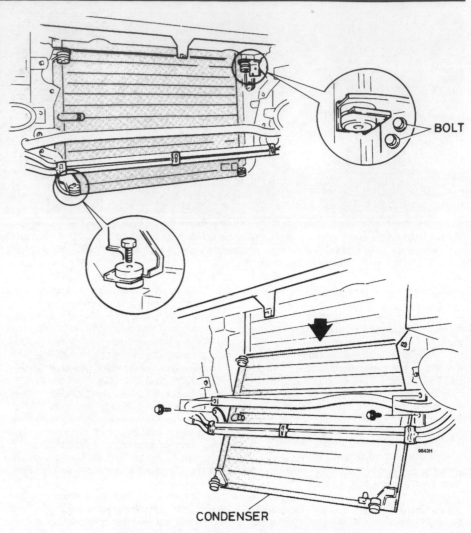

16.5a Typical condenser mounting details

open fittings immediately to keep moisture and dirt out of the system.

5   Remove the hood latch (if necessary) and condenser mounting bolts **(see illustrations)** and lift the condenser out.

6   Install the condenser, brackets and bolts, making sure the rubber cushions fit on the mounting points properly.

7   Reconnect the refrigerant lines, using new O-rings where needed.

8   Reinstall the remaining parts in the reverse order of removal.

9   Have the system evacuated, charged and leak tested by the shop that discharged it.

Chapter 4
Fuel and exhaust systems

Contents

Specifications

Torque specifications

	Ft-lbs
Fuel injection service bolt	9
Carburetor mounting nuts	15
Throttle body mounting nuts	16
Fuel rail mounting nuts	9

1   General information

Some vehicles covered by this manual are equipped with a feedback carburetor. Others are equipped with an electronic port fuel injection system. In 1984, all vehicles were equipped with a three-barrel feedback carburetor. In 1985, some models were again equipped with the three-barrel carburetor, while other models were equipped with an optional electronic port fuel injection system. This system was offered from 1985 on. In 1986, the three-barrel carburetor was replaced by a two-barrel unit.

All models are equipped with an electric fuel pump. On all 1984 and 1985 models, the pump is located in front of the left rear wheel; on 1986 and later models, it's located inside the fuel tank.

The exhaust system consists of a header pipe, a catalytic converter, an exhaust pipe and a muffler. Each of these components is replaceable. For further information regarding the catalytic converter, refer to Chapter 6.

2   Fuel pressure relief (fuel-injected models)

Refer to illustration 2.2
Warning: *Gasoline is extremely flammable, so take extra precautions when working on any part of the fuel system. Don't smoke or allow open flames or bare light bulbs in or near the work area. And don't work in a garage if a natural gas appliance such as a water heater or clothes dryer is present.*
1   Detach the cable from the negative battery terminal.
2   You'll need two wrenches for this procedure: One to loosen the service bolt at the top of the fuel filter and another to hold the special banjo bolt into which the service bolt is installed **(see illustration)**.

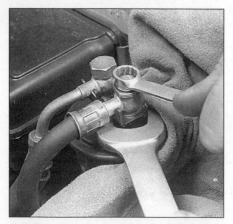

2.2 To relieve the fuel pressure on a fuel-injected vehicle, you'll need one wrench to loosen the service bolt on top of the fuel filter and another wrench to hold the special banjo bolt into which the service bolt is installed

3   Place a shop rag over the service bolt.
4   While holding the special banjo bolt, slowly loosen the service bolt one complete turn.
5   Always replace the washer between the service bolt and the special banjo bolt whenever the service bolt is loosened to relieve fuel pressure. Tighten the service bolt to the specified torque.

3   Fuel pump/fuel pressure - check

Warning: *Gasoline is extremely flammable, so take extra precautions when you work on any part of the fuel system. Don't smoke or allow open flames or bare light bulbs in or near the work area. And don't work in a garage if a natural gas appliance such as a water heater or clothes dryer is present.*

Carburetor-equipped vehicles
Fuel pump operational check
Note: *On 1984 and 1985 models, the fuel pump is located underneath the vehicle, immediately ahead of the left rear wheel. On 1986 and later models, its located inside the fuel tank.*
1   Set the parking brake and have an assistant turn the ignition switch to the On position while you listen at the fuel pump. You should hear a whirring sound, lasting for a couple of seconds. Start the engine. The whirring sound should now be continuous (although harder to hear with the engine running).
2   If there is no whirring sound, either the fuel pump or the fuel cutoff relay circuit is defective. Check the cut-off relay circuit first (proceed to Step 8).

Fuel pressure check
Refer to illustration 3.5
3   If you suspect low fuel pressure, first check for a leaking, clogged or otherwise damaged fuel line or a clogged fuel filter (see Chapter 1).
4   Remove the fuel cut-off relay from the fuse box (see Chapter 12).
5   Bridge the 1st terminal to the 2nd terminal on the fuse box where the fuel cut-off relay plugs in **(see illustration)**.
6   Detach the fuel line at the fuel filter (see Chapter 1) and attach a pressure gauge in its place.
7   Turn the ignition switch to the On position until pressure stabilizes, then turn the key off. The pressure should be 2.4 to 3.4 psi. If it's not, replace the fuel pump and recheck the pressure.

Fuel pump cut-off relay check
8   The fuel pump cut-off relay switches the fuel pump on any time ignition pulsations are present at the negative terminal of the ignition coil and cuts off electrical current to the pump when the engine stops running. The relay allows fuel to flow only when the ignition switch is in the On position or the engine is running.

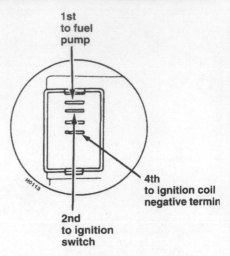

3.5 Here's how the fuel cut-off relay terminals in the fuse box are numbered - note that some models have terminals that are laid out horizontally; in that case, the terminals are numbered from left to right instead of from top to bottom (as shown here)

9   With the ignition switch off, remove the fuel cut-off relay from the fuse panel (see Chapter 12).
10   Touch the positive probe of a voltmeter to the 2nd terminal in the fuse panel **(see illustration 3.5)** and the negative probe to ground. Turn the ignition switch to On. The voltmeter should indicate battery voltage.
11   If the meter indicates no voltage:
a)   *Make sure you're touching the probe to the 2nd terminal.*
b)   *Check the fuse (see Chapter 12)*
c)   *Check for continuity between the 2nd terminal and the ignition switch.*

12   If voltage is present, touch the positive probe of the voltmeter to the 4th terminal in the fuse panel and touch the negative probe to ground. Turn the ignition switch to On. The voltmeter should indicate battery voltage.
13   If the meter indicates no voltage, check the blue wire circuit between the fuse panel 4th terminal and the ignition coil negative terminal. Repair the circuit as necessary.
14   If voltage is present, bridge the 1st and 2nd terminals **(see illustration 3.5)** together with a jumper wire, then turn the ignition switch to On. The fuel pump should come on.
15   If battery voltage was available in steps 10 and 12, but the fuel pump didn't come on, bridge the 1st and 2nd terminals as described in the previous step. Detach the wires from the fuel pump (see Section 4) and attach the positive probe of the voltmeter to the black and yellow wire and the negative probe to the black wire. Turn the ignition switch to On and verify there is voltage present.

a)   *If there is no voltage present, check for continuity between the yellow wire and the 2nd terminal and between the black wire and ground.*
b)   *If voltage is present, replace the relay.*

3.17 Remove the service bolt from the top of the fuel filter and attach a fuel pressure gauge

Fuel-injected vehicles

Pressure check

Refer to illustration 3.17

16　Relieve the system fuel pressure (see Section 2).

17　Remove the service bolt from the top of the fuel filter and attach a fuel pressure gauge **(see illustration)**.

18　Start the engine. Detach the vacuum hose from the pressure regulator (see Section 13). With the engine idling, measure the fuel pressure. It should be 33 to 39 psi.

19　If the fuel pressure is not within specification, check the following:

　a) *If the pressure is higher than specified, check for a faulty regulator (see Section 13) or a pinched or clogged fuel return hose or pipe.*

　b) *If the pressure is lower than specified:*
　　1) *Inspect the fuel filter - make sure it's not clogged.*
　　2) *Look for a pinched or clogged fuel hose between the fuel tank and the fuel pump.*

　　3) *Check the pressure regulator for a malfunction (see Section 13).*
　　4) *Look for leaks in the fuel line.*
　　5) *Look for a pinched, broken or disconnected regulator vacuum hose.*

20　If there are no problems with any of the above-listed components, check the fuel pump (see below).

Fuel pump check

21　If you suspect a problem with the fuel pump, verify the pump actually runs: Have an assistant turn the ignition switch to On - you should hear a brief whirring noise as the pump comes on and pressurizes the system. Have the assistant start the engine. This time you should hear a constant whirring sound from the pump (but it's more difficult to hear with the engine running).

22　If the pump does not come on (makes no sound), proceed to the next step.

23　Jack up the rear of the vehicle and place it securely on jackstands.

24　Remove the left rear wheel.

25　Remove the fuel pump cover (see Section 4) and detach the black and black/yellow wires (make sure the ignition switch is turned off before disconnecting the wires).

26　Touch the positive probe of a voltmeter to the black/yellow wire and the negative probe to the black wire, then turn on the ignition switch and verify there is voltage available.

27　If voltage is available, replace the fuel pump (see Section 4).

28　If no voltage is available, check the main relay (see below).

Main relay check

Refer to illustration 3.29

29　To test the main relay, first remove it from its location next to the under-dash fuse panel **(see illustration)**.

30　Using a pair of jumper wires, connect

the battery positive terminal to the No. 4 relay terminal and the battery negative terminal to the No. 8 terminal, then check for continuity between the No. 5 and No. 7 terminals. If there's no continuity, replace the relay.

31　Connect the battery positive terminal to the No. 5 relay terminal and the battery negative terminal to the No. 2 terminal and verify there's continuity between the No. 1 and No. 3 terminals. If there isn't, replace the relay.

32　Connect the battery positive terminal to the No. 3 relay terminal and the negative battery terminal to the No. 8 terminal. Verify there's continuity between the No. 5 and No. 7 terminals. If there is no continuity, replace the relay.

4　Fuel pump - removal and installation

Warning: *Gasoline is extremely flammable, so take extra precautions when working on any part of the fuel system. Don't smoke or allow open flames or bare light bulbs in or near the work area. And don't work in a garage if a natural gas appliance such as a water heater or clothes dryer is present.*

1984 and 1985 vehicles

Refer to illustrations 4.5a, 4.5b, 4.6 and 4.9

1　Detach the cable from the negative battery terminal.

2　If the vehicle is fuel-injected, relieve the fuel pressure (see Section 2).

3　Jack up the rear of the vehicle and place it securely on jackstands.

4　Remove the left rear wheel (see Chapter 1).

5　Remove the fuel pump shield retaining bolts and detach the shield **(see illustrations)**.

4

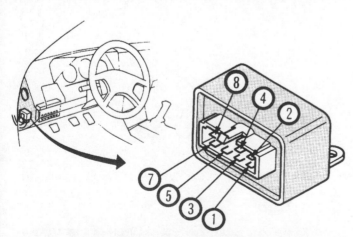

3.29 The main relay is located under the dash near the fuse box - refer to the terminal number when testing the relay

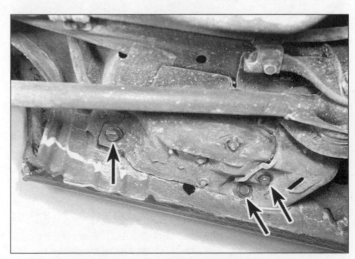

4.5a On an externally mounted fuel pump, remove the bolts (arrows) and detach the shield to gain access to the pump (carburetor type pump shown)

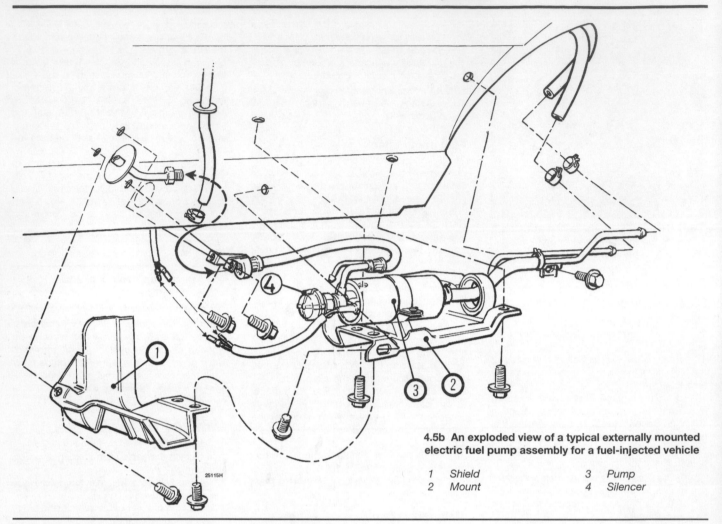

4.5b An exploded view of a typical externally mounted electric fuel pump assembly for a fuel-injected vehicle

1   Shield   *3   Pump*
2   Mount   *4   Silencer*

6   Using a pair of small clamps, pinch off the fuel lines **(see illustration)**.
7   Detach the fuel lines and electrical leads from the fuel pump.
8   Unbolt the pump from its mounting bracket and remove it.
9   Installation is the reverse of removal. If the vehicle is fuel injected, be sure to replace the crush washer between the fuel hose and the pump **(see illustration)**.

10   After you have installed the new pump, have an assistant turn the ignition switch to On two or three times while you watch for any leaks where the fuel lines are attached to the pump.

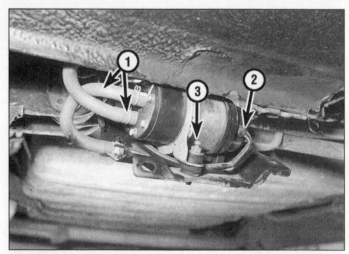

4.6 A typical externally-mounted electric fuel pump assembly - to remove it, pinch off the fuel lines at the points indicated (1), detach the electrical leads (2) and remove the two mounting bolts (3) (only one mounting bolt is visible in this photo)

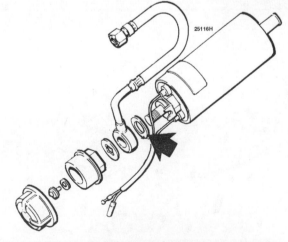

4.9 An exploded view of the hose assembly on a 1984/1985 fuel-injection type pump - whenever you remove the pump, replace the crush washer (arrow)

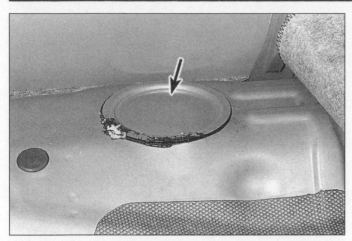

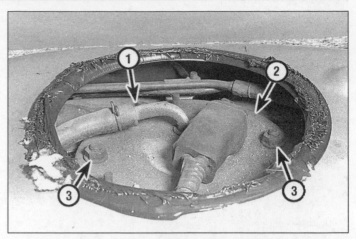

4.12 To get at an in-tank fuel pump, pull back the carpet from the left side of the trunk and remove the access cover (arrow)

4.13 To remove the in-tank pump, detach the fuel line (1), electrical connector (2) and mounting nuts (3), then pull the pump out of the tank

1986 on

Refer to illustrations 4.12 and 4.13

11   Detach the cable from the negative battery terminal.

12   Open the trunk, pull back the carpeting and pry out the left maintenance access cover from the floor of the trunk **(see illustration)**.

13   Detach the fuel lines and the electrical connector for the sending unit **(see illustration)**.

14   Remove the fuel pump/sending unit assembly mounting nuts **(see illustration 4.13)**.

15   Remove the fuel pump from the tank.
Note: *If the pump is difficult to extract, you may have to lower the tank slightly to get it out (see Section 5).*

16   Installation is the reverse of removal.

5   Fuel tank - removal and installation

Refer to illustrations 5.6 and 5.9
Note: *The following procedure is much easier to perform if the fuel tank is empty. Some tanks have a drain plug for this purpose. If the tank does not have a drain plug, simply run the engine until the tank is empty.*
Warning: *Gasoline is extremely flammable, so take extra precautions when you work on any part of the fuel system. Don't smoke or allow open flames or bare light bulbs in or near the work area. And don't work in a garage if a natural gas appliance such as a water heater or clothes dryer is present. While performing any work on the fuel tank, wear safety glasses and have a dry chemical (Class*

B) fire extinguisher on hand. If you spill any fuel on your skin, rinse it off immediately with soap and water.

1   Remove the fuel tank filler cap to relieve fuel tank pressure.

2   If the vehicle is fuel-injected, relieve the fuel system pressure (see Section 2).

3   Detach the cable from the negative terminal of the battery.

4   If the tank still has fuel in it, you can drain it at the fuel feed line after raising the vehicle. If the tank has a drain plug, remove it and drain the fuel into an approved gasoline container.

5   Raise the vehicle and place it securely on jackstands.

6   Label, then disconnect the fuel lines, the vapor return line and the fuel filler hose **(see illustration)**.

4

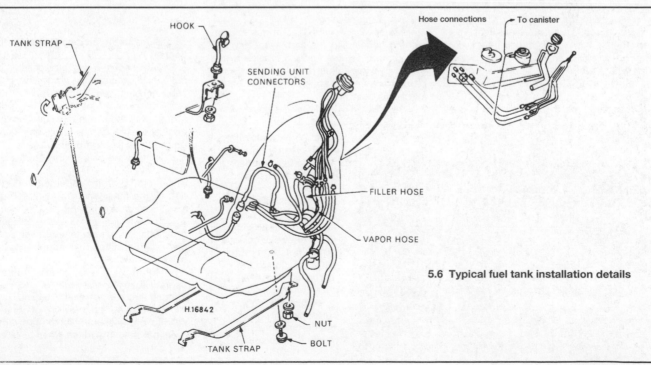

5.6 Typical fuel tank installation details

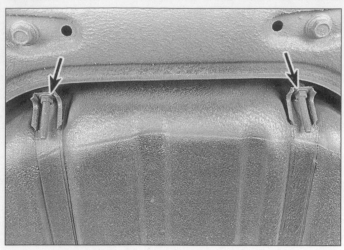

5.9 Remove the nuts (arrows) and drop the fuel tank retaining straps down

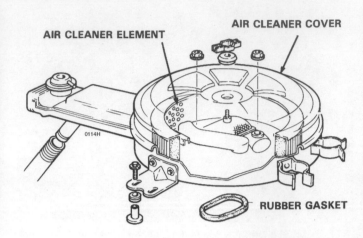

7.4a An exploded view of a typical air cleaner assembly used on early carburetor-equipped vehicles

7   Siphon the fuel from the tank at the fuel feed - not the return - line.

8   Support the fuel tank with a floor jack or jackstands. Position a piece of wood between the jack head and the fuel tank to protect the tank.

9   Disconnect both fuel tank retaining straps and pivot them down until they are hanging out of the way **(see illustration)**.

10   Lower the tank enough to disconnect the electrical wires and ground strap from the fuel pump/fuel gauge sending unit, if you have not already done so.

11   Remove the tank from the vehicle.

12   Installation is the reverse of removal.

6   Fuel tank cleaning and repair - general information

1   All repairs to the fuel tank or filler neck should be carried out by a professional who has experience in this critical and potentially dangerous work. Even after cleaning and flushing of the fuel system, explosive fumes can remain and ignite during repair of the tank.

2   If the fuel tank is removed from the vehicle, it should not be placed in an area where sparks or open flames could ignite the fumes coming out of the tank. Be especially careful inside garages where a natural gas-type appliance is located, because the pilot light could cause an explosion.

7   Air cleaner - removal and installation

Carburetor-equipped vehicles

Refer to illustrations 7.4a and 7.4b

1   Detach the cable from the negative battery terminal.

2   Remove the wing nut(s) from the air cleaner cover and detach the cover and filter element (see Chapter 1).

3   Label, then detach all hoses attached to the air cleaner housing.

4   Remove the nuts that attach the air cleaner housing to the carburetor and the bolts that attach the housing bracket to the valve cover **(see illustrations)**. Remove the protective screen (if equipped) and lift off the air cleaner housing.

5   Installation is the reverse of removal.

Fuel-injected vehicles

Refer to illustration 7.8

6   Detach the cable from the negative battery terminal.

7   Remove the air cleaner cover and filter element (see Chapter 1).

8   Label, then detach all hoses from the air cleaner base **(see illustration)**.

9   Remove the mounting nuts and detach the base.

10   Installation is the reverse of removal.

8   Throttle cable - replacement

Carburetor-equipped vehicles

Refer to illustrations 8.3, 8.8 and 8.10

1   Detach the cable from the negative battery terminal.

2   Remove the air cleaner assembly (see Section 7).

3   Push back the boot and loosen the locknut until it is beyond the groove in the throttle cable housing **(see illustration)**.

4   Pull back the cable until the groove is aligned with the slot in the mounting bracket, then slide the cable out of the mounting bracket **(see illustration 8.3)**.

5   Detach the cable end from the throttle link.

6   Working from underneath the dash, detach the other end of the cable from the accelerator pedal rod arm.

7   Detach the cable from all retaining bracket(s) on the camshaft cover and from any retaining clips that attach it to the TV cable, if equipped.

8   Rotate the firewall cable grommet 90 degrees **(see illustration)**, then pull the cable through the firewall from the engine side.

9   Installation is the reverse of removal. Be sure to apply sealant to the firewall cable grommet mating surface when installing the new cable.

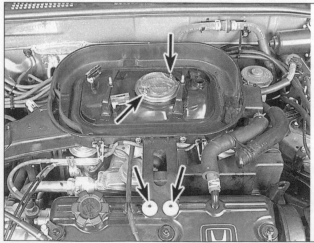

7.4b When removing the air cleaner housing from a later model carburetor-equipped vehicle, clearly label and detach all hoses attached to the base, then remove the bolts from the valve cover and the nuts that attach the housing to the carburetor (arrows) - note that this model is equipped with a protective screen over the carburetor, which must also be removed

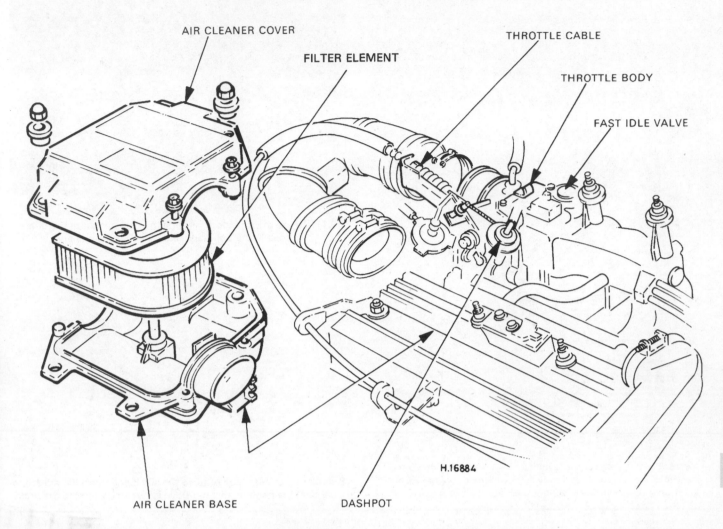

AIR CLEANER COVER

FILTER ELEMENT

THROTTLE CABLE

THROTTLE BODY

FAST IDLE VALVE

AIR CLEANER BASE

DASHPOT

H.16884

7.8 An exploded view of a typical air cleaner assembly used on fuel-injected vehicles

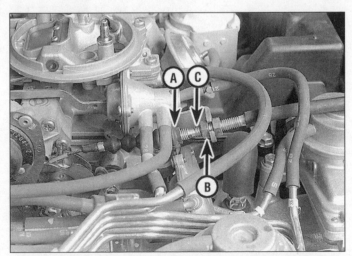

8.3 To detach the throttle cable from the throttle bracket on a carburetor-equipped vehicle, push back the cable boot (A), loosen the cable adjustment locknut (B) until it's beyond the groove in the cable housing (C), then align the groove with the slot in the mounting bracket and pull out the cable

8.8 To detach the throttle cable (arrow) from the firewall, rotate the grommet 90 degrees and pull it out of the firewall (be sure to use sealant when installing the grommet on the new cable or it may leak)

4

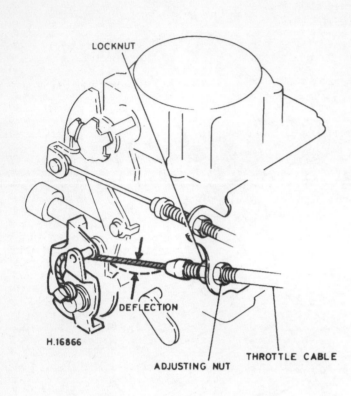

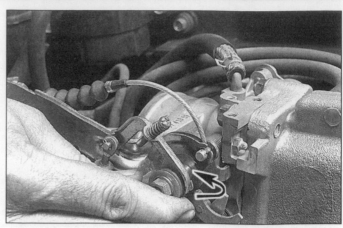

8.14 Rotate the throttle shaft until the cable is out of the guide groove in the bellcrank and detach the cable end

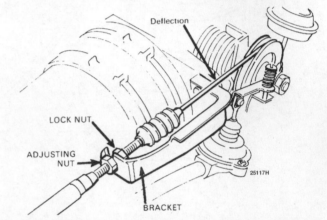

8.10 To adjust the throttle cable on a carburetor-equipped vehicle, loosen the locknut, turn it until the cable has about 3/16 to 3/8 inch deflection, then tighten the locknut

8.18 Lift up the cable to remove the slack, then turn the adjusting nut until the cable housing groove is 1/8-inch from the bracket

10   To adjust the cable:

a) *Verify that the throttle cable operates smoothly. It must not bind or stick.*

b) *Start the engine and check the cable deflection at the throttle linkage (see illustration). It should be about 3/16 to 3/8-inch. If the deflection isn't within specifications, loosen the locknut, turn the adjusting nut until the deflection is within specifications and tighten the locknut.*

c) *After the cable is correctly adjusted, have an assistant help you verify that the throttle valve opens all the way when you push the accelerator pedal to the floor and that it returns to the idle position when you release the accelerator.*

Fuel injected vehicles

Refer to illustrations 8.14 and 8.18

11   Detach the cable from the negative battery terminal.

12   Remove the fresh air duct between the throttle body and the air cleaner assembly (see Section 7).

13   Loosen the locknut and remove the throttle cable from its bracket (see illustration 8.3).

14   Rotate the throttle shaft bellcrank until the cable is out of its guide groove in the bellcrank (see illustration) and detach the cable from the bellcrank.

15   Working from underneath the dash, detach the cable from the accelerator pedal.

16   To free the cable from the firewall, rotate the rubber grommet (see illustration 8.8) about 90 degrees, pull the grommet from the firewall and pull the cable through the firewall from the engine compartment side.

17   Installation is the reverse of removal.

18   To adjust the cable (see illustration):

a) *Lift up on the cable to remove any slack.*

b) *Turn the adjusting nut until the groove in the throttle cable housing is 1/8-inch from the cable bracket.*

c) *Tighten the locknut and check cable deflection at the throttle linkage. Deflection should be 3/16 to 3/8-inch on 1984 and 1985 models and 3/8 to 1/2-inch on 1986 and later models. If deflection is not within specifications, loosen the locknut and turn the adjusting nut until the deflection is as specified.*

d) *After you have adjusted the throttle cable, have an assistant help you verify that the throttle valve opens all the way when you depress the accelerator pedal to the floor and that it returns to the idle position when you release the accelerator. Verify the cable operates smoothly. It must not bind or stick.*

e) *If the vehicle is equipped with an automatic transaxle, adjust the TV cable (see Chapter 7B).*

f) *If the vehicle is equipped with cruise control, have the cruise control cable adjusted by a dealer.*

9   Carburetor - removal and installation

Warning: *Gasoline is extremely flammable so take extra precautions when you work on any part of the fuel system. Don't smoke or allow open flames or bare light bulbs in or near the work area. And don't work in a garage if a natural gas appliance such as a water heater or clothes dryer is present.*

Removal

1   Remove the fuel filler cap to relieve fuel tank pressure.
2   Remove the air cleaner from the carburetor. Be sure to label all vacuum hoses attached to the air cleaner housing.
3   Disconnect the throttle cable from the throttle lever (see Section 8).
4   If the vehicle is equipped with an automatic transaxle, disconnect the TV cable from the throttle lever (see Chapter 7B).
5   Clearly label all vacuum hoses and fittings, then disconnect the hoses.
6   Disconnect the fuel line from the carburetor.
7   Label the wires and terminals, then unplug all wire harness connectors.
8   Remove the mounting fasteners and detach the carburetor from the intake manifold. Remove the carburetor mounting gasket. Stuff a shop rag into the intake manifold openings.

Installation

9   Use a gasket scraper to remove all traces of gasket material and sealant from the intake manifold (and the carburetor, if it's being reinstalled), then remove the shop rag from the manifold openings. Clean the mating surfaces with lacquer thinner or acetone.
10   Place a new gasket on the intake manifold.
11   Position the carburetor on the gasket and install the mounting fasteners.
12   To prevent carburetor distortion or damage, tighten the fasteners to the specified torque in a criss-cross pattern, 1/4-turn at a time.
13   The remaining installation steps are the reverse of removal.
14   Check and, if necessary, adjust the idle speed (see Chapter 1).
15   If the vehicle is equipped with an automatic transaxle, refer to Chapter 7B for the TV cable adjustment procedure.
16   Start the engine and check carefully for fuel leaks.

10   Carburetor diagnosis and overhaul - general information

Warning: *Gasoline is extremely flammable so take extra precautions when you work on any part of the fuel system. Don't smoke or allow open flames or bare light bulbs in or near the work area. And don't work in a garage if a natural gas appliance such as a water heater or clothes dryer is present.*

Diagnosis

1   A thorough road test and check of carburetor adjustments should be done before any major carburetor service work. Specifications for some adjustments are listed on the Vehicle Emissions Control Information (VECI) label found in the engine compartment.
2   Carburetor problems usually show up as flooding, hard starting, stalling, severe backfiring and poor acceleration. A carburetor that's leaking fuel and/or covered with wet looking deposits definitely needs attention.
3   Some performance complaints directed at the carburetor are actually a result of loose, out-of-adjustment or malfunctioning engine or electrical components. Others develop when vacuum hoses leak, are disconnected or are incorrectly routed. The proper approach to analyzing carburetor problems should include the following items:

a) *Inspect all vacuum hoses and actuators for leaks and correct installation (see Chapters 1 and 6).*
b) *Tighten the intake manifold and carburetor mounting nuts/bolts evenly and securely.*
c) *Perform a cylinder compression test (see Chapter 2).*
d) *Clean or replace the spark plugs as necessary (see Chapter 1).*
e) *Check the spark plug wires (see Chapter 1).*
f) *Inspect the ignition coil primary wires.*
g) *Check the ignition timing (follow the instructions printed on the Emissions Control Information label).*
h) *Check the fuel pump pressure/volume (see Chapter 4).*
i) *Check the air control diaphragm in the air cleaner for proper operation (see Chapter 1).*
j) *Check/replace the air filter element (see Chapter 1).*
k) *Check the PCV system (see Chapter 6).*
l) *Check/replace the fuel filter (see Chapter 1). Also, the strainer in the tank could be restricted.*
m) *Check for a plugged exhaust system.*
n) *Check EGR valve operation (see Chapter 6).*
o) *Check the choke-it should be completely open at normal engine operating temperature (see Chapter 1).*
p) *Check for fuel leaks and kinked or dented fuel lines (see Chapters 1 and 4).*
q) *Check accelerator pump operation with the engine off (remove the air cleaner cover and operate the throttle as you look into the carburetor throat - you should see a stream of gasoline enter the carburetor).*
r) *Check for incorrect fuel or bad gasoline.*
s) *Check the valve clearances (if applicable) and camshaft lobe lift (see Chapters 1 and 2)*
t) *Have a dealer service department or repair shop check the electronic engine and carburetor controls.*

4   Diagnosing carburetor problems may require that the engine be started and run with the air cleaner off. While running the engine without the air cleaner, backfires are possible. This situation is likely to occur if the carburetor is malfunctioning, but just the removal of the air cleaner can lean the fuel/air mixture enough to produce an engine backfire. **Warning:** *Do not position any part of your body, especially your face, directly over the carburetor during inspection and servicing procedures. Wear eye protection!*

Overhaul

5   Once it's determined that the carburetor needs an overhaul, several options are available. If you're going to attempt to overhaul the carburetor yourself, first obtain a good quality carburetor rebuild kit (which will include all necessary gaskets, internal parts, instructions and a parts list). You'll also need some special solvent and a means of blowing out the internal passages of the carburetor with air.
6   An alternative is to obtain a new or rebuilt carburetor. They are readily available from dealers and auto parts stores. Make absolutely sure the exchange carburetor is identical to the original. A tag is usually attached to the top of the carburetor or a number is stamped on the float bowl. It will help determine the exact type of carburetor you have. When obtaining a rebuilt carburetor or a rebuild kit, make sure the kit or carburetor matches your application exactly. Seemingly insignificant differences can make a large difference in engine performance.
7   If you choose to overhaul your own carburetor, allow enough time to disassemble it carefully, soak the necessary parts in the cleaning solvent (usually for at least one-half day or according to the instructions listed on the carburetor cleaner) and reassemble it, which will usually take much longer than disassembly. When disassembling the carburetor, match each part with the illustration in the carburetor kit and lay the parts out in order on a clean work surface. Overhauls by inexperienced mechanics can result in an engine which runs poorly or not at all. To avoid this, use care and patience when disassembling the carburetor so you can reassemble it correctly.
8   Because carburetor designs are constantly modified by the manufacturer in order to meet increasingly more stringent emissions regulations, it isn't feasible to include a step-by-step overhaul of each type. You'll receive a detailed, well-illustrated set of instructions with any carburetor overhaul kit; they will apply in a more specific manner to the carburetor on your vehicle.

11   Fuel injection system - general information

Refer to illustration 11.1

The Programmed Fuel Injection (PGM-FI) system **(see illustration)** consists of three sub-systems: air intake, electronic control and fuel delivery.

Air intake system

The air intake system consists of the air cleaner, the air intake pipe, the throttle body, the idle control system, the fast idle mecha-

4

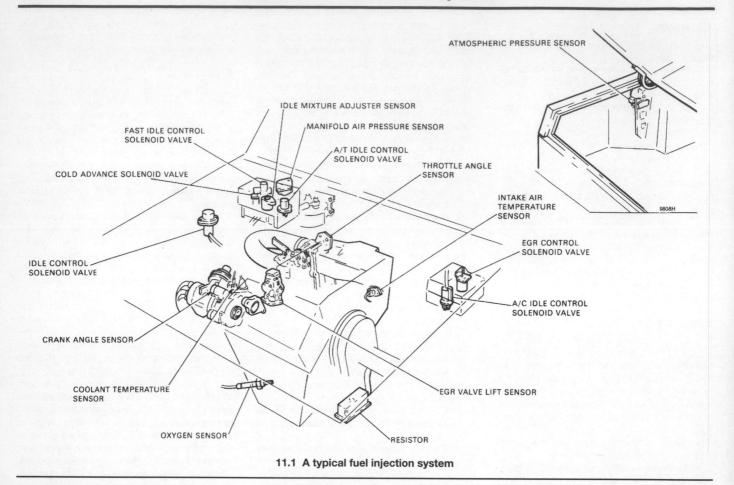

11.1 A typical fuel injection system

nism and the intake manifold. A resonator in the air intake tube provides silencing as air is drawn into the system.

The throttle body is a two-barrel, side-draft design with the primary air horn at the top. The lower portion of the throttle body is heated by engine coolant to prevent icing in cold weather. A throttle sensor attached to the throttle shaft senses changes in throttle opening. To slow the movement of the throttle valve as it closes, a dashpot is added to vehicles equipped with a manual transaxle.

When the engine is idling, the air-fuel ratio is controlled by the idle control system, which consists of the Electronic Control Unit (ECU), the idle control, fast idle, A/T idle control and A/C idle control solenoid valves. The first three of these solenoid valves alter the amount of air bypassed into the air intake manifold. The A/C idle control solenoid valve opens the A/C idle control valve when the air conditioning system is turned on.

When the idle speed is low because of electrical or other loads on the engine, the idle control solenoid valve opens to allow extra air into the intake manifold. This additional air allows the idle speed to increase to its normal speed. The valve also reduces fast idle speed during warm-up, once the coolant temperature has surpassed 104 degrees F. Finally, to prevent rough running after the engine starts, the valve is opened during cranking and immediately after starting to

provide additional air into the intake manifold.

The fast idle control solenoid valve also opens when the engine is cold to prevent erratic idling by passing additional air to the intake manifold to raise the idle speed. The fast idle control solenoid valve is energized by the coolant temperature and atmospheric pressure sensors. The valve is open below 105 degrees F at sea level and below 104 degrees F at high altitude.

When the automatic transaxle is in gear, the idle speed tends to go down. The A/T idle control solenoid valve compensates for this by sending more air to the intake in order to maintain the correct idle speed.

If the air conditioning system is on, the A/C idle control solenoid valve opens to increase air flow and maintain the normal idle speed.

In 1988, these four idle control valves were replaced by the Electronic Air Control Valve (EACV) and the Fast Idle Valve. Like the solenoid valves in the idle control system described above, these valves change the amount of air bypassed into the intake manifold in response to changes in an electrical signal from the ECU.

After the engine starts, the EACV opens. The amount of air is increased to raise the idle speed about 150 to 250 rpm. When the coolant temperature is low, the EACV is opened to obtain the proper fast idle speed. The amount of bypassed air is controlled in

relation to the coolant temperature. When the coolant temperature is below 122 degrees F, it also activates the fast idle valve to prevent the idle speed from dropping.

Electronic control system

The electronic control system consists of an eight-bit microprocessor (computer) and nine sensors:

The crank angle sensor, which is an integral part of the distributor assembly, consists of two rotors (TDC and CYL) and a pickup for each rotor. The distributor is driven off the end of the camshaft, and the rotors are coupled to the distributor shaft, so they turn together as a unit as the cam rotates. The CYL pickup detects the position of the No. 1 cylinder as the base for sequential injection; the TDC pickup determines the injection timing for each cylinder. The TDC pickup also monitors engine speed to help determine the basic discharge duration for different operating conditions.

The manifold air pressure (MAP) sensor converts manifold air pressure readings into electrical voltage signals and sends them to the ECU. This data, along with the data from the TDC and CYL sensors, enables the ECU to determine the duration during which fuel is injected.

The atmospheric pressure (PA) sensor converts atmospheric pressures into voltage signals and sends them to the ECU. These

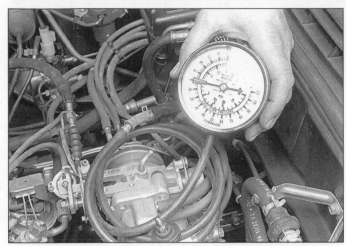

12.1 Detach the vacuum hose from the top of the throttle body (that goes to the evaporative canister) and attach a vacuum gauge in its place

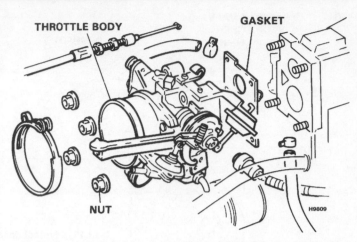

12.13 An exploded view of a typical fuel injection throttle body

signals enable the ECU to modify the basic fuel discharge duration to compensate for changes in the atmospheric pressure.

The coolant temperature (TW) sensor uses a temperature dependent diode (thermistor) to measure differences in the coolant temperature. The resistance of the thermistor decreases with a rise in coolant temperature. The ECU uses this input to increase or decrease the fuel discharge duration.

The intake air temperature (TA) sensor, which is located in the intake manifold, is also a thermistor. In operation, it's similar to the TW sensor but has a lower thermal capacity for quicker response time.

The throttle angle sensor is a variable resistor. The sensor is mounted on the end of the throttle valve shaft. As the throttle valve is rotated, the resistance varies, altering the output voltage to the control unit, which in turn alters the fuel discharge duration.

The oxygen sensor monitors the oxygen content in the exhaust gas and sends a variable voltage signal to the ECU, which alters the fuel discharge duration.

The purpose of the idle mixture adjuster (IMA) sensor is to permit adjustment for the correct air-fuel ratio at idle after an injector is replaced. Turning the adjuster alters the voltage signal to the ECU, which in turn changes the fuel discharge duration.

When the ignition key is turned to Start, the starter switch sends a signal to the ECU, which increases the amount of fuel injected, in accordance with the engine temperature. The amount of fuel injected is gradually reduced once the engine is started.

Fuel delivery system

The fuel delivery system consists of eight components: The fuel pump, the pressure regulator, four injectors, the resistor and the main relay.

The fuel pump, which is located immediately forward of the left rear wheel, is an inline, direct drive type. Fuel is drawn through a filter into the pump, flows past the armature

through the one-way valve and is delivered to the injectors. A relief valve prevents excessive pressure build-up by opening in the event of a blockage in the discharge side and allowing fuel to flow from the high to the low pressure side.

The pressure regulator maintains a constant fuel pressure to the injectors. The spring chamber of the pressure regulator is connected to the intake manifold to constantly maintain the fuel pressure at 36 psi higher than the pressure in the manifold. When the difference between the fuel pressure and manifold pressure exceeds this figure, the diaphragm is pushed upward and excess fuel is fed back to the fuel tank through the return line.

The four injectors are solenoid-actuated, constant stroke, pintle types consisting of a solenoid, plunger, needle valve and housing. When current is applied to the solenoid coil, the needle valve raises and pressurized fuel fills the injector housing and squirts out the nozzle. The needle valve lift and the fuel pressure are constant, so the injection quantity is determined by the length of time the valve is open, i.e. the length of time during which current is supplied to the solenoid coils.

Because it determines opening and closing intervals - which in turn determine the air-fuel mixture ratio - injector timing must be quite accurate. To attain the best possible injector response, the current rise time, when voltage is being applied to each injector coil, must be as short as possible. The number of windings in the coil has therefore been reduced to lower the inductance in the coil. However, this creates low coil resistance, which could compromise the durability of the coil. The flow of current in the coil is therefore restricted by a resistor installed in the injector wire harness.

The main relay, which is installed adjacent to the fuse box, is a direct coupler type which contains the relays for the electronic control unit power supply and the fuel pump power supply.

12 Throttle body - component check and replacement

Throttle body
Check
Refer to illustration 12.1

1   On top of the throttle body, locate the vacuum hose that goes to the canister. Detach it from the throttle body and attach a vacuum gauge in its place **(see illustration)**.
2   Start the engine and warm it to its normal operating temperature (wait until the cooling fan comes on twice). Verify the gauge indicates no vacuum.
3   Open the throttle slightly from idle and verify that the gauge indicates vacuum.
4   Stop the engine and verify the throttle cable and valve operate smoothly without binding or sticking.
5   If the throttle cable or valve binds or sticks, check for a build-up of sludge on the cable or throttle shaft.
6   If a build-up of sludge is evident, try removing it with carburetor cleaner or a similarly suitable solvent.
7   If cleaning fails to remedy the problem, replace the throttle body.

Replacement
Refer to illustration 12.13

8   Detach the cable from the negative battery terminal.
9   Remove the air duct that connects the air cleaner assembly to the throttle body.
10 Label, then detach, all vacuum hoses from the throttle body.
11 Detach the throttle cable (see Section 8) and, if equipped, TV cable (see Chapter 7B).
12 Detach the coolant hoses from the throttle body.
13 Remove the four mounting nuts and detach the throttle body and gasket **(see illustration)**.
14 Installation is the reverse of removal. Be sure to adjust the throttle cable (see Section 8) and, if equipped, the TV cable (see Chapter 7B).

4

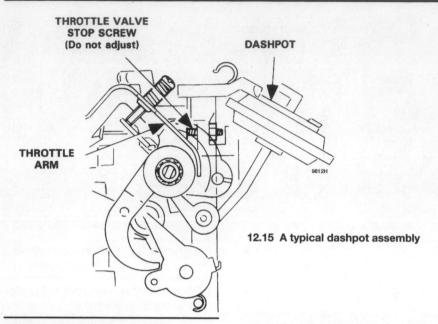

12.15 A typical dashpot assembly

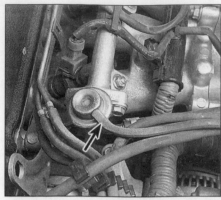

13.3 To check the fuel pressure regulator, detach the vacuum hose (arrow) and verify the fuel pressure rises

Throttle control (dashpot) system check 1985 and 1986 vehicles)

Refer to illustration 12.15

15   The dashpot **(see illustration)** slows the closing of the throttle valve during gear shifting or deceleration.

16   Slowly open the throttle arm until the dashpot rod is raised up as far as it will go.

17   Release the throttle arm and measure the time until the throttle arm contacts the stop screw. This should take about 1/4 to two seconds.

a)   *If the time is over two seconds, replace the dashpot check valve and re-check it.*

b)   *If the rod doesn't operate, check for binding in the linkage or a clogged check valve or vacuum line. If they're okay, replace the dashpot.*

13   Fuel pressure regulator - check and replacement

Warning: *Gasoline is extremely flammable, so take extra precautions when you work on any part of the fuel system. Don't smoke or allow open flames or bare light bulbs in or near the work area. And don't work in a garage if a natural gas appliance such as a water heater or clothes dryer is present.*

Check

Refer to illustration 13.3

1   Inspect the fuel system for pinched or broken vacuum hoses.

2   Test the fuel pressure (see Section 3). If the pressure is not as specified, check the fuel pump first (see Section 3), then check the regulator.

3   Detach the vacuum hose from the regulator **(see illustration)** and verify the fuel pressure rises. If the fuel pressure doesn't rise, reattach the hose and pinch it. If the pressure still doesn't rise, replace the regulator.

Replacement

Refer to illustration 13.6

4   Detach the cable from the negative battery terminal.

5   Relieve the system fuel pressure (see Section 2).

6   Detach the vacuum hose and fuel return hose from the regulator **(see illustration)**.

7   Remove the two bolts and detach the regulator.

8   Installation is the reverse of removal. Be sure to use a new O-ring. Apply clean engine oil to the O-ring and install it in its proper position. Be sure you don't damage the O-ring when you install the regulator.

14   Fuel injector - check and replacement

Warning: *Gasoline is extremely flammable, so take extra precautions when you work on any part of the fuel system. Don't smoke or allow open flames or bare light bulbs in or near the work area. And don't work in a garage if a natural gas appliance such as a water heater or clothes dryer is present.*

Check

Refer to illustrations 14.2 and 14.3

1   Start the engine and warm it to its normal operating temperature.

2   With the engine idling, unplug the injectors one-at-a-time **(see illustration)** and note the change in idle speed. If the idle speed drop is almost the same for each cylinder, the injectors are operating correctly. If unplugging a particular injector fails to change the idle speed, proceed to the next step.

3   Check the injector electrical connector with a voltmeter **(see illustration)**.

a)   *If the voltage fluctuates between zero and two volts, replace the injector (see below).*

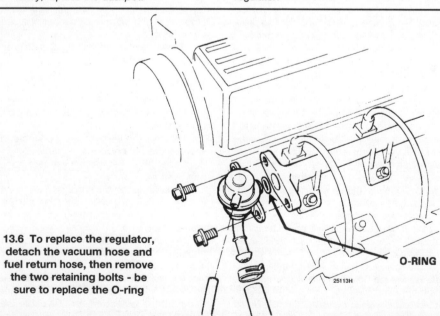

13.6 To replace the regulator, detach the vacuum hose and fuel return hose, then remove the two retaining bolts - be sure to replace the O-ring

O-RING

14.2 Before unplugging an injector connector, use a scribe (shown) or a small screwdriver to pry the spring clip loose

14.3 With the engine running, check for voltage at the injector electrical connector

14.10 To replace an injector - or simply remove the fuel rail assembly - remove the nut (arrow) and detach the two ground cables from the intake manifold

b) *If there is no voltage, check the injector resistor (see Section 15).*
c) *If the injector resistor is operating normally, check the wiring between the resistor and the injector and between the injector and the ECU for a short circuit, break in the wire or bad connection.*
d) *If there is voltage at the electrical connector, but the injector is malfunctioning, listen to the clicking sound of each injector with a stethoscope. If the suspect injector isn't making the same clicking sound as the other injectors, replace it (see below), then recheck it.*

4   With the engine stopped, unplug the injector electrical connector and measure the resistance between the terminals of the injector. It should be between 1.5 and 2.5 ohms. If the resistance is not as specified, replace the injector (see below).

Replacement
Refer to illustrations 14.10, 14.11, 14.12, 4.13 and 14.17
5   Detach the cable from the negative battery terminal.
6   Relieve the fuel pressure (see Section 2).

7   Remove the air cleaner assembly (see Section 7).
8   Unplug the injector connector(s) **(see illustration 14.2)**.
9   Detach the vacuum hose and fuel return hose from the fuel pressure regulator (see Section 13).
10   Detach the two ground cables from the intake manifold **(see illustration)**.
11   Detach the fuel lines **(see illustration)**.
12   Remove the mounting nuts **(see illustration)** and detach the fuel rail and injectors.
13   Remove the injector(s) from the fuel rail and remove and discard the seal ring(s) **(see illustration)**. Note the location of the injector O-ring and cushion ring, then remove and dis-

card them. **Note:** *Whether you're replacing an injector or a leaking O-ring, it's a good idea to remove all the injectors from the fuel rail and replace all the O-rings and cushion rings.*
14   Coat the new cushion ring(s) with fresh engine oil and slide it/them onto the injector(s).
15   Coat the new O-ring(s) with fresh engine oil and place it/them on the injector(s), then insert each injector into its corresponding bore in the fuel rail.
16   Coat the new seal ring(s) with fresh engine oil and press it/them into the injector bore(s) in the intake manifold.

4

14.11 Remove the crown nut (1) and detach the pressure line, then remove the hose clamp and detach the return line (2)

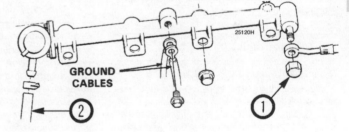

14.12 Remove the fuel rail mounting nuts (arrows), then pull the fuel rail assembly and injectors off the manifold

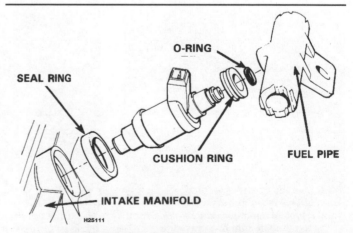

14.13 An exploded view of the injector assembly - note the relationship of the injector to the seal ring, cushion ring and O-ring to ensure proper reassembly

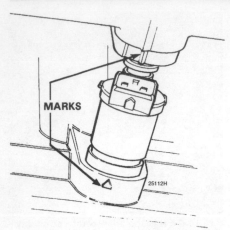

14.17 Be sure the mark on each injector connector is aligned with the mark on the intake manifold

17   Install the injector and fuel rail assembly on the intake manifold. Make sure the center-line of the electrical connector on each injector is aligned with its corresponding mark on the intake manifold **(see illustration)**. Tighten the fuel rail mounting nuts to the specified torque.

18   The remainder of installation is the reverse of removal.

19   After the injector/fuel rail assembly installation is complete, turn the ignition switch to On, but don't operate the starter (this activates the fuel pump for about two seconds, which builds up fuel pressure in the fuel lines and the fuel rail). Repeat this about two or three times, then check the fuel lines, rail and injectors for fuel leakage.

15   Injector resistor - check

Refer to illustration 15.2, 15.3 and 15.4

1   Detach the cable from the negative battery terminal.

2   Locate the injector resistor **(see illustration)**. It's on the left side of the engine com-

partment, below and in front of the cruise control assembly.

3   To get at the electrical connector for the resistor, you must detach the mounting bracket for the wire harness connectors behind the cruise control assembly **(see illustration)** and set the bracket and connectors aside (it's not necessary to detach anything).

4   Trace the electrical lead from the resistor back to its connector and unplug it **(see illustration)**.

5   Check the resistance between the power supply connector terminal and each of the other four terminals in the connector **(see illustration 15.4)**. Resistance for each of the four checks should be about 5 to 7 ohms.

6   If the indicated resistance isn't within specification, replace the resistor.

16   Fuel control system - general information

1   Numerous devices and systems are employed on the vehicles covered by this manual to alter basic fuel flow parameters during noncruising conditions such as warm-up, acceleration or deceleration.

2   Because of the complexity of the checking and diagnostic procedures and the special equipment necessary to carry out these procedures, diagnosis of the fuel control system is best left to a dealer.

17   Exhaust system servicing - general information

Refer to illustrations 17.1 and 17.6
Warning: *Inspection and repair of exhaust system components should be done only after enough time has elapsed after driving the vehicle to allow the system components to cool completely. Also, when working under the vehicle, make sure it is securely supported on jackstands.*

1   The exhaust system **(see illustration)** consists of the exhaust manifold(s), the catalytic converter, the muffler, the tailpipe and all connecting pipes, brackets, hangers and clamps. The exhaust system is attached to the body with mounting brackets and rubber hangers. If any of the parts are improperly installed, excessive noise and vibration will be transmitted to the body.

Muffler and pipes

2   Conduct regular inspections of the exhaust system to keep it safe and quiet. Look for any damaged or bent parts, open seams, holes, loose connections, excessive corrosion or other defects which could allow exhaust fumes to enter the vehicle. Also check the catalytic converter when you inspect the exhaust system (see below). Deteriorated exhaust system components should not be repaired; they should be replaced with new parts.

3   If the exhaust system components are extremely corroded or rusted together, welding equipment will probably be required to remove them. The convenient way to accomplish this is to have a muffler repair shop remove the corroded sections with a cutting torch. If, however, you want to save money by doing it yourself (and you don't have a welding outfit with a cutting torch), simply cut off the old components with a hacksaw. If you have compressed air, special pneumatic cutting chisels can also be used. If you do decide to tackle the job at home, be sure to wear safety goggles to protect your eyes from metal chips and work gloves to protect your hands.

4   Here are some simple guidelines to follow when repairing the exhaust system:

 a) *Work from the back to the front when removing exhaust system components.*

 b) *Apply penetrating oil to the exhaust system component fasteners to make them easier to remove.*

 c) *Use new gaskets, hangers and clamps when installing exhaust systems components.*

15.2 A typical injector resistor - look for it on the left side of the engine compartment, below and in front of the cruise control

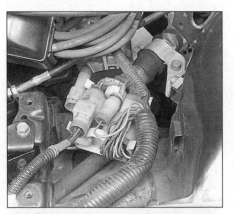

15.3 To get at the electrical connector for the injector resistor, you'll have to remove the harness mounting bracket from the cruise control assembly and put it and the harness connectors aside

15.4 To check the injector resistor, measure the resistance between the power supply terminal (arrow) and the other four terminals in the connector - resistance should be about 5 to 7 ohms

d) *Apply anti-seize compound to the threads of all exhaust system fasteners during reassembly.*

e) *Be sure to allow sufficient clearance between newly installed parts and all points on the underbody to avoid over-heating the floor pan and possibly damaging the interior carpet and insulation. Pay particularly close attention to the catalytic converter and heat shield.*

Catalytic converter

Warning: *The converter gets very hot during operation. Make sure it's cooled down before you touch it.*

Note: *See Chapter 6 for more information on the catalytic converter.*

5   Periodically, inspect the heat shield for cracks, dents and loose or missing fasteners.

6   Remove the heat shield **(see illustration)** an inspect the converter for cracks or other damage.

7   If the converter must be replaced, remove the mounting nuts from the flanges at each end, detach the rubber mounts and separate the converter from the exhaust system (you should be able to push the exhaust pipes at each end out of the way to clear the converter studs.

8   Installation is the reverse of removal. Be sure to use new gaskets.

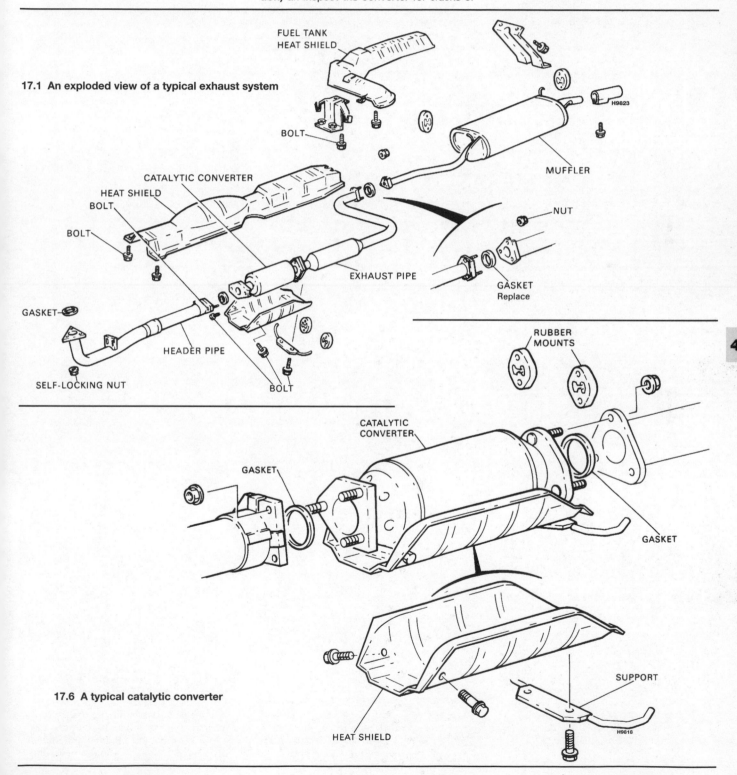

17.1 An exploded view of a typical exhaust system

17.6 A typical catalytic converter

Notes

Chapter 5
Engine electrical systems

Contents

5

Specifications

Coil

1984 and 1985

Primary resistance	1.06 to 1.24 ohms
Secondary resistance	4 to 11 k-ohms

1986 on

Primary resistance (between terminals A and D)	1.2 to 1.5 ohms
Secondary resistance (between terminal A and high tension terminal)	9 to 13.6 k-ohms
Resistance between terminals B and D	Approximately 2.2 k-ohms
Radio condenser capacitance	0.38 to 0.56 microfarads

Charging system

Alternator brush minimum length	1/4-inch

1   General information

The engine electrical systems include all ignition, charging and starting components. Because of their engine-related functions, these components are discussed separately from chassis electrical devices such as the lights, the instruments, etc. (which are included in Chapter 12).

Always observe the following precautions when working on the electrical systems:

a) *Be extremely careful when servicing engine electrical components. They are easily damaged if checked, connected or handled improperly.*

b) *Never leave the ignition switch on for long periods of time with the engine off.*

c) *Don't disconnect the battery cables while the engine is running.*

d) *Maintain correct polarity when connecting a battery cable from another vehicle during jump starting.*

e) *Always disconnect the negative cable first and hook it up last or the battery may be shorted by the tool being used to loosen the cable clamps.*

It's also a good idea to review the safety related information regarding the engine electrical systems located in the Safety First section near the front of this manual before beginning any operation included in this Chapter.

2   Battery - emergency jump starting

Refer to the *Booster battery (jump) starting* procedure at the front of this manual.

3   Battery cables - check and replacement

1   Periodically inspect the entire length of each battery cable for damage, cracked or burned insulation and corrosion. Poor battery cable connections can cause starting problems and decreased engine performance.

2   Check the cable-to-terminal connections at the ends of the cables for cracks, loose wire strands and corrosion. The presence of white, fluffy deposits under the insulation at the cable terminal connection is a sign that the cable is corroded and should be replaced. Check the terminals for distortion, missing mounting bolts and corrosion.

3   When removing the cables, always disconnect the negative cable first and hook it up last or the battery may be shorted by the tool used to loosen the cable clamps. Even if only the positive cable is being replaced, be sure to disconnect the negative cable from the battery first (see Chapter 1 for further information regarding battery cable removal).

4   Disconnect the old cables from the battery, then trace each of them to their opposite ends and detach them from the starter

4.2 To remove the battery, detach the negative, then the positive cable clamps from their respective terminals, remove the two nuts (arrows), then detach the hold-down clamp

solenoid and ground terminals. Note the routing of each cable to ensure correct installation.

5   If you are replacing either or both of the old cables, take them with you when buying new cables. It is vitally important that you replace the cables with identical parts. Cables have characteristics that make them easy to identify: positive cables are usually red,

larger in cross-section and have a larger diameter battery post clamp; ground cables are usually black, smaller in cross-section and have a slightly smaller diameter clamp for the negative post.

6   Clean the threads of the solenoid or ground connection with a wire brush to remove rust and corrosion. Apply a light coat of battery terminal corrosion inhibitor, or petroleum jelly, to the threads to prevent future corrosion.

7   Attach the cable to the solenoid or ground connection and tighten the mounting nut/bolt securely.

8   Before connecting a new cable to the battery, make sure that it reaches the battery post without having to be stretched.

9   Connect the positive cable first, followed by the negative cable.

4   Battery - removal and installation

Refer to illustration 4.2

1   **Caution:** *Always disconnect the negative cable first and hook it up last or the battery may be shorted by the tool being used to loosen the cable clamps.* Disconnect both cables from the battery terminals.

2   Remove the battery hold down clamp **(see illustration)**.

3   Lift out the battery. Be careful - it's heavy. **Note:** *Battery straps and handlers are available at most auto parts stores for a reasonable price. They make it easier to remove and carry the battery.*

4   While the battery is out, inspect the carrier (tray) for corrosion (see Chapter 1).

5   If you are replacing the battery, make sure you get one that's identical, with the

same dimensions, amperage rating, cold cranking rating, etc.

6   Installation is the reverse of removal.

5   Ignition system - general information

Warning: *Transistorized electronic ignition systems generate considerably higher voltage than conventional systems. Be extra careful when servicing these ignition systems.*

The electronic ignition system consists of the ignition switch, battery, coil, distributor, spark plug wires and spark plugs.

All distributors are driven by the camshaft. Earlier distributors employ centrifugal and vacuum advance systems; later distributors are advanced and retarded by the electronic control unit. Several distributors are used on the vehicles covered by this manual: Fuel injected models use a Toyo Denso distributor. Carbureted models may be equipped with either a Hitachi or a Toyo Denso distributor. Both units are similar - the primary difference between the two is the physical location of the components such as the igniter, reluctor, stator, magnet, etc. For example, the igniter on the Hitachi is located inside the distributor, underneath the rotor; on the Toyo Denso, the igniter is located on the outside of the distributor housing. Fuel-injected models employ a crank angle sensor, which is located between the distributor and the cylinder head.

6   Ignition system - check

1   Attach an inductive timing light to each plug wire, one at a time, and crank the engine.

a) *If the light flashes, voltage is reaching the plug.*

b) *If the light does not flash, proceed to the next Step.*

2   Inspect the spark plug wire(s), distributor cap, rotor and spark plug(s) (see Chapter 1).

3   If the engine still won't start, check the ignition coil (see Section 7).

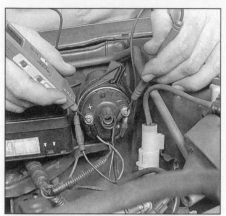

7.3 Checking the resistance between the coil primary terminals (1984 and 1985 vehicles)

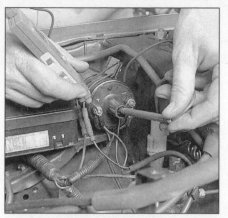

7.4 Checking the resistance between the coil positive primary terminal and the high tension terminal (1984 and 1985 vehicles)

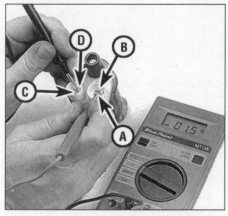

7.13 Checking the resistance between primary terminals A and D (1986 and later vehicles) (coil removed for clarity)

7 Ignition coil - check and replacement

1984 and 1985
Check

Refer to illustrations 7.3 and 7.4

1   Make sure the ignition switch is off for the following checks.
2   Remove the rubber coil boot (cover) and detach the high tension lead from the secondary terminal.
3   Using an ohmmeter, touch the probes to the positive and negative terminals of the coil primary winding **(see illustration)**, measure the resistance and compare your reading to the specified primary resistance.
4   Touch the probes to the secondary winding terminal and the primary winding positive terminal **(see illustration)**, measure the resistance and compare your reading to the specified resistance.
5   The above figures will vary somewhat with the temperature of the coil. The specified resistance values are for a coil temperature of about 70-degrees F.
6   If the coil fails either check, replace it.

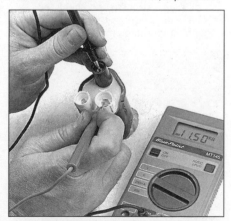

7.14 Checking the resistance between primary terminal A and the high tension terminal (1986 and later vehicles) (coil removed for clarity)

Replacement

7   Detach the cable from the negative battery terminal.
8   Detach the electrical leads from the primary and secondary terminals and detach the coil high tension lead.
9   Loosen the coil mounting clamp screw and remove the coil.
10   Installation is the reverse of removal.

1986 on
Check

Refer to illustrations 7.13 and 7.14

11   Make sure the ignition switch is off for the following tests.
12   Unplug the primary and secondary connectors and the coil high tension lead.
13   Using an ohmmeter, touch the probes to terminals A and D of the primary winding **(see illustration)**, measure the resistance between them and compare your reading to the specified resistance.
14   Touch the probes to terminal A and the secondary winding terminal **(see illustration)**, measure the resistance and compare your reading to the specified resistance.
15   Touch the probes to terminals B and D **(see illustration 7.13)**, measure the resistance

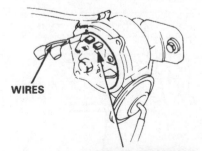

8.2 To test the igniter unit on a Hitachi distributor, unplug the wires and check the resistance between the two igniter terminals

and compare your reading to the specified resistance.
16   The above figures will vary somewhat with coil temperature. The specified resistance values are for a coil temperature of about 70-degrees F.
17   If the coil passes all three checks, it's okay. Plug in the connectors. If it fails any of the above checks, replace it.

Replacement

18   Detach the cable from the negative battery terminal.
19   Unplug the primary connectors and detach the high tension lead from the coil.
20   Remove the two coil mounting bolts and detach the coil from its mounting bracket.
21   Installation is the reverse of removal.

8 Igniter - check and replacement

Note: *If your distributor has a cover on the side like the one shown in illustration 8.7a, it's a Toyo Denso distributor. If not, it's a Hitachi.*

Hitachi

Refer to illustration 8.2

1   Remove the distributor cap (see Chapter 1).
2   Unplug the wires from the igniter **(see illustration)**.
3   With the ignition switch on, check the voltage between the blue wire and body ground, then between the black/yellow wire and body ground. There should be battery voltage for both checks. If not, there is a fault elsewhere in the ignition system.
4   With the wires still disconnected, check continuity in both directions between the two igniter terminals with an ohmmeter set on the R X 100 scale. There should be continuity in only one direction. If there is continuity in neither direction or both directions, replace the igniter (proceed to the next step)
5   Remove the two screws that secure the igniter to the distributor and lift out the igniter.
6   Installation is the reverse of removal. Be sure to reconnect the igniter wires.

5

8.7a To remove the igniter on a Toyo Denso distributor, remove the two screws and lift off the igniter cover . . .

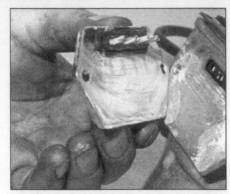

8.7b . . . then unplug the igniter from the distributor base

Toyo Denso

Refer to illustrations 8.7a, 8.7b and 8.8

7   Remove the igniter cover and unplug the igniter unit from the distributor (**see illustrations**).

8   With the ignition switch on, check the voltage between the blue 1 terminal and body ground, then between the black/yellow terminal and body ground (**see illustration**). There should be battery voltage for both checks.

9   Connect a jumper wire between the blue 2 and green terminals on the igniter unit (**see illustration 8.8**). With the ohmmeter scale set to R X 100, check for continuity in both directions between the black/yellow and blue 1 terminals. There should be continuity in only one direction.

10   Replace the igniter if it fails any of the above tests.

9   Radio condenser - check and replacement

Refer to illustration 9.1

Note: *The radio condenser is a device that reduces ignition noise in the radio. It is included in this chapter because it can prevent the engine from running if it fails.*

1   If you own or have access to a condenser tester, check the capacitance of the condenser (**see illustration**) and compare your reading with the specified capacitance. If you don't have a condenser tester, or access to one, take the condenser to a television repair shop and have it tested.

2   If the indicated capacitance isn't within specification, replace the condenser.

10   Distributor - removal and installation

Refer to illustrations 10.4, 10.6a, 10.6b, 10.9 and 10.10

Removal

1   Detach the cable from the negative battery terminal.

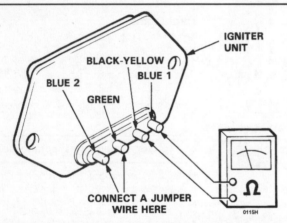

8.8 To check the igniter on a Toyo Denso distributor, measure the voltage between the blue 1 terminal and body ground and between the black/yellow terminal and body ground; then connect a jumper wire between the blue 2 and green terminals and check for continuity in both directions between the black-yellow and blue 1 terminals

9.1 The radio condensor (arrow) is mounted on the shock tower at the right rear of the engine compartment - if you have a condenser checker, hook it up as shown and check the condenser; if you don't have one, remove the condensor and have it checked by a television repair shop

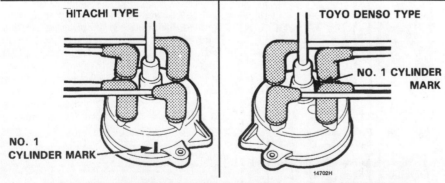

10.4 Look for a raised No. 1 on the distributor cap - that's where the rotor should be pointing when you remove the distributor

10.6a Make one mark directly underneath the rotor tip . . .

2   Detach the vacuum hose from the vacuum advance diaphragm on the distributor.
3   Detach the primary leads from the coil.
4   Look for a raised "1" on the distributor cap **(see illustration)**. This marks the location for the number one cylinder spark plug wire terminal. If the cap does not have a mark for the number one terminal, locate the number one spark plug and trace the wire back to the terminal on the cap.
5   Remove the distributor cap (see Chapter 1) and turn the engine over until the rotor is pointing toward the number one spark plug terminal (see locating TDC procedure in Chapter 2).
6   Make a mark on the edge of the distributor base directly below the rotor tip and in line with it (if the rotor on your engine has more than one tip, use the center one for reference). Also, mark the distributor base and the cylinder head to ensure the distributor is installed correctly **(see illustrations)**.
7   Unplug the igniter leads (see Section 8).
8   Remove the distributor hold down bolts and pull out the distributor. **Caution:** *DO NOT turn the crankshaft while the distributor is out of the engine, or the alignment marks will be useless.*

Installation

Note: *If the crankshaft has been moved while the distributor is out, the number one piston must be repositioned at TDC. This can be done by feeling for compression pressure at the number one plug hole as the crankshaft is turned. Once compression is felt, align the ignition timing zero mark with the pointer.*
9   Install a new O-ring on the distributor housing **(see illustration)**.
10   Insert the distributor into the cylinder head in exactly the same relationship to the head that it was when removed. **Note:** *The lugs on the end of the distributor and the corresponding grooves in the camshaft end are offset to eliminate the possibility of installing the distributor 180-degrees out of time* **(see illustration)**.
11   Recheck the alignment marks between the distributor base and the cylinder head to

10.6b ... and another between the distributor base and the cylinder head (arrow)

verify the distributor is in the same position it was in before removal. Also check the rotor to see if it's aligned with the mark you made on the distributor.
12   Loosely install the hold-down bolts.
13   Attach the igniter leads.
14   Install the distributor cap.
15   Reattach the spark plug wires to the plugs (if removed).
16   Connect the cable to the negative terminal of the battery.
17   Check the ignition timing (see Chapter 1) and tighten the distributor hold-down bolts securely.

11   Reluctor air gap - check and adjustment

Refer to illustrations 11.3a and 11.3b
1   Detach the cable from the negative battery terminal.
2   Remove the distributor cap and rotor (see Chapter 1).
3   Using a non-magnetic feeler gauge, verify the air gaps between the stator and reluctor are equal **(see illustrations)**.
a)   *If your vehicle is equipped with a Hitachi distributor and the gaps aren't equal,*

10.9 Put a new O-ring (arrow) on the bottom of the distributor housing before installing the distributor

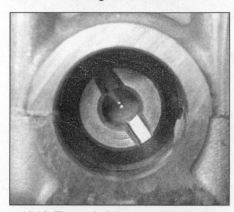

10.10 The end of the camshaft has an offset groove which matches the lugs on the distributor shaft - this ensures you won't install the distributor 180-degrees out of phase

loosen the screws **(see illustration 11.3a)** *and move the stator until the air gaps are equal. Tighten the screws, then recheck the gaps to make sure they are still equal.*
b)   *If your vehicle is equipped with a Toyo Denso distributor and the gaps aren't equal, check for damage to the stator or reluctor. If any damage to the stator is evident, replace the distributor; if there is damage to the reluctor, replace it (see Section 12).*

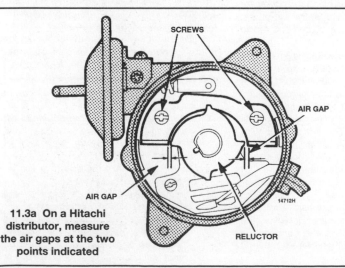

11.3a On a Hitachi distributor, measure the air gaps at the two points indicated

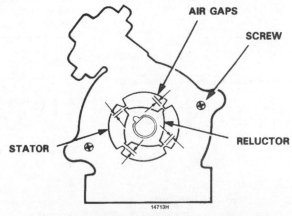

11.3b On a Toyo Denso distributor, measure the air gaps at the four points indicated

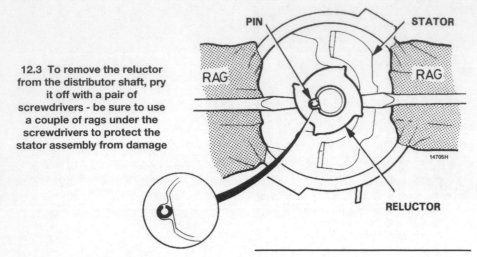

12.3 To remove the reluctor from the distributor shaft, pry it off with a pair of screwdrivers - be sure to use a couple of rags under the screwdrivers to protect the stator assembly from damage

PIN   STATOR

RAG   RAG

RELUCTOR

14705H

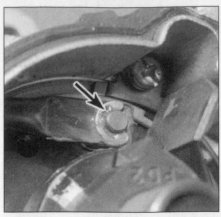

13.6 To remove the vacuum advance diaphragm, first remove the C-clip (arrow) that attaches it to the breaker plate

13.7 Diaphragm mounting screws (arrows) (Toyo Denso distributor shown - Hitachi distributor similar)

12   Reluctor - replacement

Refer to illustration 12.3

1   Detach the cable from the negative battery terminal.
2   Remove the distributor cap (see Chapter 1).
3   Remove the reluctor by prying it off with a pair of small screwdrivers **(see illustration)**. Be careful - using excessive force to pry off the reluctor may result in a damaged stator.
4   Installation is the reverse of removal. Make sure you install the new reluctor with the number or letter manufacturing code facing up and the gap in the pin facing away from the shaft.

13   Vacuum advance diaphragm - check and replacement

Check

1   Detach the cable from the negative battery terminal.
2   Remove the distributor cap.
3   Detach the vacuum hose(s) from the vacuum advance diaphragm on the distributor and attach a vacuum pump to the fitting. If there are two hoses, attach the pump where the outer hose connects.
4   Turn the breaker plate right and left to check for freedom of movement.
5   Apply a gradual vacuum while watching the breaker plate. Verify the breaker plate operates smoothly - there should be no binding.

 a)   *If there's binding, find the source of the binding and free the breaker plate.*
 b)   *If the vacuum pump gauge indicates a loss of vacuum, the diaphragm is defective and must be replaced.*

Replacement

Refer to illustrations 13.6 and 13.7

6   Remove the vacuum advance diaphragm arm C-clip **(see illustration)**.
7   Remove the diaphragm mounting screws **(see illustration)**.
8   Detach the diaphragm arm, then pull the diaphragm out of the distributor.
9   Installation is the reverse of removal.

14   Centrifugal advance - check

1   Detach the vacuum hose(s) from the vacuum advance diaphragm and plug it (them).
2   Connect a timing light in accordance with the manufacturer's instructions.
3   Start the engine and increase the engine speed from idle to about 2500 RPM. The timing mark (T) should appear to move past the pointer toward the firewall, indicating an increase in ignition advance. If it doesn't, check the centrifugal advance mechanism for sticking or binding.

15   Charging system - general information and precautions

The charging system includes the alternator, an internal voltage regulator, a charge indicator, the battery, a fusible link and the wiring between all the components. The charging system supplies electrical power for the ignition system, the lights, the radio, etc. The alternator is driven by a drivebelt at the left end of the engine.

The purpose of the voltage regulator is to limit the alternator's voltage to a preset value. This prevents power surges, circuit overloads, etc., during peak voltage output.

The fusible link is a short length of insulated wire integral with the engine compartment wiring harness. The link is four wire gauges smaller in diameter than the circuit it protects. Production fusible links and their identification flags are identified by the flag color. See Chapter 12 for additional information regarding fusible links.

The charging system doesn't ordinarily require periodic maintenance. However, the drivebelt, battery and wires and connections should be inspected at the intervals outlined in Chapter 1.

The dashboard warning light should come on when the ignition key is turned to On, but it should go off immediately after the engine is started. If it remains on, there is a malfunction in the charging system (see Section 16). Some vehicles are also equipped with a voltmeter. If the voltmeter indicates abnormally high or low voltage, check the charging system (see Section 16).

Be very careful when making electrical circuit connections to a vehicle equipped with an alternator and note the following:

 a)   *When reconnecting wires to the alternator from the battery, be sure to note the polarity.*
 b)   *Before using arc welding equipment to repair any part of the vehicle, disconnect the wires from the alternator and the battery terminals.*
 c)   *Never start the engine with a battery charger connected.*
 d)   *Always disconnect both battery leads before using a battery charger.*
 e)   *The alternator is turned by an engine drivebelt which could cause serious injury if your hands, hair or clothes become entangled in it with the engine running.*

f) Because the alternator is connected directly to the battery, it could arc or cause a fire if overloaded or shorted out.

g) Wrap a plastic bag over the alternator and secure it with rubber bands before steam cleaning the engine.

16 Charging system - check

1 If a malfunction occurs in the charging circuit, don't automatically assume that the alternator is causing the problem. First check the following items:

a) Check the drivebelt tension and condition (Chapter 1). Replace it if it's worn or deteriorated.

b) Make sure the alternator mounting and adjustment bolts are tight.

c) Inspect the alternator wiring harness and the connectors at the alternator and voltage regulator. They must be in good condition and tight.

d) Check the fusible link (if equipped) located between the starter solenoid and the alternator. If it's burned, determine the cause, repair the circuit and replace the link (the vehicle won't start and/or the accessories won't work if the fusible link blows). Sometimes a fusible link may look good, but still be bad. If in doubt, remove it and check for continuity.

e) Start the engine and check the alternator for abnormal noises (a shrieking or squealing sound indicates a bad bearing).

f) Check the specific gravity of the battery electrolyte. If it's low, charge the battery (doesn't apply to maintenance free batteries).

g) Make sure the battery is fully charged (one bad cell in a battery can cause overcharging by the alternator).

h) Disconnect the battery cables (negative first, then positive). Inspect the battery posts and the cable clamps for corrosion. Clean them thoroughly if necessary (see Chapter 1). Reconnect the cable to the negative terminal.

i) With the key off, connect a test light between the negative battery post and the disconnected negative cable clamp.

  1) If the test light does not come on, reattach the clamp and proceed to the next step.

  2) If the test light comes on, there is a short (drain) in the electrical system of the vehicle. The short must be repaired before the charging system can be checked.

  3) Disconnect the alternator wiring harness.

    a) If the light goes out, the alternator is bad.

    b) If the light stays on, pull each fuse until the light goes out (this will tell you which component is shorted).

2 Using a voltmeter, check the battery voltage with the engine off. If should be approximately 12-volts.

3 Start the engine and check the battery

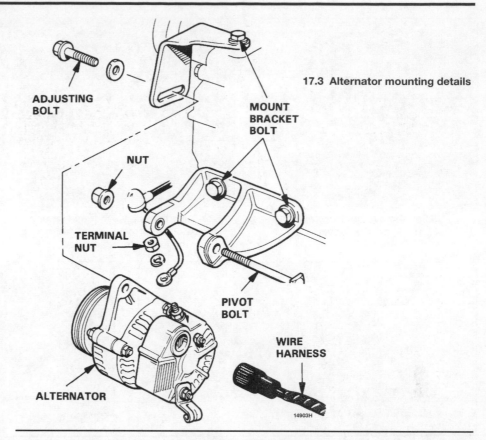

17.3 Alternator mounting details

voltage again. It should now be approximately 14-to-15 volts.

4 Turn on the headlights. The voltage should drop, and then come back up, if the charging system is working properly.

5 If the voltage reading is more than the specified charging voltage, replace the voltage regulator (refer to Section 18). If the voltage is less, the alternator diode(s), stator or rectifier may be bad or the voltage regulator may be malfunctioning.

17 Alternator - removal and installation

Refer to illustration 17.3
Note: To gain access to the alternator, it may be necessary to disconnect the left drive shaft from the steering knuckle.

1 Detach the cable from the negative terminal of the battery. Raise the vehicle. Support it securely on jackstands and remove the left driveaxle from the steering knuckle (see Chapter 8).

2 Detach the wire harness from the alternator.

3 Loosen the alternator adjusting bolt and pivot bolt nut, then detach the drivebelt **(see illustration)**.

4 Remove the adjusting and pivot bolts and separate the alternator from the engine. If necessary, remove the upper and lower mount brackets.

5 If you are replacing the alternator, take the old one with you when purchasing a

replacement unit. Make sure the new/rebuilt unit looks identical to the old alternator. Look at the terminals - they should be the same in number, size and location as the terminals on the old alternator. Finally, look at the identification numbers - they will be stamped into the housing or printed on a tag attached to the housing. Make sure the numbers are the same on both alternators.

6 Many new/rebuilt alternators DO NOT have a pulley installed, so you may have to switch the pulley from the old unit to the new/rebuilt one. When buying an alternator, find out the shop's policy regarding pulleys - some shops will perform this service free of charge.

7 Installation is the reverse of removal.

8 After the alternator is installed, adjust the drivebelt tension (see Chapter 1).

9 Check the charging voltage to verify proper operation of the alternator (see Section 16).

18 Voltage regulator and alternator brushes - replacement

Refer to illustrations 18.2a, 18.2b, 18.3, 18.4a, 18.4b, 18.5 and 18.7
Note: Don't attempt to overhaul the alternator. If replacing the brushes and regulator does not solve the alternator problem, take the alternator to a dealer and have it rebuilt or exchange it as a core for a rebuilt unit.

1 Remove the alternator (see Section 17) and place it on a clean workbench.

5

18.2a Remove the three nuts from the rear cover

18.2b Take the nut, washer and terminal insulator off terminal B and remove the alternator rear cover

18.3 Once the rear cover is removed, remove the five screws (arrows) that retain the voltage regulator and the brush holder

18.4a Remove the brush holder, . . .

18.4b . . . then remove the regulator

2   Remove the three rear cover nuts, the nut and terminal insulator and the rear cover **(see illustrations)**.
3   Remove the five voltage regulator and brush holder retaining screws **(see illustration)**.
4   Remove the brush holder and the regulator from the rear end frame **(see illustrations)**. If you are only replacing the regulator, proceed to Step 8, install the new unit, reassemble the alternator and install it on the engine (see Section 17). If you are going to replace the brushes, proceed with the next Step.
5   Measure the exposed length of each brush **(see illustration)** and compare it to the specified minimum length. If the length of either brush is less than the specified minimum, replace the brushes.
6   Make sure that each brush moves smoothly in the brush holder.

7   Install the brush holder by depressing each brush with a small screwdriver to clear the shaft **(see illustration)**.
8   Install the voltage regulator and brush holder screws into the rear frame.
9   Install the rear cover and tighten the three nuts securely.
10   Install the terminal insulator and tighten it with the nut.
11   Install the alternator (see Section 17).

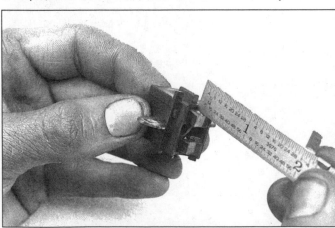

18.5 Measure the exposed length of the brushes and compare your measurements to the specified minimum length to determine whether they should be replaced

18.7 To install the brush holder, depress each brush with a small screwdriver to clear the shaft

19 Starting system - general information and precautions

The sole function of the starting system is to turn over the engine quickly enough to allow it to start.

The starting system consists of the battery, the starter motor, the starter solenoid and the wires connecting them. The solenoid is mounted directly on the starter motor.

The solenoid/starter motor assembly is installed on the lower part of the engine, next to the transmission bellhousing.

When the ignition key is turned to the Start position, the starter solenoid is actuated through the starter control circuit. The starter solenoid then connects the battery to the starter. The battery supplies the electrical energy to the starter motor, which does the actual work of cranking the engine.

The starter motor on some vehicles equipped with a manual transmission can only be operated when the clutch pedal is depressed; the starter on all vehicles equipped with an automatic transmission can only be operated when the transmission selector lever is in Park or Neutral.

Always observe the following precautions when working on the starting system:

a) *Excessive cranking of the starter motor can overheat it and cause serious damage. Never operate the starter motor for more than 30 seconds at a time without pausing to allow it to cool for at least two minutes.*

b) *The starter is connected directly to the battery and could arc or cause a fire if mishandled, overloaded or shorted out.*

c) *Always detach the cable from the negative terminal of the battery before working on the starting system.*

20 Starter motor - in-vehicle check

Note: *Before diagnosing starter problems, make sure the battery is fully charged.*

1   If the starter motor does not turn at all when the switch is operated, make sure the shift lever is in Neutral or Park (automatic transmission) or the clutch pedal is depressed (manual transmission).
2   Make sure the battery is charged and all cables, both at the battery and starter solenoid terminals, are clean and secure.
3   If the starter motor spins but the engine is not cranking, the overrunning clutch in the starter motor is slipping and the starter motor must be replaced.
4   If, when the switch is actuated, the starter motor does not operate at all but the solenoid clicks, then the problem lies with either the battery, the main solenoid contacts or the starter motor itself (or the engine is seized).
5   If the solenoid plunger cannot be heard when the switch is actuated, the battery is bad, the fusible link is burned (the circuit is open) or the solenoid itself is defective.
6   To check the solenoid, connect a jumper lead between the battery (+) and the ignition switch wire terminal (the small terminal) on the solenoid. If the starter motor now operates, the solenoid is OK and the problem is in the ignition switch, neutral start switch or the wiring.
7   If the starter motor still does not operate, remove the starter/solenoid assembly for disassembly, testing and repair.
8   If the starter motor cranks the engine at an abnormally slow speed, first make sure that the battery is charged and that all terminal connections are tight. If the engine is partially seized, or has the wrong viscosity oil in it, it will crank slowly.
9   Run the engine until normal operating temperature is reached, then disconnect the coil wire from the distributor cap and ground it on the engine.
10   Connect a voltmeter positive lead to the positive battery post and connect the negative lead to the negative post.
11   Crank the engine and take the voltmeter readings as soon as a steady figure is indicated. Do not allow the starter motor to turn for more than 30 seconds at a time. A reading of 9 volts or more, with the starter motor turning at normal cranking speed, is normal. If the reading is 9 volts or more but the cranking speed is slow, the motor is faulty. If the reading is less than 9 volts and the cranking speed is slow, the solenoid contacts are probably burned, the starter motor is bad, the battery is discharged or there is a bad connection.

21 Starter motor - removal and installation

1   Detach the cable from the negative terminal of the battery.
2   Clearly label, then disconnect the wires from the terminals on the starter motor and solenoid.
3   Remove the mounting bolts and detach the starter.
4   Installation is the reverse of removal.

22 Starter solenoid - removal and installation

1   Disconnect the cable from the negative terminal of the battery.
2   Remove the starter motor (see Section 21).
3   Disconnect the large wire from the solenoid to the starter motor terminal.
4   Remove the screws which secure the solenoid to the starter motor gear housing and detach the solenoid from the gear housing.
5   While the solenoid is removed, check the overrunning clutch by sliding it along its shaft. If it doesn't move freely, or if the clutch slips when you rotate the armature while holding the drive gear, replace the clutch assembly. If the gear is worn or damaged, replace the complete overrunning clutch assembly (the gear isn't available separately). If the starter gear teeth are damaged, you should also inspect the flywheel or driveplate ring gear for damage.
6   Installation is the reverse of removal.

5

Notes

Chapter 6
Emission control systems

Contents

1 General information

Refer to illustrations 1.6a and 1.6b

To prevent pollution of the atmosphere from incompletely burned and evaporating gases, and to maintain good driveability and fuel economy, a number of emission control systems are incorporated. They include the:

Feedback Control system
Exhaust Gas Recirculation (EGR) system
Secondary air supply/air injection system
Fuel evaporative control system
Positive Crankcase Ventilation (PCV) system
Intake air temperature control system
Catalytic converter

The Sections in this Chapter include general descriptions, checking procedures within the scope of the home mechanic and component replacement procedures (when possible) for each of the systems listed above.

Before assuming that an emissions control system is malfunctioning, check the fuel and ignition systems carefully. The diagnosis of some emission control devices requires specialized tools, equipment and training. If checking and servicing become too difficult or if a procedure is beyond your ability, consult a dealer service department. Remember, the most frequent cause of emissions problems is simply a loose or broken vacuum hose or wire, so always check the hose and wiring connections first.

This doesn't mean, however, that emission control systems are particularly difficult to maintain and repair. You can quickly and easily perform many checks and do most of

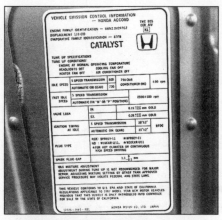

1.6a The Vehicle Emission Control Information (VECI) label provides essential tune-up specifications like idle speed and fast idle, spark plug types, etc.

the regular maintenance at home with common tune-up and hand tools. **Note:** *Because of a Federally mandated extended warranty which covers the emission control system components, check with your dealer about warranty coverage before working on any emissions-related systems. Once the warranty has expired, you may wish to perform some of the component checks and/or replacement procedures in this Chapter to save money.*

Pay close attention to any special precautions outlined in this Chapter. It should be noted that the illustrations of the various systems may not exactly match the system installed on your vehicle because of changes made by the manufacturer during production

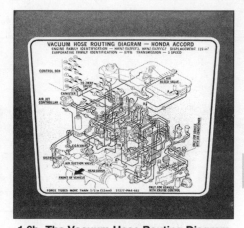

1.6b The Vacuum Hose Routing Diagram tells you what emission control devices the vehicle is equipped with, gives you their approximate locations and provides a vacuum hose routing schematic, which is helpful when you're looking for leaks and disconnected or misrouted hoses

or from year-to-year.

A Vehicle Emissions Control Information (VECI) label is attached to the underside of the hood **(see illustration)**. This label contains important emissions specifications and adjustment information. A second label, the Vacuum Hose Routing Diagram, **(see illustration)** provides a vacuum hose schematic with emissions components identified. When servicing the engine or emissions systems, the VECI label and the vacuum hose routing diagram in your particular vehicle should always be checked for up-to-date information.

6

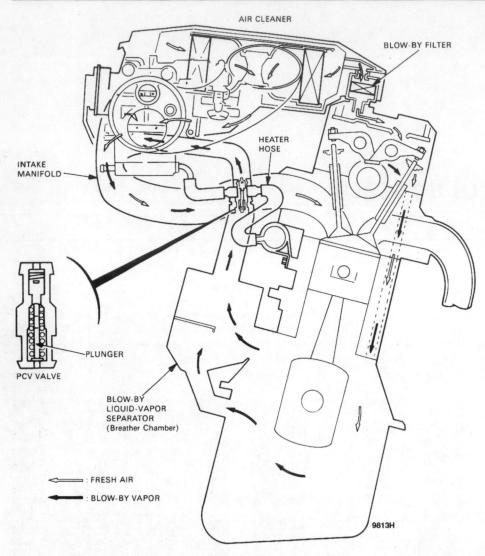

2.1 **A typical Positive Crankcase Ventilation (PCV) system (carbureted vehicle shown, fuel-injected vehicles similar)**

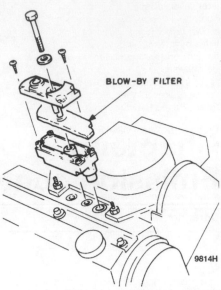

2.2 **An exploded view of the PCV filter assembly on a fuel-injected vehicle**

2   Every evaporative system employs a canister filled with activated charcoal to absorb fuel vapors. The means by which these vapors are controlled, however, varies considerably from one system to another. The following descriptions of typical systems for carbureted and fuel injected vehicles should provide you enough information to understand the system on your vehicle.

Carbureted vehicles

Note: *The following description is not intended as a specific description of the evaporative system on your particular vehicle. Rather, it is intended as a general description of a typical system used on carbureted vehicles. Although the following components are most likely all used on your particular system, there may also be other devices, not included here, which are unique to your system.*

3   The fuel filler cap is fitted with a two-way valve as a safety device. The valve vents fuel vapors to the atmosphere if the evaporative control system fails.

4   Another two-way valve, mounted on the fuel tank, regulates fuel vapor flow from the fuel tank to the charcoal canister, based on the pressure or vacuum caused by temperature changes.

5   After passing through the two-way valve, fuel vapor is carried by vent hoses to the charcoal canister in the engine compartment. The activated charcoal in the canister absorbs and stores these vapors.

6   An air vent cut-off diaphragm, mounted on the carburetor, vents fuel vapors from the float chambers to the charcoal canister when the engine is off.

7   When the engine is running and warmed to a pre-set temperature, a thermo valve on top of the canister closes, allowing a purge control diaphragm valve in the charcoal can-

2   Positive Crankcase Ventilation (PCV) system

Refer to illustrations 2.1 and 2.2

1   The Positive Crankcase Ventilation (PCV) system **(see illustration)** reduces hydrocarbon emissions by scavenging crankcase vapors. It does this by circulating fresh air from the air cleaner through the crankcase, where it mixes with blow-by gases and is then rerouted through a PCV valve to the intake manifold.

2   The main components of the PCV system for all vehicles are the PCV valve, a blow-by filter and the vacuum hoses connecting these two components with the engine. On carbureted vehicles, the blow-by filter is on the side of the air cleaner housing; on fuel-injected vehicles, it's mounted on the camshaft cover **(see illustration)**.

3   To maintain idle quality, the PCV valve

restricts the flow when the intake manifold vacuum is high. If abnormal operating condition (such as piston ring problems) arise, the system is designed to allow excessive amounts of blow-by gases to flow back through the crankcase vent tube into the air cleaner to be consumed by normal combustion.

4   Checking and replacement of the PCV valve and filter is covered in Chapter 1.

3   Fuel evaporative control system

General description

Refer to illustrations 3.1a and 3.1b

1   The fuel evaporative control system **(see illustrations)** absorbs fuel vapors and, during engine operation, releases them into the engine intake where they mix with the incoming air-fuel mixture.

ister to be opened by intake manifold vacuum. Fuel vapors from the canister are then drawn through the purge control diaphragm valve by intake manifold vacuum.

8   When the engine isn't running, the fuel passages in the main and slow primary fuel metering system are cut off by solenoid valves to prevent the fuel in the float chamber from entering the carburetor bore.

Fuel-injected vehicles

Note: *The following description is not intended as a specific description of the evaporative system on your particular vehicle. Rather, it is a general description of a typical system used on fuel-injected vehicles. Although the following components are most likely all used on your particular system, there may also be other devices, not included here, which are unique to your system.*

9   When fuel vapor pressure in the fuel tank exceeds a pre-set level, a two-way valve on the fuel tank opens and allows the fuel vapors to flow to the charcoal canister.

10   The charcoal canister temporarily stores fuel vapors until they can be purged from the charcoal canister into the engine and burned.

11   Canister purging is controlled by a vapor purge control diaphragm which is opened or closed by a thermo valve. When the engine coolant temperature is below about 131 degrees F, the thermo valve provides no manifold vacuum to the purge control diaphragm. When the temperature exceeds 131 degrees F, the thermo valve directs manifold vacuum to the purge control diaphragm, which admits ported vacuum to the canister and draws fresh air through the canister into a port on the throttle body.

Checking

Note: *Complete checking of the fuel evaporative control system is beyond the scope of the home mechanic. Fortunately, the evaporative control system, like all emission control systems, is protected by a Federally-mandated extended warranty (5 years or 50,000 miles at the time this manual was written). The fuel evaporative system probably won't fail during the service life of the vehicle; however, if it does, the hoses or charcoal canister are usually to blame.*

Hoses

12   Always check the hoses first. A disconnected, damaged or missing hose is the most likely cause of a malfunctioning evaporative system. Refer to the Vacuum Hose Routing Diagram (attached to the underside of the hood) to determine whether the hoses are correctly routed and attached. Repair any damaged hoses or replace any missing hoses as necessary.

Charcoal canister

13   Detach the canister from the firewall.
14   Detach the intake tube hose (refer to the Vacuum Hose Routing Diagram attached to the underside of the hood) and put your fin-

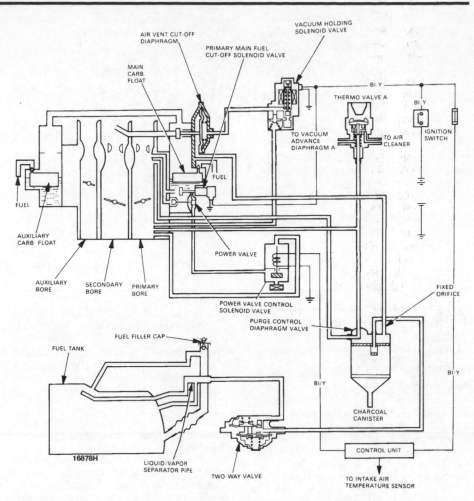

3.1a Schematic for a typical fuel evaporative control system on a carbureted vehicle

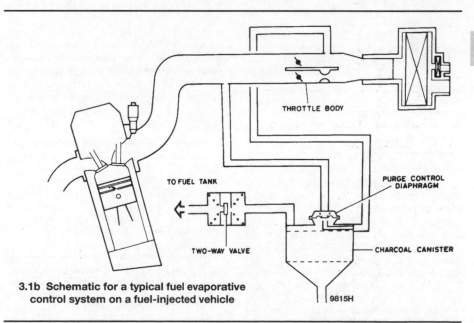

3.1b Schematic for a typical fuel evaporative control system on a fuel-injected vehicle

ger on the end of the canister inlet fitting.
15   Warm the engine to normal operating temperature, then increase the engine speed to 2500 rpm. If the canister is functioning correctly, air will be drawn into the canister through the inlet tube and you will feel suction. If you don't feel suction, replace the canister.

6

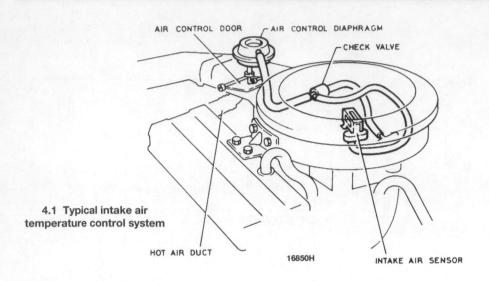

4.1 Typical intake air temperature control system

AIR CONTROL DOOR — AIR CONTROL DIAPHRAGM — CHECK VALVE — HOT AIR DUCT — 16850H — INTAKE AIR SENSOR

4   Intake air temperature control system

General description

Refer to illustration 4.1

1   The air temperature control system **(see illustration)** provides heated intake air during warm-up, then maintains a uniform inlet air temperature of about 100 degrees by mixing warm and cool air. This allows leaner fuel/air mixture settings for the carburetor, which reduces emissions and improves driveability.

2   Two fresh air inlets - one hot and one cold - are used. The balance between the two is controlled by an air control diaphragm, which operates an air control door in the air cleaner.

3   When the underhood temperature is cold, warm air radiating off the exhaust manifold is trapped by a shroud which fits over the manifold and routed up through a hot air duct through the door into the air cleaner. This provides warm air for the carburetor, resulting in better driveability and faster warm-up. As the temperature inside the air cleaner

rises, the air control door is gradually closed by the vacuum motor (which, in turn is controlled by an intake air sensor inside the air cleaner) and the air cleaner draws air through an outside air duct instead. The result is a consistent intake air temperature.

Checking

Note: *This check is done with the engine off. Make sure the engine is cold before beginning this test.*

4   Always check the vacuum source and the integrity of all vacuum hoses between the source and the air control diaphragm before beginning the following test. Do not proceed until they're okay.

5   Apply the parking brake and block the wheels.

6   Detach, but do not remove, the air cleaner housing and element (see Chapter 4).

7   Turn the air cleaner housing upside down so the air control door is visible. The door should be open. If it isn't, it might be binding or sticking. Make sure that it's not rusted in an open or closed position by attempting to move it by hand. If it's rusted, it

can usually be freed by cleaning and oiling the hinge. If it fails to work properly after servicing, replace it.

8   If the air control door is okay but the motor still fails to operate correctly, check carefully for a leak in the hose leading to it. Check the vacuum source to and from the intake air sensor with a hand vacuum pump. If no leak is found, replace the vacuum motor.

Component replacement

Refer to illustration 4.9

9   To remove the air control diaphragm, twist it 90 degrees and pull straight up **(see illustration)**.

5   Ignition timing control system

General description

Refer to illustrations 5.1a and 5.1b

1   The ignition timing control system **(see illustrations)** alters ignition timing during and after engine warm-up to reduce emissions, maximize fuel economy and enhance performance.

Checking

2   Warm the engine to its normal operating temperature.

3   Attach a tachometer in accordance with the manufacturer's instructions.

4   Detach the hose from the vacuum advance diaphragm on the distributor and attach a vacuum gauge to the hose. If there are two hoses, attach the gauge to the inner hose (closest to the distributor).

5   Start the engine, allow it to idle and verify there is vacuum.

   a If there is vacuum, go to the next Step.

   b If no vacuum is indicated on the gauge, check the hose connections between the distributor and the carburetor insulator block for leaks or blockage.

6   Attach a hand vacuum pump/gauge to the hose fitting on the vacuum advance diaphragm and hook up a timing light in

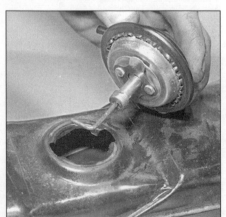

4.9 The air control diaphragm is easy to replace - simply twist it 90 degrees and pull out

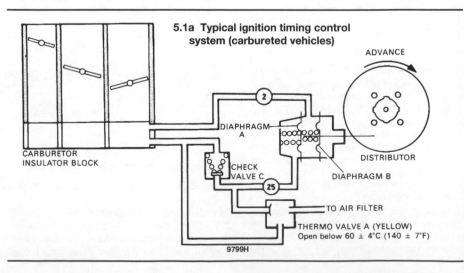

5.1a Typical ignition timing control system (carbureted vehicles)

CARBURETOR INSULATOR BLOCK — DIAPHRAGM A — CHECK VALVE C — ADVANCE — DISTRIBUTOR — DIAPHRAGM B — TO AIR FILTER — THERMO VALVE A (YELLOW) Open below 60 ± 4°C (140 ± 7°F) — 9799H

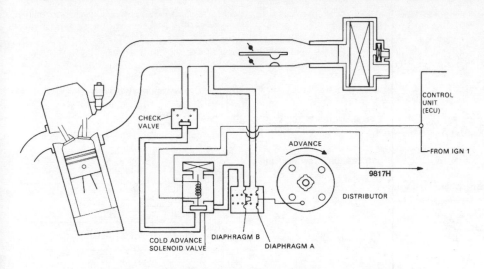

5.1b Typical ignition timing control system (fuel-injected vehicles)

accordance with the manufacturer's instructions. Start the engine and apply 20 in-Hg of vacuum. The ignition timing should advance and vacuum should remain steady.

a If the timing advances, the system is okay. Detach the tachometer and reattach the vacuum hose.

b If the timing doesn't advance and the vacuum doesn't remain steady, the diaphragm is leaking. Replace it (see Chapter 4) and recheck.

c If the vacuum remains steady but the timing does not advance, stop the engine and remove the distributor cap. Verify that the breaker plate turns freely by turning it left and right. If there's no evidence of binding, replace the vacuum

advance diaphragm (see Chapter 4) and recheck it.

---

6 Throttle control system

Refer to illustration 6.1

General description

1 To reduce emissions and provide easier starting, a throttle controller **(see illustration)** holds the throttle open slightly to admit extra air during starting, shifting and deceleration.

2 When the engine is running above idle speed, ported vacuum in the carburetor is applied to the throttle controller through a

dashpot check valve. On deceleration, this vacuum is bled off through an orifice in the dashpot check valve, gradually diminishing until the throttle closes entirely.

3 When the engine is cranked during start-up, the cranking opener solenoid valve is activated to allow intake manifold vacuum into the diaphragm to ensure the proper throttle opening angle.

Checking

Throttle controller

4 Detach the vacuum hose from the throttle controller, attach a hand vacuum pump to the hose fitting and apply 8 in-Hg vacuum. Engine speed should rise to about 2000 rpm within one minute.

a If the speed is lower than specified, widen the adjusting slot in the controller lever with a screwdriver.

b If the speed is higher than specified, narrow the adjusting slot in the lever with needle nose pliers.

c If the speed can't be adjusted or the diaphragm won't hold vacuum, replace the throttle controller and recheck.

Cranking opener solenoid valve

5 Perform the check described in Steps 4 and 5 above.

6 Ground the coil secondary wire to prevent the engine from starting. Turn the ignition key to Start. The throttle controller arm should retract when you crank the engine. If it doesn't, check all the hoses in the system for damage and proper routing (refer to the Vacuum Hose Routing Diagram on the underside of the vehicle's hood). If all hoses are in good condition and properly routed, take the vehicle to a dealer service department for further checking.

6

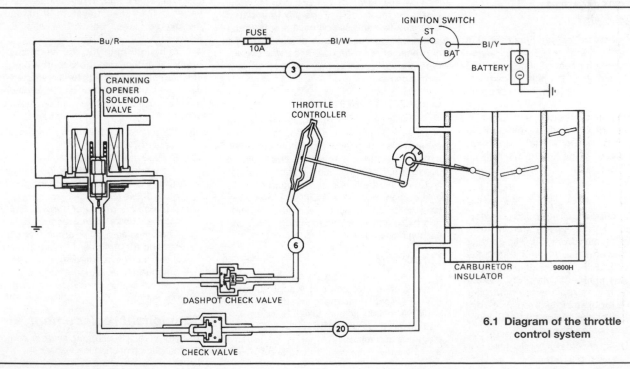

6.1 Diagram of the throttle control system

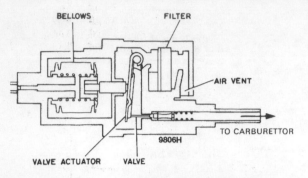

7.1 Cutaway view of a typical air jet controller

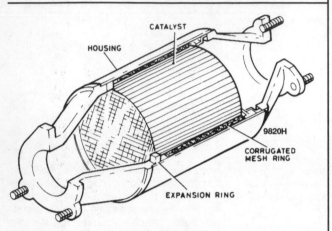

8.1 Cutaway view of a typical catalytic converter used on the vehicles covered by this manual

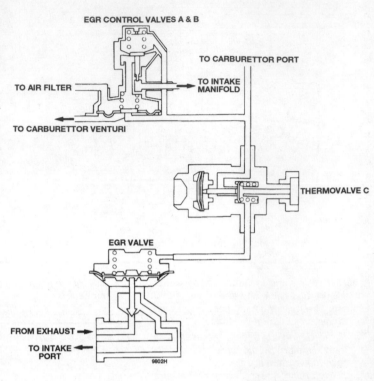

9.2 Typical EGR system on a carbureted vehicle

7 Air jet controller

General description

Refer to illustration 7.1

1 The air jet controller **(see illustration)** is an atmospheric pressure sensing device which controls the amount of airflow into the slow and main air jets of the primary carburetor bore and the slow air jet of the secondary carburetor bore.

2 As atmospheric pressure is reduced by increasing altitude, the bellows expands to open the valve in the air jet controller, increasing air flow to the jets to maintain an optimum air/fuel ratio.

Checking

3 A malfunctioning air jet controller normally causes an excessively rich mixture (black smoke coming from the tailpipe) and poor engine performance when operating the vehicle at high altitudes. If you suspect the air jet controller is malfunctioning, the easiest way to check it is to replace the controller and see if the problem is resolved. The controller is located on the engine side of the firewall next to the control box.

8 Catalytic converter

Refer to illustration 8.1

Note: *Because of a Federally mandated extended warranty which covers emissions-related components such as the catalytic converter, check with a dealer service department before replacing the converter at your own expense.*

General description

1 The catalytic converter **(see illustration)** is an emission control device added to the exhaust system to reduce pollutants from the exhaust gas stream. There are two types of converters. The conventional oxidation catalyst reduces the levels of hydrocarbon (HC) and carbon monoxide (CO). The three-way catalyst lowers the levels of oxides of nitrogen (NOx) as well as hydrocarbons (HC) and carbon monoxide (CO).

Checking

2 The test equipment for a catalytic converter is expensive and highly sophisticated. If you suspect that the converter on your vehicle is malfunctioning, take it to a dealer or authorized emissions inspection facility for diagnosis and repair.

3 Whenever the vehicle is raised for servicing of underbody components, check the converter for leaks, corrosion, dents and other damage. Check the welds/flange bolts that attach the front and rear ends of the converter to the exhaust system. If damage is discovered, the converter should be replaced.

4 Although catalytic converters don't break too often, they do become plugged. The easiest way to check for a restricted converter is to use a vacuum gauge to diagnose the effect of a blocked exhaust on intake vacuum.

a) *Open the throttle until the engine speed is about 2000 RPM.*

b) *Release the throttle quickly.*

c) *If there is no restriction, the gauge will quickly drop to not more than 2 in-Hg or more above its normal reading.*

d) *If the gauge does not show 5 in-Hg or more above its normal reading, or seems to momentarily hover around its highest reading for a moment before it returns, the exhaust system, or the converter, is plugged (or an exhaust pipe is bent or dented, or the core inside the muffler has shifted).*

Component replacement

5 Refer to the exhaust system removal and installation section in Chapter 4.

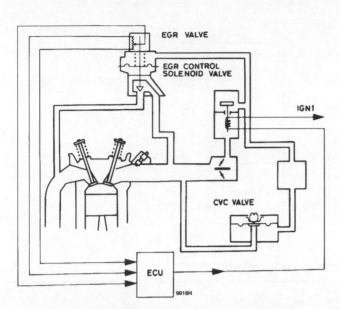

9.3 Typical EGR system on a fuel-injected vehicle

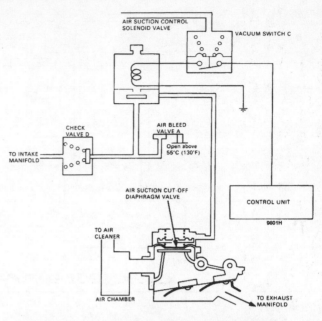

10.1 Typical secondary air supply system

9 Exhaust gas recirculation (EGR) system

General description

Refer to illustrations 9.2 and 9.3

1   The EGR system reduces oxides of nitrogen by recirculating exhaust gas through the EGR valve and intake manifold into the combustion chambers.

2   On carbureted vehicles, the EGR system **(see illustration)** consists of the EGR valve, a pair of control valves and a thermo valve. The EGR valve, which is operated by ported vacuum via the two control valves, recirculates gases in accordance with engine load (intake air volume). To eliminate recirculation at idle, the vacuum signal is ported above the idle throttle position. During cold engine operation, the thermo valve opens, bleeding off ported vacuum and keeping the EGR valve closed. When the engine coolant temperature exceeds the set temperature of the thermo valve, it closes and ported vacuum is applied to the EGR valve and control valve A. This opens the EGR valve and allows exhaust gas into the intake manifold. Control valve B is normally closed. When manifold vacuum reaches a set level, the valve opens, allowing venturi vacuum to enter control valve A and the EGR valve.

3   On fuel-injected vehicles, the EGR system **(see illustration)** consists of the EGR valve, the CVC valve, the EGR control solenoid valve, the Electronic Control Unit (ECU) and various sensors. The ECU memory is programmed to produce the ideal EGR valve lift for each operating condition. An EGR valve lift sensor detects the amount of EGR valve lift and sends this information to the ECU. The ECU then compares it with the ideal EGR valve lift, which is determined by data received from the other sensors. If there's any difference between the two, the ECU triggers the EGR control solenoid valve to reduce the amount of vacuum applied to the EGR valve.

Checking

EGR valve

4   Start the engine and allow it to idle.

5   Detach the vacuum hose from the EGR valve and attach a hand vacuum pump in its place.

6   Apply vacuum to the EGR valve. Vacuum should remain steady and the engine should run poorly.

  a   *If vacuum doesn't remain steady and the engine doesn't run poorly, replace the EGR valve and recheck it.*

  b   *If vacuum remains steady but the engine doesn't run poorly, remove the EGR valve and check the valve and the intake manifold for blockage. Clean or replace as necessary and recheck.*

EGR system (carbureted vehicles)

7   Detach the vacuum hose from the EGR valve and attach a vacuum gauge to the hose.

8   Start the engine and warm it to its normal operating temperature (wait for the electric cooling fan to come on).

9   Remove the control box from the firewall (it's attached with four bolts), then remove the control box cover (it's held on by four screws). Vacuum at the EGR hose should be as follows:

  a   *At idle, there should be no vacuum. If there is, replace the EGR control valve and check the vacuum hose routing (refer to the Vacuum Hose Routing diagram on the underside of the hood).*

  b   *At 4500 rpm, there should be 2 to 6 in-Hg*

of vacuum. If there isn't, check for vacuum at the inlet and outlet of the thermo valve. If there is vacuum at the inlet but none at the outlet, replace the thermo valve. If there is no vacuum at the inlet, check the routing of the vacuum hoses and repair or replace them as necessary.

  c   *At 4500 rpm with the vacuum bleed hose pinched, there should be less than 2 in-Hg. If there is more, replace the EGR control valve and check the vacuum hose routing.*

  d   *During rapid acceleration, there should be 2 to 6 in-Hg. If there isn't, check for vacuum at the thermo valve inlet and outlet. If there's vacuum at the inlet but not at the outlet, replace the thermo valve. If there's no vacuum at the inlet, check the routing of the vacuum hoses and repair or replace them as necessary.*

  e   *During deceleration, there should be no vacuum.*

EGR system (fuel-injected vehicles)

10   Checking the EGR system on fuel-injected vehicles requires special tools and equipment. Take the vehicle to a dealer service department for checking.

10 Secondary air supply/air injection system

General description

Refer to illustration 10.1

1   The secondary air supply system **(see illustration)** is designed to improve emission control performance by introducing fresh air from the air cleaner into the exhaust manifold through the air suction cut-off diaphragm valve.

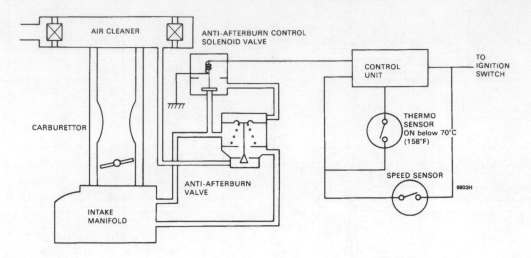

11.1 Typical anti-afterburn/mixture control system

Checking

2   Checking the secondary air supply system is best left to a dealer service department.

11 Anti-afterburn valve/mixture control system

General description

Refer to illustration 11.1

1   The anti-afterburn valve/mixture control system **(see illustration)** prevents an excessively rich mixture during shifting and deceleration by supplying fresh air to the intake manifold.

Checking

2   Checking the anti-afterburn valve/mixture control system is best left to a dealer service department.

12 Feedback control system

General description

Refer to illustration 12.1

1   The feedback control system **(see illustration)** maintains the proper air/fuel mixture ratio for varying operating conditions by altering the amount of extra air supplied to the intake manifold.

Checking

2   This system requires special tools and test equipment for proper diagnosis. Checking the system is best left to a dealer service department.

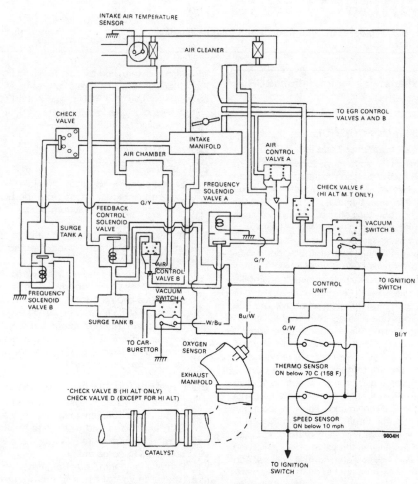

12.1 Typical feedback control system

Chapter 7 Part A
Manual transaxle

Contents

Specifications

Clearances

Fifth gear-to-shoulder on spacer collar
- Standard .... 0.001 to 0.005 in (0.03 to 0.13 mm)
- Service limit .... 0.01 in (0.25 mm)

Fifth/reverse shift shaft pin-to-reverse shift fork
- Standard .... 0.002 to 0.014 in (0.05 to 0.35 mm)
- Service limit .... 0.02 in (0.5 mm)

Reverse idler gear-to-reverse idler gear shift fork
- Standard .... 0.008 to 0.04 in (0.2 to 1.0 mm)
- Service limit .... 0.07 in (1.7 mm)
- Reverse shift fork slot .... 0.278 to 0.285 in (7.05 to 7.25 mm)
- Reverse shift fork fingers .... 0.46 to 0.48 in (11.8 to 12.1 mm)

Synchronizer ring-to-gear
- Standard
  - 1984 and 1985 .... 0.033 in to 0.043 in (0.85 to 1.10 mm)
  - 1986 on .... 0.029 to 0.047 in (0.73 to 1.18 mm)
- Service limit (all models) .... 0.016 in to (0.4 mm)

Shift fork-to-synchronizer sleeve
- Standard .... 0.014 to 0.026 in (0.35 to 0.65 mm)
- Service limit .... 0.039 in (1.0 mm)

Transaxle housing bearing snap-ring (dimension A)
- Mainshaft .... 0.118 to 0.314 in (3.0 to 8.0 mm)
- Countershaft .... 0.276 to 0.279 in (7.0 to 7.1 mm)
- Differential pinion gear backlash .... 0.002 to 0.006 in (0.05 to 0.15 mm)
- Differential thrust washer available thicknesses ...... 0.028 in (0.70 mm)
  - 0.030 in (0.75 mm)
  - 0.031 in (0.80 mm)
  - 0.033 in (0.85 mm)
  - 0.035 in (0.90 mm)
  - 0.037 in (0.95 mm)
  - 0.039 in (1.00 mm)

Mainshaft

End play	0.004 to 0.014 in (0.10 to 0.35 mm)
Third gear shoulder-to-second gear shoulder	
Standard	0.0012 to 0.0071 in (0.03 to 0.18 mm)
Service limit	0.012 in (0.3 mm)
Fourth gear shoulder-to-spacer collar	
Standard	0.0012 to 0.0071 in (0.03 to 0.18 mm)
Service limit	0.012 in (0.3 mm)
Fifth gear shoulder-to-spacer collar	
Standard	0.0012 to 0.0051 in (0.03 to 0.13 mm)
Service limit	0.01 in (0.25 mm)
Mainshaft ball bearing-to-spacer washer	0.0 to 0.004 in (0.0 to 0.1 mm)
Replacement washers	
A	0.074 to 0.075 in (1.88 to 1.92 mm)
B	0.076 to 0.078 in (1.94 to 1.98 mm)
C	0.079 to 0.080 in (2.00 to 2.04 mm)
D	0.081 to 0.082 in (2.06 to 2.10 mm)
E	0.083 to 0.085 in (2.12 to 2.16 mm)
Outside diameter	
Standard	
At point A	1.0238 to 1.0243 in (26.004 to 26.017 mm)
At point B	1.2592 to 1.2598 in (31.984 to 32.00 mm)
At point C	0.9835 to 0.9840 in (24.980 to 24.993 mm)
Service limit	
At point A	1.022 in (25.95 mm)
At point B	1.257 in (31.93 mm)
At point C	0.98 in (24.93 mm)
Runout	
Standard	0.0016 in (0.04 mm)
Service limit	0.004 in (0.10 mm)

Countershaft

End play	0.004 to 0.014 in (0.10 to 0.35 mm)
First gear shoulder-to-thrust washer	0.001 to 0.003 in (0.03 to 0.08 mm)
Replacement washers	
A	0.080 to 0.082 in (2.02 to 2.04 mm)
B	0.079 to 0.080 in (2.00 to 2.02 mm)
C	0.078 to 0.079 in (1.98 to 2.00 mm)
D	0.077 to 0.078 in (1.96 to 1.98 mm)
Third gear shoulder-to-second gear shoulder	
Standard	0.0012 to 0.004 in (0.03 to 0.1 mm)
Service limit	0.007 in (0.18 mm)
Countershaft outside diameter	
Standard	
A	1.2992 to 1.2998 in (33.000 to 33.015 mm)
B	1.3380 to 1.3386 in (33.984 to 34.000 mm)
C	0.9835 to 0.9840 in (24.980 to 24.993 mm)
Service limit	
A	1.297 in (32.95 mm)
B	1.336 in (33.93 mm)
C	0.981 in (24.93 mm)

Gearshift mechanism

Selector arm collar-to-shim	0.0004 to 0.008 in (0.01 to 0.2 mm)
Available shims	
A	0.031 in (0.8 mm)
B	0.039 in (1.0 mm)
C	0.047 in (1.2 mm)
D	0.055 in (1.4 mm)
E	0.063 in (1.6 mm)
Shift arm-to-shift guide	
Standard	0.004 to 0.012 in (0.1 to 0.3 mm)
Service limit	0.024 in (0.6 mm)
Shift guide slot	0.311 to 0.315 in (7.9 to 8.0 mm)
Selector arm-to-interlock	
Standard	0.002 to 0.010 in (0.05 to 0.25 mm)
Service limit	0.03 in (0.7 mm)
Selector arm finger gap	0.396 to 0.400 in (10.05 to 10.15 mm)

Shift arm-to-shift rod guide
   Standard.. 0.002 to 0.010 in (0.05 to 0.25 mm)
   Service limit... 0.03 in (0.5 mm)
Slot in shift rod guide... 0.469 to 0.472 in (11.9 to 12.0 mm)
Selector arm-to-shift rod guide
   Standard.. .0.002 to 0.01 in (0.05 to 0.25 mm)
   Service limit... 0.002 in (0.05 mm)
Tab on selector arm.. 0.469 to 0.472 in (11.9 to 12.0 mm)

Gear thicknesses

Second gear
   Standard.. 1.198 to 1.200 in (30.42 to 30.47 mm)
   Service limit... 1.192 in (30.3 mm)
Third gear
   1984 through 1986
      Standard.. 1.158 to 1.160 in (29.42 to 29.47 mm)
      Service limit... 1.15 in (29.3 mm)
   1987 on
      Standard.. 1.237 to 1.239 in (31.42 to 31.47 mm)
      Service limit... 1.232 in (31.30 mm)
Fourth gear
   1984 through 1986
      Standard.. 1.158 to 1.160 in (29.42 to 29.47 mm)
      Service limit... 1.15 in (29.3 mm)
   1987 on
      Standard.. 1.237 to 1.239 in (31.42 to 31.47 mm)
      Service limit... 1.232 in (31.30 mm)
Fifth gear
   1984 through 1986
      Standard.. 1.06 to 1.062 in (26.92 to 26.97 mm)
      Service limit... 1.06 in (26.8 mm)
   1987 on
      Standard.. 1.276 to 1.239 in (32.42 to 32.47 mm)
      Service limit... 1.272 in (32.30 mm)

Torque specifications

	Ft-lbs	Nm
Lubricant filler plug	33	45
Drain plug	29	39
Gear shift rod fork bolt	16	22
Torque rod front mounting bolt	7	9
Mainshaft locknut (left-hand thread)	65	88
Countershaft locknut	65	88
Shift rod guide bolt	22	30
Shift rod holder bolts	13	18
Mainshaft bearing retainer bolt	21	28
Backup light switch	18	24
Transaxle-to-clutch housing bolts	21	28
Detent ball retaining screws	16	22
Transaxle end cover bolts	9	12
Differential ring gear bolts (left-hand thread)	76	103

1 General information

The vehicles covered by this manual are equipped with either a five-speed manual transaxle or a four-speed automatic transaxle. Information on the manual transaxle is included in this Part of Chapter 7. Service procedures for the automatic transaxle are contained in Chapter 7, Part B.

The manual transaxle is a compact, two piece, lightweight aluminum alloy housing containing both the transmission and differential assemblies.

2 Oil seal replacement

1 Oil leaks frequently occur due to wear of the driveaxle oil seals, and/or the speedometer drive gear oil seal and O-ring. Replacement of these seals is relatively easy, since the repairs can usually be performed without removing the transaxle from the vehicle.

2 The driveaxle oil seals are located at the sides of the transaxle, where the driveaxles are attached. If leakage at the seal is suspected, raise the vehicle and support it securely on jackstands. If the seal is leaking, lubricant will be found on the sides of the transaxle.

3 Refer to Chapter 8 and remove the driveaxles.

4 Using screwdriver or pry bar, carefully pry the oil seal out of the transaxle bore.

5 If the oil seal cannot be removed with a screwdriver or pry bar, a special oil seal removal tool (available at auto parts stores) will be required.

6 Using a large section of pipe or a large deep socket as a drift, install the new oil seal. Drive it into the bore squarely and make sure it's completely seated.

7A

7   Install the driveaxle(s). Be careful not to damage the lip of the new seal.

8   The speedometer cable and driven gear housing is located on the transaxle housing. Look for lubricant around the cable housing to determine if the O-ring is leaking.

9   Disconnect the speedometer cable from the transaxle.

10   Using a hook, remove the seal.

11   Using a small socket as a drift, install the new seal.

12   Install a new O-ring on the driven gear housing and reinstall the speedometer cable assembly.

3   Transaxle mount - check and replacement

Refer to illustration 3.1

1   Insert a large screwdriver or prybar between the mount and the transaxle and pry up **(see illustration)**.

2   The transaxle should not move more than about 1/2 to 3/4-inch away from the mount. If it does, replace the mount.

3   To replace the mount, support the transaxle with a jack, remove the nuts and bolts and remove the mount. It may be necessary to raise the transaxle slightly to pro-

vide enough clearance to remove the mount.

4   Installation is the reverse of removal.

4   Shift assembly - removal and installation

Refer to illustration 4.1

1   From under the vehicle, remove the retaining bolts from the ends and lower the shift rod and torque rod from the vehicle **(see illustration)**.

2   Inside the vehicle, remove the shift knob, console and shift lever boot.

3   Also from inside the vehicle, remove the screws from the shift lever plate and lift the gear shift lever assembly out.

4   Installation is the reverse of removal. Prior to installation, lubricate the contact surfaces of the assembly with general purpose grease.

5   Manual transaxle - removal and installation

Removal

1   Disconnect the negative cable from the battery.

2   Raise the vehicle and support it securely on jackstands.

3   Drain the transaxle lubricant (see Chapter 1).

4   Disconnect the shift and clutch linkage from the transaxle.

5   Detach the speedometer cable and wire harness connectors from the transaxle.

6   Remove the exhaust system components as necessary for clearance.

7   Support the engine. This can be done from above with an engine hoist, or by placing a jack (with a block of wood as an insulator) under the engine oil pan. The engine must remain supported at all times while the transaxle is out of the vehicle!

8   Remove any chassis or suspension components that will interfere with transaxle removal (see Chapter 10).

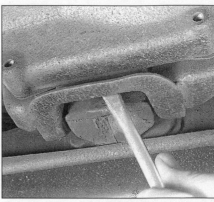

3.1 Pry on the transaxle mount to check for movement

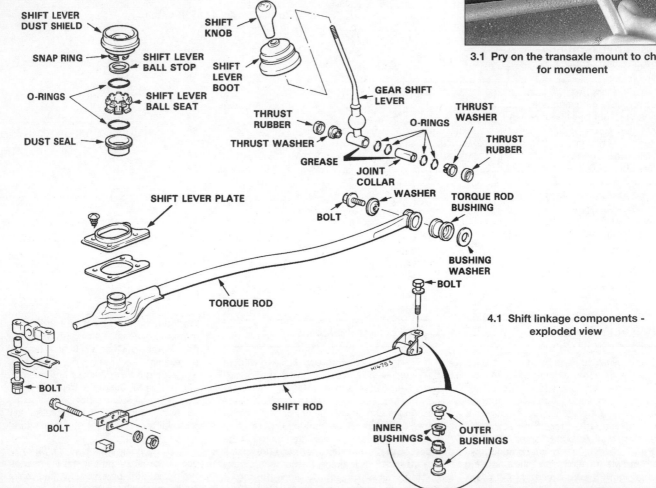

4.1 Shift linkage components - exploded view

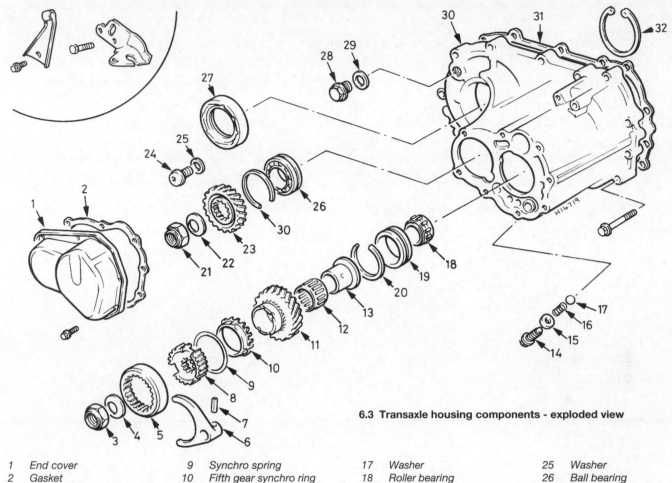

6.3 Transaxle housing components - exploded view

1	End cover	9	Synchro spring	17	Washer	25	Washer
2	Gasket	10	Fifth gear synchro ring	18	Roller bearing	26	Ball bearing
3	Locknut (left-hand thread)	11	Fifth gear mainshaft	19	Bearing outer race	27	Oil seal
4	Spring washer	12	Needle bearing	20	Snap-ring (60 mm)	28	Oil filler plug
5	Fifth gear synchro sleeve	13	Spacer collar	21	Locknut	29	Washer (20 mm)
6	Fifth gear shift fork	14	Retaining screw	22	Spring washer	30	Transaxle housing
7	Spring pin	15	Washer	23	Countershaft fifth gear	31	Gasket
8	Fifth gear synchro hub	16	Spring	24	Drain plug	32	Snap-ring

9 Disconnect the driveaxles from the transaxle (see Chapter 8).

10 Support the transaxle with a jack, then remove the bolts securing the transaxle to the engine.

11 Remove the transaxle mount nuts and bolts.

12 Remove the starter (see Chapter 5).

13 Make a final check that all wires and hoses have been disconnected from the transaxle, then carefully pull the transaxle and jack away from the engine.

14 Once the input shaft is clear, lower the transaxle and remove it from under the vehicle. **Caution:** *Do not depress the clutch pedal while the transaxle is out of the vehicle.*

15 With the transaxle removed, the clutch components are now accessible and can be inspected. In most cases, new clutch components should be routinely installed when the transaxle is removed.

Installation

16 If removed, install the clutch components (see Chapter 8).

17 With the transaxle secured to the jack with a chain, raise it into position behind the engine, then carefully slide it forward, engaging the input shaft with the clutch plate hub splines. Do not use excessive force to install the transaxle - if the input shaft does not slide into place, readjust the angle of the transaxle so it is level and/or turn the input shaft so the splines engage properly with the clutch plate hub.

18 Install the transaxle-to-engine bolts. Tighten the bolts securely.

19 Install the transaxle mount nuts or bolts.

20 Install the starter (see Chapter 5).

21 Install the chassis and suspension components which were removed. Tighten all nuts and bolts securely.

22 Remove the jacks supporting the transaxle and engine.

23 Install the various items removed previously, referring to Chapter 8 for installation of the driveaxles and Chapter 4 for information regarding the exhaust system components.

24 Make a final check that all wires, hoses, linkages and the speedometer cable have been connected and that the transaxle has been filled with lubricant to the proper level (see Chapter 1).

25 Connect the negative battery cable. Road test the vehicle for proper operation and check for leaks.

6 Manual transaxle - overhaul

Disassembly

Transaxle and clutch housings

Refer to illustrations 6.3, 6.12, 6.16 and 6.18

1 Before starting to disassemble the transaxle, clean the exterior with a water soluble degreaser. This will make it easier to handle and will reduce the possibility of getting dirt and other contaminants inside the transaxle.

2 Place the transaxle on a workbench.

3 Remove the end cover **(see illustration)**.

4 Measure the end play between the spacer collar and the fifth gear shoulder on

7A

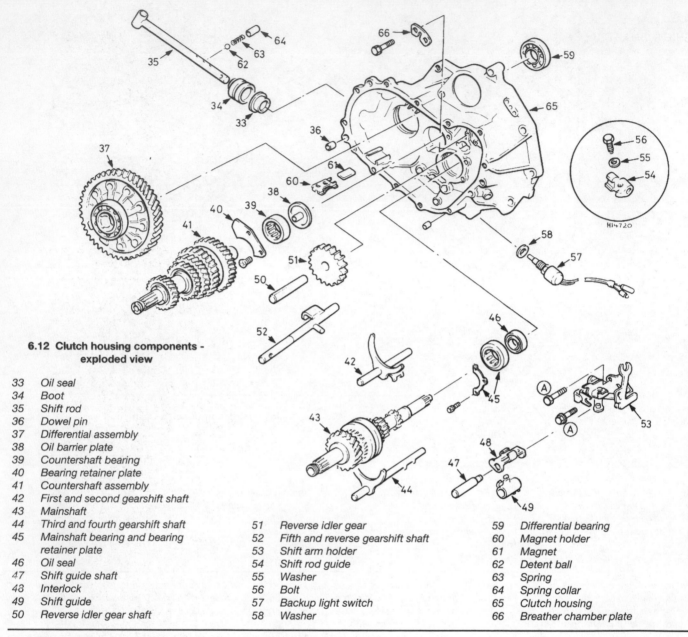

**6.12 Clutch housing components -
exploded view**

33   *Oil seal*
34   *Boot*
35   *Shift rod*
36   *Dowel pin*
37   *Differential assembly*
38   *Oil barrier plate*
39   *Countershaft bearing*
40   *Bearing retainer plate*
41   *Countershaft assembly*
42   *First and second gearshift shaft*
43   *Mainshaft*
44   *Third and fourth gearshift shaft*
45   *Mainshaft bearing and bearing
      retainer plate*
46   *Oil seal*
47   *Shift guide shaft*
48   *Interlock*
49   *Shift guide*
50   *Reverse idler gear shaft*

51   *Reverse idler gear*
52   *Fifth and reverse gearshift shaft*
53   *Shift arm holder*
54   *Shift rod guide*
55   *Washer*
56   *Bolt*
57   *Backup light switch*
58   *Washer*

59   *Differential bearing*
60   *Magnet holder*
61   *Magnet*
62   *Detent ball*
63   *Spring*
64   *Spring collar*
65   *Clutch housing*
66   *Breather chamber plate*

both the main and countershafts, as a reference for reassembly **(see illustration 6.3)**.
5   Bend back the locking tabs on the locknuts of both shafts.
6   Before the nuts can be removed, the gears will have to be locked in position. One method is to remove the spring roll pin from the fifth gear shift fork and shaft, select a gear other than fifth, then select fifth gear. This will lock the gears.
7   Remove the locknuts, noting the mainshaft locknut has a left-hand thread.
8   If not already done, drive out the spring pin securing the fifth gear shift fork to the shift shaft.
9   Remove the shift fork, mainshaft fifth gear, synchronizer sleeve, hub, ring and spring washer as one unit.
10   Remove the countershaft fifth gear.
11   Remove the three retaining screws,

springs and detent balls from the side of the transaxle housing.
12   Remove the backup light switch **(see illustration)**.
13   Remove the bolts securing the transaxle housing to the clutch housing.
14   A special housing puller is required (available from a Honda dealer) for separating the two housings. If this is not available, gently tap the transaxle housing using a soft-faced hammer, until the housings separate. Do not attempt to pry them apart, because the faces of the aluminum housings are easily damaged. If they are damaged, lubricant leaks will result.
15   Lift off the transaxle housing from the clutch housing. The mainshaft bearing will remain on the shaft and the countershaft bearing will remain in the housing.
16   Using feeler gauges, measure the clear-

ance between the fifth/reverse shift shaft pin and the reverse shift fork, comparing the results with the specifications **(see illustration)**.
17   If the specifications are exceeded, measure the width of the slot in the reverse shift fork.
18   Measure the clearance between the reverse/idler gear and the reverse shift fork **(see illustration)**.
19   If the specifications are exceeded, pull out the reverse collar and its shaft and measure the distance between the fingers on the reverse shift fork.
20   Replace any worn parts so that tolerances are maintained.
21   Place the transaxle in Neutral.
22   Remove the mainshaft bearing retainer plate and pull out the shift guide shaft **(see illustration 6.12)**.

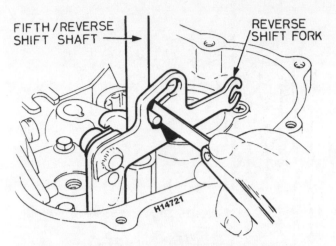

6.16 Use a feeler gauge to measure the clearance between the fifth/reverse shift shaft pin and the reverse shift fork

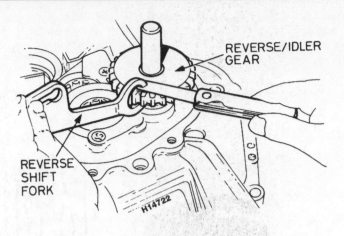

6.18 Measuring the clearance between the reverse/idler gear and the reverse shift fork

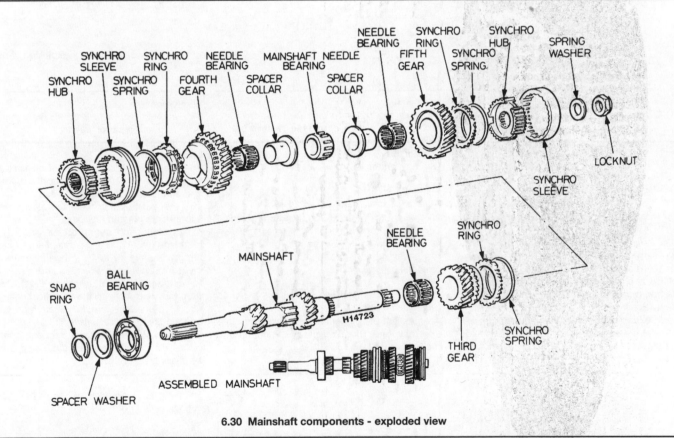

6.30 Mainshaft components - exploded view

23   If still in place, pull out the reverse idler gear and shaft.
24   Pull the third/fourth and first/second gear shift shafts up to shift into fourth and second.
25   Remove the fifth and reverse shift shaft by pulling it up, while at the same time lifting the reverse shift fork.
26   Tilt the interlock and shift guide to the side, then lift them out.
27   The mainshaft and countershaft, together with first/second and third/fourth

shift shafts, may now be lifted out as an assembly.

Mainshaft
Refer to illustration 6.30
28   Before disassembling the mainshaft, measure the end play of the gears, as described in Steps 70 through 79.
29   Replace any worn components.
30   Slide each component off the shaft, removing the snap-rings as necessary **(see illustration)**.

31   Keep each component in its relative position (so they can be reassembled identically) and inspect each component, as described in Steps 34 through 38.

Countershaft
Refer to illustration 6.32
32   Disassemble the countershaft **(see illustration)** in the same manner as the mainshaft.
33   Measure the end play tolerances as described in Steps 91 through 93. Do not mix any components from the mainshaft and countershaft assemblies.

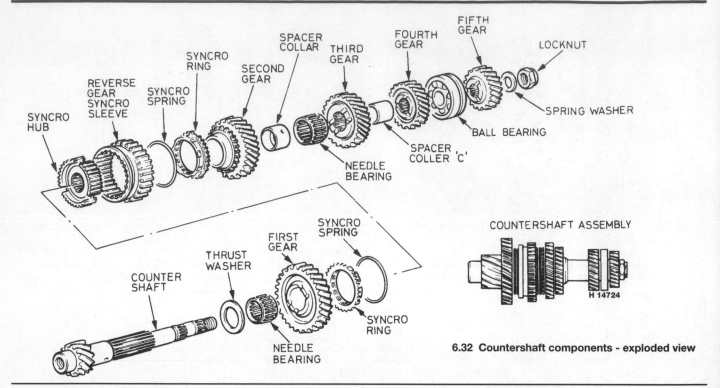

6.32 Countershaft components - exploded view

Inspection (mainshaft and countershaft components)

Note: *Before inspecting any components, be sure to wash them in solvent and dry them thoroughly. Keep all components in their relative order, taking care not to mix the mainshaft and countershaft components.*

Mainshaft

Refer to illustrations 6.35 and 6.37

34   With all the components removed from the shaft and cleaned, inspect the shaft splines and gear teeth for wear, cracks, pitting and chipping.

35   Make sure the oil passageways are clean and free from restrictions **(see illustration)**.

36   The outside diameter of the shaft should be measured at points A, B and C **(see illustration 6.35)** to detect any radial wear.

37   The shaft should also be checked for runout with a dial indicator **(see illustration)**.

38   Shafts which exceed the wear or runout limits in the specifications should be replaced with new ones.

Countershaft

Refer to illustrations 6.39a and 6.39b

39   Inspect the countershaft **(see illustrations)** in the same manner as the mainshaft.

40   Any shaft which exceeds the wear or runout limits in specifications should be replaced with new ones.

Gears and synchronizer rings

Refer to illustration 6.41

41   Inspect each gear and synchronizer ring assembly **(see illustration)** as described in the following Steps.

42   Inspect the inside of the synchronizer ring for wear.

43   Inspect the teeth on both the synchronizer ring and gear for wear.

44   Inspect the thrust surface on the gear hub for wear.

45   Inspect the cone surface on first and second countershaft gears and third, fourth and fifth mainshaft gears for wear.

46   Inspect the gear teeth for uneven wear, scoring, cracks and chipping.

47   Install each synchronizer ring on its matching gear cone and rotate it until it stops (approximately 10 to 20°), then measure the clearance between the ring and gear with feeler gauges **(see illustration 6.41)**. Compare the clearances to the specifications.

48   Replace any synchronizer rings worn beyond the specifications.

49   Remove the ring from the gear, coat all parts with oil and reassemble, using a new synchronizer spring.

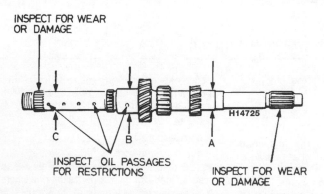

6.35 Inspect the mainshaft for damage and measure it for wear at the points shown

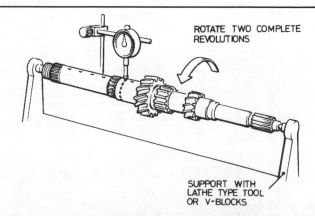

6.37 Check the mainshaft for runout at the point shown - rotate it two complete revolutions to be sure of an accurate reading

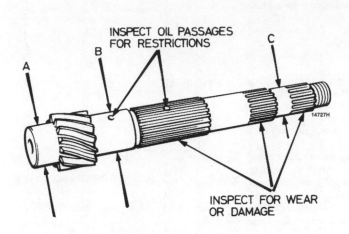

6.39a Inspect the countershaft for damage and measure it for wear at the points shown

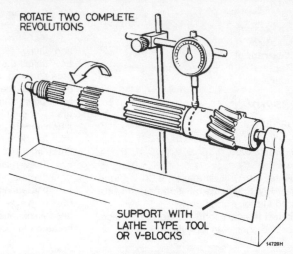

6.39b Check the countershaft for runout at the point shown - rotate it two complete revolutions to be sure of an accurate reading

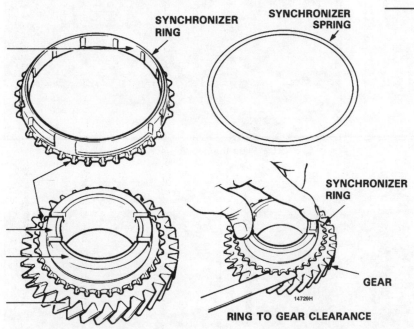

6.41 Check the gear and synchronizer ring for wear at the indicated points (arrows) - check synchronizer ring-to-gear clearance with feeler gauges at the point shown

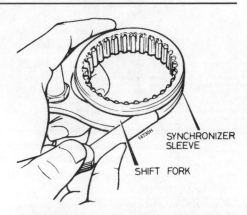

6.50 Check the shift fork-to-synchronizer sleeve clearance with a feeler gauge

Synchronizer sleeve and hub

Refer to illustrations 6.50 and 6.53

50   Measure the clearance between the fingers of each shift fork and its synchronizer sleeve using feeler gauges. Compare each measurement with the specifications **(see illustration)**.

51   If worn beyond the service limits, replace the synchronizer sleeve with a new one.

52   Note that the tolerances are the same for all three synchronizer sleeves.

53   Inspect each hub and sleeve for wear **(see illustration)**. Replace worn components with new ones as necessary.

54   Install the synchronizer sleeve onto its hub and check for freedom of movement.

Needle and roller bearings

55   Inspect each bearing for signs of overheating, indicated by bluing or discoloration.

56   Excessive wear in the bearings is indicated by a rattling noise when the bearing is shaken.

57   Although the three needle bearing assemblies are identical, they should be reinstalled in their original positions.

7A

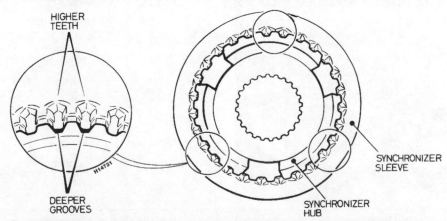

6.53 Check the synchronizer sleeve and hub for wear at the points shown

Gears

Refer to illustration 6.58

58 Measure the thickness of each gear **(see illustration)**.

59 Replace any gears which are worn beyond limits.

Reassembly

Mainshaft

Refer to illustrations 6.61, 6.62, 6.63a, 6.63b, 6.64a, 6.64b, 6.65, 6.66, 6.70, 6.73, 6.76 and 6.79

60 Refer to illustration 6.30 during reassembly to ensure all components are replaced in their correct order.

61 install the mainshaft ball bearing, spacer washer and snap-ring **(see illustration)**.

62 Slide on the needle bearing **(see illustration)**.

63 Install third gear and its synchro ring and spring **(see illustrations)**.

64 Install the synchronizer hub and sleeve **(see illustrations)**.

65 Install the remaining synchronizer ring and spring, then slide on fourth gear, the needle roller bearing, and the spacer collar **(see illustration)**.

66 Install the mainshaft roller bearing **(see illustration)**.

67 The remaining components are installed after the main and countershaft assemblies are installed in the transaxle housing.

68 However, to establish correct clearances, you must install the remaining components on the mainshaft and tighten the lock-

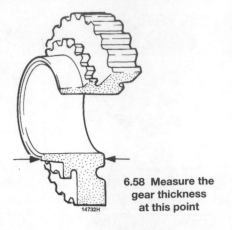

6.58 Measure the gear thickness at this point

6.61 Install the ball bearing, spacer washer and snap-ring on the mainshaft

6.62 Slide the needle bearing onto the shaft

6.63a Install third gear . . .

6.63b . . . and its synchro ring and spring

6.64a Install the synchro hub . . .

6.64b . . . and its sleeve

6.65 Slide fourth gear, its needle bearing and spacer collar onto the shaft

6.66 Install the roller bearing

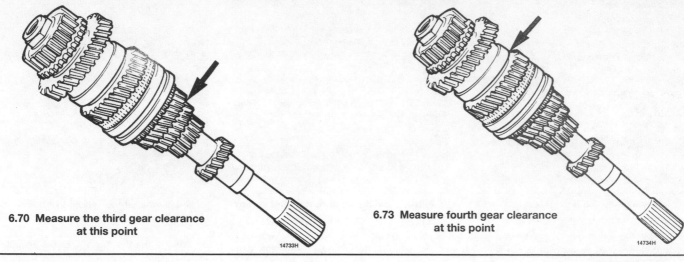

6.70 Measure the third gear clearance at this point

6.73 Measure fourth gear clearance at this point

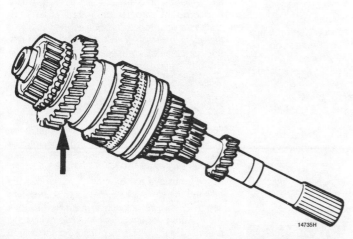

6.76 Measure fifth gear clearance at this point

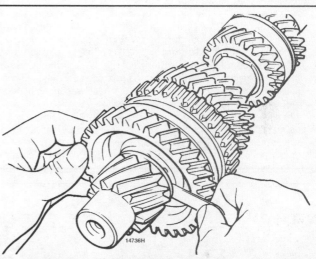

6.79 Use a feeler gauge to measure the mainshaft ball bearing clearance

nut to the specified torque. Do not over torque or incorrect clearances may result.

69 Now carry out the following clearance checks, comparing your results with the specifications.

70 Measure the clearance between the shoulder on third gear and the shoulder on second gear **(see illustration)**.

71 If out of limits, measure the thickness of third gear, and replace as necessary.

72 If third gear thickness is within limits, install a new synchronizer hub.

73 Measure the clearance between the spacer collar and the shoulder on fourth gear **(see illustration)**.

74 If the fourth gear-to-spacer collar is out

of limits, measure the thickness of fourth gear and replace it with a new one if necessary.

75 If fourth gear thickness is within limits, install a new synchronizer hub.

76 Measure the clearance between the spacer collar and the shoulder on fifth gear **(see illustration)**.

77 If out of limits, measure the thickness of fifth gear.

78 If fifth gear thickness is less than specified, replace fifth gear.

79 Measure the clearance between the spacer washer and the mainshaft ball-bearing **(see illustration)**. If out of tolerance, install a new spacer washer of suitable thickness. Refer to the Specifications Section for available sizes.

Countershaft

Refer to illustrations 6.80, 6.81, 6.82a, 6.82b, 6.83, 6.84, 6.85, 6.86, 6.87a and 6.87b

80 Install the thrust washer on the countershaft **(see illustration)**.

81 Slide on the needle bearing **(see illustration)**.

82 Install first gear, followed by its synchro ring and spring **(see illustrations)**.

7A

6.80 Install the thrust washer on the countershaft

6.81 Slide the roller bearing against the thrust washer

6.82a Install first gear . . .

6.82b . . . and its synchro ring and spring

6.83 Install the synchro hub and reverse gear

83 Install the synchro hub and reverse gear synchro sleeve **(see illustration)**.
84 Slide the needle roller bearing onto the shaft **(see illustration)**.
85 Install the synchro spring, synchro ring and second gear **(see illustration)**.
86 Install third gear **(see illustration)**.
87 Slide on the spacer collar and fourth gear **(see illustrations)**.
88 The remaining components are installed after the mainshaft and countershaft are installed in the transaxle housing.
89 However, as with the mainshaft, these components must be assembled on the shaft and the locknut installed and tightened to the

specified torque to carry out the following measurements. Do not over torque the locknut or incorrect tolerances may result.
90 Refer to illustration 6.32 and the specifications when making these checks.
91 Measure the clearance between the first gear thrust washer and the shoulder on first gear, installing the proper thickness thrust washer as necessary if the tolerances cannot be met.
92 Measure the clearance between the shoulder on third gear and the shoulder on second gear.
93 If the clearance is out of limits, measure the thickness of second gear, replacing sec-

ond gear if the thickness is below specification.
94 After all clearances have been checked and brought into limits, reassemble both main and countershafts and recheck all clearances.
95 Once all clearances are correct, remove the fifth gear components and reinstall the bearings in the transaxle housing.

Clutch housing bearing and seal

Refer to illustration 6.96
96 Refer to the accompanying illustration for the countershaft bearing and mainshaft oil seal installation details in the clutch housing **(see illustration)**.
97 To remove the bearing, first remove the bearing retainer plate. Note that the two securing screws are center punched to lock them, so an impact driver may be needed to remove them. Don't forget to center punch the screws and the retaining plate when reinstalling.
98 Pull the bearing from the housing, then lift out the plastic oil guide plate.
99 Clean out the bearing housing and the oil guide plate, wash the bearing in solvent and dry it thoroughly.
100 Inspect the bearing for signs of wear, discoloration due to overheating and cracking or scoring of the rollers.
101 Reinstall the plastic oil guide plate.

6.84 Slide the needle bearing onto the shaft

6.85 The synchro ring and second gear fit over the bearing

6.86 Third gear installation

6.87a Slide the spacer collar onto the shaft . . .

6.87b . . . then fit the gear over it

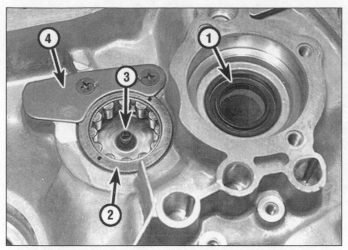

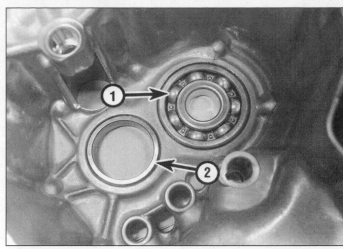

6.96 Here's where the countershaft bearing and mainshaft oil seal are located in the clutch housing

1	*Mainshaft oil seal*	3	*Oil guide plate*
2	*Bearing*	4	*Bearing retainer plate*

6.107 Here's where the countershaft ball bearing and mainshaft bearing outer race are located in the transaxle housing

1	*Ball bearing*	2	*Mainshaft bearing outer race*

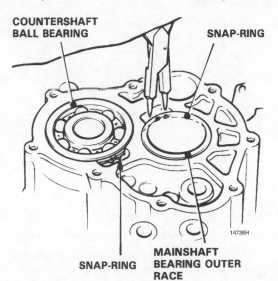

6.108 Snap-ring pliers are required when removing the countershaft ball bearing and mainshaft bearing outer race from the mainshaft

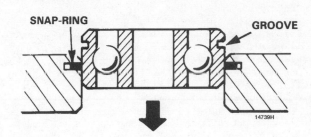

6.110 The groove in the ball bearing must engage the snap-ring

6.111 Dimension A must be correct for the transaxle housing bearing to be seated securely (refer to the specifications for the correct dimension)

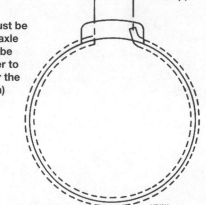

102 To reinstall the bearing, first liberally coat it with clean engine oil. Then, with a block of wood positioned under the housing, use a hammer and a socket or a piece of pipe of the same diameter as the bearing to drive the bearing all the way into the housing bore.
103 Reinstall the bearing retainer plate and center punch the screws to the plate.
104 Pry out the mainshaft oil seal using a screwdriver, being careful not to damage the housing.
105 The lips on the new oil seal must face toward the bearing.
106 Coat the seal with clean engine oil and, again using a socket or piece of pipe of the same diameter as the seal, gently tap the seal into the housing. Take care to install the seal squarely.

Transaxle housing bearing and seal
Refer to illustrations 6.107, 6.108, 6.110 and 6.111
107 Refer to the accompanying illustration for details of the countershaft ball bearing and the mainshaft bearing outer race installation in the transaxle housing.
108 Both components are held in place by snap-rings and are removed by first expanding the snap-rings using snap-ring pliers, then lifting out the component **(see illustration)**.
109 Do not expand the snap-rings any more than is necessary to remove the bearings, and avoid damaging the housing during this operation.
110 To install the components, place them in position, expand the snap-rings so the bearings can enter the housings, then push the

bearings down by hand, feeling for the click indicating the snap-ring has snapped into the groove on the bearing **(see illustration)**. The bearing is installed with the part number facing out.
111 As a check that the snap-ring is positioned correctly, measure dimension A **(see illustration)** and compare it to the specification.
112 If dimension A is not within specification, either reseat the bearing and snap-ring or replace the snap-ring.

7A

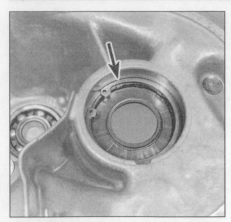

6.116 The differential oil seal is retained in the housing by a snap-ring (arrow)

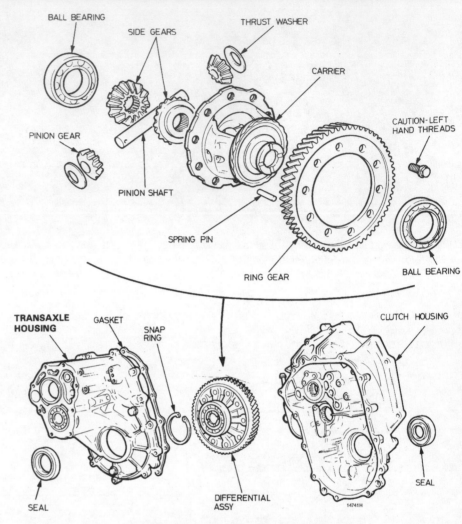

6.121 Differential unit installation details

Differential oil seals

Refer to illustration 6.116

113 To replace the differential oil seals, the transaxle components and differential assembly must first be removed from the transaxle housings (differential removal begins at Step 121).

114 Both seals should be replaced whenever the transaxle assembly is disassembled.

115 To remove the seal in the clutch housing, use a hammer and a socket or piece of pipe to drive the seal from the housing.

116 Similarly, drive out the seal from the transaxle housing, but first remove the snap-ring **(see illustration)**.

117 Installation is the reverse of removal, but note the following.

118 The transaxle housing oil seal is installed with its part number side facing away from the snap-ring.

119 The clutch housing seal is installed with the part number side facing away from the bearing.

120 If the differential bearings or carrier was replaced, a snap-ring of suitable thickness to give the correct clearance between the snap-ring and the bearing outer race will have to be selected and installed.

Differential assembly

Refer to illustrations 6.121, 6.122, 6.123, 6.141 and 6.142

121 The differential assembly will have already been lifted out of the transaxle housing, together with the transmission gears,

shafts and shift mechanism **(see illustration)**.

122 Before proceeding any further with disassembly, the backlash in the pinion gears should be checked, as shown **(see illustration)**.

123 Backlash can be brought within limits by

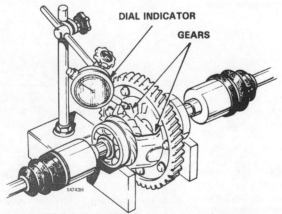

6.122 Differential backlash measurement details

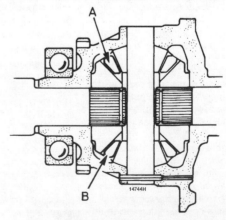

6.123 Check the differential at points A and B

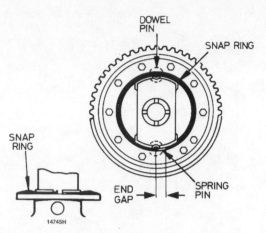

6.141 Correct alignment of the differential snap-ring and spring pin

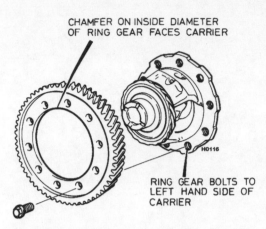

6.142 Differential ring gear installation details

installing thicker thrust washers behind the pinion gears **(see illustration).**

124 The thrust washers on each side should be of equal thickness.

Refer to the specifications for thrust washer sizes and backlash tolerances.

125 If the backlash cannot be brought within specification by installing thicker thrust washers, the differential will have to be completely dismantled and inspected, as described in the following paragraphs. At this point, consider obtaining a new or rebuilt unit.

126 Inspect the ball bearings **(see illustration 6.121)** for wear, discoloration due to overheating and roughness during rotation.

127 If the ball bearings are in reasonable condition and backlash is not excessive, the unit may be reinstalled. If further disassembly is necessary, proceed as follows.

128 Use a bearing puller to remove the two ball bearings.

129 The ring gear bolts have left-handed threads. Remove these and the ring gear, then inspect the teeth for wear and damage.

130 Remove the pinion shaft spring pin with a pin punch and hammer, then remove the pinion shaft, pinion gears and thrust washers.

131 Inspect all parts for wear, scoring, overheating, burrs and damage, replacing any that are defective.

132 Coat all gears with moly-based grease before reassembly.

133 Place the side gears in the carrier.

134 Position the pinion gears in place, exactly opposite each other and in mesh with the side gears, then install a thrust washer of selected thickness behind each gear. Remember, the thrust washers must be of equal thickness.

135 Rotate the gears until the shaft holes in the pinion gears line up with those on the carrier.

136 Insert the pinion shaft, lining up the spring pin hole with the hole in the carrier.

137 Install a new spring pin, using a punch and hammer.

138 Check the backlash of both pinion

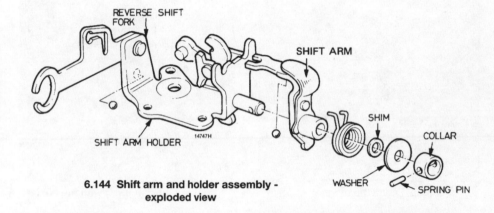

6.144 Shift arm and holder assembly - exploded view

gears, as described above.

139 If the tolerances cannot be met using thicker washers, replace the pinion gears, and, if this fails, replace the side gears.

140 If backlash is still excessive, replace the entire carrier assembly.

141 The snap-ring should be installed so that it covers the spring pin securing the pinion shaft **(see illustration).**

142 Install the ring gear and tighten the bolts (which have left-hand threads) to the specified torque **(see illustration).**

143 The procedure for reinstalling the differential is in Steps 171 through 177.

Gearshift mechanism

Refer to illustrations 6.144, 6.145, 6.148, 6.150, 6.160a, 6.160b, 6.161, 6.162a, 6.162b, 6.163a, 6.163b, 6.164a, 6.164b, 6.164c, 6.165, 6.167, 6.169a and 6.169b

144 The shift arm and holder assembly is bolted into the transaxle housing **(see illustration).**

145 Before removing it, measure the clearance between the end collar and the shim **(see illustration)** and compare your measurement with the specifications. If the clearance is greater than specified, install a thicker shim. Refer to the Specifications for details.

146 To remove the selector arm from the holder for shimming, use a pin punch to drive out the spring pin **(see illustration 6.144).**

147 Use a new spring pin during reassembly.

148 Measure the shift arm-to-shift guide clearance and, if it is greater than specified,

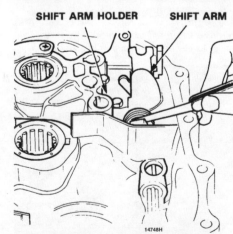

6.145 Check the shift arm holder and collar-to-shim clearance with a feeler gauge

7A

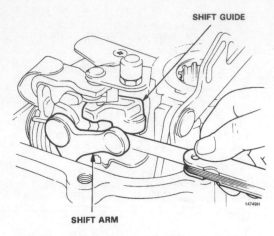

6.148 Measure the shift arm-to-guide clearance

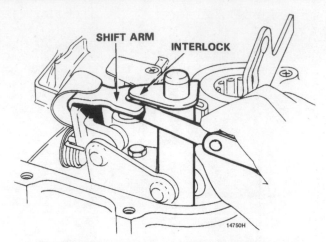

6.150 Measure the selector arm-to-interlock clearance

6.160a Install the magnet . . .

6.160b . . . and secure it with the holder

6.161 Insert the shift rod

measure the width of the slot in the shift guide **(see illustration)**.

149 If the slot is wider than specified, replace the shift guide.

150 Check the selector arm-to-interlock clearance and, if it is not as specified, measure the gap between the selector arm fingers **(see illustration)**.

151 If specifications cannot be met, replace the selector arm.

152 If further disassembly is required, first remove the main and countershaft assemblies, as described earlier in this Section.

153 Remove the three bolts and lift out the shift arm holder.

154 Inspect the shift rod for damage.

155 To remove the shift rod for further inspection or to replace the shift rod oil seal and rubber boot, remove the shoulder bolt.

156 This will release the shift rod guide, and the rod may be pulled from the housing.

157 Make sure not to lose the detent ball and spring as the shift rod clears the detent hole.

158 Pry out the shift rod oil seal and press in a new oil seal.

159 Remove the old rubber boot from the

shift rod, lubricate the inside of the new boot with grease, then install it on the shift rod.

160 Remove and clean the magnet and its holder, then reinstall them **(see illustrations)**.

161 Reinstall the shift rod in the housing **(see illustration)**.

162 Replace the detent spring in its housing, followed by the detent ball **(see illustrations)**.

163 Depress the ball and spring and push the shift rod into place **(see illustrations)**.

164 Install the shift rod guide and shoulder bolt, then snap the rubber boot over the oil seal **(see illustrations)**.

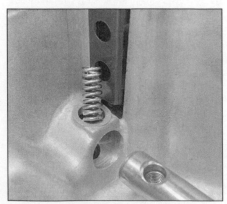

6.162a Install the detent spring . . .

6.162b . . . followed by the detent ball

6.163a Depress the ball and spring, . . .

6.163b . . . then push the rod through the housing

6.164a Install the shift rod guide and bolt . . .

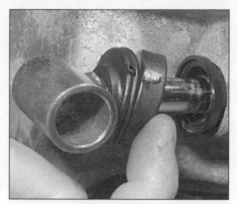

6.164b . . . then snap the rubber boot . . .

6.164c . . . over the oil seal

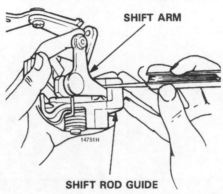

6.165 Measure the clearance between the shift arm and shift rod guide with a feeler gauge

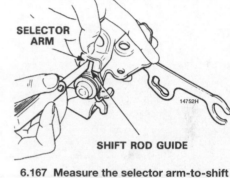

6.167 Measure the selector arm-to-shift rod guide clearance

165 Check the clearance between the shift arm and shift rod guide. If it's out of specification, measure the width of the slot in the shift rod guide **(see illustration)**.

166 If the width of the slot is beyond the service limit, replace the shift rod guide.

167 Check the selector arm-to-shift rod guide clearance and, if the clearance isn't as specified, measure the width of the tab on the selector arm **(see illustration)**.

168 If the width is greater than specified, replace the arm.

169 Reinstall the shift arm holder assembly and tighten the three bolts **(see illustrations)**.

170 The remainder of the selector mechanism is installed during reassembly of the transaxle unit.

Final transaxle reassembly

Refer to illustrations 6.176, 6.177a, 6.177b, 6.178, 6.181, 6.183, 6.185, 6.187, 6.188, 6.189, 6.191, 6.192, 6.193a, 6.193b, 6.194, 6.195a, 6.195b, 6.196a, 6.196b, 6.197, 6.198, 6.200 and 6.201

171 Make sure the countershaft ball bearing

and mainshaft bearing outer race are installed correctly in the transaxle housing.

172 Ensure the countershaft roller bearing and mainshaft oil seal are installed correctly in the clutch housing.

173 Make sure the shift rod is installed correctly, the magnetic oil filter is installed and the oil-smeared pipe screen is in position.

174 If not already done, install the shift arm holder.

175 Check that the differential oil seals are installed correctly. Reassembly may now begin.

176 Install the differential assembly in the clutch housing **(see illustration)**.

7A

6.169a Install the shift arm holder assembly . . .

6.169b . . . and secure it with the three bolts (arrows)

6.176 Lower the differential assembly into the housing

6.177a Lower the main and countershaft assemblies into place . . .

6.177b . . . until they are seated in the housing

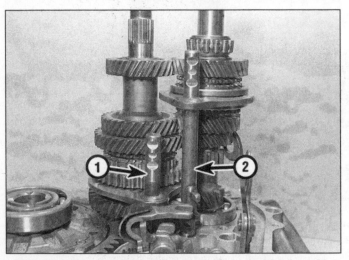

6.178 Install the first and second gear shift shaft (1) followed by the third and fourth gear shift shaft (2)

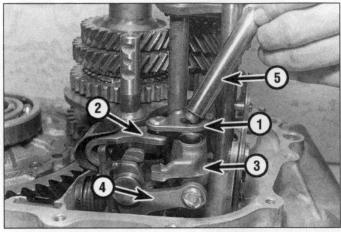

6.181 Selector installation details

1	Interlock	4	Shift arm
2	Selector arm	5	Fifth and reverse shift
3	Shift guide		shaft

177 Install the main and countershaft assemblies, meshing them together as they go into position **(see illustrations)**.

178 Install the first and second, then the third and fourth gearshift shafts **(see illustration)**.

179 The main and countershaft assemblies may have to be lifted up slightly to allow the gearshift shafts to be positioned.

180 When positioning the gearshift shafts, it may also be helpful to place the shift forks in second and fourth gear.

181 Lift the mainshaft and install the interlock in the selector arm **(see illustration)**.

182 Return the shift rod to Neutral, then hook the interlock into the selector arm, first

6.183 The fifth and reverse shift shaft pin should be located in the reverse shift fork slot (arrow)

6.185 Measure the distance the shift guide shaft extends above the interlock (arrows)

6.187 Install the mainshaft bearing retainer plate (arrow) - when tightening the retaining bolts, you must use a twelve-point socket

6.188 Correct installation of the reverse idler gear and shaft

6.189 Screw the backup light switch into the case - don't forget the washer!

correct assembly.

187 Install the mainshaft bearing retainer plate **(see illustration)**.

188 Install the reverse idler gear and shaft **(see illustration)**.

189 Install the backup light switch, using a new washer, and tighten it to the specified torque **(see illustration)**.

190 Place a new gasket in position on the clutch housing and ensure the dowel pins are installed.

191 Place the transaxle in third gear to position the shift guide shaft correctly for reassembly, then install the transaxle housing, making sure the main and countershafts line up with the bearings, and that the housing locates over the dowel pins **(see illustration)**.

192 Tighten the retaining bolts to the specified torque, in the sequence shown **(see illustration)**.

193 Install the three detent balls, springs, washers and retaining bolts. Tighten the retaining bolts to the specified torque **(see illustrations)**.

194 Install the countershaft fifth gear with the high side facing down **(see illustration)**.

and second gearshift shaft and third and fourth gearshift shaft.

183 Hook the shift guide into the shift arm, then install the fifth and reverse shift shaft, making sure its pin locates in the reverse shift fork slot **(see illustration)**.

184 Finally, install the shift guide shaft so

that it bottoms securely in place in the clutch housing.

185 The end of the shift guide shaft should not extend more than 1/2-inch (12 mm) above the interlock **(see illustration)**.

186 If the guide shaft does extend above the specified distance, check all components for

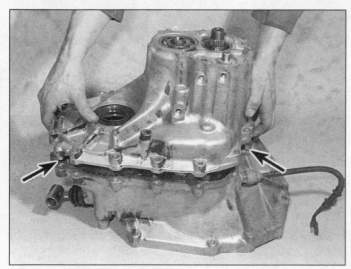

6.191 Lower the housing into place over the dowel pins (arrows)

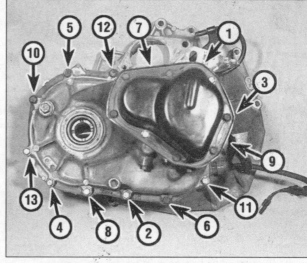

6.192 Tighten the bolts in this sequence

7A

6.193a Place each steel ball in the case . . .

6.193b . . . and secure it with its spring and retaining screw

6.194 Install the countershaft fifth gear

6.195a Install the spacer collar onto the mainshaft . . .

6.195b . . . followed by the needle bearing

6.196a Install the fifth gear synchro components . . .

6.196b . . . and the shift fork

6.197 Install the main and countershaft spring washers and retaining nuts

6.198 Using a hammer and a punch, drive a new spring pin into the fifth gear shift fork

195 Install the spacer collar and needle bearing over the mainshaft **(see illustrations)**.

196 Install the mainshaft fifth gear, synchro ring, spring, hub and sleeve onto the mainshaft **(see illustration)**. At the same time, install the shift fork on the sleeve and over the shaft **(see illustration)**.

197 Install the spring washers on both the countershaft and mainshaft, concave side facing down, and install the retaining nuts **(see illustration)**.

198 Install a new spring pin in the fifth gear shift fork and drive it in with a hammer and punch **(see illustration)**.

199 Keep the transaxle from rotating, then tighten the locknuts on the counter and mainshafts to the specified torques. Back the nuts off, then retighten them to the same torque.

200 Stake the locking collar of the nuts into the slots on the shafts **(see illustration)**.

201 Set a new end cover gasket in place **(see illustration)**, install the end cover and tighten the retaining nuts to the specified torque.

6.200 Use a punch and hammer to stake each locking collar

6.201 Position a new gasket as shown when installing the end cover

Chapter 7 Part B
Automatic transaxle

Contents

Specifications

General

Throttle Valve (TV) cable end-to-locknut A clearance	3.366 in (85.5 mm)
Throttle valve (TV) cable free play at transaxle lever	0.078 to 0.157 in (2 to 4 mm)

Torque specifications

	Ft-lbs	Nm
Transaxle-to-engine bolts	33	45
Torque converter-to-driveplate bolts	9	12

1   General information

All vehicles covered in this manual come equipped with either a 5-speed manual transaxle or a 4-speed automatic transaxle. All information on the automatic transaxle is included in this Part of Chapter 7. Information for the manual transaxle can be found in Part A of this Chapter.

Due to the complexity of the automatic transaxles covered in this manual and the need for specialized equipment to perform most service operations, this Chapter contains only general diagnosis, routine maintenance, adjustment and removal and installation procedures.

If the transaxle requires major repair work, it should be left to a dealer service department or an automotive or transmission repair shop. You can, however, remove and install the transaxle yourself and save the expense, even if the repair work is done by a transmission shop.

2   Diagnosis - general

Note: *Automatic transaxle malfunctions may be caused by five general conditions: poor engine performance, improper adjustments, hydraulic malfunctions, mechanical malfunc-*tions *or malfunctions in the computer or its signal network. Diagnosis of these problems should always begin with a check of the easily repaired items: Fluid level and condition (Chapter 1), shift linkage adjustment and throttle linkage adjustment. Next, perform a road test to determine if the problem has been corrected or if more diagnosis is necessary. If the problem persists after the preliminary tests and corrections are completed, additional diagnosis should be done by a dealer service department or transmission repair shop. Refer to the Troubleshooting section at the front of this manual for transaxle problem diagnosis.*

Preliminary checks

1   Drive the vehicle to warm the transaxle to normal operating temperature.
2   Check the fluid level as described in Chapter 1:
a) *If the fluid level is unusually low, add enough fluid to bring the level within the designated area of the dipstick, then check for external leaks.*
b) *If the fluid level is abnormally high, drain off the excess, then check the drained fluid for contamination by coolant. The presence of engine coolant in the automatic transmission fluid indicates that a failure has occurred in the internal radiator walls that separate the coolant from the transmission fluid (see Chapter 3).*
c) *If the fluid is foaming, drain it and refill the transaxle, then check for coolant in the fluid or a high fluid level.*
3   Check the engine idle speed. **Note:** *If the engine is malfunctioning, do not proceed with the preliminary checks until it has been repaired and runs normally.*
4   Check the throttle valve cable for freedom of movement. Adjust it if necessary (see Section 5). **Note:** *The throttle valve cable may function properly when the engine is shut off and cold, but it may malfunction once the engine is hot. Check it cold and at normal engine operating temperature.*
5   Inspect the shift linkage (see Section 3). Make sure that it's properly adjusted and that the linkage operates smoothly.

Fluid leak diagnosis

6   Most fluid leaks are easy to locate visually. Repair usually consists of replacing a seal or gasket. If a leak is difficult to find, the following procedure may help.
7   Identify the fluid. Make sure it's transmission fluid and not engine oil or brake fluid (automatic transmission fluid is a deep red color).
8   Try to pinpoint the source of the leak. Drive the vehicle several miles, then park it over a large sheet of cardboard. After a minute or two, you should be able to locate the leak by determining the source of the fluid dripping onto the cardboard.

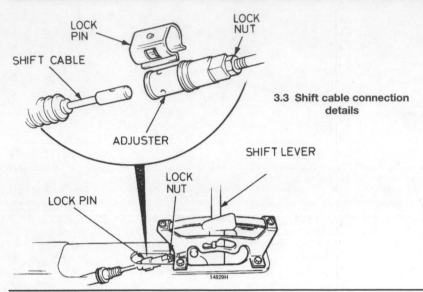

3.3 Shift cable connection details

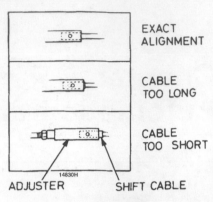

3.4 The shift cable is properly adjusted when the holes in the adjuster and shift cable are lined up

9   Make a careful visual inspection of the suspected component and the area immediately around it. Pay particular attention to gasket mating surfaces. A mirror is often helpful for finding leaks in areas that are hard to see.

10   If the leak still cannot be found, clean the suspected area thoroughly with a degreaser or solvent, then dry it.

11   Drive the vehicle for several miles at normal operating temperature and varying speeds. After driving the vehicle, visually inspect the suspected component again.

12   Once the leak has been located, the cause must be determined before it can be properly repaired. If a gasket is replaced but the sealing flange is bent, the new gasket will not stop the leak. The bent flange must be straightened.

13   Before attempting to repair a leak, check to make sure that the following conditions are corrected or they may cause another leak. **Note:** *Some of the following conditions cannot be fixed without highly specialized tools and expertise. Such problems must be referred to a transmission shop or a dealer service department.*

Gasket leaks

14   Check the end cover periodically. Make sure the bolts are tight, no bolts are missing and the gasket is in good condition.

15   If the end cover gasket is leaking, the fluid level or the fluid pressure may be too high, the vent may be plugged, the end cover bolts may be too tight, the sealing surface of the end cover or transaxle housing may be damaged, the gasket may be damaged or the transaxle casting may be cracked or porous. If sealant instead of gasket material has been used to form a seal between the end cover and the transaxle housing, it may be the wrong sealant.

Seal leaks

16   If a transaxle seal is leaking, the fluid level or pressure may be too high, the vent may be plugged, the seal bore may be

damaged, the seal itself may be damaged or improperly installed, the surface of the shaft protruding through the seal may be damaged or a loose bearing may be causing excessive shaft movement.

17   Make sure the dipstick guide pipe seal is in good condition and the pipe is properly seated. Periodically check the area around the speedometer gear or sensor for leakage. If transmission fluid is evident, check the O-ring for damage. Also inspect the side gear shaft oil seals for leakage. Case leak.

18   If the case itself appears to be leaking, the casting is porous and will have to be repaired or replaced.

19   Make sure the oil cooler hose fittings are tight and in good condition.

Fluid comes out vent pipe or guide pipe

20   If this condition occurs, the transaxle is overfilled, there is coolant in the fluid, the case is porous, the dipstick is incorrect, the vent is plugged or the drain back holes are plugged.

3   Shift linkage - check and adjustment

Refer to illustrations 3.3 and 3.4

Check

1   Try to start the engine in each shift lever position; the starter should operate in Park and Neutral only. If the starter does not operate in Park or Neutral or operates in any position other than Park and Neutral, the shift linkage is in need of adjustment or the Neutral start switch is defective (see Section 4).

Adjustment

2   Remove the center console (see Chapter 11).

3   Place the shift lever in D4 or Reverse and remove the lock pin from the adjuster **(see illustration)**.

4   Make sure the hole in the adjuster is perfectly aligned with hole in the shift cable **(see illustration)**. There are two holes in the end of the shift cable, positioned 90 degrees apart, allowing cable adjustment in 1/4-turn increments.

5   If the cable holes are not aligned perfectly, loosen the locknut on the adjuster **(see illustration 3.3)** and turn the adjuster until the hole in the adjuster is perfectly aligned with the hole in the shift cable.

6   Tighten the locknut and install the lock pin. If the pin binds when you install it, readjust the cable.

7   Try to start the engine in each shift lever position; the starter should operate in the Park and Neutral only.

8   Reinstall the center console (see Chapter 11).

4   Neutral start switch - check and replacement

Refer to illustrations 4.2 and 4.3

1   Try to start the engine in each shift lever position; the starter should operate in Park and Neutral only. If the starter does not operate, or operates in any position other than Park or Neutral, first check the shift linkage adjustment (see Section 3). If the shift linkage is properly adjusted and the problem persists, check the Neutral start switch which, on these models, incorporates the backup light switch as well.

2   Remove the center console (see Chapter 11) and unplug the connector from the Neutral start switch. Check the connector for continuity with the shift lever in each position **(see illustration)**.

3   If the continuity is not as specified, replace the switch. Do this by removing the two retaining bolts and detaching the switch from the gearshift selector mounting bracket **(see illustration)**.

4   When installing the new switch, place the switch slider and shift lever in Neutral, place the switch in place over the actuator pin and tighten the bolts securely **(see illustration 4.3)**.

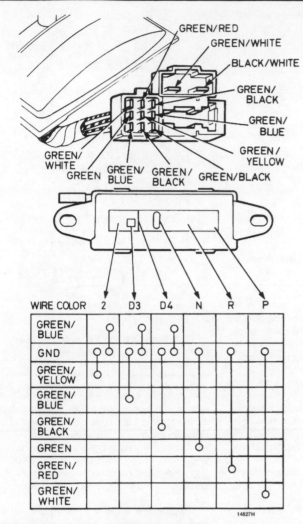

WIRE COLOR	2	D3	D4	N	R	P
GREEN/BLUE		○	○	○		
GND	○○	○○	○○	○	○	○
GREEN/YELLOW	○					
GREEN/BLUE		○				
GREEN/BLACK			○			
GREEN				○		
GREEN/RED					○	
GREEN/WHITE						○

SWITCH POSITION

WIRE COLOR	N	R	P
BLACK/WHITE	○		○
GREEN/BLACK		○	
BLACK/WHITE	○		○
GREEN/BLACK			

4.2 Make the continuity checks indicated in these two charts - the Neutral start switch must be in the indicated position for each check (for example, when checking continuity between ground and green/yellow, the switch must be in the 2 position)

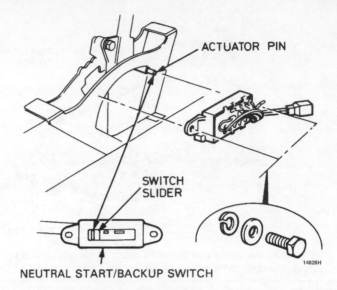

4.3 To install the Neutral start/backup switch, position the switch slider as shown, place the switch over the actuator pin and install the retaining bolts

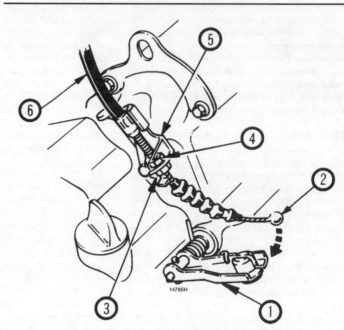

5.3a TV cable details - to remove the cable, loosen locknut B, slide the TV cable out of the bracket, then slide the TV cable end out of the TV control lever

1   TV control lever
2   TV cable end
3   Locknut B
4   Locknut A
5   TV cable bracket
6   TV cable

7B

5   Throttle Valve (TV) cable - adjustment (fuel-injected models)

Refer to illustrations 5.3a, 5.3b and 5.8
Note: You need a special tool to adjust the TV cable bracket on carbureted models, so TV cable adjustment on carbureted models is best left to a dealer service department or a repair shop.

1   Before beginning this procedure, the engine must be at normal operating temperature (the cooling fan must come on at least twice), the idle speed must be correct (see Chapter 1) and the throttle cable must be properly adjusted (see Chapter 4).

1984 and 1985

2   Attach a three-pound (approximately) weight to the throttle pedal. Raise and release the pedal to take up the cable free play.

3   Disconnect the TV cable from the transaxle (see illustration), lay the end on the shock tower and adjust the distance between the cable end and locknut A to the specified distance (see illustration).
4   Reinstall the TV cable on the transaxle.
5   Depress the throttle pedal and check that the cable moves freely.
6   Start the engine and make sure the movement of the fuel injection throttle link is synchronized with the TV cable movement.

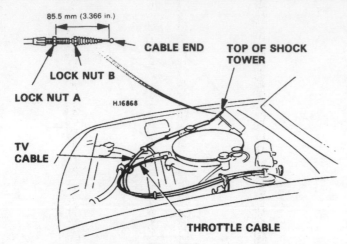

5.3b Secure the upper end of the TV cable as shown, lay the end on top of the shock tower and adjust the locknut A-to-cable end distance (see the specifications)

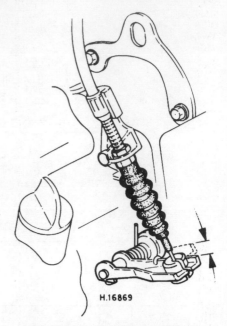

5.8 Measure the TV lever free play at the point shown

The TV cable should start to move as the engine speed increases.

7   If the lever moves before the engine speed increases, turn locknut A counter-clockwise **(see illustration 5.3a)**, then tighten locknut B. If the lever moves after the engine speed increases, loosen locknut B, turn locknut A clockwise then tighten locknut B.

8   Remove the weight from the throttle pedal and check that the free play at the TV cable end is as specified **(see illustration)**. If it's not, readjust the cable.

1986 on

9   Loosen locknuts A and B on the TV cable at the bracket **(see illustration 5.3a).**

10   Push down on the TV cable lever on the transaxle, hold it down and check the TV cable free play at the fuel injection unit throttle link. If there is any free play, remove it by turning locknut A until none can be felt at the throttle link.

11   Continue to the press down on the TV cable lever and pull on the throttle link at the fuel injection unit. The throttle link and TV cable lever should move at precisely the same time.

12   Have an assistant depress the throttle pedal and hold it to the floor. Check the free play at the control lever **(see illustration 5.8)**. If it's not as specified, readjust the cable.

6   Automatic transaxle - removal and installation

Removal

1   Disconnect the negative cable from the battery.

2   Raise the vehicle and support it securely on jackstands.

3   Drain the transaxle fluid (see Chapter 1).

4   Remove the torque converter cover.

5   Mark the torque converter and the drive-plate with white paint so they can be installed

in the same relative position.

6   Remove the eight torque converter-to-driveplate bolts. Turn the crankshaft pulley bolt for access to each bolt.

7   Remove the starter motor (see Chapter 5).

8   Disconnect the driveaxles from the transaxle (see Chapter 8).

9   Disconnect the speedometer cable.

10   Disconnect the wire harness from the transaxle.

11   On models so equipped, disconnect the vacuum hose(s).

12   Remove any exhaust components which will interfere with transaxle removal (see Chapter 4).

13   Disconnect the TV cable (see Section 5).

14   Disconnect the shift linkage.

15   Support the engine using a hoist from above or a jack and a block of wood under the oil pan to spread the load.

16   Support the transaxle with a jack - preferably a special jack made for this purpose. Safety chains will help steady the transaxle on the jack.

17   Remove any chassis or suspension components which will interfere with transaxle removal.

18   Remove the bolts securing the transaxle to the engine.

19   Remove the transaxle mount nuts and bolts (see Chapter 7A).

20   Lower the transaxle slightly and disconnect and plug the transaxle cooler lines.

21   Move the transaxle back to disengage it from the engine block dowel pins and make sure the torque converter is detached from the driveplate. Secure the torque converter to the transaxle so it will not fall out during removal. Lower the transaxle from the vehicle.

Installation

22   Prior to installation, make sure the torque converter hub is securely engaged in the pump.

23   With the transaxle secured to the jack, raise it into position. Be sure to keep it level so the torque converter does not slide out. Connect the fluid cooler lines.

24   Turn the torque converter to line up the bolt holes in the converter and driveplate. The white paint mark on the torque converter and the driveplate made in Step 5 must line up.

25   Move the transaxle forward carefully until the dowel pins and the torque converter are engaged.

26   Install the transaxle housing-to-engine bolts. Tighten them securely.

27   Install the torque converter-to-driveplate bolts. Tighten the bolts to the specified torque.

28   Install the transaxle and any suspension and chassis components which were removed. Tighten the bolts and nuts to the specified torque.

29   Remove the jacks supporting the transaxle and the engine.

30   Install the starter motor (see Chapter 5).

31   Connect the vacuum hose(s) (if equipped).

32   Connect the shift and TV linkage.

33   Plug in the transaxle electrical connectors.

34   Install the torque converter cover.

35   Connect the driveaxles (see Chapter 8).

36   Connect the speedometer cable.

37   Adjust the shift linkage and TV cable (see Sections 3 and 5).

38   Install any exhaust system components that were removed or disconnected.

39   Lower the vehicle.

40   Fill the transaxle (see Chapter 1), run the vehicle and check for fluid leaks.

Chapter 8
Clutch and driveaxles

Contents

Specifications

General

Driveaxle standard length (A in illustration 9.16a)

1984	
Left	31.874 to 32.051 in (809 to 813.5 mm)
Right	20.251 to 20.43 in (514 to 518.5 mm)
1985	
Left (manual transaxle)	30.692 to 30.869 in (779 to 783.5 mm)
Left (automatic transaxle)	31.000 to 31.185 in (787 to 791.5 mm)
Right	19.542 to 19.71 in (496 to 500.5 mm)
1986 on	
Left (manual transaxle)	31.787 to 31.894 in (805 to 809.5 mm)
Left (automatic transaxle)	31.992 to 32.17 in (812 to 816.5 mm)
Right	19.936 to 20.113 in (506 to 510.5 mm)

Torque specifications

	Ft-lbs	Nm
Pressure plate-to-flywheel bolts	19	26
Release fork-to-release shaft bolt	19	26
Driveaxle hub nut	137	186
Wheel lug nuts	See Chapter 1	

8

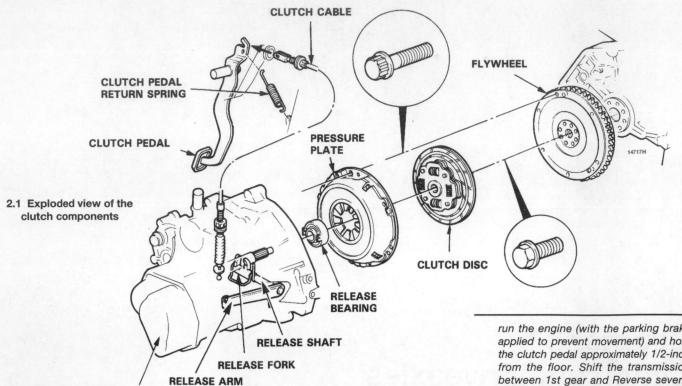

2.1 Exploded view of the clutch components

1 General information

The information in this Chapter deals with the components from the transaxle end of the engine to the front wheels, except for the transaxle, which is dealt with in the previous Chapter. For the purposes of this Chapter, these components are grouped into two categories: Clutch and driveaxles. Separate Sections within this Chapter offer general descriptions and checking procedures for components in each of the two groups.

Since nearly all the procedures covered in this Chapter involve working under the vehicle, make sure it's securely supported on sturdy jackstands or on a hoist where the vehicle can be easily raised and lowered.

2 Clutch - description and check

Refer to illustration 2.1

1   All vehicles with a manual transmission use a single dry plate, diaphragm spring type clutch **(see illustration)**. The clutch disc has a splined hub which allows it to slide along the splines of the transmission input shaft. The clutch and pressure plate are held in contact by spring pressure exerted by the diaphragm in the pressure plate.

2   The clutch release system is operated mechanically. The mechanical release system includes the clutch pedal, a clutch cable which actuates the clutch release fork and the release bearing.

3   When the clutch pedal is depressed, the clutch cable pulls against the outer end of the

clutch release fork arm. As the shaft pivots, the fork pushes against the release bearing. The bearing pushes against the fingers of the diaphragm spring of the pressure plate assembly, which in turn releases the clutch plate.

4   Terminology can be a problem when discussing the clutch components because common names are in some cases different from those used by the manufacturer. For example, the driven plate is also called the clutch plate or disc, the clutch release bearing is sometimes called a throwout bearing, the release fork is sometimes called the release lever.

5   Other than to replace components with obvious damage, some preliminary checks should be performed to diagnose clutch problems. These checks assume the transaxle is in good working condition.

a)   *The first check should be of the clutch cable adjustment. If there is too much slack in the cable, the clutch won't release completely, making gear engagement difficult or impossible. Refer to Section 5 for the adjustment procedure.*

b)   *To check "clutch spin down time," run the engine at normal idle speed with the transmission in Neutral (clutch pedal up - engaged). Disengage the clutch (pedal down), wait several seconds and shift the transmission into Reverse. No grinding noise should be heard. A grinding noise would most likely indicate a problem in the pressure plate or the clutch disc.*

c)   *To check for complete clutch release,*

run the engine (with the parking brake applied to prevent movement) and hold the clutch pedal approximately 1/2-inch from the floor. Shift the transmission between 1st gear and Reverse several times. If the shift is rough, the clutch cable is in need of adjustment (see Section 5) or a clutch component has failed.

d)   *Visually inspect the pivot bushing at the top of the clutch pedal to make sure there is no binding or excessive play.*

e)   *A clutch pedal that is difficult to operate is most likely caused by a faulty clutch cable. Check the cable where it enters the housing for frayed wires, rust and other signs of corrosion. If it looks good, lubricate the cable with penetrating oil. If pedal operation improves, the cable is worn out and should be replaced.*

3 Clutch components - removal, inspection and installation

Warning: *Dust produced by clutch wear and deposited on clutch components may contain asbestos, which is hazardous to your health. DO NOT blow it out with compressed air and DO NOT inhale it. DO NOT use gasoline or petroleum-based solvents to remove the dust. Brake system cleaner should be used to flush the dust into a drain pan. After the clutch components are wiped clean with a rag, dispose of the contaminated rags and cleaner in a covered, marked container.*

Removal

Refer to illustration 3.5

1   Access to the clutch components is normally accomplished by removing the transaxle, leaving the engine in the vehicle. If the engine is being removed for major overhaul, check the clutch for wear and replace worn components as necessary. However,

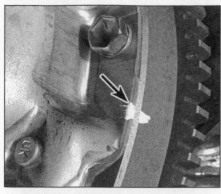

3.5 Index the pressure plate to the flywheel (just in case you're going to reuse the same pressure plate)

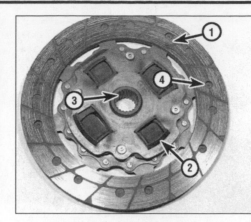

3.9 The clutch disc

1 **Lining** - this will wear down in use
2 **Springs** - check for cracking and deformation
3 **Splined hub** - the splines must not be worn and should slide smoothly on the transaxle input shaft splines
4 **Rivets** - these secure the lining and will damage the flywheel or pressure plate if allowed to contact the surfaces

NORMAL FINGER WEAR

EXCESSIVE WEAR

EXCESSIVE FINGER WEAR

BROKEN OR BENT FINGERS

3.11 Replace the pressure plate if excessive wear is noted

the relatively low cost of the clutch components compared to the time and trouble spent gaining access to them warrants their replacement anytime the engine or transaxle is removed, unless they are new or in near perfect condition. The following procedures are based on the assumption the engine will stay in place.

2 Referring to Chapter 7 Part A, remove the transaxle from the vehicle. Support the engine while the transaxle is out. Preferably, an engine hoist should be used to support it from above. However, if a jack is used underneath the engine, make sure a piece of wood is positioned between the jack and oil pan to spread the load. **Caution:** *The pickup for the oil pump is very close to the bottom of the oil pan. If the pan is bent or distorted in any way, engine oil starvation could occur.*

3 The clutch fork and release bearing can remain attached to the transaxle housing for the time being.

4 To support the clutch disc during removal, install a clutch alignment tool through the clutch disc hub.

5 Carefully inspect the flywheel and pressure plate for indexing marks. The marks are usually an X, an O or a white letter. If they cannot be found, scribe or paint marks yourself so the pressure plate and the flywheel will be in the same alignment during installation **(see illustration)**.

6 Turning each bolt a little at a time, loosen the pressure plate-to-flywheel bolts. Work in a criss-cross pattern until all spring pressure is relieved. Then hold the pressure

plate securely and completely remove the bolts, followed by the pressure plate and clutch disc.

Inspection

Refer to illustrations 3.9 and 3.11

7 Ordinarily, when a problem occurs in the clutch, it can be attributed to wear of the clutch driven plate assembly (clutch disc). However, all components should be inspected at this time.

8 Inspect the flywheel for cracks, heat checking, grooves and other obvious defects. If the imperfections are slight, a machine shop can machine the surface flat and smooth, which is highly recommended regardless of the surface appearance. Refer to Chapter 2 for the flywheel removal and installation procedure.

9 Inspect the lining on the clutch disc. There should be at least 1/16-inch of lining above the rivet heads. Check for loose rivets, distortion, cracks, broken springs and other obvious damage **(see illustration)**. As mentioned above, ordinarily the clutch disc is routinely replaced, so if in doubt about the condition, replace it with a new one.

10 The release bearing should also be replaced along with the clutch disc (see Section 4).

11 Check the machined surfaces and the diaphragm spring fingers of the pressure plate **(see illustration)**. If the surface is grooved or otherwise damaged, replace the pressure plate. Also check for obvious damage, distortion, cracking, etc. Light glazing

can be removed with medium grit emery cloth. If a new pressure plate is required, new and factory-rebuilt units are available.

Installation

Refer to illustration 3.13

12 Before installation, clean the flywheel and pressure plate machined surfaces with brake cleaner, lacquer thinner or acetone. It's important that no oil or grease is on these surfaces or the lining of the clutch disc. Handle the parts only with clean hands.

13 Position the clutch disc and pressure plate against the flywheel with the clutch held in place with an alignment tool **(see illustration)**. Make sure it's installed properly (most replacement clutch plates will be marked "fly-

3.13 Center the clutch disc in the pressure plate with a clutch alignment tool

8

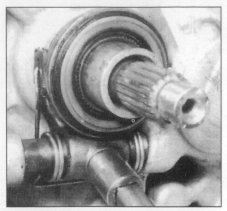

4.2 Remove the clutch release bearing fork bolt, then slide the release shaft out of the transaxle housing (assembly removed from transaxle for clarity)

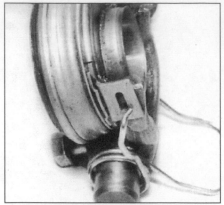

4.3 To release the bearing from the fork, pull the ends of the retaining spring out

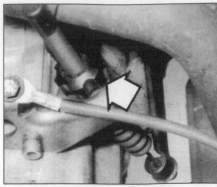

5.2a Loosen the adjuster wheel (arrow) to provide enough slack in the cable to unhook it

wheel side" or something similar - if not marked, install the clutch disc with the damper springs toward the transaxle).

14   Tighten the pressure plate-to-flywheel bolts only finger tight, working around the pressure plate.

15   Center the clutch disc by ensuring the alignment tool extends through the splined hub and into the pocket in the crankshaft. Wiggle the tool up, down or side-to-side as needed to center the disc. Tighten the pressure plate-to-flywheel bolts a little at a time, working in a crisscross pattern to prevent distorting the cover. After all of the bolts are snug, tighten them to the specified torque. Remove the alignment tool.

16   Using high-temperature grease, lubricate the inner groove of the release bearing (refer to Section 4). Also place grease on the release lever contact areas and the transaxle input shaft bearing retainer.

17   Install the clutch release bearing as described in Section 4.

18   Install the transaxle and all components removed previously. Tighten all fasteners to the proper torque specifications.

4   Clutch release bearing and fork - removal, inspection and installation

Refer to illustrations 4.2 and 4.3

Warning: *Dust produced by clutch wear and deposited on clutch components may contain asbestos, which is hazardous to your health. DO NOT blow it out with compressed air and DO NOT inhale it. DO NOT use gasoline or petroleum-based solvents to remove the dust. Brake system cleaner should be used to flush the dust into a drain pan. After the clutch components are wiped clean with a rag, dispose of the contaminated rags and cleaner in a covered, marked container.*

Removal

1   Remove the transaxle from the vehicle (see Chapter 7, Part A) and clean the clutch

housing as described in the Warning above.
2   Remove the clutch release bearing fork-to-release shaft bolt **(see illustration)** and slide the shaft out of the transaxle housing to free the release bearing.
3   Slide the bearing and fork off the transaxle input shaft. To separate the bearing from the fork, pull the spring ends out, disengaging them from the slots in the bearing locating tabs **(see illustration)**.

Inspection

4   Check the release fork, release shaft and lever for excessive wear, replacing them if necessary.
5   Inspect the bearing for damage, wear and cracks. Hold the center of the bearing and spin the outer race. If the bearing doesn't turn smoothly or if it's noisy, replace it with a new one. It's common practice to replace the bearing with a new one whenever a clutch job is performed, to decrease the possibility of a bearing failure in the future.

Installation

6   Wipe the old grease from the release bearing, if the bearing is to be reused. Do not clean it by immersing it in solvent; it's packed with grease and sealed at the factory and would be ruined if solvent got into it. Fill the groove in the inner diameter of the bearing with high temperature grease.
7   Replace the bearing on the release fork, making sure the spring ends completely engage with the bearing locating tabs.
8   Lubricate the release shaft with multi-purpose grease, position the release fork/bearing assembly in the transaxle housing and install the release shaft. Align the hole in the fork with the threaded hole in the shaft and install the bolt and washer. Tighten the bolt to the specified torque.
9   Work the release shaft arm by hand to verify smooth operation of the release shaft and bearing. The remainder of installation is the reverse of the removal procedure. Don't forget to adjust the clutch release cable, as described in Section 5.

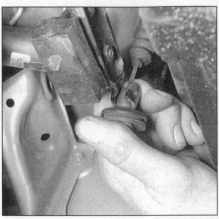

5.2b To disconnect the cable from the release lever arm, pull up on the lever and pass the cable through the slot in the arm

5   Clutch cable - removal, installation and adjustment

Refer to illustrations 5.2a, 5.2b and 5.3

Removal

1   Disconnect the cable from the negative terminal of the battery.
2   Loosen the clutch cable adjuster wheel **(see illustration)** to provide slack in the cable, then unhook the cable end from the release arm **(see illustration)**.
3   Pry the cable housing out of the hole in the firewall.
4   Working inside the vehicle, disconnect the cable from the top of the clutch pedal. Pull the cable through the firewall, into the engine compartment.

Installation

5   Feed the cable through the firewall and hook the cable end to the top of the clutch pedal. Push the cable housing into the hole in the firewall until it's completely seated.
6   Route the cable into position on the bracket on the transaxle. Connect the cable end to the release arm.

Adjustment

7   Refer to Chapter 1 for the clutch cable adjustment procedure.

8   Reconnect the battery cable.

6   Clutch pedal - removal and installation

Removal

1   Disconnect the cable from the negative terminal of the battery.

2   Loosen the clutch cable adjuster wheel (see Section 5) to provide enough slack to unhook the cable end from the clutch pedal.

3   Unhook the pedal return spring from the pedal.

4   Working under the dash, remove the E-clip or nut which secures the pedal to the pivot shaft. Slide the pedal off the shaft.

Installation

5   Installation is the reverse of the removal procedure. Apply a thin coat of multi-purpose grease to the pivot shaft before sliding the pedal onto it. When assembly is complete, adjust the clutch cable as described in Chapter 1.

7   Driveaxles, constant velocity (CV) joints and boots - check

1   The driveaxles, CV joints and boots should be inspected periodically and whenever the vehicle is raised for any reason. The most common symptom of driveaxle or CV joint failure is knocking or clicking noises when turning.

2   Raise the vehicle and support it securely on jackstands.

3   Inspect the CV joint boots for cracks, leaks and broken retaining bands. If lubricant leaks out through a hole or crack in the boot, the CV joint will wear prematurely and require replacement. Replace any damaged boots immediately (see Section 9). It's a good idea to disassemble, clean, inspect and repack the CV joint whenever replacing a CV joint boot, to ensure that the joint is not contaminated with moisture or dirt, which would cause premature CV joint failure.

4   Check the entire length of each axle to make sure they aren't cracked, dented, twisted or bent.

5   Grasp each axle and rotate it in both directions while holding the CV joint housings to check for excessive movement, indicating worn splines or loose CV joints.

6   If a boot is damaged or loose, remove the driveaxle as described in Section 8. Disassemble and inspect the CV joint as outlined in Section 9. **Note:** *Some auto parts stores carry "split" type replacement boots, which can be installed without removing the driveaxle from the vehicle. This is a convenient alternative; however, it's recommended that the driveaxle be removed and the CV joint disassembled and cleaned to ensure that the joint is free from contaminants such as moisture and dirt, which will accelerate CV joint wear.*

8   Driveaxles - removal and installation

Refer to illustrations 8.1, 8.7, 8.9 and 8.16

Removal

1   Remove the wheel cover center cap (not all models) and loosen the hub nut **(see illustration)**. Loosen the wheel lug nuts, raise the front of the vehicle and support it securely on jackstands. Remove the front wheel.

2   Remove the driveaxle hub nut. To prevent the hub from turning, place a pry bar between two of the wheel studs, then loosen the nut.

3   Drain the transaxle gear lubricant or automatic transmission fluid (see Chapter 1).

4   If you are working on a 1986 or later model, remove the damper fork from the strut/shock absorber assembly and the suspension lower arm (see Chapter 10).

5   Remove the lower arm-to-steering knuckle balljoint stud nut or pinch bolt and separate the lower arm from the steering knuckle (see Chapter 10, if necessary).

8.1 Break the hub nut loose while the wheel is still on the ground

6   Pull out on the steering knuckle and hub until the end of the driveaxle is clear, then maneuver the axle out of the way. Support the end of the axle with a piece of wire to avoid unnecessary strain on the inner CV joint.

7   Carefully pry the inner end of the axle from the transaxle, using a large pry bar positioned between the transaxle housing and the CV joint housing **(see illustration)**.

8   Support the CV joints and carefully remove the driveaxle from the vehicle.

Installation

9   Pry the old spring clip from the inner end of the driveaxle and install a new one **(see illustration)**. Lubricate the differential seal with multi-purpose grease, raise the driveaxle into position while supporting the CV joints and insert the splined end of the inner CV joint into the differential side gear. Seat the shaft in the side gear by firmly pushing in on the driveaxle.

10   Apply a light coat of multi-purpose grease to the outer CV joint splines, pull out on the strut/steering knuckle assembly and install the stub axle into the hub.

11   Connect the lower arm to the steering knuckle and install the balljoint stud nut or pinch bolt.

12   Install the damper fork.

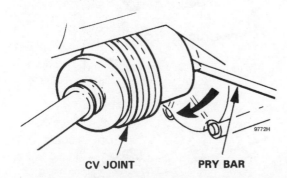

8.7 Using a pry bar, pop the inner CV joint out of the transaxle - be careful not to damage the transaxle case or seal or leaks could develop

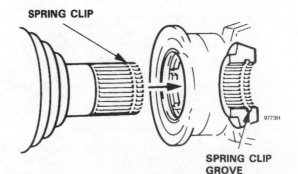

8.9 Always replace the spring clip on the inner CV joint stub shaft before reinstalling the driveaxle

8

13   Install the hub nut. Lock the disc so it cannot turn, as described in Step 2, and tighten the hub nut securely.

14   Grasp the inner CV joint housing (not the driveaxle) and pull out to make sure the axle has seated securely in the transaxle.

15   Install the wheel and lower the vehicle. Tighten the lug nuts to the specified torque.

16   Tighten the hub nut to the specified torque and stake the collar of the nut into the groove **(see illustration)**. Install the wheel cover center cap.

17   Refill the transaxle with the proper type and amount of lubricant (see Chapter 1).

9   Driveaxle boot replacement and CV joint overhaul

Refer to illustrations 9.3a, 9.3b, 9.6, 9.11, 9.12, 9.13a, 9.13b, 9.14, 9.15, 9.16a, 9.16b and 9.16c

Note: *If the CV joints exhibit signs of wear indicating the need for an overhaul (usually due to torn boots), explore all options before beginning the job. Complete rebuilt driveaxles are available on an exchange basis, which eliminates much time and work. Whichever route you choose to take, check on the cost and availability of parts before disassembling the vehicle.*

1   Remove the driveaxle (refer to Section 8).

2   Paint match marks on the inner joint housing and driveaxle.

3   Pry the outer (larger) clamps loose with a small screwdriver **(see illustrations)** and

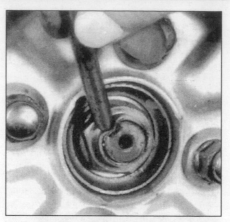

8.16 After the driveaxle hub nut has been tightened to the specified torque, stake the collar of the nut into the groove in the stub shaft - this will prevent the nut from coming loose

slide them off the ends of the driveaxle. Cut the inner (smaller) clamps and the damper clamp (right driveaxle only) with a pair of diagonal cutters and discard them.

4   Separate the inner joint housing from the spider **(see illustration 9.3b)**.

5   Remove the spider outer snap-ring by prying it off with a screwdriver.

6   Punch match marks on the spider and the end of the driveaxle **(see illustration)**. Index each of the three roller assemblies to the spider with pieces of numbered tape so they can be returned to their original positions. Remove the roller assemblies.

9.3a   The large boot clamps can be pried open with a small screwdriver

7   Remove the spider from the driveaxle. The inner snap-ring can now be pried off with a screwdriver.

8   Slide the inner joint boot and the outer joint boot off the driveaxle.

9   Thoroughly clean the inner and outer CV joints with solvent and dry them with compressed air, if available. **Note:** *Because the outer joint cannot be disassembled, it is difficult to wash away all the old grease and to rid the bearing of solvent once it's clean. But it is imperative that the job be done thoroughly, so take your time and do it right.*

10   Inspect the inner spider for signs of wear or damage. If the spider is obviously worn or damaged, replace it, along with the housing, as an assembly.

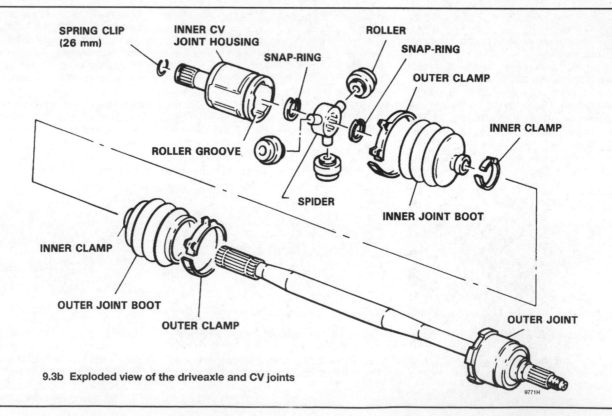

9.3b   Exploded view of the driveaxle and CV joints

9.6 Use a center punch to make match marks (arrows) on the spider and the driveaxle to ensure they are reassembled properly

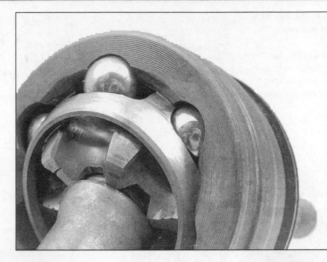

9.11 After the old grease has been rinsed away and the cleaning solvent has been blown out with compressed air, rotate the outer CV joint through its full range of motion and inspect the bearing surfaces for wear or damage - if the race, cage, or any of the bearings look damaged, replace the driveaxle/outer joint assembly

9.12 Wrap the splined area of the axle with vinyl tape to prevent damage to the boots when installing them

9.13a Install the inner snap-ring on the axleshaft

11 Bend the outer CV joint housing at an angle to the driveaxle to expose the bearings, inner race and cage (see illustration). Inspect the bearing surfaces for signs of wear. If the bearings are damaged or worn, replace the driveaxle.

12 Slide the new outer boot onto the driveaxle. It's a good idea to wrap vinyl tape around the splines of the shaft to prevent damage to the boot (see illustration). When

the boot is in position, pack the joint with as much grease as it will hold and put the rest into the boot (the grease is included in the boot kit). Slide the boot on the rest of the way and install the new clamps.

13 Slide the inner boot onto the driveaxle, followed by the inner snapring (see illustration). Make sure the snap-ring is completely seated in the groove. Align the match marks you made before removing the joint and slide

the spider onto the driveaxle (see illustration). Install the outer snap-ring.

14 Lubricate the three roller assemblies with constant velocity joint grease and install them in their original positions on the tripod joint spider (see illustration).

15 Fill the inner joint housing with grease and install it over the spider, making sure the previously applied match marks are lined up (see illustration). Slide the boot into place

9.13b Install the spider on the axleshaft, making sure the punch marks are lined up, then install the outer snap-ring

9.14 Install the roller assemblies on the spider in their original positions

9.15 Pack the inner CV joint housing with grease and slide it over the spider, making sure the previously applied alignment marks match up

8

and equalize the pressure inside the boot by inserting a small screwdriver between the boot and joint.

16   Measure the driveaxle standard length and make sure the boot is not stretched, contracted or distorted in any way **(see illustration)**. Tighten the boot clamps **(see illustrations)**.

17   Install the driveaxle (Section 8).

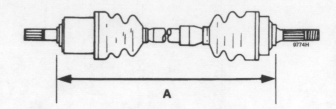

9.16a Before tightening the boot clamp, adjust the driveaxle length (A) to the dimension listed in the specifications

9.16b To install the new clamps, bend the tang down . . .

9.16c . . . and flatten the tabs to hold it in place

Chapter 9 Brakes

Contents

Specifications

General

Parking brake lever travel	
1984 and 1985	4 to 8 clicks
1986 on	7 to 11 clicks
Power brake booster pushrod-to-master cylinder piston	
clearance (with a vacuum of 20 in-Hg applied	
to booster)...	0.0 to 0.016 in (0.0 to 0.4 mm)
Front disc brakes	
Brake pad minimum thickness	See Chapter 1
Disc thickness	
1988 and 1989 LX-i and SE-i	
Standard	0.83 in (21 mm)
Minimum*	3/4-inch (19 mm)
All others	
Standard	3/4-inch (19 mm)
Minimum*	0.67 in (17 mm)
Thickness variation (parallelism)	0.0006 in (0.015 mm)
Runout limit..	0.004 in (0.10 mm)

Rear disc brakes

Brake pad minimum thickness	See Chapter 1
Disc thickness	
Standard..	0.39 in (10.0 mm)
Minimum*	0.31 in (8.0 mm)
Thickness variation (parallelism)	0.0006 in (0.015 mm)
Runout limit..	0.006 in (0.15 mm)

Refer to marks stamped on the disc (they supersede information printed here)

Drum brakes

Brake lining thickness.. See Chapter 1
Drum diameter
     Standard... 7.87 in (200 mm)
     Maximum*... 7.91 in (201 mm)

* Refer to marks cast into the drum (they supersede information printed here)

Brake pedal

Pedal height (measured from the floor, without the floor mat)
     1984 and 1985 .... 7.36 in (187 mm)
     1986 on .... 8.07 in (205 mm)
Pedal free play... 0.04 to 0.20 in (1 to 5 mm)

Torque specifications   **Ft-lbs** (unless otherwise indicated)

Front brake caliper mounting bolts
     1984 and 1985 20
     1986 on (except LX-i and SE-i models)............................ 33
     1988 on LX-i and SE-i models 24
Front brake caliper mounting bracket bolts
     1984 and 1985 56
     1986 on (except LX-i and SE-i models)............................ 53
     1988 on LX-i and SE-i models 56
Brake hose-to-caliper banjo bolt (front or rear) 25
Rear brake caliper guide bolts.. 17
Rear brake caliper mounting bracket bolts 28
Rear wheel spindle nuts (1986 and later
     models with drum brakes).. 134
Wheel cylinder
     Nuts .... 72 in-lbs
     Bolts .... 84 in-lbs
Brake backing plate bolts.. 28
Master cylinder mounting nuts
     1984 and 1985 .... 60 in-lbs
     1986 on .... 132 in-lbs
Power brake booster mounting nuts .... 108 in lbs

1   General information

Refer to illustration 1.3

General

     All vehicles covered by this manual are equipped with hydraulically operated power assisted brake systems. All front brake systems are disc type, while the rear brakes are either disc or drum type.
     All brakes are self-adjusting. The front and rear disc brakes automatically compensate for pad wear, while the rear drum brakes incorporate an adjustment mechanism which is activated as the brakes are applied, either through the pedal or the parking brake lever.
     The hydraulic system is a diagonally split design, meaning there are separate circuits for the left front/right rear and the right front/left rear brakes **(see illustration)**. If one circuit fails, the other circuit will remain functional and a warning indicator will light up on the dashboard when a substantial amount of brake fluid is lost, showing that a failure has occurred.

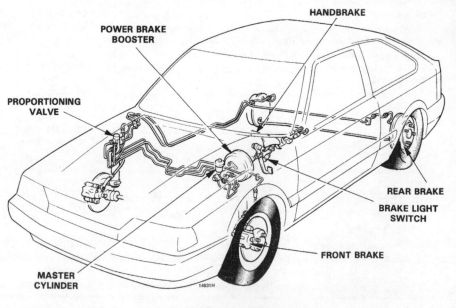

1.3 Schematic of the brake system

2.5 Using a large C-clamp, push the piston back into the caliper - note that one end of the clamp is on the flat area on the back side of the caliper and the other end (screw end) is pressing on the outer brake pad

2.6a Before removing anything, spray the caliper and brake pads with brake cleaner to remove the dust produced by brake pad wear - DO NOT blow the dust off with compressed air!

Master cylinder

The master cylinder is located under the hood, mounted to the power brake booster, and is best recognized by the large fluid reservoir on top. The fluid reservoir is a removable plastic cup, secured to the master cylinder by a clamp.

The master cylinder is designed for the "split system" mentioned earlier and has separate primary and secondary piston assemblies, the piston nearest the firewall being the secondary piston.

Proportioning valves

The proportioning valve assembly is bolted to the right strut tower. It incorporates two separate valves - one valve for each circuit.

The proportioning valves regulate the hydraulic pressure to the rear brakes during heavy braking to eliminate rear wheel lockup. Under normal braking conditions they allow full pressure to the rear brake system until a predetermined pedal pressure is reached. Above that point, the pressure to the rear brakes is limited.

The proportioning valve is not serviceable - if a problem develops with the valve, it must be replaced as an assembly.

Power brake booster

The power brake booster, utilizing engine manifold vacuum and atmospheric pressure to provide assistance to the hydraulically operated brakes, is mounted on the firewall in the engine compartment.

Parking brake

The parking brake mechanically operates the rear brakes only. On drum brake models the parking brake cables pull on a lever attached to the brake shoe assembly, causing the shoes to expand against the drum. On models with rear disc brakes, the

cables pull on levers that are attached to screw-type actuators in the caliper housings, which apply force to the caliper pistons, clamping the brake pads against the brake disc.

Precautions

There are some general cautions and warnings involving the brake system on this vehicle:

a) *Use only brake fluid conforming to DOT 3 specifications.*

b) *The brake pads and linings may contain asbestos fibers which are hazardous to your health if inhaled. Whenever you work on brake system components, clean all parts with brake system cleaner or denatured alcohol. Do not allow the fine dust to become airborne.*

c) *Safety should be paramount whenever any servicing of the brake components is performed. Do not use parts or fasteners which are not in perfect condition, and be sure that all clearances and torque specifications are adhered to. If you are at all unsure about a certain procedure, seek professional advice. Upon completion of any brake system work, test the brakes carefully in a controlled area before putting the vehicle into normal service.*

If a problem is suspected in the brake system, don't drive the vehicle until it's fixed.

---

2 Front disc brake pads - replacement

Refer to illustrations 2.5 and 2.6a through 2.6i

Warning: *Disc brake pads must be replaced on both wheels at the same time - never replace the pads on only one wheel. Also, the dust created by the brake system may con-*

tain asbestos, which is harmful to your health. Never blow it out with compressed air and don't inhale any of it. An approved filtering mask should be worn when working on the brakes. Do not, under any circumstances, use petroleum based solvents to clean brake parts. Use brake cleaner or denatured alcohol only!

Note: *When servicing the disc brakes, use only high quality, nationally recognized name brand pads.*

1   Remove the cap from the brake fluid reservoir.

2   Loosen the wheel lug nuts, raise the front of the vehicle and support it securely on jackstands.

3   Remove the front wheels. Work on one brake assembly at a time, using the assembled brake for reference if necessary.

4   Inspect the brake disc carefully as outlined in Section 4. If machining is necessary, follow the information in that Section to remove the disc, at which time the calipers and pads can be removed as well.

5   Push the piston back into the bore to provide room for the new brake pads. A C-clamp can be used to accomplish this **(see illustration)**. As the piston is depressed to the bottom of the caliper bore, the fluid in the master cylinder will rise. Make sure it doesn't overflow. If necessary, siphon off some of the fluid.

6   Follow the accompanying illustrations, beginning with 2.6a, for the actual pad replacement procedure. Be sure to stay in order and read the caption under each illustration.

7   When reinstalling the caliper, be sure to tighten the mounting bolts to the specified torque. After the job has been completed, firmly depress the brake pedal a few times to bring the pads into contact with the disc.

8   Check for fluid leakage and make sure the brakes operate normally before driving in traffic.

9

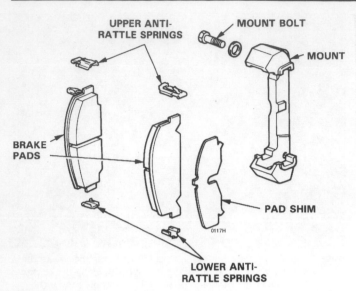

2.6b Front brake pads and related components - exploded view

2.6c Remove the lower caliper mounting bolt and pivot the caliper up, off of the brake pads

2.6d Slide the pads and shims out of the caliper mounting bracket

2.6e Remove the anti-rattle springs and check them for cracks, replacing them with new ones if necessary

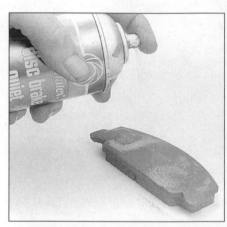

2.6f Before installing the pads, apply a coat of disc brake anti-squeal compound to the backing plates of the pads - follow the manufacturer's instructions on the label

2.6g Smear a little silicone grease on the anti-rattle springs

2.6h Install the inner brake pad and shim in the caliper mounting bracket (the inner pad is the one with the wear indicator at the top of the pad)

2.6i Install the outer brake pad and shim, swing the caliper down into position and tighten the lower caliper mounting bolt to the specified torque

3 Front disc brake caliper - removal, overhaul and installation

Refer to illustrations 3.1a, 3.1b, 3.3a, 3.3b, 3.4, 3.6, 3.7, 3.12 and 3.14

Warning: *Dust created by the brake system may contain asbestos, which is harmful to your health. Never blow it out with compressed air and don't inhale any of it. An approved filtering mask should be worn when working on the brakes. Do not, under any circumstances, use petroleum-based solvents to clean brake parts. Use brake cleaner or denatured alcohol only!.*

Note: *If an overhaul is indicated (usually because of fluid leakage) explore all options before beginning the job. New and factory rebuilt calipers are available on an exchange basis, which makes this job quite easy. If it's decided to rebuild the calipers, make sure a rebuild kit is available before proceeding. Always rebuild the calipers in pairs - never rebuild just one of them.*

Removal

1   Disconnect the brake line from the caliper and plug it to keep contaminants out of the brake system and to prevent losing any more brake fluid than is necessary **(see illustrations)**.

2   Remove the caliper mounting bolts and lift the caliper from the mount. On 1986 and later models, rotate the caliper up and slide it off the caliper pin.

Overhaul

3   To overhaul the caliper, remove the rubber boot ring and the rubber boot (1984 and 1985 models only) **(see illustrations)**. Before you remove the piston, place a wood block between the piston and caliper to prevent damage as it is removed.

4   To remove the piston from the caliper, apply compressed air to the brake fluid hose

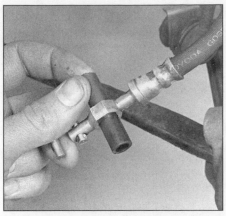

3.1a Remove the brake hose-to-caliper banjo bolt - use new sealing washers when reconnecting the fitting

3.1b Using a piece of rubber hose of the appropriate diameter, plug the brake line fitting

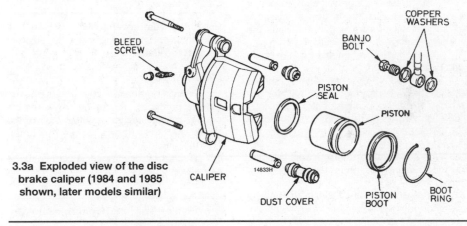

3.3a Exploded view of the disc brake caliper (1984 and 1985 shown, later models similar)

BLEED SCREW

COPPER WASHERS

BANJO BOLT

PISTON SEAL

PISTON

CALIPER

14833H

DUST COVER

PISTON BOOT

BOOT RING

connection on the caliper body **(see illustration)**. Use only enough pressure to ease the piston out of its bore. **Warning:** *Be careful not to place your fingers between the piston and the caliper as the piston may come out with some force. On 1986 and later models, remove the piston boot.*

5   Inspect the mating surfaces of the

piston and caliper bore wall. If there is any scoring, rust, pitting or bright areas, replace the complete caliper unit with a new one.

6   If these components are in good condition, remove the rubber piston seal from the caliper bore using a wooden or plastic tool **(see illustration)**. Metal tools may damage the cylinder bore.

3.3b On 1984 and 1985 models, use a small screwdriver to remove the boot ring

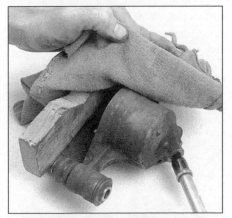

3.4 With the caliper padded to catch the piston, use compressed air to force the piston out of its bore - make sure your hands or fingers are not between the piston and the caliper

3.6 The piston seal should be removed with a plastic or wooden tool to avoid damage to the bore and seal groove - a pencil will do the job

9

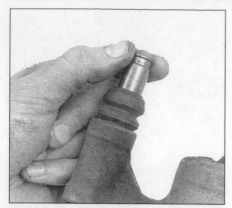

3.7 On each side of the caliper, push the mounting bolt sleeves through the boot and pull them free, then remove the dust boots

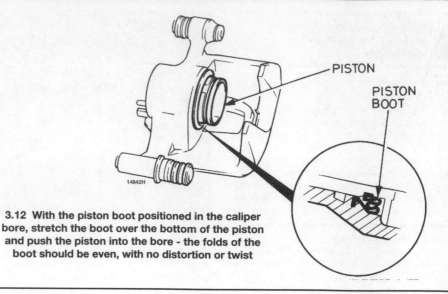

3.12 With the piston boot positioned in the caliper bore, stretch the boot over the bottom of the piston and push the piston into the bore - the folds of the boot should be even, with no distortion or twist

7   Push the mounting bolt sleeves out of the caliper ears **(see illustration)** and remove the rubber boots from both ends. Slide the bushing sleeves out of the caliper ears.

8   Wash all the components in clean brake fluid or alcohol.

9   To reassemble the caliper, you should already have the correct rebuild kit for the vehicle. **Note:** *During reassembly, apply silicone-based grease (supplied with the rebuild kit) between the sliding bushing and the bushing sleeve.*

10   Submerge the new piston seal in brake fluid and install it in the lower groove in the caliper bore.

11   On 1986 and later models, install the piston boot in the upper groove in the caliper bore.

12   Lubricate the piston with clean brake fluid and position it squarely in the caliper bore, then apply firm (but not excessive) pressure to install it. On 1986 and later models, make sure the piston boot seats in the groove in the piston **(see illustration)**.

13   Install the new rubber boot and retaining ring (pre-1986 models).

14   Lubricate the sliding bushings and sleeves with silicone-based grease (supplied in the kit) and push them into the caliper ears.

Install the dust covers. Also lubricate the caliper upper mounting pin with silicone grease **(see illustration)**.

Installation

15   Install the caliper by reversing the removal procedure. Remember to replace the copper sealing washer on either side of the brake line fitting (they should be included with the rebuild kit).

16   Bleed the brake system according to the procedure in Section 12.

---

4   Brake disc - inspection, removal and installation

Note: *This procedure applies to both the front and rear brake discs (on vehicles so equipped).*

Inspection

Refer to illustrations 4.2a, 4.2b, 4.3, 4.4a, 4.4b, 4.5a, 4.5b and 4.6

1   Loosen the wheel lug nuts, raise the vehicle and support it securely on jackstands.

Remove the wheel and install two lug nuts with 3 mm thick washers under them to hold the disc in place (if the two disc retaining screws are still in place, this will be unnecessary). If the rear brake disc is being worked on, release the parking brake.

2   Remove the front or rear brake caliper as outlined in Section 3 or Section 6, respectively. It is not necessary to disconnect the brake hose. After removing the caliper bolts, suspend the caliper out of the way with a piece of wire **(see illustration)**. Remove the two caliper mounting bracket-to-steering knuckle bolts **(see illustration)** and remove the mounting bracket.

3   Visually inspect the disc surface for scoring or damage. Light scratches and shallow grooves are normal after use and may not always be detrimental to brake operation, but deep scoring - over 0.015 inch (0.38 mm) - requires disc removal and refinishing by an automotive machine shop. Be sure to check both sides of the disc **(see illustration)**. If pulsating has been noticed during application of the brakes, suspect disc runout.

4   To check disc runout, place a dial indicator at a point about 1/2-inch from the outer

3.14 Apply a thin film of silicone grease to the upper mounting pin

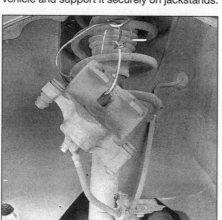

4.2a Secure the caliper out of the way with a piece of wire - DO NOT let the caliper hang by the brake hose

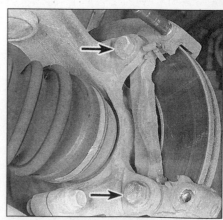

4.2b The caliper mounting bracket is fastened to the steering knuckle with two bolts (arrows)

4.3 The brake pads on this vehicle were obviously neglected, as they wore down to the rivets; the rivets then cut deep grooves into the disc, and now the disc must be replaced

4.4a With two lug nuts (with washers underneath) or the disc retaining screws installed to hold the brake disc in place, rotate the disc and check the runout with a dial indicator - if the reading exceeds the maximum allowable runout limit, the disc will have to be machined or replaced

4.4b Using a swirling motion, remove the glaze from the disc with emery cloth or sandpaper

4.5a The minimum allowable thickness is stamped into the disc

4.5b A micrometer is used to measure disc thickness

edge of the disc **(see illustration)**. Set the indicator to zero and turn the disc. The indicator reading should not exceed the specified allowable runout limit. If it does, the disc

4.6 If the disc is stuck, thread two bolts into the holes in the disc and tighten them

should be refinished by an automotive machine shop. **Note:** *It is recommended that the discs be resurfaced regardless of the dial indicator reading, as this will impart a smooth finish and ensure a perfectly flat surface, eliminating any brake pedal pulsation or other undesirable symptoms related to questionable discs. At the very least, if you elect not to have the discs resurfaced, remove the glazing from the surface with emery cloth or sandpaper using a swirling motion* **(see illustration)**.

5   It is absolutely critical that the disc not be machined to a thickness under the specified minimum allowable disc refinish thickness. The minimum wear (or discard) thickness is cast into the inside of the disc **(see illustration)**. The disc thickness can be checked with a micrometer **(see illustration)**.

Removal

Refer to illustration 4.6

6   Remove the two lug nuts which were put on to hold the disc in place (or the two

disc retaining screws, if present) and remove the disc from the hub. If the disc is stuck to the hub and won't come off, thread two bolts into the holes provided **(see illustration)** and tighten them. Alternate between the bolts, turning them a couple of turns at a time, until the disc is free.

Installation

7   Place the disc in position over the threaded studs.

8   Install the caliper mounting bracket, brake pads and caliper over the disc. Tighten the mounting bracket and caliper bolts to the specified torque.

9   Install the wheel, then lower the vehicle to the ground. Depress the brake pedal a few times to bring the brake pads into contact with the disc. Bleeding of the system will not be necessary unless the fluid hose was disconnected from the caliper. Check the operation of the brakes carefully before placing the vehicle into normal service.

9

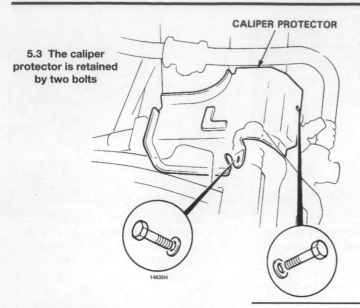

5.3 The caliper protector is retained by two bolts

14835H

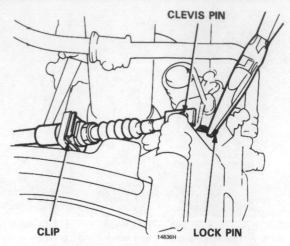

CLEVIS PIN

CLIP   LOCK PIN

14836H

5.4 Pull out the lock pin with a pair of pliers, then remove the clevis pin, which will free the parking brake cable from the caliper actuator lever

5   Rear disc brake pads - replacement

Refer to illustrations 5.3, 5.4, 5.5, 5.6 and 5.9

Warning: *Disc brake pads must be replaced on both rear wheels at the same time - never replace the pads on only one wheel. Also, the dust created by the brake system may contain asbestos, which is harmful to your health. Never blow it out with compressed air and don't inhale any of it. An approved filtering mask should be worn when working on the brakes. Do not, under any circumstances, use petroleum based solvents to clean brake parts. Use brake cleaner or denatured alcohol only!*

Note: *When servicing brakes, use only high quality, nationally recognized name brand pads.*

1   Remove the master cylinder reservoir cap and siphon out approximately half of the brake fluid.

2   Loosen the rear wheel lug nuts, raise the rear of the vehicle and support it securely on jackstands. Remove the wheels.

3   Remove the caliper protector **(see illustration)**.

4   Remove the lock pin from the parking brake cable-to-actuator lever clevis pin **(see illustration)** and disconnect the cable from the lever.

5   Remove the two caliper guide bolts **(see illustration)** and lift the caliper from its mounting bracket. Hang it out of the way with a piece of wire - don't let it hang by the brake hose.

6   Lift off the pad spring, then remove the pads and shims from the caliper bracket. Remove the pad guides from the bracket **(see illustration)**.

7   Before installing the new pads, apply a thin coat of disc brake anti-squeal compound to the backing plates of the pads, following the manufacturer's instructions.

8   Position the pad guides in the caliper mounting bracket, then install the new pads and the guides. The pad with the small tab on its backing plate must be installed on the inside of the disc.

9   Before the caliper is installed, the piston must be retracted until it bottoms in the bore. A pair of needle-nose pliers with the tips engaged in two of the cut-outs in the top of the piston can be used to turn the piston

clockwise, which will cause it to retract **(see illustration)**. Now the piston will have to be positioned so one of the cut-outs will mesh with the tab on the inner brake pad when the caliper is installed. Use the needle-nose pliers to adjust it accordingly. If the piston dust boot becomes distorted when the piston is turned, turn the piston in the opposite direction to restore its shape, but be sure the cut-out will still line up. This may take a few attempts to set the piston in the right position.

10   Position the pad spring over the pads, then install the caliper, tightening the guide bolts to the specified torque.

11   Connect the parking brake cable to the lever on the caliper and install a new lock pin.

12   Install the caliper protector.

13   Install the wheel and lug nuts, lower the vehicle and tighten the lug nuts to the torque specified in Chapter 1.

14   Check the brake fluid level and add fluid, if necessary (see Chapter 1).

15   Apply and release the brake pedal and the hand brake lever several times to bring the pads into contact with the brake discs. Check the operation of the brakes in an isolated area before driving the vehicle in traffic.

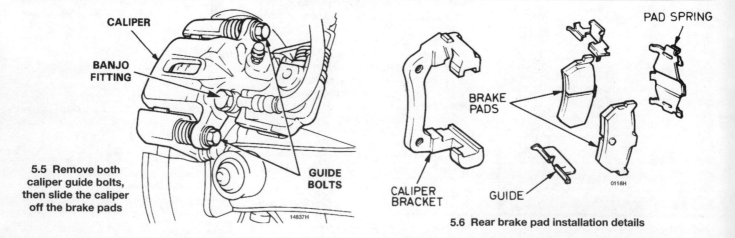

CALIPER

BANJO FITTING

GUIDE BOLTS

14837H

5.5 Remove both caliper guide bolts, then slide the caliper off the brake pads

PAD SPRING

BRAKE PADS

CALIPER BRACKET   GUIDE

0118H

5.6 Rear brake pad installation details

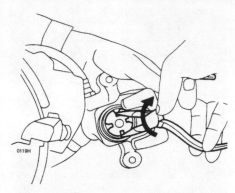

5.9 A pair of needle-nose pliers can be used to screw the caliper piston into the bore

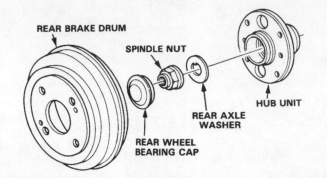

7.3 Rear wheel bearing, hub and brake drum (1986 and later models) - exploded view

6 Rear disc brake caliper - removal, overhaul and installation

Warning: *Disc brake pads must be replaced on both rear wheels at the same time - never replace the pads on only one wheel. Also, the dust created by the brake system may contain asbestos, which is harmful to your health. Never blow it out with compressed air and don't inhale any of it. An approved filtering mask should be worn when working on the brakes. Do not, under any circumstances, use petroleum based solvents to clean brake parts. Use brake cleaner or denatured alcohol only!*

Removal

1   Loosen the wheel lug nuts, raise the rear of the vehicle and support it securely on jackstands. Remove the wheel.
2   Disconnect the fluid hose from the caliper by removing the banjo fitting bolt. Discard the sealing washers on each side of the fitting - they must be replaced with new ones when reassembling.
3   Follow Steps 3 through 5 in the previous Section, as caliper removal is part of the brake pad replacement procedure.

Overhaul

4   Due to the need for special tools and expertise and the relatively complex design of the rear brake caliper/parking brake actuator assembly, the overhaul procedure should be performed by a dealer service department or a repair shop.

Installation

5   To install the caliper, follow Steps 9 through 13 in the previous Section, then bleed the brakes as described in Section 12.

7 Drum brake shoes - replacement

Refer to illustrations 7.3, 7.4a through 7.4s and 7.5

Warning: *Drum brake shoes must be replaced on both wheels at the same time - never replace the shoes on only one wheel. Also, the dust created by the brake system*

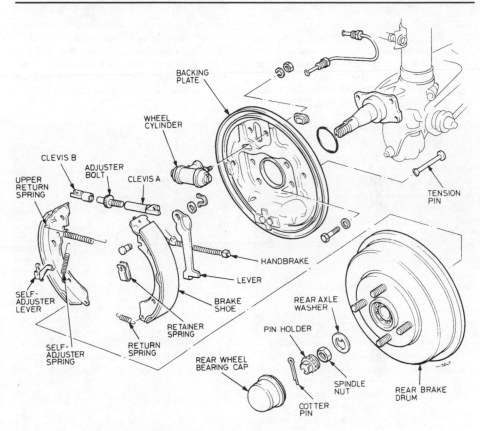

7.4a Exploded view of a typical rear drum brake assembly

may contain asbestos, which is harmful to your health. Never blow it out with compressed air and don't inhale any of it. An approved filtering mask should be worn when working on the brakes. Do not, under any circumstances, use petroleum based solvents to clean brake parts. Use brake cleaner or denatured alcohol only!
Caution: *Whenever the brake shoes are replaced, the return and hold-down springs should also be replaced. Due to the continuous heating/ cooling cycle that the springs are subjected to, they lose their tension over a period of time and may allow the shoes to drag on the drum and wear at a much faster rate than normal. When replacing the rear brake shoes, use only high quality nationally recognized brand-name parts.*

1   Loosen the wheel lug nuts, raise the rear

of the vehicle and support it securely on jackstands. Block the front wheels to keep the vehicle from rolling.
2   Release the parking brake.
3   Remove the wheel and the brake drum.
Note: *See Chapter 1 - "Rear wheel bearing check, repack and adjustment" for the 1985 and earlier model brake drum removal procedure. 1986 and later model brake drums simply pull straight off the axle flanges once the securing screws (if still installed) are removed. Also, when replacing brake shoes on 1986 and later models, remove the rear wheel bearing cap, spindle nut and washer, then slide off the hub unit (see illustration). This will make the procedure much easier.*

4   Follow the accompanying illustrations (7.4a through 7.4s) for the inspection and replacement of the brake shoes. Be sure to

9

7.4b Before removing anything, clean the brake assembly with brake cleaner and allow it to dry - position a drain pan under the brake to catch the residue- DO NOT USE COMPRESSED AIR TO BLOW THE DUST FROM THE PARTS!

7.4c Push down on the retainer spring with a screwdriver, then turn the tension pin to align its blade with the slot in the retainer spring - the spring should pop off (repeat this on the other spring)

7.4d Pull the shoe assembly down and over the spindle

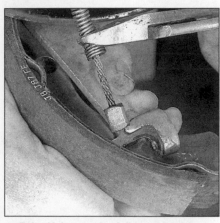

7.4e Using a pair of diagonal cutting pliers, pull back on the parking brake cable spring and squeeze the pliers just enough to grip the cable, holding the spring in the compressed position (be careful not to cut the cable); unhook the cable end from the parking brake lever

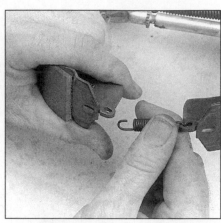

7.4f With the brake shoe assembly on a clean working surface, unhook the lower return spring from the shoes

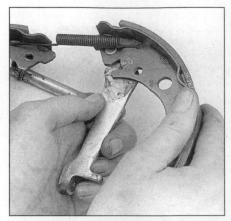

7.4g Swing the parking brake lever away from the trailing shoe, which will force the adjuster bolt clevis out of its groove in the shoe; the two shoes can now be separated

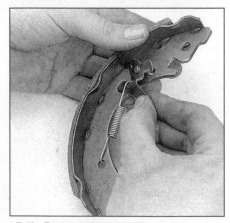

7.4h Remove the self adjuster lever and spring from the leading shoe

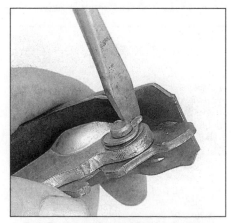

7.4i Pry open the parking brake lever retaining clip and separate the lever from the shoe; be careful not to lose the wave washer that is under the clip

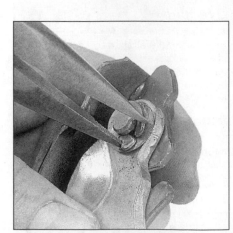

7.4j Put the new trailing shoe on the lever, place the wave washer over the pin, then install the retaining clip; crimp the ends of the clip together with a pair of needle-nose pliers

7.4k Clean the adjuster bolt and clevis, then lubricate the threads and ends with high-temperature grease

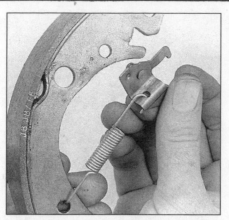

7.4l Connect the self adjuster lever spring to the leading brake shoe, then insert the pin on the lever into its hole in the shoe

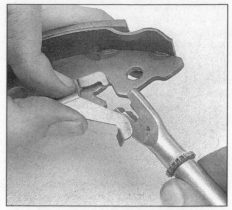

7.4m Insert the short clevis of the adjuster bolt into its slot in the leading shoe, making sure it catches the self adjuster lever

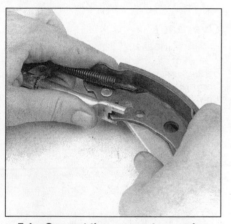

7.4n Connect the upper return spring between the two shoes, pry the lower ends of the shoes apart and insert the clevis at the other end of the adjuster bolt into the slot in the shoe; notice the position of the stepped portion of the clevis opening

7.4o Bring the lower ends of the shoes together and install the lower return spring

7.4p Lubricate the brake shoe contact areas on the backing plate with high temperature grease

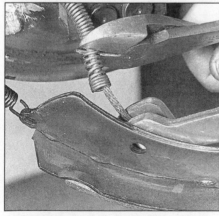

7.4q Compress the parking brake cable spring, hold it in position and connect the cable end to the parking brake lever

7.4r Place the brake shoe assembly against the backing plate and slide it up, engaging the upper ends of the shoes in the slots in the wheel cylinder pistons

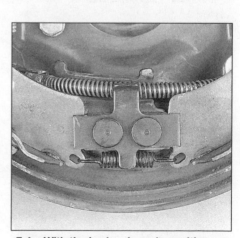

7.4s With the brake shoes in position on the backing plate, pass the tension pins through the holes in the backing plate and brake shoes, then install the retainer springs (see illustration 7.4c) - make sure the parking brake cable spring and the lower return spring are seated behind the anchor plate, as shown here

9

stay in order and read the caption under each illustration. All four rear brake shoes must be replaced at the same time, but to avoid mixing up parts, work on only one brake assembly at a time.

5   Before reinstalling the drum it should be checked for cracks, score marks, deep scratches and hard spots, which will appear as small discolored areas. If the hard spots cannot be removed with fine emery cloth or if any of the other conditions listed above exist, the drum must be taken to an automotive machine shop to have it turned. **Note:** *Professionals recommend resurfacing the drums whenever a brake job is done. Resurfacing will eliminate the possibility of out-of-round drums. If the drums are worn so much that they can't be resurfaced without exceeding the maximum allowable diameter (stamped into the drum)* **(see illustration)**, *then new ones will be required. At the very least, if you elect not to have the drums resurfaced, remove the glazing from the surface with sandpaper or emery cloth using a swirling motion.*

6   Install the brake drum (1984 and 1985

models). On 1986 and later models, install the hub and bearing unit, using a new spindle nut. Tighten the nut to the specified torque and install the brake drum.

7   Mount the wheel, install the lug nuts, then lower the vehicle.

8   Make a number of forward and reverse stops to adjust the brakes until satisfactory pedal action is obtained.

9   Check brake operation before driving the vehicle in traffic.

8   Wheel cylinder - removal, overhaul and installation

Note: *If an overhaul is indicated (usually because of fluid leakage or sticky operation) explore all options before beginning the job. New wheel cylinders are available, which makes this job quite easy. If it's decided to rebuild the wheel cylinder, make sure that a rebuild kit is available before proceeding. Never overhaul only one wheel cylinder-always rebuild both of them at the same time.*

Removal

Refer to illustration 8.4

1   Raise the rear of the vehicle and support it securely on jackstands. Block the front wheels to keep the vehicle from rolling.

2   Remove the brake shoe assembly (see Section 7).

3   Remove all dirt and foreign material from around the wheel cylinder.

4   Unscrew the brake line fitting **(see illustration)**. Don't pull the brake line away from the wheel cylinder.

5   Remove the wheel cylinder mounting fasteners **(see illustration 8.4)**.

6   Detach the wheel cylinder from the brake backing plate and place it on a clean workbench. Immediately plug the brake line to prevent fluid loss and contamination. **Note:** *If the brake shoe linings are contaminated with brake fluid, install new brake shoes and clean the drums with brake cleaner.*

Overhaul

Refer to illustration 8.7

7   Remove the bleed screw, dust covers, pistons, piston cups and spring assembly from the wheel cylinder body **(see illustration)**.

8   Clean the wheel cylinder with brake fluid, denatured alcohol or brake system cleaner. **Warning:** *Do not, under any circumstances, use petroleum based solvents to clean brake parts!*

9   Use compressed air to remove excess fluid from the wheel cylinder and to blow out the passages.

10   Check the cylinder bore for corrosion and score marks. Crocus cloth can be used to remove light corrosion and stains, but the cylinder must be replaced with a new one if the defects cannot be removed easily, or if the bore is scored.

11   Lubricate the new cups with brake fluid.

12   Assemble the wheel cylinder components. Make sure the cup lips face in.

7.5 The maximum diameter is cast into the drum

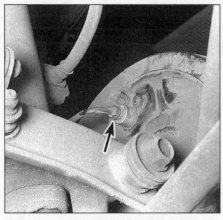

8.4 Unscrew the brake line fitting (arrow), then remove the two mounting nuts or bolts

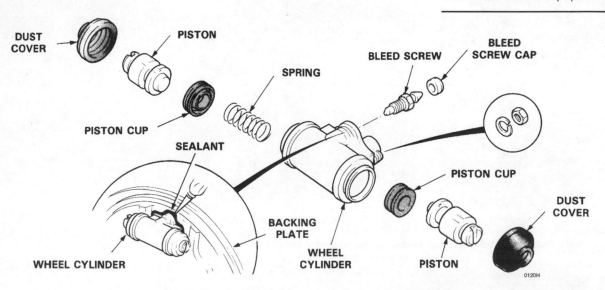

8.7 Exploded view of the rear wheel cylinder components

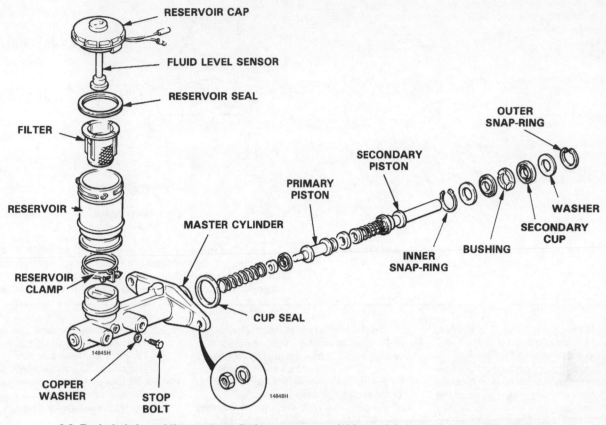

9.8 Exploded view of the master cylinder components (1984 model shown, later models similar)

Installation

13 Apply silicone sealant to the mating surface of the wheel cylinder and the brake backing plate, place the cylinder in position and install the fasteners.

14 Connect the brake line and tighten the fitting. Install the brake shoe assembly.

15 Bleed the brakes (see Section 12).

16 Check brake operation before driving the vehicle in traffic.

9   Master cylinder - removal, overhaul and installation

Note: *Before deciding to overhaul the master cylinder, check on the availability and cost of a new or factory rebuilt unit and also the availability of a rebuild kit.*

Removal

1 The master cylinder is located in the engine compartment, mounted to the power brake booster.

2 Remove as much fluid as you can from the reservoir with a syringe.

3 Place rags under the fluid fittings and prepare caps or plastic bags to cover the ends of the lines once they are disconnected. **Caution:** *Brake fluid will damage paint. Cover all body parts and be careful not to spill fluid during this procedure.*

4 Loosen the tube nuts at the ends of the

brake lines where they enter the master cylinder. To prevent rounding off the flats on these nuts, the use of a flare nut wrench, which wraps around the nut, is preferred.

5 Pull the brake lines slightly away from the master cylinder and plug the ends to prevent contamination.

6 Disconnect the electrical connector at the master cylinder, then remove the nuts attaching the master cylinder to the power booster. Pull the master cylinder off the studs and out of the engine compartment. Again, be careful not to spill the fluid as this is done.

Overhaul

Refer to illustrations 9.8, 9.9, 9.10 and 9.12

7 Before attempting the overhaul of the

master cylinder, obtain the proper rebuild kit, which will contain the necessary replacement parts and also any instructions which may be specific to your model.

8 Loosen the reservoir clamp and pull the reservoir off the master cylinder body **(see illustration)**.

9 Remove the outer snap-ring, followed by the stop plates, secondary cups and bushing **(see illustration)**.

10 Place the cylinder in a vise and use a punch or Phillips screwdriver to depress the secondary piston assembly until the internal components bottom against the other end of the master cylinder **(see illustration)**. Hold the pistons in this position and remove the stop bolt on the side of the master cylinder.

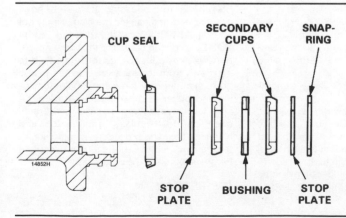

9.9 Order of assembly of the secondary cups, stop plates, bushing and snap-ring

9

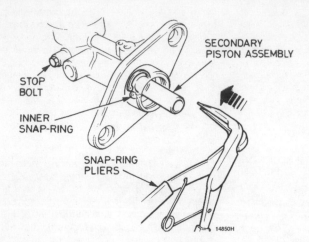

9.10 Push in on the secondary piston assembly and remove the inner snap-ring with snap-ring pliers

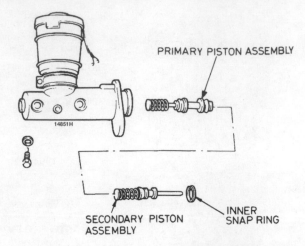

9.12 The master cylinder primary and secondary piston assemblies can be removed from the cylinder once the snap-ring has been removed - it may be necessary to tap the open end of the cylinder on a block of wood to eject the piston assemblies

11   While still holding the pistons in the bottomed position, carefully remove the inner snap-ring (see illustration 9.10).

12   The internal components can now be removed from the cylinder bore (see illustration). Make a note of the proper order of the components so they can be returned to their original locations. Note: *The two springs are of different tension, so pay particular attention to their order.*

13   Carefully inspect the bore of the master cylinder. Any deep scoring or other damage will mean a new master cylinder is required. DO NOT attempt to hone the master cylinder.

14   Replace all parts included in the rebuild kit, following any instructions in the kit. Clean all reused parts with clean brake fluid only. During assembly, lubricate all parts liberally with clean brake fluid. Be sure to tighten all fittings and connections to the specified torque.

15   Push the assembled components into the bore, bottoming them against the end of the master cylinder, then install the stop bolt and a new copper washer. A screwdriver can be used to bottom the components, but be careful not to scratch the bore.

16   Install the new inner snap-ring, making sure it is seated properly in the groove.

17   Lubricate the cup seal, secondary cups and bushing with clean brake fluid. Install them, along with the stop plates, in the master cylinder (see illustration 9.9). Install the snap-ring.

18   Install the reservoir and clamp, tightening it securely.

19   Before installing the new master cylinder it should be bench bled. Because it will be necessary to apply pressure to the master cylinder piston and, at the same time, control flow from the brake line outlets, it is recommended that the master cylinder be mounted in a vise, with the jaws of the vise clamping on the mounting flange.

20   Insert threaded plugs into the brake line outlet holes and snug them down so that there will be no air leakage past them, but not so tight that they cannot be easily loosened.

21   Fill the reservoir with brake fluid of the recommended type (see Chapter 1).

22   Remove one plug and push the piston assembly into the master cylinder bore to expel the air from the master cylinder. A large Phillips screwdriver can be used to push on the piston assembly.

23   To prevent air from being drawn back into the master cylinder, the plug must be replaced and snugged down before releasing the pressure on the piston assembly.

24   Repeat the procedure until only brake fluid is expelled from the brake line outlet hole. When only brake fluid is expelled, repeat the procedure with the other outlet hole and plug. Be sure to keep the master cylinder reservoir filled with brake fluid to prevent the introduction of air into the system.

25   Since high pressure is not involved in the bench bleeding procedure, an alternative to the removal and replacement of the plugs with each stroke of the piston assembly is available. Before pushing in on the piston assembly, remove the plug as described in Step 22. Before releasing the piston, however, instead of replacing the plug, simply put your finger tightly over the hole to keep air from being drawn back into the master cylinder. Wait several seconds for brake fluid to be drawn from the reservoir into the piston bore, then depress the piston again, removing your finger as brake fluid is expelled. Be sure to put your finger back over the hole each time before releasing the piston, and when the bleeding procedure is complete for that outlet, replace the plug and snug it before going on to the other port.

Installation

26   Install the master cylinder over the studs

on the power brake booster and tighten the attaching nuts only finger tight at this time.

27   Thread the brake line fittings into the master cylinder. Since the master cylinder is still a bit loose, it can be moved slightly in order for the fittings to thread in easily. Do not strip the threads as the fittings are tightened.

28   Fully tighten the mounting nuts and the brake fittings.

29   Fill the master cylinder reservoir with fluid, then bleed the master cylinder (only if the cylinder has not been bench bled) and the brake system as described in Section 12. To bleed the cylinder on the vehicle, have an assistant pump the brake pedal several times and then hold the pedal to the floor. Loosen the fitting nut to allow air and fluid to escape. Repeat this procedure on both fittings until the fluid is clear of air bubbles. Test the operation of the brake system carefully before placing the vehicle in normal service.

10 Proportioning valve - general information

1   The proportioning valve is mounted on the right side strut tower (see illustration 1.3). Its purpose is to limit hydraulic pressure to the rear brakes under heavy braking conditions to prevent rear wheel lockup.

2   The valve is not serviceable and if a problem is suspected with it, it must be checked by a dealer service department or repair shop equipped with the necessary pressure gauges.

3   If the valve is known to be defective, it can be replaced by unscrewing the brake lines (using a flare nut wrench, if available) and unbolting the valve from the strut tower. After the new valve is installed, bleed the complete brake system as described in Section 12.

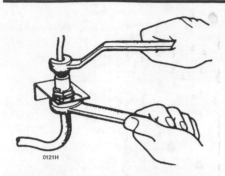

11.4 A backup wrench must be used to keep the hose from turning, otherwise the steel brake line will twist

11 Brake lines and hoses - inspection and replacement

Refer to illustration 11.4

1 About every six months the flexible hoses which connect the steel brake lines with the rear brakes and front calipers should be inspected for cracks, chafing of the outer cover, leaks, blisters, and other damage.

2 Replacement steel and flexible brake lines are commonly available from dealer parts departments and auto parts stores. Do not, under any circumstances, use anything other than genuine steel lines or approved flexible brake hoses as replacement items.

3 When installing the brake line, leave at least 0.75 in (19 mm) clearance between the line and any moving or vibrating parts.

4 When disconnecting a hose and line, first remove the spring clip. Then, using a normal wrench to hold the hose and a flare-nut wrench to hold the tube, make the disconnection **(see illustration)**. Use the wrenches in the same manner when making a connection, then install the clip. **Note:** *Make sure the tube passes through the center of the grommet.*

5 When disconnecting two hoses, use normal wrenches on the hose fittings. When connecting two hoses, make sure they are

12.8 When bleeding the brakes, a hose is connected to the bleed screw at the caliper or wheel cylinder and then submerged in brake fluid - air will be seen as bubbles in the tube and container (all air must be expelled before moving to the next wheel)

not twisted or strained.

6 Steel brake lines are usually retained along their span with clips. Always remove these clips completely before removing a fixed brake line. Always reinstall these clips, or new ones if the old ones are damaged, when replacing a brake line, as they provide support and keep the lines from vibrating, which can eventually break them.

12 Brake hydraulic system - bleeding

Refer to illustration 12.8

Warning: *Wear eye protection when bleeding the brake system. If the fluid comes in contact with your eyes, immediately rinse them with water and seek medical attention.*

1 Bleeding the hydraulic system is necessary to remove any air that manages to find its way into the system when it's been opened during removal and installation of a hose, line, caliper or master cylinder. It will probably be necessary to bleed the system at all four brakes if air has entered the system due to low fluid level, or if the brake lines have been disconnected at the master cylinder.

2 If a brake line was disconnected only at a wheel, then only that caliper or wheel cylinder must be bled.

3 If a brake line is disconnected at a fitting located between the master cylinder and any of the brakes, that part of the system served by the disconnected line must be bled.

4 Remove any residual vacuum from the brake power booster by applying the brake several times with the engine off.

5 Remove the master cylinder reservoir cover and fill the reservoir with brake fluid. Reinstall the cover. **Note:** *Check the fluid level often during the bleeding operation and add fluid as necessary to prevent the fluid level from falling low enough to allow air bubbles into the master cylinder.*

6 Have an assistant on hand, as well as a supply of new brake fluid, a clear container partially filled with clean brake fluid, a length of 3/16-inch plastic, rubber or vinyl tubing to fit over the bleed screw and a wrench to open and close the bleed screw.

7 Beginning at the left front wheel, loosen the bleed screw slightly, then tighten it to a point where it is snug but can still be loosened quickly and easily.

8 Place one end of the tubing over the

bleed screw and submerge the other end in brake fluid in the container **(see illustration)**.

9 Have the assistant pump the brakes slowly a few times to get pressure in the system, then hold the pedal firmly depressed.

10 While the pedal is held depressed, open the bleed screw just enough to allow a flow of fluid to leave the screw. Watch for all bubbles to exit the submerged end of the tube. When the fluid flow slows after a couple of seconds, close the screw and have your assistant release the pedal.

11 Repeat Steps 9 and 10 until no more air is seen leaving the tube, then tighten the bleed screw and proceed to the right rear wheel, the right front wheel and the left rear wheel, in that order, and perform the same procedure. Be sure to check the fluid in the master cylinder reservoir frequently.

12 Never use old brake fluid. It contains moisture which will deteriorate the brake system components.

13 Refill the master cylinder with fluid at the end of the operation.

14 Check the operation of the brakes. The pedal should feel solid when depressed, with no sponginess. If necessary, repeat the entire process. **Warning:** *Do not operate the vehicle if you are in doubt about the effectiveness of the brake system.*

13 Power brake booster - check, removal and installation

Operating check

Refer to illustration 13.2

1 Depress the brake pedal several times with the engine off and make sure there is no change in the pedal reserve distance.

2 Depress the pedal and start the engine. If the pedal goes down slightly, operation is normal **(see illustration)**.

Air tightness check

Refer to illustration 13.3

3 Start the engine and turn it off after one or two minutes. Depress the brake pedal several times slowly. If the pedal goes down farther the first time but gradually rises after the second or third depression, the booster is air tight **(see illustration)**.

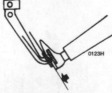

13.2 Push down on the brake pedal, then start the engine - the brake pedal should go down slightly, indicating normal booster operation

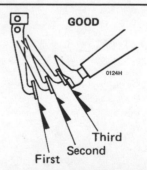

13.3 With the engine turned off, the pedal should build up with each pump if the booster is functioning properly

9

4   Depress the brake pedal while the engine is running, then stop the engine with the pedal depressed. If there is no change in the pedal reserve travel after holding the pedal for 30 seconds, the booster is air tight.

Removal

Refer to illustration 13.7

5   Power brake booster units should not be disassembled. They require special tools not normally found in most automotive repair stations or shops. They are fairly complex and because of their critical relationship to brake performance it is best to replace a defective booster unit with a new or rebuilt one.

6   To remove the booster, first remove the brake master cylinder as described in Section 9.

7   Locate the pushrod clevis pin connecting the booster to the brake pedal **(see illustration)**. This is accessible from under the dash panel in front of the driver's seat.

8   Remove the clevis pin retaining clip with pliers and pull out the pin.

9   Holding the clevis with pliers, disconnect the clevis locknut with a wrench. The clevis is now loose.

10   Disconnect the hose leading from the engine to the booster. Be careful not to damage the hose when removing it from the booster fitting.

11   Remove the four nuts and washers holding the brake booster to the firewall. You may need a light to see these, as they are up under the dash area.

12   Slide the booster straight out from the firewall until the studs clear the holes and pull the booster, brackets and gaskets from the engine compartment area.

Installation

Refer to illustrations 13.14a and 13.14b

13   Installation procedures are basically the reverse of those for removal. Tighten the clevis locknut securely and the booster mounting nuts to the specified torque.

14   If the power booster unit is being replaced, the clearance between the master

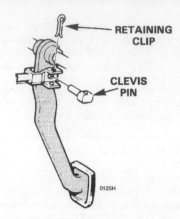

13.7 Remove the retaining clip, then pull out the clevis pin

cylinder piston and the pushrod in the vacuum booster must be measured. Using a depth micrometer or vernier calipers, measure the distance from the seat (recessed area) in the master cylinder piston to the master cylinder mounting flange. Next, apply a vacuum of 20 in-Hg to the booster (using a hand vacuum pump) and measure the distance from the end of the vacuum booster pushrod to the mounting face of the booster

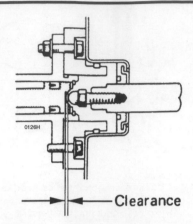

13.14a The booster pushrod-to-master cylinder clearance must be as specified - if there is interference between the two, the brakes may drag; if there is too much clearance, there will be excessive brake pedal travel

(including gasket, if used) where the master cylinder mounting flange seats. Subtract the two measurements to get the clearance **(see illustration)**. If the clearance is more or less than specified, loosen the star locknut and turn the adjuster on the power booster

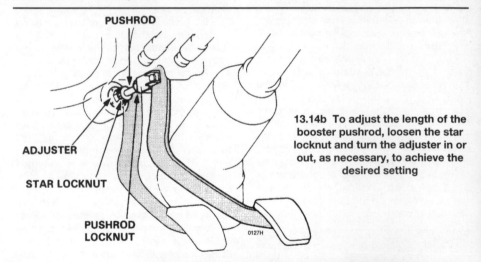

13.14b To adjust the length of the booster pushrod, loosen the star locknut and turn the adjuster in or out, as necessary, to achieve the desired setting

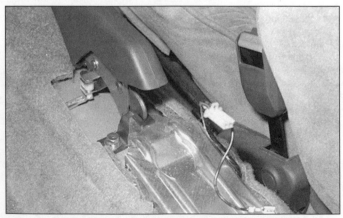

14.2 After removing the console trim, remove the equalizer cover plate

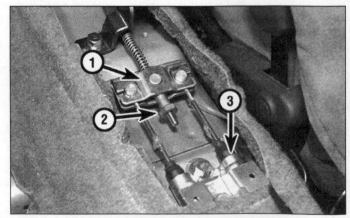

14.4 Parking brake equalizer and adjuster

1   Equalizer   2   Adjuster nut   3   Cable clamp

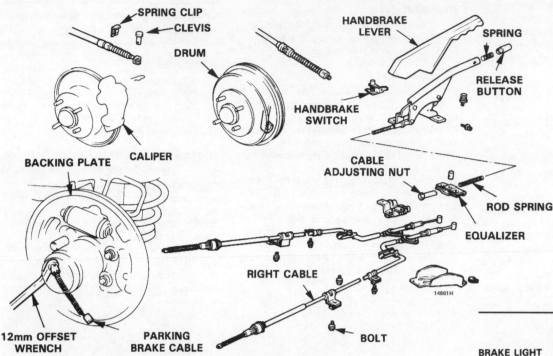

15.4 Parking brake cables and related components

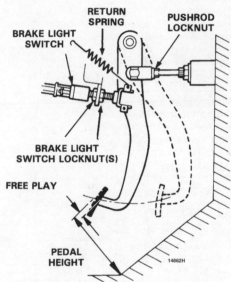

16.3 The brake pedal height is adjusted by loosening the booster pushrod locknut and turning the pushrod - remove the floormats before measuring the pedal height

pushrod until the clearance is within the specified limit **(see illustration)**. After adjustment, tighten the locknut.

15 A second method to measure the pushrod-to-piston clearance is to install the master cylinder to the vacuum booster with a small piece of modeling clay placed on the end of the pushrod. Make sure the gasket is in place when making this trial fit. Remove the master cylinder and measure the resulting impression left in the clay. Again adjust as needed to meet the specification. This method may require several trial and-error fits to reach the proper clearance.

16 After the final installation of the master cylinder and brake hoses and lines, the brake pedal height and free play must be adjusted and the system must be bled. See the appropriate Sections of this Chapter for the procedures.

14 Parking brake - adjustment

Refer to illustrations 14.2 and 14.4

1 Refer to Chapter 11 and remove the console trim around the parking brake lever.
2 Remove the parking brake equalizer cover plate **(see illustration)** to gain access to the equalizer.
3 Block the front wheels, raise the rear of the vehicle and support it securely on jackstands. Apply the parking brake lever until you hear one click.
4 Turn the adjuster nut on the equalizer **(see illustration)** clockwise while rotating the rear wheels. Stop turning the nut when the

brakes just start to drag on the rear wheels.
5 Release the parking brake lever and check to see that the brakes don't drag when the rear wheels are turned. The travel on the parking brake lever should be as listed in the Specifications when properly adjusted.
6 Lower the vehicle and reinstall the equalizer cover plate and console trim.

15 Parking brake cable(s) - replacement

Refer to illustration 15.4

1 Block the front wheels and loosen the rear wheel lug nuts. Raise the rear of the vehicle and support it securely on jackstands.
2 On vehicles with rear drum brakes, remove the brake drum(s) (see Section 7).
3 Following the procedure in the previous Section, loosen the equalizer adjuster nut. Remove the cable clamp from the cable housing **(see illustration 14.4)** and unhook the cable from the equalizer.
4 On models with rear drum brakes, remove the brake shoes and disconnect the cable end from the lever on the trailing brake shoe (see Section 7). Depress the tangs on the cable housing retainer and pass the cable through the backing plate. You can do this by passing an offset 12 mm box end wrench over the end of the cable and onto the retainer. This will compress the tangs in all at once **(see illustration)**.
5 On models with rear disc brakes, remove the clip and clevis to disconnect the cable end from the actuator lever on the

caliper, then remove the spring clip to free the cable housing from the support bracket **(see illustration 15.4)**.
6 Unbolt the cable housing clamps from the underbody, noting how the cable is routed, then remove the cable from the vehicle. It may be necessary to remove the exhaust pipe heat shield bolts at the rear to allow cable removal.
7 If both cables are to be removed, repeat the above steps to remove the remaining cable.
8 Installation is the reverse of the removal procedure. After the cable(s) are installed, be sure to adjust them according to the procedure described in Section 14.

9

16   Brake pedal - removal, installation and adjustment

Refer to illustration 16.3

Removal

1   Disconnect the cable from the negative battery terminal.

2   Disconnect the power brake booster pushrod from the brake pedal (see Section 13).

3   Working underneath the dash, unhook the pedal return spring from the pedal **(see illustration)**.

4   Remove the E-clip or nut from the left end of the pedal pivot shaft, then slide the shaft to the right far enough to allow the pedal to drop down. If the vehicle you are working on is equipped with a manual transmission, insert a rod or long bolt in from the left side while sliding the pivot shaft out. This will support the clutch pedal in the absence of the pivot shaft.

Installation

5   Before installing the pedal, lubricate the shaft with multi-purpose grease. Installation is the reverse of the removal procedure.

Adjustment

6   Loosen the brake light switch locknut and unscrew the switch so it no longer makes contact with the pedal.

7   Loosen the brake booster pushrod locknut and turn the pushrod in or out until the pedal height is as specified **(see illustration 16.3)**. Tighten the locknut.

8   Check the pedal free play by lightly depressing the pedal with your finger. The distance the pedal travels before resistance is encountered is the free play. If it is not as specified, readjust the booster pushrod to obtain the desired free play.

9   Adjust the brake light switch as described in the next Section.

17   Brake light switch - removal, installation and adjustment

Removal

1   Disconnect the electrical connector from the switch.

2   Remove the locknut on the pedal side of the switch **(see illustration 16.3)** and unscrew the switch from the bracket.

Installation and adjustment

3   Installation of the brake light switch is the reverse of the removal procedure.

4   To adjust the switch, back off the locknut on the connector side of the switch and screw the switch in until the plunger at the end is completely depressed by the brake pedal.

5   Unscrew the switch one-half turn and tighten the locknut.

6   Verify the brake lights operate when the pedal is depressed and go off when the pedal is released.

Chapter 10
Suspension and steering systems

Contents

Specifications

Steering

Steering wheel free play (measured at rim)	0.4 in (10.0 mm) maximum
Steering effort (measured with spring scale)	
Manual	3.3 lbs
Power assisted	
Sedan	4.0 lbs
Hatchback	5.0 lbs

Torque Specifications — Ft-lbs

Front suspension

Radius rod-to-front crossmember nuts	32
Radius rod-to-lower arm nuts	40
Lower arm pivot bolt	
1984 and 1985	36
1986 on	40
Lower arm balljoint-to-steering knuckle pinch bolt (1984 and 1985 models)	40
Lower arm-to-steering knuckle balljoint stud nut (1986 on)	40
Upper arm-to-body nuts	53
Upper arm balljoint stud nut	32
Strut/shock absorber-to-steering knuckle pinch bolt (1984 and 1985 models)	47

10

Torque Specifications

Ft-lbs

Front suspension (continued

Shock absorber/coil spring assembly-to-damper fork pinch bolt (1986 on)	32
Strut/shock absorber and coil spring assembly upper mounting nuts.................................	28
Damper fork-to-lower arm nut (1986 on).........................	47
Strut/shock absorber and coil spring assembly damper shaft nut	
1984 and 1985	33
1986 on	22

Rear suspension

Radius rod-to-body nuts	47
Radius rod-to-hub carrier nuts	51
Suspension lower arm inner pivot bolt (1984 and 1985 models)...	40
Suspension lower arm-to-hub carrier nut (1984 and 1985 models)...	60
Strut/shock absorber-to-hub carrier pinch bolt..............	40
Trailing arm-to-mounting bracket pivot bolt nuts (1986 on)...................	47
Trailing arm mounting bracket-to-body bolts (1986 on).........................	47
Trailing arm-to-rear knuckle nuts	17
Lower arm inner pivot bolt (1986 on)	
Short arm...	40
Long arm	47
Lower arm-to-knuckle bolts (1986 on)	47
Upper arm-to-body bolts (1986 on)...............................	28
Upper arm balljoint stud nut	32
Hub assembly nut (1986 on)*.......................................	134
Brake backing plate-to-hub carrier bolts (1984 and 1985 models)............................	22
Brake backing plate-to-knuckle (1986 on)	28
Strut/shock absorber upper mounting nuts	
1984 and 1985	16
1986 on	28
Strut damper shaft nut...	16
Shock absorber/coil spring assembly-to-knuckle bolt (1986 on)	40

Steering

Steering wheel mounting nut...	36
Steering shaft U-joint-to-steering gear input shaft pinch bolt	
1984 and 1985	22
1986 on	16
Steering gear mounting bracket bolts	16
Tie-rod end-to-steering knuckle nuts............................	32

Always use a new nut

1   General information

Refer to illustrations 1 .2a 1.2b, 1.3 and 1.4

The vehicles covered by this manual, while very similar in most respects, have two different suspension designs.

On 1984 and 1985 models, a Macpherson strut style suspension was used front and rear. This design is comprised of a strut/shock absorber/coil spring assembly (which also supports the steering knuckle and hub assembly), a lower arm and a radius rod, which support the bottom end of the steering knuckle (on the front suspension) or the rear wheel hub carrier (on the rear suspension) **(see illustrations)**. A stabilizer bar attached to the lower arms and connected to the frame minimizes body roll.

In 1986, these vehicles underwent a major change in suspension design. Later vehicles are suspended at all four wheels by what at first appears to be a Macpherson strut assembly, but is actually only a shock absorber/coil spring assembly, serving no role in supporting the steering knuckle (or the rear knuckle). As in the previous front suspension design, a lower arm and radius rod are used to hold the bottom end of the steering knuckle, but an upper arm has been added to locate the top of the steering knuckle **(see illustration)**. A stabilizer bar is also used, as in the previous design.

The rear suspension on the 1986 and later vehicles is similar to the front, but uses a trailing arm in place of a radius rod, and two unequal length lower arms to give lateral support **(see illustration)**.

Steering on all models is through a rack and pinion steering gear. Although some of these vehicles were produced with manual steering gear assemblies, most of them are equipped with power-assisted steering, which employs an engine-driven hydraulic pump, a speed sensor and the necessary hoses connected to the steering gear. The amount of power assist is regulated by the transaxle-mounted speed sensor, which provides full power steering at low vehicle speeds, but reduces the amount of assist as the vehicle speed increases, thereby transmitting improved "road feel" to the driver.

Frequently, when working on the suspension or steering system components, you may come across fasteners which seem impossible to loosen. These fasteners on the underside of the vehicle are continually sub-

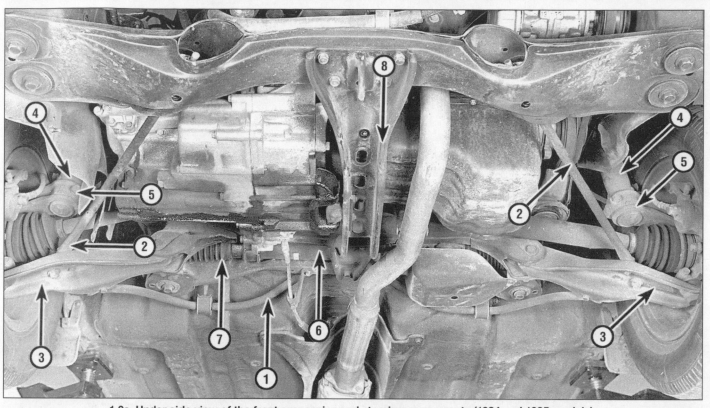

1.2a Under side view of the front suspension and steering components (1984 and 1985 models)

1	Stabilizer bar	4	Front strut/shock absorber and coil spring assembly
2	Radius rod		
3	Lower arm	5	Steering knuckle

6	Steering gear
7	Steering gear boot
8	Engine center support beam

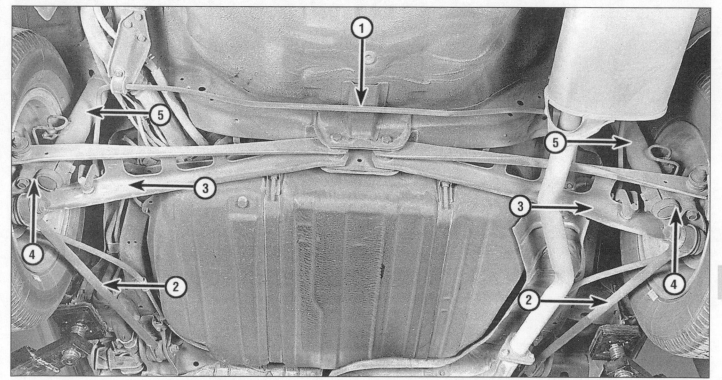

1.2b Under side view of the rear suspension components (1984 and 1985 models)

1	Stabilizer bar	3	Lower arm	5	Strut/shock absorber and coil spring assembly
2	Radius rod	4	Rear wheel hub carrier		

10

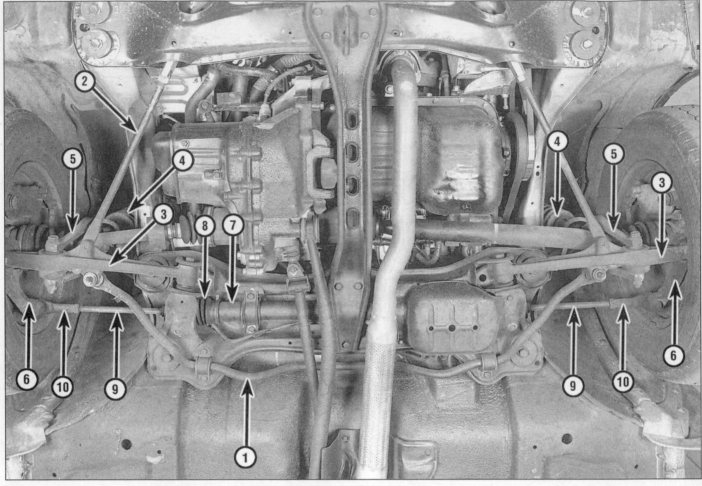

1.3 Under side view of the front suspension and steering components (1986 and later models)

1	Stabilizer bar	5	Damper fork	10	Toe-rod end
2	Radius rod	6	Steering knuckle		
3	Lower arm	7	Steering gear boot		
4	Shock absorber/coil spring assembly	9	Tie-rod		

Note: The upper arm is not visible in this photograph

jected to water, road grime, mud, etc., and can become rusted or "frozen," making them extremely difficult to remove, To unscrew these stubborn fasteners without damaging them (or other components), be sure to use lots of penetrating oil and allow it to soak in for a while. Using a wire brush to clean exposed threads will also ease removal of the nut or bolt and prevent damage to the threads. Sometimes a sharp blow with a hammer and punch is effective in breaking the bond between a nut and bolt threads, but care must be taken to prevent the punch from slipping off the fastener and ruining the threads. Heating the stuck fastener and surrounding area with a torch sometimes helps too, but isn't recommended because of the obvious dangers associated with fire. Long breaker bars and extension, or "cheater," pipes will increase leverage, but never use an extension pipe on a ratchet - the ratcheting mechanism could be damaged. Sometimes, turning the nut or bolt in the tightening (clockwise) direction first will help to brake it loose.

Fasteners that require drastic measures to unscrew should always be replaced with new ones.

Since most of the procedures that are dealt with in this chapter involve jacking up the vehicle and working underneath it, a good pair of jackstands will be needed. A hydraulic floor jack is the preferred type of jack to lift the vehicle, and it can also be used to support certain components during various operations. **Warning:** *Never, under any circumstances, rely on a jack to support the vehicle while working on it. Whenever any of the suspension or steering fasteners are loosened or removed they must be inspected and, if necessary, replaced with new ones of the same part number or of original equipment quality and design. Torque specifications must be followed for proper reassembly and component retention. Never attempt to heat or straighten any suspension or steering components. Instead, replace any bent or damaged part with a new one.*

2   Front stabilizer bar and bushings - removal and installation

Refer to illustrations 2.2a, 2.2b and 2.3

Removal

1   Apply the parking brake. Raise the front of the vehicle and support it securely on jackstands.
2   Remove the stabilizer bar-to-lower arm nuts or bolts, noting how the spacers, washers and bushings are positioned **(see illustrations)**.
3   Remove the stabilizer bar bracket bolts and detach the bar from the vehicle **(see illustration)**.
4   Pull the U brackets off the stabilizer bar and inspect the bushings for cracks, hardness and other signs of deterioration. If the bushings are damaged, replace them. Using a wire brush, clean the areas on the bracket where the bushings ride.

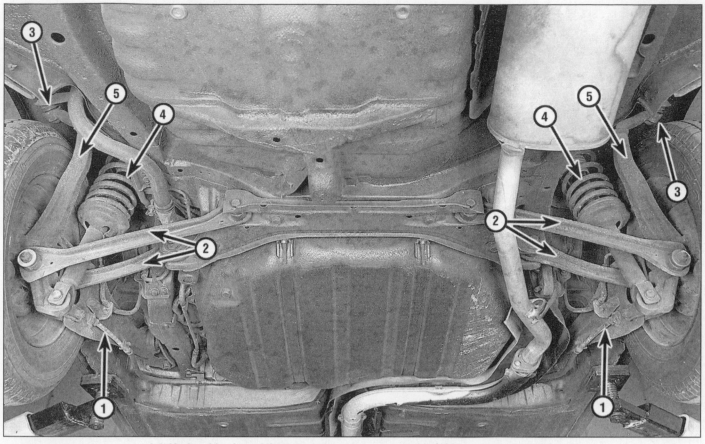

1.4 Under side view of the rear suspension components (1986 and later models)

1 Trailing arm
2 Lower arm
3 Upper arm (barely visible)
4 Rear shock absorber/coil
    spring assembly
5 Knuckle

Installation

5 Position the stabilizer bar bushings on the bar. A light coat of vegetable oil will ease installation of the bushings and U-bolt brackets (don't use petroleum-based lubricants or brake fluid - they will damage the rubber).

6 Push the brackets over the bushings and raise the bar up to the frame. **Note:** *The offset in the bar must face up.* Install the bracket bolts, but don't tighten them com- pletely at this time.

7 Install the stabilizer bar-to-lower arm bushings and/or fasteners. Tighten the fas- teners securely.

8 Tighten the bracket bolts.

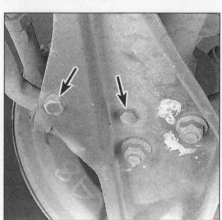

2.2a The stabilizer bar on 1984 and 1985 models is retained to the lower arm by two bolts and nuts (arrows)

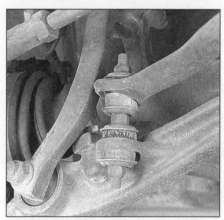

2.2b The stabilizer bar on 1986 and later models is connected to the lower arm by a rubber insulator link - it can be disconnected at the top or the bottom (by removing the respective nut) or removed completely for bushing replacement

2.3 Remove the stabilizer bar bracket bolt (arrow) and unhook the bracket from the mount (1985 model shown - 1986 and later models use a bolt on each side of the bracket)

10

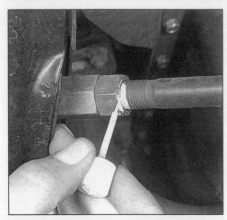

3.2 Mark the position of the adjuster nut on the radius rod - if the rod is to be replaced, measure the distance from the nut to the rod-to-lower arm mounting bolt hole (be sure to measure precisely, since the length of this rod is critical to front end alignment)

3   Front radius rod - removal and installation

Refer to illustrations 3.2, 3.3a and 3.3b
Warning: *Whenever any of the suspension or steering fasteners are loosened or removed, they must be inspected and, if necessary, replaced with new ones of the same part number or of original equipment quality and design. Torque specifications must be followed for proper reassembly and component retention.*
Note: *The following procedure is applicable to either the right or left radius rod.*

Removal

1   Loosen the wheel lug nuts, raise the front of the vehicle and support it securely on jackstands. Remove the wheel.
2   If you are working on a 1986 or later vehicle, mark the position of the inner locknut on the rod **(see illustration)**. If the rod is to be replaced, measure the distance from the locknut to the forward mounting bolt hole, instead.
3   Remove the radius rod-to-front crossmember nut and the two bolts that secure the other end of the rod to the lower arm **(see illustrations)**.
4   Remove the large washer and rubber bushing from the front of the rod, then pull the rod straight back out of the crossmember.
5   Check the rod for cracks and bending. If the rod is distorted at all, it must be replaced - don't try to straighten it. Inspect the bushings for wear, cracking, hardness and general deterioration, replacing them if necessary.

Installation

6   Before installing the rod, or if installing a new one, thread the inner locknut onto the rod the previously measured distance or to the paint mark (1986 and later models only).

3.3a Remove the large nut (arrow) at the front crossmember, followed by the washer and rubber bushing

7   Assemble the inner washer, rubber bushing and sleeve on the rod and insert it into its hole in the crossmember. Install the two bolts and nuts that secure the rod to the lower arm and tighten them to the specified torque.
8   Install the outer rubber bushing, washer and nut on the front of the rod, but don't tighten it fully yet.
9   Install the wheel and lug nuts, lower the vehicle and tighten the lug nuts to the specified torque.
10   Tighten the outer radius rod nut to the specified torque.
11   It would be a good idea to drive the vehicle to an alignment shop to have the front wheel alignment checked and, if necessary, adjusted on 1986 and later models only).

4   Front suspension lower arm - removal, inspection and installation

Refer to illustrations 4.5, 4.6 and 4 7
Warning: *Whenever any of the suspension or steering fasteners are loosened or removed, they must be inspected and, if necessary, replaced with new ones of the same part number or of original equipment quality and design. Torque specifications must be followed for proper reassembly and component retention.*

Removal

1   Loosen the wheel lug nuts on the side of the vehicle to be disassembled, raise the front of the vehicle, support it securely on jackstands and remove the wheel.
2   Remove the radius rod-to-lower arm nuts and bolts (see illustration 3.3b).
3   Disconnect the stabilizer bar from the lower arm (see Section 2).
4   On 1986 and later models, remove the damper fork-to-lower arm bolt (see Section 7).
5   If you are working on a 1984 or 1985 model, remove the balljoint pinch bolt and

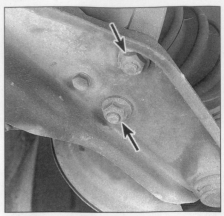

3.3b On 1984 and 1985 models, the radius rod is fastened to the lower arm by two nuts and bolts (arrows); on 1986 and later models, two bolts are used

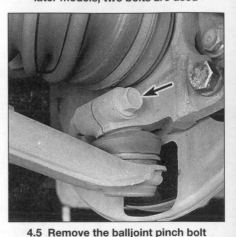

4.5 Remove the balljoint pinch bolt (arrow) and separate the lower arm from the steering knuckle

pull the lower arm down, separating it from the steering knuckle **(see illustration)**.
6   On 1986 and later models, remove the cotter pin, loosen the castellated nut a few turns and break the lower arm loose from the

4.6 On 1986 and later models, a puller is required to separate the lower arm from the balljoint; notice how the nut has been loosened, but not removed - this will prevent the components from separating violently

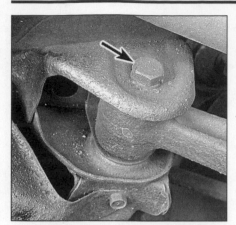

4.7 Remove the lower arm inner pivot bolt (arrow) (1986 model shown, other models similar)

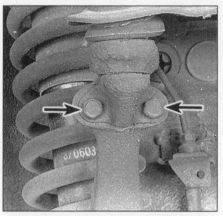

5.2 To expose the balljoint stud nut, remove the two bolts (arrows) that secure the balljoint shield to the knuckle

5.4 Unscrew the two upper arm-to-body nuts (arrows)

balljoint using a two-jaw puller **(see illustration)**. Remove the nut and separate the two components.

7   Remove the bolt from the lower control arm inner pivot and pull the arm from the crossmember **(see illustration)**. If necessary, use a prybar to pry the arm out of the mount.

Inspection

8   Check the lower arm for distortion and the bushing for wear, damage and deterioration. Replace the arm if it's damaged or bent. If the inner pivot bushing is worn, take the lower arm to a dealer service department or a repair shop, as special tools are required to replace the bushing. On 1984 and 1985 models, there is a balljoint at the outer end of the lower arm. If it's worn or damaged, the lower arm must be replaced.

Installation

9   Place the lower arm in its mount on the crossmember. Install the bolt, but don't tighten it completely yet.
10   Connect the lower arm to the steering knuckle and tighten the bolt or nut to the specified torque. **Note:** *On 1984 and 1985 models, the groove in the balljoint stud must line up with the pinch bolt hole in the steering knuckle. On 1986 and later models, tighten the nut an additional amount, if necessary, to line up a slot in the nut with the hole in the balljoint - never loosen the nut to align the hole. Install a new cotter pin.*
11   Attach the radius rod to the lower arm and tighten the nuts to the specified torque.
12   On 1986 and later models, connect the damper fork to the lower arm and install the bolt and nut, tightening the nut to the specified torque.
13   Connect the stabilizer bar to the lower arm (see Section 2).
14   Place a jack under the balljoint, with a block of wood on the jack head to act as a cushion. Raise the lower arm to simulate normal ride height, then tighten the lower arm pivot bolt to the specified torque.
15   Lower the jack and install the wheel and lug nuts.

16   Lower the vehicle and tighten the lug nuts to the specified torque. Recheck your work. It would be a good idea to drive the car to an alignment shop to have the front end alignment checked and, if necessary, adjusted.

---

5   Front suspension upper arm - removal and Installation (1986 and later models)

Refer to illustrations 5.2 and 5.4
Warning: *Whenever any of the suspension or steering fasteners are loosened or removed, they must be inspected and, if necessary, replaced with new ones of the same part number or of original equipment quality and design. Torque specifications must be followed for proper reassembly and component retention.*

Removal

1   Loosen the wheel lug nuts, raise the front of the vehicle and support it securely on jackstands. Remove the wheel.
2   Remove the upper balljoint shield **(see Illustration)**.
3   Loosen the upper balljoint stud nut a few turns, then separate the upper arm from the steering knuckle with a two-jaw puller. After this is done, wire the steering knuckle to the coil spring to prevent the knuckle from falling out, which could overextend the inner constant velocity joint.
4   From inside the engine compartment, unscrew the two upper arm-to-body nuts **(see illustration)** and remove the arm from inside the fenderwell.
5   Check the bushings for cracking and deterioration. If they appear to be in need of replacement, remove the upper arm pivot bolt, followed by the anchor bolts and seals. Mount the arm in a vise and drive the bushings out with a drift. The new bushings can be installed by pressing them in with the jaws of the vise. Coat the bushings and seals with chassis grease. Apply a thin coat of silicone

sealant to the underside of the pivot bolt head and nut.

Installation

6   Installation is the reverse of the removal procedure. Use new upper arm-to-body nuts and be sure to tighten the fasteners to the specified torque. It would be a good idea to drive the car to an alignment shop to have the front end alignment checked and, if necessary, adjusted.

---

6   Balljoints - replacement

Warning: *Whenever any of the suspension or steering fasteners are loosened or removed, they must be inspected and, if necessary, replaced with new ones of the same part number or of original equipment quality and design. Torque specifications must be followed for proper reassembly and component retention.*

1984 and 1985 models

1   If the balljoint is damaged or worn, the entire lower arm must be replaced, as the balljoint is not removable. Refer to Section 4 for the lower arm removal and installation procedure.

1986 and later models

Upper balljoint
2   If the upper balljoint is damaged or worn, the entire upper arm must be replaced (See section 5). The upper balljoints are not available separately.

Lower balljoint
3   The lower balljoints are replaceable, but a large vise and some large sockets or sections of pipe will be required to remove and install them. If you decide not to do this yourself, you can remove the steering knuckle (see Section 8) and take it to a dealer service department or repair shop to have the balljoint replaced.

10

7.4a On 1984 and 1985 models, remove the strut-to-steering knuckle pinch bolt (arrow)

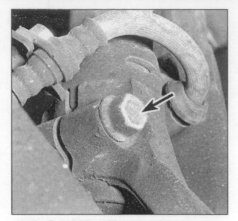

7.4b On 1986 and later models, remove the damper fork pinch bolt (arrow)

7 Front strut/shock absorber and coil spring assembly - removal, overhaul and installation

Refer to illustrations 7.4a, 7.4b, 7.5, 7.6, 7.7, 7.11, 7.12a, 7.12b and 7.20
Warning: *Whenever any of the suspension or steering fasteners are loosened or removed, they must be inspected and, if necessary, replaced with new ones of the same part number or of original equipment quality and design. Torque specifications must be followed for proper reassembly and component retention.*

Removal

1   Loosen the wheel lug nuts, raise the vehicle and support it securely on jackstands. Remove the wheel.
2   Unbolt the flexible brake hose from the strut assembly.
3   Disconnect the stabilizer bar from the lower arm (see Section 2).
4   Place a floor jack under the lower arm to support it when the strut/ shock absorber assembly is removed. Remove the strut-to-steering knuckle pinch bolt (1984 and 1985 models) or the shock absorber-to-damper fork pinch bolt **(see illustrations)**.
5   On 1984 and 1985 models, lower the jack and separate the strut/ shock absorber assembly from the steering knuckle. It may be necessary to tap down on the knuckle while lowering the jack **(see illustration)**.
6   On 1986 and later models, remove the damper fork-to-lower arm bolt and remove the fork **(see illustration)**. It may be necessary to tap the fork from the shock absorber.
7   Support the strut/shock absorber and coil spring assembly and remove the three upper mounting nuts **(see illustration)**. Remove the unit through the fenderwell.

Overhaul

8   Check the strut/shock absorber for leaking fluid, dents, cracks and other obvious

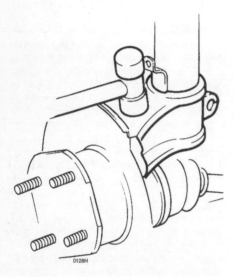

7.5 On 1984 and 1985 models, you may have to tap the steering knuckle down to get it to separate from the strut

4   If you decide to replace the balljoint(s) yourself, follow the procedure in Section 8 and remove the steering knuckle from the vehicle.
5   Remove the balljoint boot snap-ring with a pair of snap-ring pliers, then pry the boot off.
6   Obtain a piece of pipe or a large socket that will fit over the balljoint stud and rest against the lower collar on the balljoint. Also obtain a deep socket or piece of pipe that fits over the upper end of the balljoint and rests against the steering knuckle.
7   Position the above-mentioned sockets or pieces of pipe on either side of the balljoint and position this assembly between the jaws of a vise. Tighten the vise until the balljoint is forced out of the knuckle.
8   Installation of the balljoint is basically the reverse of the removal procedure, but a large deep socket or piece of pipe will be needed to accept the stud of the balljoint as it is pressed into the steering knuckle. Also, a smaller socket will be needed to push the balljoint into the bore from the upper end.
9   Use an appropriate size socket to push a new balljoint boot over the balljoint, then install the snap-ring.
10   Install the steering knuckle (see Section 8).

7.6 Remove the damper fork-to-lower arm bolt and remove the fork to provide clearance for shock/coil spring assembly removal

7.7 The strut/shock absorber assembly is mounted to the strut tower with three nuts (arrows)

damage. Check the coil spring for chips and cracks which could cause premature failure. Inspect the spring seats for hardness or general deterioration. If there is fluid leakage from the shock absorber or excessive wear or damage to any of the components, replace the strut/shock absorber and coil spring assembly or disassemble the unit and replace the defective component(s) (begin disassembly at the next Step). Rebuilt strut/shock absorber assemblies, complete with the coil springs, are available on an exchange basis, which eliminates much time and work. So, before disassembling a strut to replace individual components, check the availability of parts and the price of a complete rebuilt unit. **Warning:** *Disassembling a strut assembly is a potentially dangerous undertaking and utmost attention must be directed to the job at hand, or serious injury may result. Use only a high quality spring compressor and carefully follow the manufacturer's instructions furnished with the tool. After removing the coil spring from the strut or shock absorber, set it aside in a safe, isolated area (a steel cabinet is preferred).*

9   Mount the strut/shock absorber assembly in a vise. Line the vise jaws with wood or rags to prevent damage to the unit and tighten the vise only enough to secure the assembly.

7.11 Install the spring compressor according to the tool manufacturer's instructions and compress the spring until all pressure is relieved from the upper spring seat

SPRING COMPRESSOR

14868H

10   If you are working on a 1986 or later model, mark the relationship of the upper mount to the spring (or if the spring is being replaced, put the mark on the shock absorber body). This will ensure correct positioning of the mount when the unit is reassembled.

11   Following the tool manufacturer's instructions, install the spring compressor

(which can be obtained at most auto parts stores or equipment rental yards on a daily rental basis) on the spring and compress it sufficiently to relieve all pressure from the spring seat **(see illustration)**. This can be verified by wiggling the spring (it should move freely).

12   Remove the damper cap and unscrew the spring seat nut while holding the damper shaft with an Allen wrench to prevent it from turning **(see illustrations)**. Remove the upper shock mount, spring seat and associated washers and bearings (where applicable), noting their positions. Inspect the bearing in

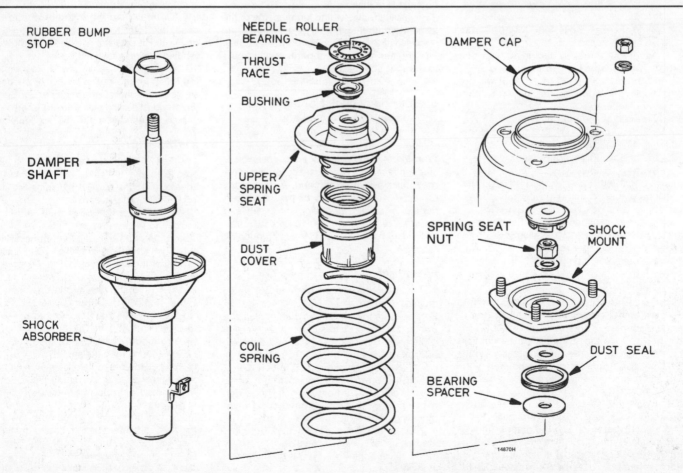

7.12a Exploded view of the strut/shock absorber and coil spring assembly (1984 and 1985 models)

RUBBER BUMP STOP

DAMPER SHAFT

SHOCK ABSORBER

NEEDLE ROLLER BEARING

THRUST RACE

BUSHING

UPPER SPRING SEAT

DUST COVER

COIL SPRING

DAMPER CAP

SPRING SEAT NUT

SHOCK MOUNT

DUST SEAL

BEARING SPACER

14870H

10

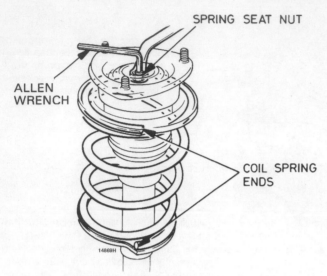

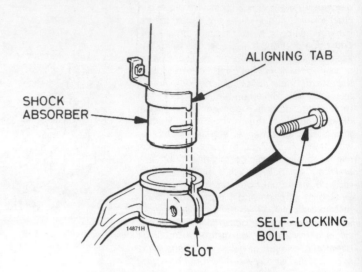

7.12b With the spring compressed, remove the damper shaft nut while holding the damper shaft with an Allen wrench

7.20 Ensure the aligning tab on the shock absorber enters the slot in the steering knuckle or damper fork

the upper mount for smooth operation (1984 and 1985 models only). If it doesn't operate smoothly, replace it.

13   Carefully lift the compressed spring from the assembly and set it in, a safe place, such as a steel cabinet. **Warning:** *Keep the ends of the spring facing away from your body!*

14   Slide the dust cover and rubber bump stop off the damper shaft.

15   Assemble the strut beginning with the rubber bump stop and the dust cover - extend the damper shaft as far as it will go and slide the components down to the strut/shock absorber body.

16   Carefully place the coil spring onto the strut/shock absorber body, with the end of the spring resting in the lowest part of the seat.

17   Install the upper spring seat, washers and bearing, followed by the upper shock mount. On 1986 and later models, align the previously applied marks on the mount and the spring (or shock absorber body).

18   Install a new spring seat nut and tighten it securely, again using the Allen wrench to prevent the damper shaft from turning. Remove the spring compressor.

Installation

19   Guide the strut/shock absorber assembly up into the fenderwell and insert the three upper mounting studs through the holes in the body. Once the studs protrude from the holes, install the nuts so the assembly won't fall, but don't tighten them completely yet. The strut is heavy and awkward, so get an assistant to help you, if possible.

20   Insert the lower end of the strut/shock absorber into the steering knuckle (1984 and"! 985 models) or into the damper fork 0 986 and later models). Make sure the aligning tab on the back of the strut/shock absorber body enters the slot in the steering knuckle or damper fork **(see illustration)**. Install a new pinch bolt and tighten it to the specified

torque.

21   On 1986 and later models, connect the damper fork to the lower arm, using a new self-locking nut. Tighten the nut to the specified torque.

22   Attach the brake hose to its bracket and tighten the bolt securely.

23   Install the wheel and lug nuts, lower the vehicle and tighten the lug nuts to the torque specified in Chapter 1.

24   Tighten the three upper mounting nuts to the specified torque.

8   Steering knuckle and hub assembly - removal and installation

Warning: *Whenever any of the suspension or steering fasteners are loosened or removed, they must be inspected and, if necessary, replaced with new ones of the same part number or of original equipment quality and design. Torque specifications must be followed for proper reassembly and component retention.*

Removal

1   Remove the wheel cover and loosen the driveaxle hub nut.

2   Loosen the wheel lug nuts, raise the front of the vehicle and support it securely on jackstands. Remove the wheel and driveaxle hub nut.

3   Following the procedure in Chapter 9, unbolt the brake caliper from the steering knuckle and hang it from the coil spring with a piece of wire. Also, remove the caliper mounting bracket and the brake disc.

4   Disconnect the tie-rod end from the steering knuckle (see Section 20).

5   Separate the lower arm from the steering knuckle (see Section 4).

6   Unbolt the brake hose from the strut/shock absorber assembly.

7   On 1984 and 1985 models, disconnect the steering knuckle from the strut by removing the pinch bolt and tapping the knuckle and hub assembly down (see Section 7).

8   On 1986 and later models, separate the top of the knuckle from the upper arm, following the procedure in Section 5.

9   Carefully pull the knuckle and hub assembly off the driveaxle. Support the driveaxle with a piece of wire to avoid overextending the inner CV joint.

10   If the bearings are worn, take the steering knuckle and hub assembly to a dealer service department or a repair shop. Special tools and expertise are required to press the hub and bearing from the steering knuckle.

Installation

11   Apply alight coat of wheel bearing grease to the driveaxle splines. Insert the driveaxle into the hub while guiding the steering knuckle into position.

12   On 1984 and 1985 models, attach the knuckle to the strut, making sure the aligning tab on the strut engages with the slot in the hub pinch joint (see illustration 7.20). Install a new pinch bolt and tighten it to the specified torque.

13   On 1986 and later models, connect the upper end of the knuckle to the upper balljoint. Tighten the balljoint stud nut to the specified torque.

14   Connect the bottom of the knuckle to the lower arm (see Section 4).

15   Install the brake disc, caliper mount and caliper (see Chapter 9).

16   Thread the hub nut onto the driveaxle and tighten it securely.

17   Install the wheel and lug nuts, lower the vehicle and tighten the lug nuts to the torque specified in Chapter 1.

18   Tighten the hub nut to the torque specified in Chapter 8, then stake the collar of the nut into the groove in the driveaxle (see illustration 8.16 in Chapter 8).

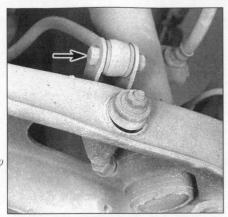

9.2 Remove the stabilizer bar-to-bracket bolt (arrow) to free it from the arm (1985 model shown); if necessary, the bracket can be removed and the rubber insulators replaced

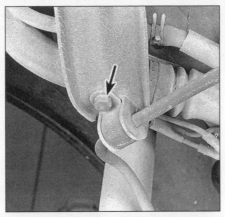

9.3 To detach the stabilizer bar from the body, remove the stabilizer bar bracket bolt (arrow) and swing the bracket down to unhook it

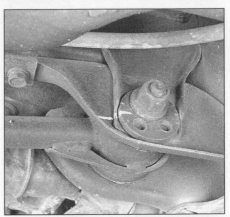

10.2 To ensure correct alignment when reassembling, mark the relationship of the toe-in adjuster to the forward mounting bracket, then remove the nut and bolt

19   It would be a good idea to drive the vehicle to an alignment shop to have the front end alignment checked and, if necessary, adjusted.

9   Rear stabilizer bar and bushings - removal and installation

Refer to illustrations 9.2 and 9.3

1   Raise the vehicle and support it securely on jackstands.
2   Disconnect the stabilizer bar from the bracket on the lower arm (1984 and 1985 models) or the stabilizer bar link (1986 and later models) **(see illustration).**
3   Remove the stabilizer bar bracket-to-body bolts **(see illustration).** Unhook the brackets from the body and remove the bar from the vehicle.
4   Check the bracket bushings for cracking, hardness and general deterioration, replacing them if necessary. Also check the lower arm bracket or link bushings for wear. Clean the areas where the bushings ride with a wire brush.

5   Installation is the reverse of the removal procedure. A light coat of vegetable oil will ease installation of the bushings and U-brackets (don't use petroleum-based lubricants or brake fluid - they will lead to premature failure of the bushing).

10   Rear radius rod - removal and installation (1984 and 1985 models)

Refer to illustrations 10.2 and 10.3
Warning: *Whenever any of the suspension or steering fasteners are loosened or removed, they must be inspected and, if necessary, replaced with new ones of the same part number or of original equipment quality and design. Torque specifications must be followed for proper reassembly and component retention.*

Removal

1   Loosen the rear wheel lug nuts, raise the rear of the vehicle and support it securely on jackstands. Remove the wheel.
2   Using a scribe or white paint, mark the

position of the toe-in adjuster on the forward mounting bracket **(see illustration).**
3   Remove the nut and bolt from each end of the radius rod and remove the rod from the vehicle **(see illustration).**

Installation

4   To install the rod, position it in its brackets and install the bolt and nut at each end of the rod, but don't tighten them yet.
5   Position a floor jack under the rear hub carrier and raise it to simulate normal ride height. Align the marks on the toe-in adjuster cam and tighten the nuts to the torque specified in Chapter 1.
6   Install the wheel and lug nuts, lower the vehicle and tighten the lug nuts to the specified torque.
7   It would be a good idea to drive the vehicle to an alignment shop to have the rear wheel alignment checked and, if necessary, adjusted.

11   Rear suspension lower arm(s) - removal and installation (1984 and 1985 models)

Refer to illustrations 11. 3 and 11. 4
Warning: *Whenever any of the suspension or steering fasteners are loosened or removed, they must be inspected and, if necessary, replaced with new ones of the same part number or of original equipment quality and design. Torque specifications must be followed for proper reassembly and component retention.*

Removal

1   Loosen the rear wheel lug nuts, raise the rear of the vehicle and support it securely on jackstands. Remove the wheel.
2   Disconnect the rear stabilizer bar from the lower arm (see Section 9).
3   Remove the lower arm-to-hub carrier nut, bolt and washers **(see illustration).** It may be necessary to drive the bolt out with a hammer and a long drift.

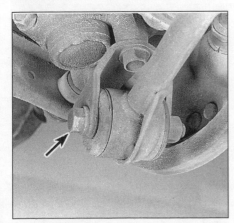

10.3 Remove the radius rod-to-rear wheel hub carrier bolt/nut (arrow)

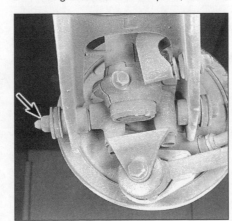

11.3 The lower arm is fastened to the rear wheel hub carrier by a long bolt (arrow), nut and washers

10

4   Support the lower arm and remove the inner pivot bolt **(see illustration)**. Remove the lower arm from the vehicle.

5   If any of the bushings in the lower arm appear to be in need of replacement (due to cracking, hardness or general deterioration), take the arm to a dealer service department or a repair shop to have new bushings installed.

Installation

6   Raise the arm up into position and install the inner pivot bolt, but don't tighten it completely yet.

7   Push the outer end of the bar into place over the rear wheel hub carrier and install the bolt and nut, but don't tighten the nut yet.

8   Attach the stabilizer bar to the lower arm (see Section 9).

9   Place a floor jack under the hub carrier and raise the rear suspension to simulate normal ride height. Tighten the fasteners to the specified torque.

10   It would be a good idea to drive the vehicle to an alignment shop to have the rear wheel alignment checked and, if necessary, adjusted.

---

12   Rear wheel hub carrier - removal and installation (1984 and 1985 models)

Refer to illustration 12.6

Warning: *Whenever any of the suspension or steering fasteners are loosened or removed, they must be inspected and, if necessary, replaced with new ones of the same part number or of original equipment quality and design. Torque specifications must be followed for proper reassembly and component retention.*

Removal

1   Loosen the rear wheel lug nuts, raise the rear of the vehicle and support it securely on jackstands. Remove the wheel.

2   Following the procedure in Chapter 1

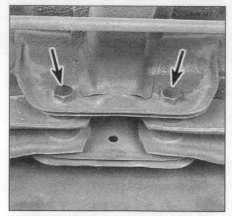

11.4 Locations of the lower arm inner pivot bolts (arrows)

under *Rear wheel bearing check, repack and adjustment,* remove the brake drum.

3   Using a flare nut wrench, unscrew the brake line fitting from the wheel cylinder (see Chapter 9). Don't pull the line away from the backing plate.

4   Remove the four brake backing plate-to-hub carrier bolts and lift the backing plate, complete with brake shoe assembly, off the hub carrier. Support the assembly out of the way with a piece of wire, then plug the open brake line to prevent excessive fluid loss and contamination.

5   Remove the radius rod-to-hub carrier bolt (see Section 10).

6   Loosen, but do not remove, the strut-to-hub carrier pinch bolt **(see illustration)**.

7   Remove the lower arm-to-hub carrier nut and bolt (see Section 11).

8   Remove the strut-to-hub carrier pinch bolt and separate the hub carrier from the strut. It may be necessary to tap the carrier off of the strut using a soft-face hammer.

9   Thoroughly clean the hub carrier with solvent, dry it off and check for cracks, especially in the area where the spindle meets the carrier. Replace the carrier if any undesirable conditions exist.

Installation

10   Slide the hub carrier onto the strut, making sure the tab on the back of the strut engages with the notch in the carrier. Install the pinch bolt, but don't tighten it completely yet.

11   Push the carrier into the lower arm and install the bolt and nut. Don't tighten the nut completely at this time.

12   Connect the trailing end of the radius rod to the carrier and install the bolt, but don't completely tighten it.

13   Tighten the strut pinch bolt to the specified torque.

14   Install the brake backing plate assembly, tightening the four bolts to the specified torque.

15   Connect the brake line and tighten the fitting securely.

16   At this time, it's a good idea to clean, check and repack the rear wheel bearings (see Chapter 1). Once that has been done, install the brake drum and adjust the wheel bearings following the procedure in Chapter 1.

17   Place a floor jack under the hub carrier and raise the rear suspension to simulate normal ride height. Tighten the radius rod-to-hub carrier bolt and the lower arm-to-hub carrier nut to the specified torque's.

18   Bleed the brakes following the procedure in Chapter 9.

19   Install the wheel and lug nuts, lower the vehicle and tighten the lug nuts to the specified torque.

---

13   Rear trailing arm - removal and Installation (1986 and later models)

Refer to illustration 13.4

Warning: *Whenever any of the suspension or steering fasteners are loosened or removed, they must be inspected and, if necessary, replaced with new ones of the same part number or of original equipment quality and design. Torque specifications must be followed for proper reassembly and component retention.*

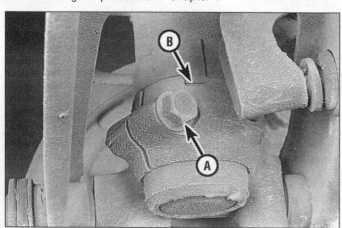

12.6 Remove the strut-to-hub carrier pinch bolt (A) - when assembling the strut to the hub carrier, make sure the tab on the strut fits into the notch in the hub carrier (B)

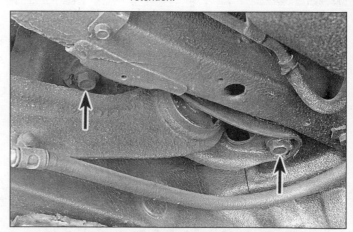

13.4 Locations of the trailing arm bracket-to-floorpan bolts (arrows)

14.2 Mark the relationship of the toe adjuster cam to the frame to ensure correct alignment when reassembling

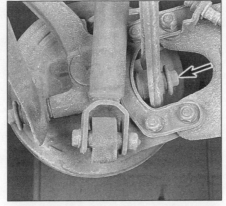

14.3 Both of the lower arms on 1986 and later models are retained to the rear knuckle by the same long bolt (arrow)

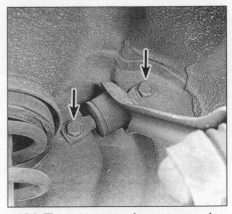

15.3 The rear suspension upper arm is fastened to the frame by two bolts (arrows)

Removal

1   Loosen the rear wheel lug nuts, raise the rear of the vehicle and support it securely on jackstands. Remove the wheel.

2   Remove the brackets that secure the brake hydraulic line and parking brake cable to the arm. Remove the brake drum and disconnect the parking brake cable from the lever (see Chapter 9). Pass the cable through the hole in the trailing arm.

3   Remove the two nuts and bolts attaching the rear of the trailing arm to the rear knuckle. Also disconnect the upper end of the stabilizer bar link from the arm (see Section 9).

4   Remove the two trailing arm bracket-to-floorpan bolts and lower the arm from the vehicle **(see illustration)**.

5   If it is necessary to remove the trailing arm bracket, unscrew the nut and remove the pivot bolt, then separate the bracket from the arm.

6   Inspect the trailing arm bushing for cracking and general deterioration. If it appears to be in need of replacement, take the arm to a dealer service department or a repair shop to have the old bushing pressed out and the new one pressed in.

Installation

7   If the bracket has been removed from the trailing arm, install it, but don't tighten the pivot bolt nut completely yet.

8   Assemble the trailing arm on the rear knuckle, installing the bolts and nuts loosely.

9   Position the trailing arm bracket on the body and install the bolts, tightening them to the specified torque (don't tighten the pivot bolt nut yet).

10   Tighten the trailing arm-to-knuckle fasteners to the specified torque.

11   Place a floor jack under the rear wheel hub carrier and raise the rear suspension to simulate normal ride height. Tighten the trailing arm pivot bolt nut to the specified torque.

12   Route the brake line and parking brake cable along the inner edge of the trailing arm and install the clips or clamps.

13   Install the wheel and lug nuts, lower the vehicle and tighten the lug nuts to the torque

specified in Chapter 1.

14   It would be a good idea to drive the vehicle to an alignment shop to have the rear wheel alignment checked and, if necessary, adjusted.

14   Rear suspension lower arm(s) - removal and installation (1986 and later models)

Refer to illustrations 14.2 and 14.3

Warning: *Whenever any of the suspension or steering fasteners are loosened or removed, they must be inspected and, if necessary, replaced with new ones of the same part number or of original equipment quality and design. Torque specifications must be followed for proper reassembly and component retention.*

Note: *This procedure can be used for either the long or short lower arm.*

Removal

1   Loosen the rear wheel lug nuts, raise the rear of the vehicle and support it securely on jackstands. Remove the wheel.

2   If you are removing the short lower arm, mark the relationship of the toe adjuster cam to the frame **(see illustration)**.

3   Remove the lower arm-to-rear knuckle nut and bolt **(see illustration)**. It may be necessary to drive the bolt out with a hammer and a long drift.

4   Remove the lower arm inner pivot bolt and detach the arm from the vehicle.

5   Check the bushings at the ends of the arm for cracking and general deterioration. If they are in need of replacement, they can be pressed out using a vise and two appropriate size sockets - one with an outside diameter slightly smaller than that of the bushing and another large enough to accept the bushing when it is pressed out. Position the sockets on each side of the bushing, then place the assembly between the jaws of a vise. Tighten the vise until the bushing is free of the arm. Install the now bushing using the same method.

Installation

6   Attach the outer end of the arm to the knuckle and install the bolt and nut, but don't tighten the nut yet.

7   Connect the inner end of the arm to its bracket on the underbody and install the bolt (and nut, if applicable). If you are installing the short arm, align the marks on the toe adjuster cam and the frame. Similarly, don't tighten the nut yet.

8   Place a floor jack under the knuckle and raise the rear suspension to simulate normal ride height. Tighten the inner pivot bolt and the lower arm-to-knuckle nut to the specified torque.

9   Install the wheel and lug nuts, lower the vehicle and tighten the lug nuts to the specified torque.

10   It would be a good idea to drive the vehicle to an alignment shop to have the rear wheel alignment checked and, if necessary, adjusted.

15   Rear suspension upper arm - removal and Installation (1986 and later models)

Refer to illustration 15.3

Warning: *Whenever any of the suspension or steering fasteners are loosened or removed, they must be inspected and, if necessary, replaced with new ones of the same part number or of original equipment quality and design. Torque specifications must be followed for proper reassembly and component retention.*

1   Loosen the rear wheel lug nuts, raise the rear of the vehicle and support it securely on jackstands. Remove the wheel.

2   Loosen the upper balljoint stud nut a couple of turns then separate the upper arm from the rear knuckle with a two-jaw puller. After this is done, wire the knuckle to the coil spring to prevent the knuckle fro failing out, which could distort the brake line.

3   Remove the two upper arm-to-body nuts **(see illustration)** and remove the arm from the fenderwell.

10

4   Installation is the reverse of the removal procedure. Be sure to tighten the fasteners to the specified torque. It would be a good idea to drive the car to an alignment shop to have the rear wheel alignment checked and, if necessary, adjusted.

16   Rear strut/shock absorber and coil spring assembly - removal, overhaul and installation

Refer to illustration 16.4

Warning: *Whenever any of the suspension or steering fasteners are loosened or removed, they must be inspected and, if necessary, replaced with new ones of the same part number or of original equipment quality and design. Torque specifications must be followed for proper reassembly and component retention.*

Removal

1   Loosen the wheel lug nuts, raise the vehicle and support it securely on jackstands. Remove the wheel.
2   Remove the rear seat back cushion to gain access to the strut/shock absorber upper mounting nuts.
3   Unbolt the flexible brake hose from the strut/shock absorber assembly.
4   Place a floor jack under the lower arm to support it when the strut/ shock absorber assembly is removed. Remove the strut-to-hub carrier pinch bolt (1984 and 1985 models) (see illustration 12.6) or the shock absorber-to-knuckle bolt on 1986 and later models) **(see illustration)**.
5   On 1984 and 1985 models, lower the jack and separate the strut/ shock absorber assembly from the steering knuckle. It may be necessary to tap, down on the knuckle while lowering the jack.
6   Support the strut/shock absorber and coil spring assembly and remove the three upper mounting nuts from the interior of the vehicle (see Illustration 7.7). Remove the unit through the fenderwell.

Overhaul

7   Refer to the overhaul procedure in Section 7, as the procedure for overhauling the rear strut/shock absorber and coil spring assembly is the same as for the front.

Installation

8   Guide the strut/shock absorber assembly up into the fenderwell and insert the three upper mounting studs through the holes in the body. Once the studs protrude from the holes, install the nuts so the assembly won't fall back through (don't tighten them completely yet). If possible, have an assistant help you, as the strut is heavy and awkward.
9   On 1984 and 1985 models, insert the lower end of the strut/shock absorber into the hub carrier. Make sure the aligning tab on the back of the strut/shock absorber body enters the notch in the carrier (see Illustration 12.6).

Install the pinch bolt and tighten it to the specified torque.
10   On 1986 and later models, connect the lower end of the shock absorber assembly to the carrier and install the bolt, tightening it to the specified torque.
11   Attach the brake hose to its bracket and tighten the bolt securely.
12   Install the wheel and lug nuts, lower the vehicle and tighten the lug nuts to the torque specified in Chapter 1.
13   Tighten the three upper mounting nuts to the specified torque.

17   Rear knuckle - removal and installation (1986 and later models)

Warning: *Whenever any of the suspension or steering fasteners are loosened or removed, they must be inspected and, if necessary, replaced with new ones of the same part number or of original equipment quality and design. Torque specifications must be followed for proper reassembly and component retention.*

Removal

1   Loosen the wheel lug nuts, raise the vehicle and support it secure[on jackstands. Remove the wheel.
2   Remove the brake drum or disc from the hub (see Chapter 9). Pr the dust cap from the hub.
3   Remove the spindle nut and washer, then slide the hub off the spin die. **Note:** *The hub is sealed and is not serviceable. If there is an roughness or play in the bearing, replace the assembly with a new one.*
4   On models with drum brakes, unscrew the brake line fitting from the wheel cylinder (see Chapter 9).
5   On models with drum brakes, remove the four brake backing plate to-knuckle bolts and lift the backing plate, complete with the brake shoes, from the knuckle. Hang the brake assembly from the coil sprig with a piece of wire - DON'T let it hang by the parking brake cable.
6   Disconnect the lower end of the shock absorber from the knuckle (see Section 16).
7   Unbolt the knuckle from the trailing arm (see Section 13).
8   Remove the bolt and nut that retain the lower arms to the knuckle (see Section 14).
9   Separate the top of the knuckle from the upper arm balljoint (see Section 15) and separate the knuckle from the vehicle. Check it thoroughly for cracks and wear, especially around the area of the spindle Replace the knuckle if it's cracked, damaged or worn.

Installation

10   Connect the top of the knuckle to the upper arm balljoint stud and tighten the nut to the specified torque.
11   Attach the trailing arm to the knuckle, tightening the fasteners to the specified

16.4 Remove the shock absorber/coil spring assembly-to-rear knuckle bolt (arrow)

torque.
12   Position the two lower arms against the knuckle, align the holes and install the lower arms-to-knuckle bolt and nut. Don't tighten the nut completely yet.
13   Fasten the lower end of the shock absorber to the knuckle, but don't completely tighten the bolt yet.
14   On vehicles equipped with drum brakes, mount the brake assembly on the backing plate and tighten the four bolts to the specified torque Connect the hydraulic line to the wheel cylinder and tighten the fitting securely.
15   Lubricate the spindle with wheel bearing grease and slide the hub into position. Install a new hub nut and tighten it to the specified torque.
16   Install the brake drum or disc (see Chapter 9).
17   Place a floor jack under the knuckle and raise the suspension to simulate normal ride height. Tighten all of the fasteners to the specified torque.
18   Bleed the brakes following the procedure described in Chapter 9.
19   Install the wheel and lug nuts. Lower the vehicle to the ground and tighten the lug nuts to the torque specified in Chapter 1.
20   It would be a good idea to drive the vehicle to an alignment shop to have the rear wheel alignment checked and, if necessary, adjusted.

18   Steering wheel - removal and installation

Refer to illustrations 18.2 and 18.4 Removal

1   Disconnect the cable from the negative battery terminal.
2   From the back side of the steering wheel, remove the four screws securing the horn cover to the steering wheel (see Illustration).
3   Unplug the wire harness connector and remove the horn cover.
4   Remove the steering wheel mounting nut. Mark the relationship of the steering

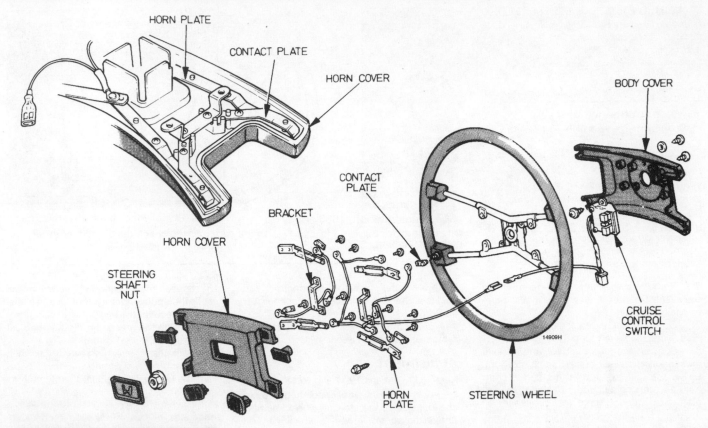

18.2 Typical steering wheel components - exploded view

18.4 Before removing the steering wheel, mark the relationship of the steering wheel hub to the steering shaft; this will ensure the wheel is not off center when installed

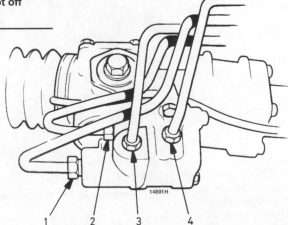

19.2 Power steering gear hydraulic line connections

1 To reservoir through cooler
2 To reservoir through speed sensor
3 To speed sensor
4 From pump

wheel hub to the steering column shaft. This will ensure correct steering wheel alignment during reassembly **(see illustration)**.
5   Pull the steering wheel straight back off the steering shaft. A steering wheel puller is not required.

Installation

6   Align the index mark on the steering wheel hub with the mark on the shaft and slip the wheel onto the shaft. Install the mounting nut and tighten it to the specified torque.
7   Plug in the electrical connector and install the horn cover.
8   Connect the negative battery cable.

19 Steering gear - removal, installation and adjustment

Note: *This procedure applies to both power and manual steering gear assemblies. When working on a vehicle equipped with a manual steering gear, simply ignore any references made to the power steering system.*

Removal

Refer to illustrations 19.2 and 19.8

1   Loosen the front wheel lug nuts, raise the front of the vehicle and support it securely on jackstands. Apply the parking brake and remove the wheels.
2   Place a drain pan under the steering gear (power steering only). Unbolt the steering gear shield. Remove the hoses/lines and cap the ends to prevent excessive fluid loss and contamination **(see illustration)**.
3   Find the steering shaft U-joint, located just above the driver's side of the floor panel, near the pedals. Mark the relationship of the U-joint to the steering gear input shaft. Remove the U-joint pinch bolt.
4   Separate the tie-rod ends from the steering knuckle arms (see Section 20).
5   Support the transaxle and remove the transaxle mount bolts (see Chapter 7A), then remove the four front and three rear bolts attaching the engine center support beam to the vehicle (see illustration 1.3). Support the beam as the final bolts are removed.

10

19.8 The steering gear is retained at each end by a mounting bracket and two bolts (arrows)

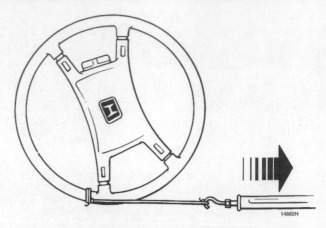

19.17 Using a spring scale, check the amount of effort required to turn the wheel

6   Remove the exhaust pipe-to-manifold bolts (see Chapter 4) and the exhaust pipe-to-engine bracket.

7   Push the steering rack all the way to the right (simulating a left turn).

8   Support the steering gear and remove the mounting bracket bolts **(see Illustration)**. Lower the unit, separate the steering shaft from the steering gear input shaft and manipulate the steering gear as necessary to remove it from the vehicle.

Installation

9   Raise the steering gear into position and connect the steering shaft, aligning the marks you made when you removed it.

10   Install the mounting brackets and bolts. Tighten them to the specified torque.

11   Connect the tie-rod ends to the steering knuckle arms (see Section 20).

12   Install the steering shaft U-joint pinch bolt and tighten it to the specified torque.

13   Connect the power steering hoses/lines to the steering gear and fill the power steer-

ing pump reservoir with the recommended fluid (see Chapter 1). Install the steering gear shield.

14   Lower the vehicle and bleed the steering system as outlined in Section 24.

Adjustment

Refer to illustrations 19.17 and 19.18

15   With the front wheels pointing straight ahead, measure the steering wheel free play (the distance the steering wheel can be turned in either direction before the front wheels start to turn). If the free play exceeds the limit shown in the specifications, check all of the steering and front suspension components for signs of wear or damage. If no wear or damage is found, adjust the steering gear as follows.

16   Raise the front of the vehicle and support it securely on jackstands.

17   Using a spring scale, check the amount of effort required to turn the steering wheel in either direction **(see illustration)**. Compare your reading with the specifications.

18   Loosen the steering rack screw locknut using the special factory tool or a modified wrench **(see illustration)**.

19   Tighten the steering rack guide adjusting screw until it just bottoms.

20   Back the adjusting screw off 451 (manual steering gear) or 35 (power steering gear) from the bottomed position, then tighten the locknut.

21   Check the steering for tightness or looseness of operation, then recheck the steering effort as described in Step 17.

22   Lower the vehicle and road test it to verify proper operation of the steering.

20   Tie-rod ends removal and installation

Refer to illustrations 20.2a, 20.2b and 20.4

Removal

1   Loosen the wheel lug nuts. Raise the front of the vehicle, support it securely, block

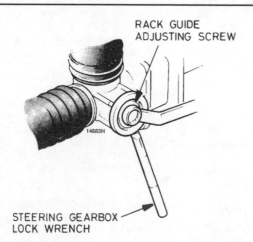

19.18 After the locknut has been loosened with the lock wrench, the rack guide can be adjusted; when tightening the locknut, hold the adjusting screw with a wrench to prevent it from turning

RACK GUIDE
ADJUSTING SCREW

STEERING GEARBOX
LOCK WRENCH

20.2a Hold the tie-rod with a wrench while loosening the jam nut

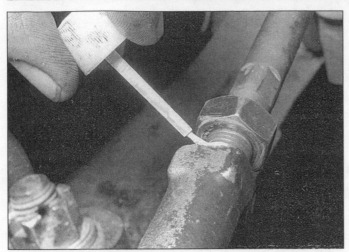

20.2b Once the jam nut has been loosened, use white paint to mark the position of the tie-rod end on the tie-rod

20.4 Use a two jaw puller to separate the tie-rod end from the spindle arm (notice the nut has been loosened, but not removed - this will prevent the components from separating violently)

the rear wheels and set the parking brake. Remove the front wheel.

2   Hold the tie-rod with a wrench and loosen the jam nut enough to mark the position of the tie-rod end in relation to the threads **(see illustrations)**.

3   Remove the cotter pin and loosen the nut on the tie-rod end stud. Don't completely remove the nut.

4   Separate the tie-rod from the steering knuckle arm with a puller **(see Illustration)**. Remove the nut and detach the tie-rod.

5   Unscrew the tie-rod end from the tie-rod.

Installation

6   Thread the tie-rod end on to the marked position and insert the tie-rod stud into the steering knuckle arm. Tighten the jam nut securely.

7   Install the castellated nut on the stud and tighten it to the specified torque. Install a new cotter pin.

8   install the wheel and lug nuts. Lower the vehicle and tighten the lug nuts to the. torque specified in Chapter 1.

9   Have the alignment checked by a dealer service department or an alignment shop.

21 Steering gear boots - replacement

1   Loosen the lug nuts, raise the front of the vehicle and support it securely on jack-stands. Apply the parking brake. Remove the wheel.

2   Refer to Section 20 and remove the tie-rod end and jam nut.

3   Remove the steering gear boot clamps and slide the boot off.

4   Before installing the new boot, wrap the threads and serration's on the end of the tie-rod with a layer of tape so the small end of the new boot isn't damaged.

5   Slide the new boot into position on the steering gear until it seats in the groove, in the steering rod. Install new clamps.

6   Remove the, tape and install the, tie-rod end (see Section 20).

7   install the wheel and lug nuts. Lower the vehicle and tighten the big nuts to the torque specified in Chapter. 1.

22 Power steering pump - removal and installation

Note: *to the complex nature of the power steering pump and the for #~!#/ tools to service it, overhaul or repair by the home mechanic Is not recommended.*

1   Loosen the adjuster bolt and remove the power steering pump drivebelt (see Chapter 1, if 'necessary).

2   Place a drain pan under the vehicle and disconnect the hoses from the pump. Plug the ends of the hoses to prevent excessive fluid loss and contamination.

3   Remove the adjusting bolt and the pivot bolt, then remove the pump from the vehicle. Be careful not to let any fluid drip on the paint.

4   Installation is the reverse of the removal procedure. Tighten the drivebelt following the procedure in Chapter 1, then bleed the power steering system (see Section 24).

23 Power steering speed sensor - removal and installation

1   Pull up the rubber boot on the speedometer cable where it enters the transaxle, remove the clip, then pull the cable from the speed sensor.

2   Disconnect and plug the hoses to the speed sensor.

3   Remove the speed, sensor-to-transaxle bolt and lift the sensor straight out of the transaxle.

4   Installation is the reverse of the removal procedure. Be sure to bleed the power steering system following the procedure in Section 24.

24 Power steering system - bleeding

1   Following any operation in which the power steering fluid lines have been disconnected, the power steering system must be bled to remove all air and obtain proper steering performance.

2   With the front wheels in the straight ahead position, check the power steering fluid level and, if low, add fluid until it reaches the lower mark on the reservoir.

3   Start the engine and allow it to run at fast idle. Recheck the fluid level and add more if necessary to reach the lower mark on the reservoir.

4   Bleed the system by turning the wheels from side-to-side, without hitting the stops. This will work the air out of the system.
Keep the reservoir full of fluid as this is done.

5   When the air is worked out of the system, return the wheels to the straight ahead position and leave the vehicle running for several more minutes before shutting it off.

6   Road test the vehicle to be sure the steering system is functioning normally and noise free.

7   Recheck the fluid level to be sure it is at the upper mark on the reservoir while the engine is at normal operating temperature. Add fluid if necessary (see Chapter 1).

25 Wheels and tires - general information

Refer to illustration 25. 1

All vehicles covered by this manual are equipped with metric-sized fiberglass or steel belted radial tires **(see illustration)**. Use of

10

METRIC TIRE SIZES

P 185 / 80 R 13

TIRE TYPE
P-PASSENGER
T-TEMPORARY
C-COMMERCIAL

ASPECT RATIO
(SECTION HEIGHT)
─────────────
(SECTION WIDTH)
70
75
80

RIM DIAMETER
(INCHES)
13
14
15

SECTION WIDTH
(MILLIMETERS)
185
195
205
ETC

CONSTRUCTION TYPE
R-RADIAL
B-BIAS - BELTED
D-DIAGONAL (BIAS)

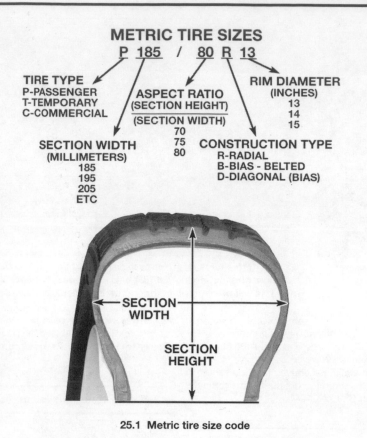

25.1 Metric tire size code

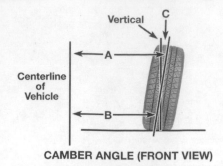

CAMBER ANGLE (FRONT VIEW)

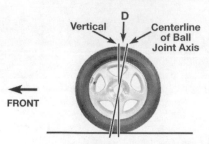

CASTER ANGLE (SIDE VIEW)

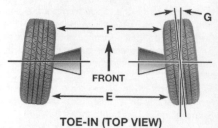

TOE-IN (TOP VIEW)

26.1 Front end alignment details

D = degrees
E - F = toe-in (measured in inches)
G = toe-in (expressed in degrees)

other size or type of tires may affect the ride and handling of the vehicle. Don't mix different types of tires, such as radials and bias belted, on the same vehicle as handling may be seriously affected. It's recommended that tires be replaced in pairs on the same axle, but if only one tire is being replaced, be sure it's the same size, structure and tread design as the other.

Because tire pressure has a substantial effect on handling and wear, the pressure on all tires should be checked at least once a month or before any extended trips (see Chapter 1).

Wheels must be replaced if they are bent, dented, leak air, have elongated bolt holes, are heavily rusted, out of vertical symmetry or if the lug nuts won't stay tight. Wheel repairs that use welding or peening are not recommended.

Tire and wheel balance is important to the overall handling, braking and performance of the vehicle. Unbalanced wheels can adversely affect handling and ride characteristics as well as tire life. Whenever a tire is installed on a wheel, the tire and wheel should be balanced by a shop with the proper equipment.

26   Wheel alignment - general information

Refer to illustration 26. 1

A wheel alignment refers to the adjustments made to the front and rear wheels so they are in proper angular relationship to the suspension and the ground. Wheels that are out of proper alignment not only affect vehicle control, but also increase tire wear. The adjustments normally required on this vehicle are caster and toe-in **(see illustration)**.

Getting the proper wheel alignment is a very exacting process, one in which complicated and expensive machines are necessary to perform the job properly. Because of this, you should have a technician with the proper equipment perform these tasks. We Will, however, use this space to give you a basic idea of what is involved with wheel alignment so you can better understand the process and deal intelligently with the shop that does the work.

Toe-in is the turning in of the wheels. The purpose of a toe specification is to ensure parallel roiling of the wheels. In a vehicle with zero toe-in, the distance between the front edges of the wheels will be the same as the distance between the rear edges of the

wheels. The actual amount of toe-in is normally only a fraction of an inch. Front wheel toe-in adjustment is controlled by the tie-rod end position on the tie-rod. Rear wheel toe-in is adjusted by turning a cam bolt on the rear radius rod (1984 and 1985 models) or the inner pivot bolt on the short lower arm (1986 and later models). Incorrect toe-in will cause the tires to wear improperly by making them scrub against the road surface.

Caster is the tilting of the top of the front steering axis from the vertical. A tilt toward the rear is positive caster and a tilt toward the front is negative caster. Front wheel caster is not adjustable on 1984 and 1985 models, but on 1986 and later models it can be adjusted by changing the position of the adjusting nuts on the radius rod.

Rear wheel caster is not adjustable. Camber is not adjustable on either the front or rear wheels.

Chapter 11   Body

Contents

Specifications

Torque specifications

	Ft-lbs	Nm
Bumper mount bolt		
1984	58	80
1985	28	39
1986 on	16	22

1   General information

These models feature a "unibody" layout, using a floor pan with front and rear frame side rails which support the body components, front and rear suspension systems and other mechanical components.

Certain components are particularly vulnerable to accident damage and can be unbolted and repaired or replaced. Among these parts are the body moldings, bumpers, the hood and trunk lid (or liftgate) and all glass.

Only general body maintenance practices and body panel repair procedures within the scope of the do-it-yourselfer are included in this Chapter.

2   Body - maintenance

1   The condition of your vehicle's body is very important, because the resale value depends a great deal on it. It's much more difficult to repair a neglected or damaged body than it is to repair mechanical components. The hidden areas of the body, such as the wheel wells, the frame and the engine compartment, are equally important, although they don't require as frequent attention as the rest of the body.

2   Once a year, or every 12,000 miles, it's a good idea to have the underside of the body steam cleaned. All traces of dirt and oil will be removed and the area can then be inspected carefully for rust, damaged brake lines, frayed electrical wires, damaged cables and other problems.

3   At the same time, clean the engine and the engine compartment with a steam cleaner or water soluble degreaser.

4   The wheel wells should be given close attention, since undercoating can peel away and stones and dirt thrown up by the tires can cause the paint to chip and flake, allowing rust to set in. If rust is found, clean down to the bare metal and apply an anti-rust paint.

5   The body should be washed about once a week. Wet the vehicle thoroughly to soften the dirt, then wash it down with a soft sponge and plenty of clean soapy water. If the surplus dirt is not washed off very carefully, it can wear down the paint.

6   Spots of tar or asphalt thrown up from the road should be removed with a cloth soaked in solvent.

7   Once every six months, wax the body and chrome trim. If a chrome cleaner is used to remove rust from any of the vehicle's plated parts, remember that the cleaner also removes part of the chrome, so use it sparingly.

3   Vinyl trim - maintenance

Don't clean vinyl trim with detergents, caustic soap or petroleum based cleaners. Plain soap and water works just fine, with a soft brush to clean dirt that may be ingrained. Wash the vinyl as frequently as the rest of the vehicle.

After cleaning, application of a high quality rubber and vinyl protectant will help prevent oxidation and cracks. The protectant can also be applied to weatherstripping, vacuum lines and rubber hoses, which often fail as a result of chemical degradation, and to the tires.

These photos illustrate a method of repairing simple dents. They are intended to supplement *Body repair - minor damage* in this Chapter and should not be used as the sole instructions for body repair on these vehicles.

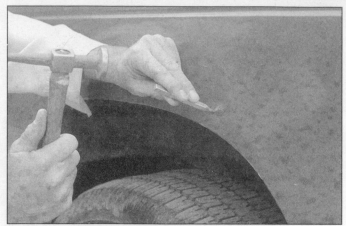

1   If you can't access the backside of the body panel to hammer out the dent, pull it out with a slide-hammer-type dent puller. In the deepest portion of the dent or along the crease line, drill or punch hole(s) at least one inch apart . . .

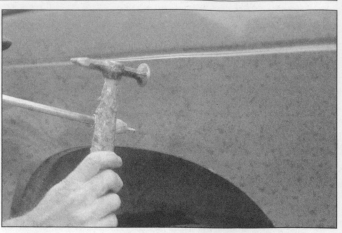

2   . . . then screw the slide-hammer into the hole and operate it. Tap with a hammer near the edge of the dent to help 'pop' the metal back to its original shape. When you're finished, the dent area should be close to its original contour and about 1/8-inch below the surface of the surrounding metal

3   Using coarse-grit sandpaper, remove the paint down to the bare metal. Hand sanding works fine, but the disc sander shown here makes the job faster. Use finer (about 320-grit) sandpaper to feather-edge the paint at least one inch around the dent area

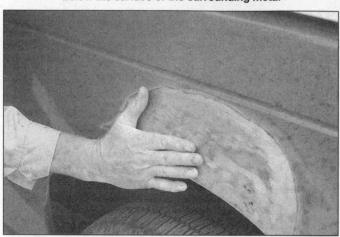

4   When the paint is removed, touch will probably be more helpful than sight for telling if the metal is straight. Hammer down the high spots or raise the low spots as necessary. Clean the repair area with wax/silicone remover

5   Following label instructions, mix up a batch of plastic filler and hardener. The ratio of filler to hardener is critical, and, if you mix it incorrectly, it will either not cure properly or cure too quickly (you won't have time to file and sand it into shape)

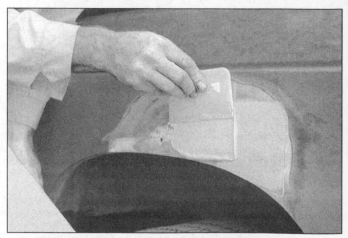

6   Working quickly so the filler doesn't harden, use a plastic applicator to press the body filler firmly into the metal, assuring it bonds completely. Work the filler until it matches the original contour and is slightly above the surrounding metal

7 Let the filler harden until you can just dent it with your fingernail. Use a body file or Surform tool (shown here) to rough-shape the filler

8 Use coarse-grit sandpaper and a sanding board or block to work the filler down until it's smooth and even. Work down to finer grits of sandpaper - always using a board or block - ending up with 360 or 400 grit

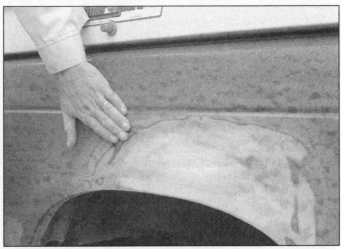

9 You shouldn't be able to feel any ridge at the transition from the filler to the bare metal or from the bare metal to the old paint. As soon as the repair is flat and uniform, remove the dust and mask off the adjacent panels or trim pieces

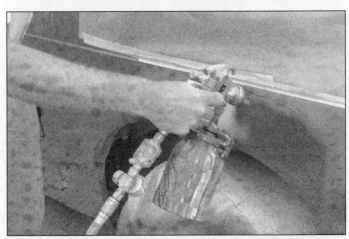

10 Apply several layers of primer to the area. Don't spray the primer on too heavy, so it sags or runs, and make sure each coat is dry before you spray on the next one. A professional-type spray gun is being used here, but aerosol spray primer is available inexpensively from auto parts stores

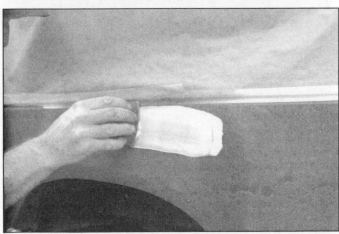

11 The primer will help reveal imperfections or scratches. Fill these with glazing compound. Follow the label instructions and sand it with 360 or 400-grit sandpaper until it's smooth. Repeat the glazing, sanding and respraying until the primer reveals a perfectly smooth surface

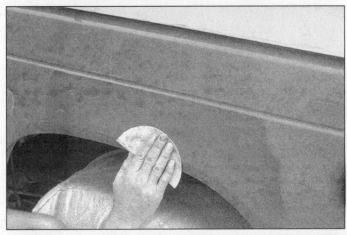

12 Finish sand the primer with very fine sandpaper (400 or 600-grit) to remove the primer overspray. Clean the area with water and allow it to dry. Use a tack rag to remove any dust, then apply the finish coat. Don't attempt to rub out or wax the repair area until the paint has dried completely (at least two weeks)

4   Upholstery and carpets - maintenance

1   Every three months remove the carpets or mats and clean the interior of the vehicle (more frequently if necessary). Vacuum the upholstery and carpets to remove loose dirt and dust.

2   Leather upholstery requires special care. Stains should be removed with warm water and a very mild soap solution. Use a clean, damp cloth to remove the soap, then wipe again with a dry cloth. Never use alcohol, gasoline, nail polish remover or thinner to clean leather upholstery.

3   After cleaning, regularly treat leather upholstery with a leather wax. Never use car wax on leather upholstery.

4   In areas where the interior of the vehicle is subject to bright sunlight, cover leather seats with a sheet if the vehicle is to be left out for any length of time.

5   Body repair - minor damage

See color photo sequence

"Repair of minor scratches"

1   If the scratch is superficial and does not penetrate to the metal of the body, repair is very simple. Lightly rub the scratched area with a fine rubbing compound to remove loose paint and built up wax. Rinse the area with clean water.

2   Apply touch-up paint to the scratch, using a small brush. Continue to apply thin layers of paint until the surface of the paint in the scratch is level with the surrounding paint. Allow the new paint at least two weeks to harden, then blend it into the surrounding paint by rubbing with a very fine rubbing compound.
Finally, apply a coat of wax to the scratch area.

3   If the scratch has penetrated the paint and exposed the metal of the body, causing the metal to rust, a different repair technique is required. Remove all loose rust from the bottom of the scratch with a pocket knife, then apply rust inhibiting paint to prevent the formation of rust in the future. Using a rubber or nylon applicator, coat the scratched area with glaze-type filler. If required, the filler can be mixed with thinner to provide a very thin paste, which is ideal for filling narrow scratches. Before the glaze filler in the scratch hardens, wrap a piece of smooth cotton cloth around the tip of a finger. Dip the cloth in thinner and then quickly wipe it along the surface of the scratch. This will ensure that the surface of the filler is slightly hollow. The scratch can now be painted over as described earlier in this section.

Repair of dents

4   When repairing dents, the first job is to pull the dent out until the affected area is as close as possible to its original shape. There is no point in trying to restore the original shape completely as the metal in the damaged area will have stretched on impact and cannot be restored to its original contours. It is better to bring the level of the dent up to a point which is about 1/8-inch below the level of the surrounding metal. In cases where the dent is very shallow, it is not worth trying to pull it out at all.

5   If the back side of the dent is accessible, it can be hammered out gently from behind using a soft-face hammer. While doing this, hold a block of wood firmly against the opposite side of the metal to absorb the hammer blows and prevent the metal from being stretched.

6   If the dent is in a section of the body which has double layers, or some other factor makes it inaccessible from behind, a different technique is required. Drill several small holes through the metal inside the damaged area, particularly in the deeper sections. Screw long, self tapping screws into the holes just enough for them to get a good grip in the metal. Now the dent can be pulled out by pulling on the protruding heads of the screws with locking pliers.

7   The next stage of repair is the removal of paint from the damaged area and from an inch or so of the surrounding metal. This is easily done with a wire brush or sanding disk in a drill motor, although it can be done just as effectively by hand with sandpaper. To complete the preparation for filling, score the surface of the bare metal with a screwdriver or the tang of a file or drill small holes in the affected area. This will provide a good grip for the filler material. To complete the repair, see the Section on filling and painting.

Repair of rust holes or gashes

8   Remove all paint from the affected area and from an inch or so of the surrounding metal using a sanding disk or wire brush mounted in a drill motor. If these are not available, a few sheets of sandpaper will do the job just as effectively.

9   With the paint removed, you will be able to determine the severity of the corrosion and decide whether to replace the whole panel, if possible, or repair the affected area. New body panels are not as expensive as most people think and it is often quicker to install a new panel than to repair large areas of rust.

10   Remove all trim pieces from the affected area except those which will act as a guide to the original shape of the damaged body, such as headlight shells, etc. Using metal snips or a hacksaw blade, remove all loose metal and any other metal that is badly affected by rust. Hammer the edges of the hole inward to create a slight depression for the filler material.

11   Wire brush the affected area to remove the powdery rust from the surface of the metal. If the back of the rusted area is accessible, treat it with rust inhibiting paint.

12   Before filling is done, block the hole in some way. This can be done with sheet metal riveted or screwed into place, or by stuffing the hole with wire mesh.

13   Once the hole is blocked off, the affected area can be filled and painted. See the following subsection on filling and painting.

Filling and painting

14   Many types of body fillers are available, but generally speaking, body repair kits which contain filler paste and a tube of resin hardener are best for this type of repair work. A wide, flexible plastic or nylon applicator will be necessary for imparting a smooth and contoured finish to the surface of the filler material. Mix up a small amount of filler on a clean piece of wood or cardboard (use the hardener sparingly). Follow the manufacturer's instructions on the package, otherwise the filler will set incorrectly.

15   Using the applicator, apply the filler paste to the prepared area. Draw the applicator across the surface of the filler to achieve the desired contour and to level the filler surface. As soon as a contour that approximates the original one is achieved, stop working the paste. If you continue, the paste will begin to stick to the applicator. Continue to add thin layers of paste at 20-minute intervals until the level of the filler is just above the surrounding metal.

16   Once the filler has hardened, the excess can be removed with a body file. From then on, progressively finer grades of sandpaper should be used, starting with a 180-grit paper and finishing with a 600-grit wet or-dry paper. Always wrap the sandpaper around a flat rubber or wooden block, otherwise the surface of the filler will not be completely flat. During the sanding of the filler surface, the wet-or-dry paper should be periodically rinsed in water. This will ensure that a very smooth finish is produced in the final stage.

17   At this point, the repair area should be surrounded by a ring of bare metal, which in turn should be encircled by the finely feathered edge of good paint. Rinse the repair area with clean water until all of the dust produced by the sanding operation is gone.

18   Spray the entire area with a light coat of primer. This will reveal any imperfections in the surface of the filler. Repair the imperfections with fresh filler paste or glaze filler and once more smooth the surface with sandpaper. Repeat this spray-and-repair procedure until you are satisfied that the surface of the filler and the feathered edge of the paint are perfect. Rinse the area with clean water and allow it to dry completely.

19   The repair area is now ready for painting. Spray painting must be carried out in a warm, dry, windless and dust free atmosphere. These conditions can be created if you have access to a large indoor work area, but if you are forced to work in the open, you will have to pick the day very carefully. If you are working indoors, dousing the floor in the work area with water will help settle the dust

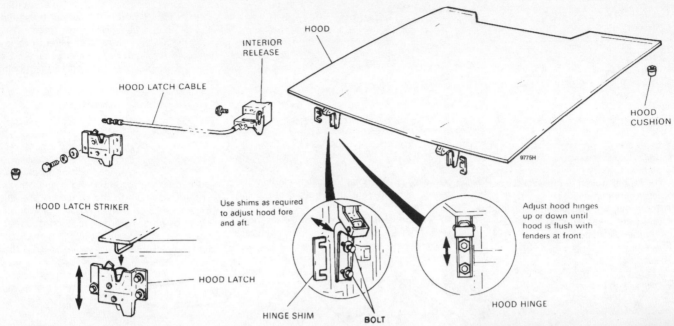

9.2a Hood installation and adjustment details (1984 and 1985 models)

which would otherwise be in the air. If the repair area is confined to one body panel, mask off the surrounding panels. This will help minimize the effects of a slight mismatch in paint color. Trim pieces such as chrome strips, door handles, etc., will also need to be masked off or removed. Use masking tape and several thicknesses of newspaper for the masking operations.

20   Before spraying, shake the paint can thoroughly, then spray a test area until the spray painting technique is mastered. Cover the repair area with a thick coat of primer. The thickness should be built up using several thin layers of primer rather than one thick one. Using 600-grit wet-or dry sandpaper, rub down the surface of the primer until it is very smooth. While doing this, the work area should be thoroughly rinsed with water and the wet-or-dry sandpaper periodically rinsed as well. Allow the primer to dry before spraying additional coats.

21   Spray on the top coat, again building up the thickness by using several thin layers of paint. Begin spraying in the center of the repair area and then, using a circular motion, work out until the whole repair area and about two inches of the surrounding original paint is covered. Remove all masking material 10 to 15 minutes after spraying on the final coat of paint. Allow the new paint at least two weeks to harden, then use a very fine rubbing compound to blend the edges of the new paint into the existing paint. Finally, apply a coat of wax.

6   Body repair - major damage

1   Major damage must be repaired by an auto body shop specifically equipped to per-

form unibody repairs. These shops have the specialized equipment required to do the job properly.

2   If the damage is extensive, the body must be checked for proper alignment or the vehicle's handling characteristics may be adversely affected and other components may wear at an accelerated rate.

3   Due to the fact that all of the major body components (hood, fenders, etc.) are separate and replaceable units, any seriously damaged components should be replaced rather than repaired. Sometimes the components can be found in a wrecking yard that specializes in used vehicle components, often at considerable savings over the cost of new parts.

7   Hinges and locks - maintenance

Once every 3000 miles, or every three months, the hinges and latch assemblies on the doors, hood and trunk (or liftgate) should be given a few drops of light oil or lock lubricant. The door latch strikers should also be lubricated with a thin coat of grease to reduce wear and ensure free movement. Lubricate the door and trunk (or liftgate) locks with spray-on graphite lubricant.

8   Fixed glass - replacement

Replacement of the windshield and fixed glass requires the use of special fast-setting adhesive/caulk materials and some specialized tools and techniques. These operations should be left to a dealer service department or a shop specializing in glass work.

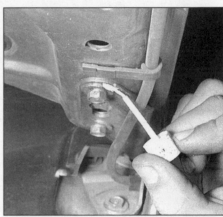

9.2b Make marks around the hood hinge bolts before loosening them (1986 and later design shown)

9   Hood - removal, installation and adjustment

Refer to illustrations 9.2a and 9.2b
Note: *The hood is heavy and somewhat awkward to remove and install - at least two people should perform this procedure.*

Removal and installation

1   Use blankets or pads to cover the fenders, front of the body (1984 and 1985 models) or cowl area (1986 and later models). This will protect the body and paint as the hood is lifted off.

2   Scribe or paint alignment marks around the bolt heads or nuts to ensure proper alignment during installation **(see illustrations)**.

3   Disconnect any cables or wire harnesses which will interfere with removal.

4   Have an assistant support the weight of the hood. Remove the hinge-to-hood nuts or bolts and shims.

11

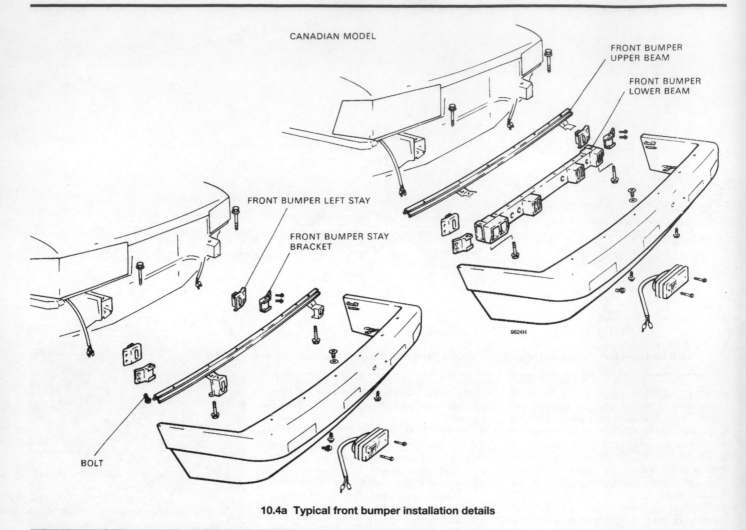

CANADIAN MODEL

FRONT BUMPER
UPPER BEAM

FRONT BUMPER
LOWER BEAM

FRONT BUMPER LEFT STAY

FRONT BUMPER STAY
BRACKET

BOLT

9824H

10.4a Typical front bumper installation details

5   Lift off the hood.
6   Installation is the reverse of removal. Be sure to reinstall the shims in their original locations.

Adjustment

7   Fore-and-aft adjustment of the hood is done by adding or removing shims between the hinge and body (1984 and 1985 models) or moving the hood after loosening the hinge-to-body bolts or nuts (1986 and later models).
8   Scribe a line around the entire hinge plate so you can judge the amount of movement.
9   Loosen the bolts or nuts and add or remove shims or move the hood into correct alignment. Move it only a little at a time. Tighten the hinge bolts or nuts and carefully lower the hood to check the alignment.
10   If necessary after installation, the entire hood latch assembly can be adjusted up-and-down as well as from side-to-side on the radiator support or firewall so the hood closes securely and is flush with the fenders. To do this, scribe a line around the hood latch mounting bolts to provide a reference point. Then loosen the bolts and reposition the latch

assembly as necessary. Following adjustment, retighten the mounting bolts.
11   Finally, adjust the hood cushions on the radiator support or hood so the hood, when closed, is flush with the fenders (1984 and 1985 models). On 1986 and later models, adjust the rear edge of the hood until it's flush with the fenders using shims under the hinge plates.
12   The hood latch assembly, as well as the hinges, should be periodically lubricated with white lithium-base grease to prevent sticking and wear.

10 Bumpers - removal and installation

Refer to illustrations 10.4a and 10.4b
1   Detach the bumper cover (if equipped).
2   Disconnect any wiring or other components that would interfere with bumper removal.
3   Support the bumper with a jack or jackstand. Alternatively, have an assistant support the bumper as the bolts are removed.
4   Remove the mounting bolts and detach the bumper **(see illustrations)**.

5   Installation is the reverse of removal.
6   Tighten the retaining bolts to the specified torque.
7   Install the bumper cover and any other components that were removed.

11 Door trim panel - removal and installation

Refer to illustrations 11.3, 11.5 and 11.8
1   Disconnect the negative cable from the battery.
2   Remove all door trim panel retaining screws and door pull/armrest assemblies.
3   On manual window regulator equipped models, remove the window crank handle **(see illustration)**. On power regulator models, pry out the control switch assembly and unplug it.
4   Insert a putty knife between the trim panel and the door and disengage the retaining clips. Work around the outer edge until the panel is free.
5   Once all of the clips are disengaged, detach the trim panel, unplug any wire harness connectors and remove the trim panel from the vehicle **(see illustration)**.

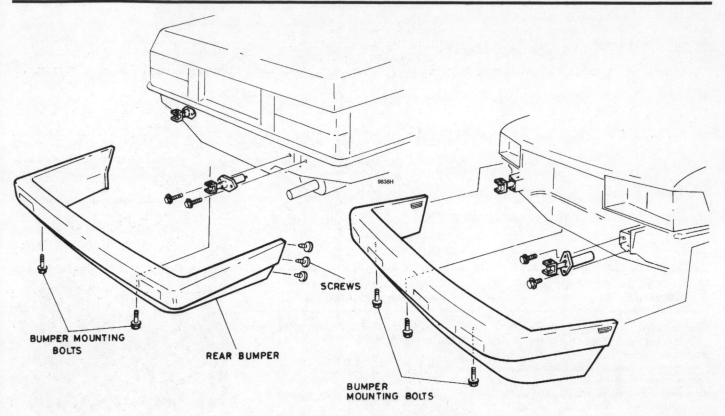

10.4b Typical rear bumper installation details

6   For access to the inner door, carefully peel back the plastic shield.

7   Prior to installation of the door panel, be sure to reinstall any clips in the panel which may have come out during the removal procedure and remain in the door itself.

8   Plug in the wire harness connectors and place the panel in position in the door. Press the door panel into place until the clips are seated and install the armrest/door pulls. Install the manual regulator crank handle (**see illustration**) or power window switch assembly.

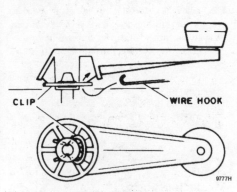

11.3 Insert a wire hook behind the manual window crank handle, remove the clip and pull the handle off

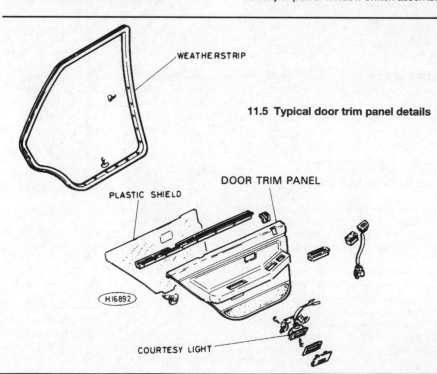

11.5 Typical door trim panel details

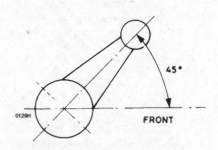

11.8 Install the crank handle so it's at a 45° angle with the window closed

11

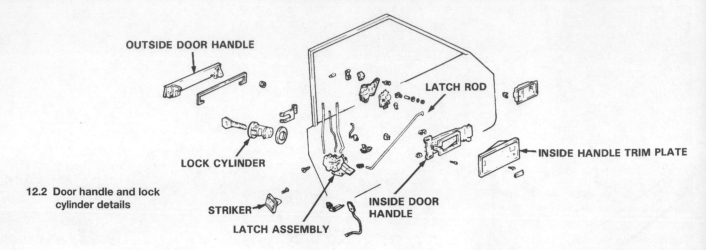

OUTSIDE DOOR HANDLE

LATCH ROD

INSIDE HANDLE TRIM PLATE

LOCK CYLINDER

STRIKER

INSIDE DOOR HANDLE

LATCH ASSEMBLY

12.2 Door handle and lock cylinder details

12   Door inside handle - removal and installation

Refer to illustration 12.2

1   Remove the door trim panel and plastic shield (see Section 11).
2   Remove the inside door handle retaining screws, disconnect the latch rod and rotate the handle out of the door **(see illustration)**.
3   Installation is the reverse of removal.

13   Door outside handle - removal and installation

1   Remove the door trim panel and plastic shield (see Section 11).
2   Disconnect the operating rods attached to the outside door handle.
3   Remove the door handle retaining nuts or bolts and detach the handle from the door **(see illustration 12.2)**.
4   Installation is the reverse of removal.

14   Door latch and lock cylinder - removal and installation

1   Remove the door trim panel and plastic shield (see Section 11).

Latch

Refer to illustration 14.4

2   Remove the inside door handle (see Section 12).
3   Disconnect the operating rods from the latch.
4   Remove the three latch retaining screws located in the end of the door **(see illustration)**.
5   Detach the latch assembly from the door.
6   Installation is the reverse of removal.

Lock cylinder

Refer to illustration 14.8

7   On 1986 and later models, remove the outside door handle (see Section 13).

14.4 Use a phillips screwdriver to remove the three latch retaining screws from the door jamb

8   Disconnect the operating rod, remove the retaining clip and withdraw the lock cylinder from the door **(see illustration)**.
9   Installation is the reverse of removal.

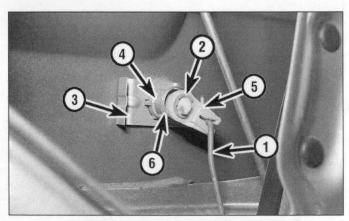

14.8 Door lock cylinder mounting details

1   *Operating rod*
2   *Lock arm-to-lock cylinder circlip*
3   *Lock cylinder-to-door retaining clip*
4   *Lock cylinder*
5   *Lock arm*
6   *Spring*

15.4a Detach the check strap by driving out the pin (arrow) with a hammer and punch, then, with an assistant supporting the door . . .

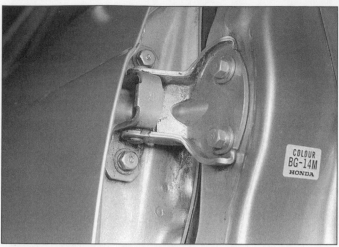

15.4b . . . remove the upper hinge bolts . . .

15.4c . . . and lower hinge bolts

15 Door - removal and installation

Refer to illustrations 15.4a, 15.4b and 15.4c

1   Remove the door trim panel (see Section 11). Disconnect any wire harness connectors and push them through the door opening so they won't interfere with door removal.

2   Place a jack or jackstand under the door or have an assistant on hand to support it when the hinge bolts are removed. **Note:** *If a jack or jackstand is used, place a rag between it and the door to protect the door's painted surfaces.*

3   Scribe around the door hinges.

4   Remove the check strap pin and hinge-to-door bolts, then carefully lift off the door **(see illustrations)**.

5   Installation is the reverse of removal.

6   Following installation of the door, check the alignment and adjust it if necessary as follows:

a) *Up-and-down and forward-and-back-ward adjustments are made by loosen-ing the hinge-to-body bolts and moving the door as necessary.*

b) *The door lock striker can also be adjusted both up-and-down and side-ways to provide positive engagement with the lock mechanism. This is done by loosening the mounting bolts and moving the striker as necessary.*

16 Door window glass - removal and installation

Refer to illustrations 16.4 and 16.5

1   Remove the door trim panel and plastic shield (see Section 11).

2   Remove the inside door handle (see Section 12).

3   Lower the window so the mounting bolts can be reached through the access hole in the door, then remove the bolts.

4   On rear doors, remove the retain-ing screws and bolts and detach the center channel and stationary glass **(see illustration)**.

5   Lift the door glass up and out of the door window slot, then tilt it and remove it from the door **(see illustration)**.

6   Installation is the reverse of removal.

17 Door window glass regulator assembly - removal, installation and adjustment

Refer to illustrations 17.4a and 17.4b

1   Remove the door trim panel and plastic shield (see Section 11).

2   Remove the inside door handle (see Section 12).

3   Remove the door window glass (see Section 16).

4   On two-door models, loosen the front stopper bolt. Remove the retaining bolts and withdraw the regulator mechanism through the access hole in the door **(see illustra-tions)**. On power window models, unplug the electrical connector.

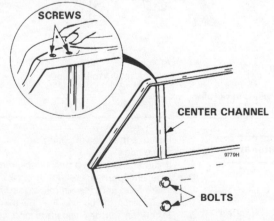

16.4 Remove the screws and bolts retaining the center channel and glass to the door

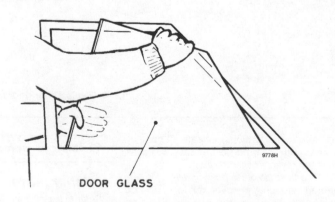

16.5 Lift the glass up out of the door while tilting it in

11

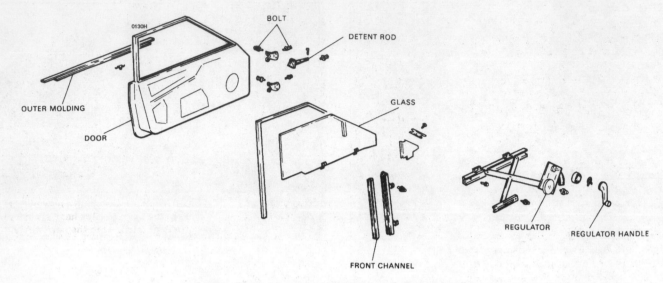

17.4a Typical front door regulator installation details

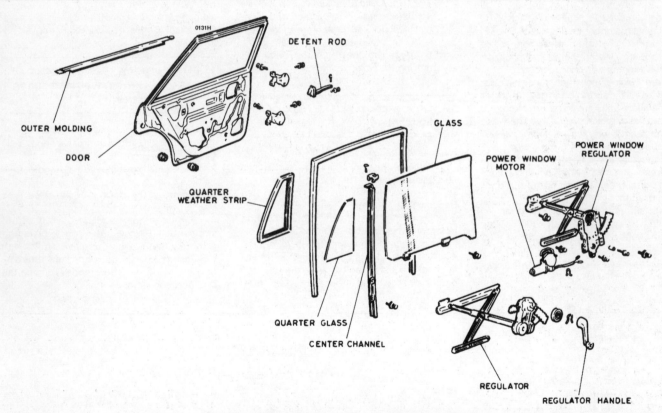

17.4b Typical rear door regulator installation details

5   Prior to installation, lubricate all contact surfaces with multi-purpose grease. Installation is the reverse of removal.

6   To adjust the glass position evenly in the opening, loosen the roller guide or motor mounting bolts. Raise the window as far as possible, making sure it's centered in its channel, then tighten the roller guide or motor mounting bolts securely.

18   Mirrors - removal and installation

Interior mirror

Refer to illustrations 18.2 and 18.4

1   Remove the rubber damper located between the mirror and windshield.

2   Pry off the mirror base cover with a screwdriver **(see illustration)**.

3   Remove the three retaining screws, then detach the mirror.

4   If you are installing a new mirror, remove the large phillips head retaining screw and detach the base from the old mirror **(see illustration)**. Transfer the base to the new mirror.

5   Place the mirror in position and install the screws. Snap the cover onto the mirror base and install the rubber damper securely between the mirror and the windshield.

Exterior mirror

Refer to illustration 18.6

6   Remove the screw, pull off the knob, then pry off the cover panel **(see illustration)**. On some later models it may be necessary to remove the door trim panel (see Section 11) for access.

7   Remove the three retaining screws and lift the mirror off. On models equipped with power mirrors, unplug the electrical connector.

8   Installation is the reverse of removal.

---

19 Trunk lid - removal, installation and adjustment

Refer to illustration 19.3

1   Open the trunk lid and cover the edges of the trunk compartment with pads or cloths to protect the painted surfaces when the lid is removed.

2   Disconnect any cables or wire harness connectors attached to the trunk lid that would interfere with removal.

3   Scribe or paint alignment marks around the hinge-to-trunk lid bolt heads **(see illustration)**.

4   While an assistant supports the trunk lid, remove the hinge-to-trunk lid bolts from both sides and lift off the trunk lid.

5   Installation is the reverse of removal. **Note:** *When reinstalling the trunk lid, align the hinge bolt flanges with the marks made during removal.*

6   After installation, close the lid and see if it's in proper alignment with the surrounding panels. Fore-and-aft and side-to-side adjustments of the lid are controlled by the position of the hinge bolts in the slots. To adjust it, loosen the hinge bolts, reposition the lid and retighten the bolts.

7   The height of the rear of the lid in relation to the surrounding body panels when closed can be adjusted by loosening the lock striker bolts, repositioning the striker and retightening the bolts. The height of the front of the lid can be adjusted by adding or removing adjusting shims (available from a dealer) between the hinges and the lid.

---

20 Liftgate - removal, installation and adjustment

Refer to illustration 20.5

1   Open the liftgate and cover the upper body area around the opening with pads or cloths to protect the painted surfaces when the liftgate is removed.

2   Disconnect all cables and wire harness connectors that would interfere with removal of the liftgate.

3   Paint or scribe around the hinge flanges.

4   While an assistant supports the liftgate, detach the support struts.

5   Remove the hinge nuts and detach the liftgate from the vehicle **(see illustration)**.

18.2 Use a screwdriver to pry off the mirror base cover

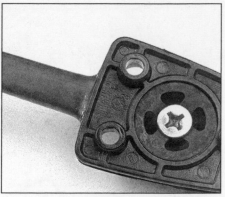

18.4 If you are installing a new mirror, remove the large phillips head screw and transfer the base to the new mirror

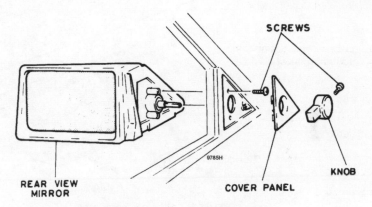

18.6 Exterior mirror mounting details

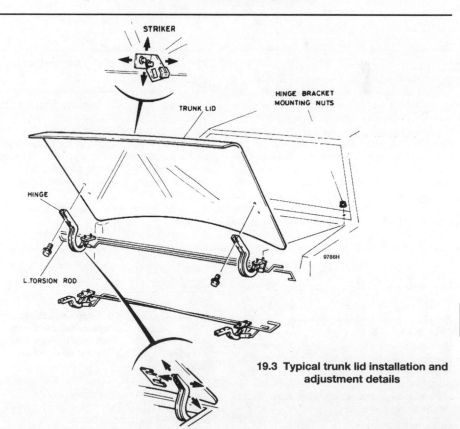

19.3 Typical trunk lid installation and adjustment details

11

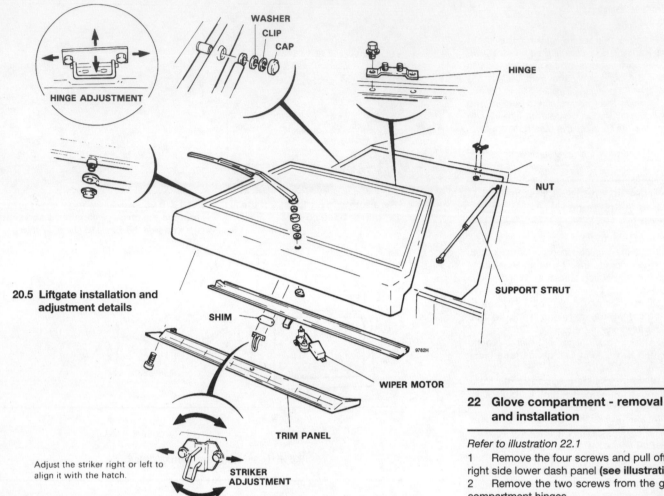

20.5 Liftgate installation and adjustment details

Adjust the striker right or left to align it with the hatch.

STRIKER ADJUSTMENT

TRIM PANEL

WIPER MOTOR

SHIM

WASHER

CLIP

CAP

HINGE

NUT

SUPPORT STRUT

HINGE ADJUSTMENT

---

6   Installation is the reverse of removal.

7   After installation, close the liftgate and make sure it's in proper alignment with the surrounding body panels. Adjustments are made by moving the position of the hinge studs in the slots. To adjust it, loosen the hinge nuts and reposition the hinges either side-to-side or fore and-aft the desired amount and retighten the nuts.

8   The engagement of the liftgate can be adjusted by loosening the lock striker bolts, repositioning the striker and retightening the bolts.

21   Center console - removal and installation

1   Disconnect the negative cable at the battery.

2   Remove the shift handle or knob.

3   Remove the retaining screws or bolts. Some screws are hidden under the cigar lighter, ashtray or under a center lid at the back of the console (which can be pried up for access).

4   Detach the console and lift it out of the vehicle.

5   Installation is the reverse of removal.

22   Glove compartment - removal and installation

Refer to illustration 22.1

1   Remove the four screws and pull off the right side lower dash panel **(see illustration)**.

2   Remove the two screws from the glove compartment hinges.

3   Working under the dashboard, remove the two horizontally-installed screws from the back upper edge of the glove compartment catch cloth.

4   Remove the vertically-installed screw from the front upper edge of the catch cloth.

5   Tilt the glove compartment to the right and pull it out.

6   Installation is the reverse of removal. Be sure to install the vertical catch cloth screw first, then the two horizontal catch cloth screws.

23   Seatbelt check

1   Check the seatbelts, buckles, latch plates and guide loops for obvious damage and signs of wear.

2   Check that the seatbelt reminder light comes on when the key is turned to the Run or Start positions. A chime should also sound.

3   The seatbelts are designed to lock up during a sudden stop or impact, yet allow free movement during normal driving. Check that the retractors return the belt against your chest while driving and rewind the belt completely when the buckle is unlatched.

4   If any of the above checks reveal problems with the seatbelts, replace parts as necessary.

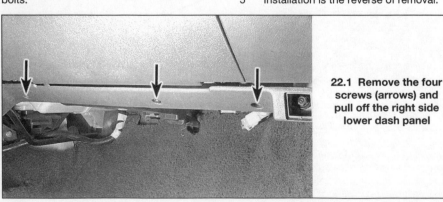

22.1 Remove the four screws (arrows) and pull off the right side lower dash panel

Chapter 12
Chassis electrical system

Contents

1 General information

The electrical system is a 12-volt, negative ground type. Power for the lights and all electrical accessories is supplied by a lead/acid-type battery which is charged by the alternator.

This Chapter covers repair and service procedures for the various electrical components not associated with the engine. Information on the battery, alternator, distributor and starter motor can be found in Chapter 5.

It should be noted that when portions of the electrical system are serviced, the negative battery cable should be disconnected from the battery to prevent electrical shorts and/or fires.

2 Electrical troubleshooting - general information

A typical electrical circuit consists of an electrical component, any switches, relays, motors, fuses, fusible links or circuit breakers related to that component and the wiring and connectors that link the component to both the battery and the chassis. To help you pinpoint an electrical circuit problem, wiring diagrams are included at the end of this book.

Before tackling any troublesome electrical circuit, first study the appropriate wiring diagrams to get a complete understanding of what makes up that individual circuit. Trouble spots, for instance, can often be narrowed down by noting if other components related

to the circuit are operating properly. If several components or circuits fail at one time, chances are the problem is in a fuse or ground connection, because several circuits are often routed through the same fuse and ground connections.

Electrical problems usually stem from simple causes, such as loose or corroded connections, a blown fuse, a melted fusible link or a bad relay. Visually inspect the condition of all fuses, wires and connections in a problem circuit before troubleshooting it.

If testing instruments are going to be utilized, use the diagrams to plan ahead of time where you will make the necessary connections in order to accurately pinpoint the trouble spot.

The basic tools needed for electrical

12

3.1a The dashboard fuse panel pulls down for access to the fuses

3.1b The engine compartment fuse block is located next to the battery, under a cover

troubleshooting include a circuit tester or voltmeter (a 12-volt bulb with a set of test leads can also be used), a continuity tester, which includes a bulb, battery and set of test leads, and a jumper wire, preferably with a circuit breaker incorporated, which can be used to bypass electrical components. Before attempting to locate a problem with test instruments, use the wiring diagram(s) to decide where to make the connections.

Voltage checks

Voltage checks should be performed if a circuit is not functioning properly. Connect one lead of a circuit tester to either the negative battery terminal or a known good ground. Connect the other lead to a connector in the circuit being tested, preferably nearest to the battery or fuse. If the bulb of the tester lights, voltage is present, which means that the part of the circuit between the connector and the battery is problem free. Continue checking the rest of the circuit in the same fashion. When you reach a point at which no voltage is present, the problem lies between that point and the last test point with voltage. Most of the time the problem can be traced to a loose connection. **Note:** *Keep in mind that some circuits receive voltage only when the ignition key is in the Accessory or Run position.*

Finding a short

One method of finding shorts in a circuit is to remove the fuse and connect a test light or voltmeter in its place to the fuse terminals. There should be no voltage present in the circuit. Move the wiring harness from side-to-side while watching the test light. If the bulb goes on, there is a short to ground somewhere in that area, probably where the insulation has rubbed through. The same test can be performed on each component in the circuit, even a switch.

Ground check

Perform a ground test to check whether a component is properly grounded. Disconnect the battery and connect one lead of a self-powered test light, known as a continuity tester, to a known good ground. Connect the other lead to the wire or ground connection being tested. If the bulb goes on, the ground is good. If the bulb does not go on, the ground is not good.

Continuity check

A continuity check is done to determine if there are any breaks in a circuit - if it is passing electricity properly. With the circuit off (no power in the circuit), a self-powered continuity tester can be used to check the circuit. Connect the test leads to both ends of the circuit (or to the "power" end and a good ground), and if the test light comes on the circuit is passing current properly. If the light doesn't come on, there is a break somewhere in the circuit. The same procedure can be used to test a switch, by connecting the continuity tester to the switch terminals. With the switch turned On, the test light should come on.

Finding an open circuit

When diagnosing for possible open circuits, it is often difficult to locate them by sight because oxidation or terminal misalignment are hidden by the connectors. Merely wiggling a connector on a sensor or in the wiring harness may correct the open circuit condition. Remember this when an open circuit is indicated when troubleshooting a circuit. Intermittent problems may also be caused by oxidized or loose connections.

Electrical troubleshooting is simple if you keep in mind that all electrical circuits are basically electricity running from the battery, through the wires, switches, relays, fuses and fusible links to each electrical component (light bulb, motor, etc.) and to ground, from which it is passed back to the battery. Any electrical problem is an interruption in the flow of electricity to and from the battery.

3   Fuses - general information

Refer to illustrations 3.1a, 3.1b and 3.3

The electrical circuits of the vehicle are protected by a combination of fuses, circuit breakers and fusible links. The two fuse blocks are located under the instrument panel on the left side of the dashboard and in the engine compartment **(see illustrations)**.

Each of the fuses is designed to protect a specific circuit, and the various circuits are identified on the fuse panel itself.

Miniaturized fuses are employed in the fuse block. These compact fuses, with blade terminal design, allow fingertip removal and replacement. If an electrical component fails, always check the fuse first. A blown fuse is easily identified through the clear plastic body. Visually inspect the element for evidence of damage **(see illustration)**. If a continuity check is called for, the blade terminal tips are exposed in the fuse body.

Be sure to replace blown fuses with the

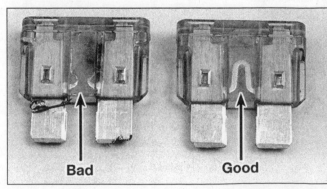

Bad   **Good**

3.3 To test for a blown fuse, pull it out and inspect it. Fuse on left is blown. Fuse on right is good

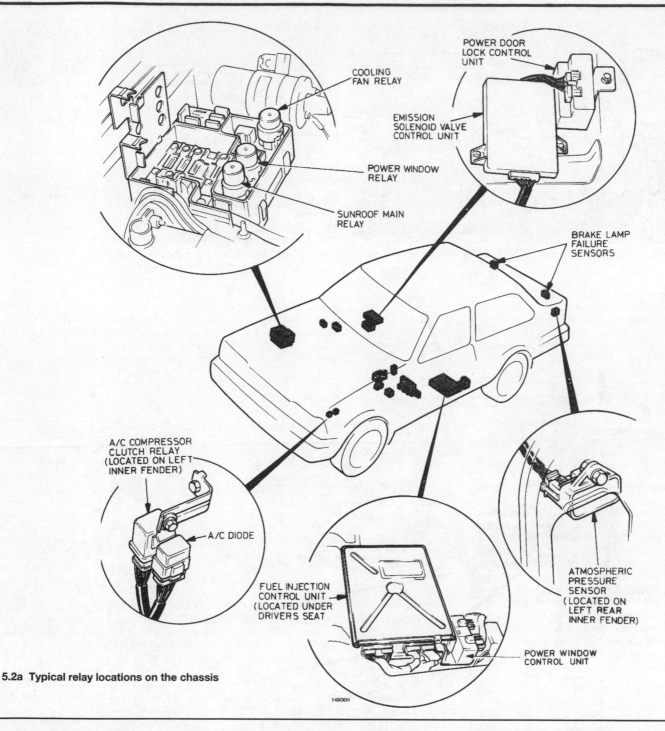

COOLING FAN RELAY

POWER WINDOW RELAY

SUNROOF MAIN RELAY

POWER DOOR LOCK CONTROL UNIT

EMISSION SOLENOID VALVE CONTROL UNIT

BRAKE LAMP FAILURE SENSORS

A/C COMPRESSOR CLUTCH RELAY (LOCATED ON LEFT INNER FENDER)

A/C DIODE

FUEL INJECTION CONTROL UNIT (LOCATED UNDER DRIVERS SEAT)

ATMOSPHERIC PRESSURE SENSOR (LOCATED ON LEFT REAR INNER FENDER)

POWER WINDOW CONTROL UNIT

5.2a Typical relay locations on the chassis

14906H

correct type. Fuses of different ratings are physically interchangeable, but only fuses of the proper rating should be used. Replacing a fuse with one of a higher or lower value than specified is not recommended. Each electrical circuit needs a specific amount of protection. The amperage value of each fuse is molded into the fuse body.

If the replacement fuse immediately fails, don't replace it again until the cause of the problem is isolated and corrected. In most cases, the cause will be a short circuit in the wiring caused by a broken or deteriorated wire.

4 Circuit breakers - general information

Circuit breakers protect components such as power windows, power door locks and headlights.

On some models the circuit breaker resets itself automatically, so an electrical overload in a circuit breaker protected system will cause the circuit to fail momentarily, then come back on. If the circuit does not come back on, check it immediately. Once the condition is corrected, the circuit breaker

will resume its normal function. Some circuit breakers must be reset manually.

5 Relays - general information

Refer to illustrations 5.2a and 5.2b

Several electrical accessories in the vehicle use relays to transmit the electrical signal to the component. If the relay is defective, that component will not operate properly.

The various relays are grouped together in several locations **(see illustrations)**.

12

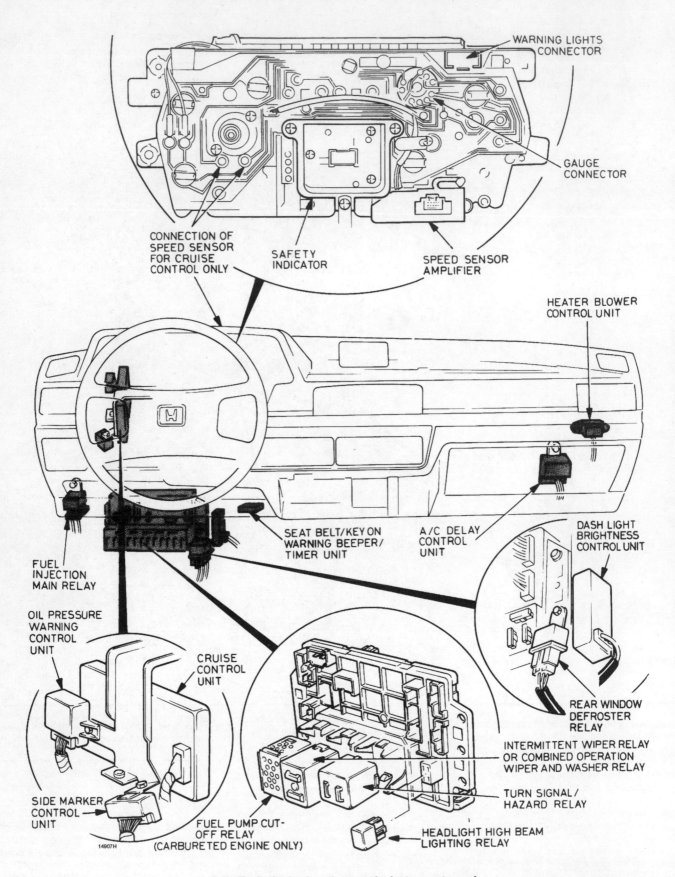

WARNING LIGHTS
CONNECTOR

GAUGE
CONNECTOR

CONNECTION OF
SPEED SENSOR
FOR CRUISE
CONTROL ONLY

SAFETY
INDICATOR

SPEED SENSOR
AMPLIFIER

HEATER BLOWER
CONTROL UNIT

FUEL
INJECTION
MAIN RELAY

SEAT BELT/KEY ON
WARNING BEEPER/
TIMER UNIT

A/C DELAY
CONTROL
UNIT

DASH LIGHT
BRIGHTNESS
CONTROL UNIT

OIL PRESSURE
WARNING
CONTROL
UNIT

CRUISE
CONTROL
UNIT

SIDE MARKER
CONTROL
UNIT

FUEL PUMP CUT-
OFF RELAY
(CARBURETED ENGINE ONLY)

REAR WINDOW
DEFROSTER
RELAY

INTERMITTENT WIPER RELAY
OR COMBINED OPERATION
WIPER AND WASHER RELAY

TURN SIGNAL/
HAZARD RELAY

HEADLIGHT HIGH BEAM
LIGHTING RELAY

14907H

5.2b Typical relay locations on the instrument panel

If a faulty relay is suspected, it can be removed and tested by a dealer service department or a repair shop. Defective relays must be replaced as a unit.

6 Steering wheel and column switches - removal and installation

Refer to illustration 6.6

1 Disconnect the negative cable from the battery.

Cruise control switches

2 Remove the retaining screws located on the back side of the steering wheel and lift off the horn cover (see Chapter 10).
3 Unplug the electrical connector, remove the retaining screws and lift off the switch(es).
4 Installation is the reverse of removal.

Combination switch

5 Remove the steering wheel (see Chapter 10).
6 Remove the steering column upper and lower covers **(see illustration)**.
7 Remove the retaining screws and lift the switch off.
8 Disconnect the switch electrical connector from the wiring harness and remove the combination switch from the vehicle.
9 Installation is the reverse of removal.

7 Ignition switch - removal and installation

1 Disconnect the negative cable from the battery.
2 Remove the steering column covers **(see illustration 6.6)**.
3 Make sure the switch is in the Lock position.
4 Unplug the switch electrical connector.

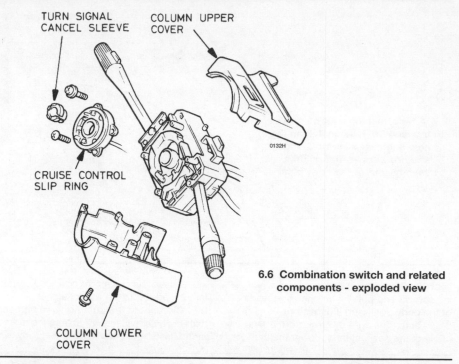

6.6 Combination switch and related components - exploded view

5 Remove the two retaining screws and lift the switch from the steering column.
6 Installation is the reverse of removal. When placing the switch in position, make sure the recess on the switch is aligned with the projection on the lock.

8 Radio and antenna - removal and installation

Refer to illustrations 8.3, 8.6 and 8.7

1 Disconnect the negative cable from the battery.

Radio

2 On 1986 and later models, remove the ashtray and ashtray holder.

3 On 1984 and 1985 models, remove the radio and mounting plate screws, lower the radio, unplug the electrical connector and antenna lead, then push the radio out of the dashboard **(see illustration)**.
4 On 1986 and later models, remove the mounting screws, lower the radio, unplug the electrical connector and antenna lead, then pull the radio out of the dashboard.
5 Installation is the reverse of removal.

Antenna

6 On manual antenna models, disconnect the antenna lead at the radio (see above). On power antenna models, extend the antenna and disconnect the cable from the antenna motor **(see illustration)**.
7 Connect a piece of string or thin wire to the antenna lead (at the radio end) or the

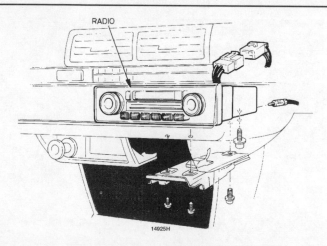

8.3 On 1984 and 1985 models, remove the screws, lower the radio mounting plate and radio, then disconnect the antenna lead and electrical connector

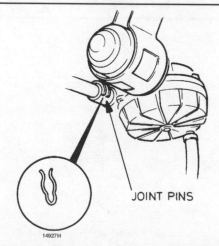

8.6 Use needle-nose pliers to pull off the joint pins, then disconnect the cable from the antenna motor

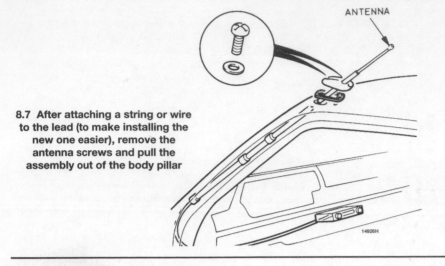

8.7 After attaching a string or wire to the lead (to make installing the new one easier), remove the antenna screws and pull the assembly out of the body pillar

9 Headlights - removal and installation

Refer to illustrations 9.4a and 9.4b

1   On retractable headlight models, raise the headlights.

2   Disconnect the negative cable from the battery.

3   Remove the retaining screws and detach the headlight bezel.

4   Remove the headlight retainer screws, taking care not to disturb the adjusting screws **(see the accompanying illustrations and illustration 10.1a or 10.1b)**.

5   Remove the retainer and pull the headlight out enough to allow the connector to be unplugged.

6   Remove the headlight.

7   To install the headlight, plug the connector in, place the headlight in position and install the retainer and screws. Tighten the screws securely.

8   Place the headlight bezel in position and install the retaining screws.

cable (at the motor end). Remove the mounting screws and pull the antenna and lead out of the body pillar **(see illustration)**.

8   Fasten the wire or string to the lead or cable of the new antenna. Lower the antenna into place while pulling the new lead or cable into the pillar with the wire or string.

9   Disconnect the string or wire and connect the antenna lead or cable to the radio or motor. Install the antenna retaining screws.

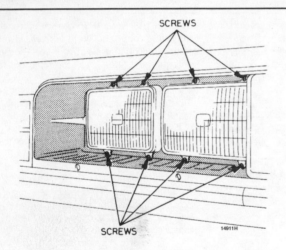

9.4a Locations of the headlight retainer screws (fixed headlight models)

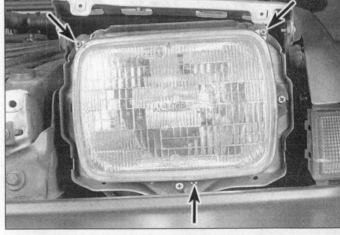

9.4b Locations of the headlight retainer screws (retractable headlight models)

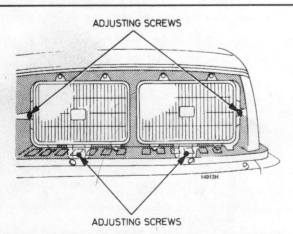

10.1a Fixed headlight adjusting screw locations - vertical adjustment is made on the bottom screws, horizontal on the side screws

10.1b Retractable headlight adjusting screw locations - (A) horizontal adjusting screw; (B) vertical adjusting screw

10 Headlights - adjustment

Refer to illustrations 10.1a, 10.1b and 10.2
Note: *The headlights must be aimed correctly. If adjusted incorrectly they could blind the driver of an oncoming vehicle and cause a serious accident or seriously reduce your ability to see the road. The headlights should be checked for proper aim every 12 months and any time a new headlight is installed or front end body work is performed. It should be emphasized that the following procedure is only an interim step which will provide temporary adjustment until the headlights can be adjusted by a properly equipped shop.*

1   Headlights have two spring-loaded adjusting screws, one on the bottom controlling up-and-down movement and one on the side controlling left-and-right movement **(see illustrations)**.

2   There are several methods of adjusting the headlights. The simplest method requires a blank wall 25 feet in front of the vehicle and a level floor **(see illustration)**.

3   Position masking tape vertically on the wall in reference to the vehicle centerline and the centerlines of both headlights.

4   Position a horizontal tape line in reference to the centerline of all the headlights. **Note:** *It may be easier to position the tape on the wall with the vehicle parked only a few inches away.*

5   Adjustment should be made with the vehicle sitting level, the gas tank half-full and no unusually heavy load in the vehicle.

6   Starting with the low beam adjustment, position the high intensity zone so it is two inches below the horizontal line and two inches to the right of the headlight vertical line. Adjustment is made by turning the bottom adjusting screw counterclockwise to raise the beam and clockwise to lower the beam. The adjusting screw on the side should be used in the same manner to move the beam left or right.

7   With the high beams on, the high intensity zone should be vertically centered with the exact center just below the horizontal line. **Note:** *It may not be possible to position the headlight aim exactly for both high and low beams. If a compromise must be made, keep in mind that the low beams are the most used and have the greatest effect on driver safety.*

8   Have the headlights adjusted by a dealer service department or service station at the earliest opportunity.

11 Bulb replacement

Refer to illustrations 11.2, 11.3a, 11.3b, 11.3c and 11.4

1   The lenses of many lights are held in place by screws, which makes it a simple procedure to gain access to the bulbs.

2   On some lights the lenses are held in place by clips. The lenses can be removed either by unsnapping them or by using a small screwdriver to pry them off **(see illustration)**.

3   Several types of bulbs are used. Some are removed by pushing in and turning them counterclockwise **(see illustrations)**. Others can simply be unclipped from the terminals or pulled straight out of the socket **(see illustration)**.

4   To gain access to the instrument panel lights **(see illustration)**, the instrument cluster will have to be removed first (see Section 13).

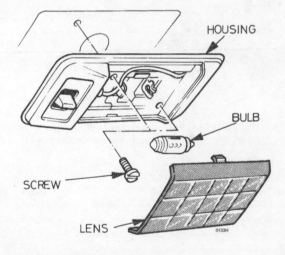

11.2 Pry off the interior light lens for access to the bulb

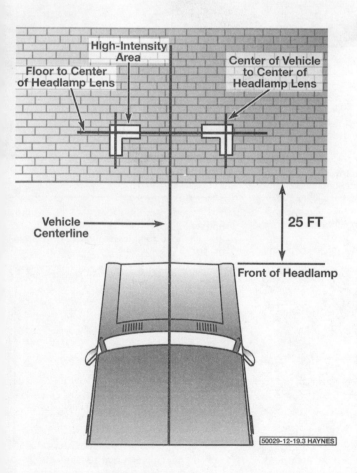

10.2 Headlight adjustment details

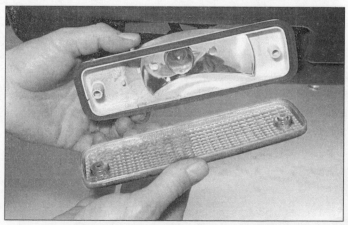

11.3a The front turn signal bulb is accessible after removing the lens

12

11.3b Remove the cover inside the vehicle for access to the tail light bulbs

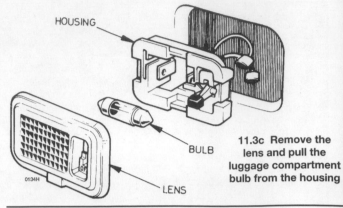

11.3c Remove the lens and pull the luggage compartment bulb from the housing

11.4 After removing the instrument cluster, flip it over and replace the bulbs by rotating them and pulling them out

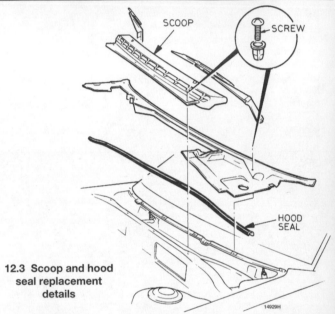

12.3 Scoop and hood seal replacement details

12 Windshield wiper motor - removal and installation

Refer to illustrations 12.3, 12.4 and 12.5

1   Disconnect the negative cable from the battery.
2   Remove the retaining nuts and detach the wiper arms.
3   Remove the scoop and hood seal from the cowl **(see illustration)**.

4   Detach the wiper linkage balljoint from the motor arm **(see illustration)**.
5   Unplug the electrical connector, remove the retaining bolts and lift the wiper motor from the engine compartment **(see illustration)**.
6   Prior to installation, lubricate the contact points of the wiper linkage with multi-purpose grease. Installation is the reverse of removal.

13 Instrument cluster - removal and installation

1   Disconnect the negative cable from the battery.
2   Remove the steering wheel (see Chapter 10).

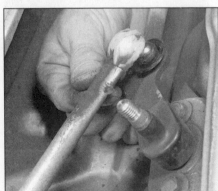

12.4 Pull up sharply on the wiper linkage to detach the balljoint

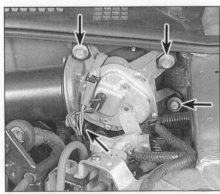

12.5 After unplugging the electrical connector, remove the retaining bolts (arrows) and separate the wiper motor from the firewall (one bolt is not visible in this photo)

13.4a On 1984 and 1985 models, remove the three bezel retaining screws from the top . . .

13.4b . . . and the two from the bottom

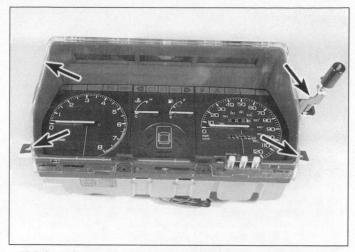

13.5 Locations of the cluster retaining screws - 1984 and 1985 models (cluster shown removed for clarity)

13.6 To disconnect the speedometer cable, press in on the clips (arrows)

13.8 To remove an instrument cluster switch on a 1986 or later model, insert a screwdriver at the bottom of the switch, between the switch and the cluster, then push gently down on the screwdriver and pull the switch out

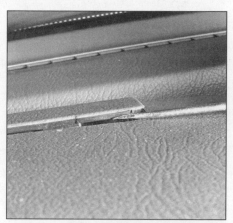

13.9 For access to the instrument cluster upper retaining screws, pry off the lid at the top of the cluster housing

3   Remove the steering column upper and lower covers **(see illustration 6.6)**.

1984 and 1985

Refer to illustrations 13.4a, 13.4b, 13.5 and 13.6

4   Remove the bezel retaining screws **(see illustrations)**.
5   Insert a screwdriver between the cluster and bezel and pry the bezel off. Wrap the tip of the screwdriver with tape to avoid scratching the cluster lens. Remove the cluster retaining screws **(see illustration)**.
6   Pull the cluster out, unplug the wiring connectors and disconnect the speedometer cable from the instrument cluster **(see illustration)**.
7   Installation is the reverse of removal.

1986 on

Refer to illustrations 13.8 and 13.9

8   Remove the instrument cluster switches by prying up at the bottom of each with a screwdriver **(see illustration)**. Pull the switches out and unplug the electrical connectors.

9   Pry out the lid at the top rear of the cluster housing with a screwdriver **(see illustration)**, then remove the two retaining screws located under the lid.
10   Remove the four retaining screws at the base of the cluster, accessible through the switch openings.
11   Pull the cluster out and unplug the wiring harness connector. Disconnect the speedometer cable **(see illustration 13.6)** to free the cluster.
12   Installation is the reverse of removal.

14   Instrument panel - removal and installation

Refer to illustrations 14.3, 14.5 and 14.8

1   Disconnect the negative cable from the battery.
2   Remove the steering wheel (see Chapter 10) and the steering column upper and lower covers **(see illustration 6.6)**.

14.3 To lower the steering column, remove the steering column mounting bracket bolts (arrows)

1984 and 1985

3   Remove the steering column mounting bracket bolts and lower the steering column **(see illustration)**.
4   Remove the instrument cluster (see Section 13).

12

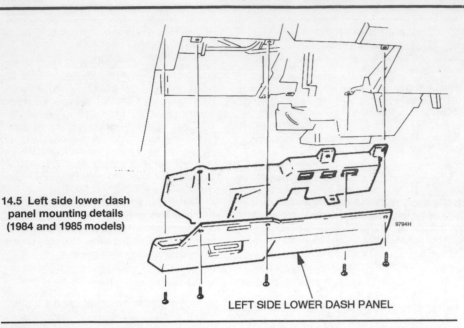

14.5 Left side lower dash panel mounting details (1984 and 1985 models)

LEFT SIDE LOWER DASH PANEL

any electrical connectors. Pull the instrument panel straight back while supporting it so it doesn't drop when it comes off the guide pin.

19   Installation is the reverse of removal.

15   Power door lock system - description and check

The power door lock system operates the door lock actuators mounted in each door. The system consists of the switches, actuators and associated wiring. Since special tools and techniques are required to diagnose the system, it should be left to a dealer service department or a repair shop. However, it is possible for the home mechanic to make simple checks of the wiring connections and actuators for minor faults which can be easily repaired. These include:

a) *Check the system fuse and/or circuit breaker.*

b) *Check the switch wires for damage and loose connections. Check the switches for continuity.*

c) *Remove the door panel(s) and check the actuator wiring connections to see if they're loose or damaged. Inspect the actuator rods (if equipped) to make sure they aren't bent or damaged. Inspect the actuator wiring for damaged or loose connections. The actuator can be checked by applying battery power momentarily. A discernible click indicates that the solenoid is operating properly.*

5   Remove the left side lower dash panel and the fuse box cover **(see illustration)**.

6   Remove the air conditioner and heater control assembly (see Chapter 3).

7   Remove the center access panel, clock and ashtray assembly.

8   Remove the retaining bolts, nuts and screws and unplug any electrical connectors. Support the instrument panel, pull it off the guide pin and remove it from the vehicle **(see illustration)**.

9   Installation is the reverse of removal.

1986 on

10   Remove instrument cluster (see Section 13).

11   Remove the dashboard lower panel and ashtray assembly.

12   Remove the combination switch (see Section 6).

13   Unplug the wiring harnesses.

14   Remove the hood release handle, but do not disconnect the control cable.

15   Remove the air conditioner and heater control assembly (see Chapter 3).

16   Remove the coin box, radio (see Section 8), cigarette lighter and any other components which would interfere with removal.

17   Disconnect the radio antenna cable (vehicles equipped with power antennas) (see Section 8).

18   Remove the retaining bolts and unplug

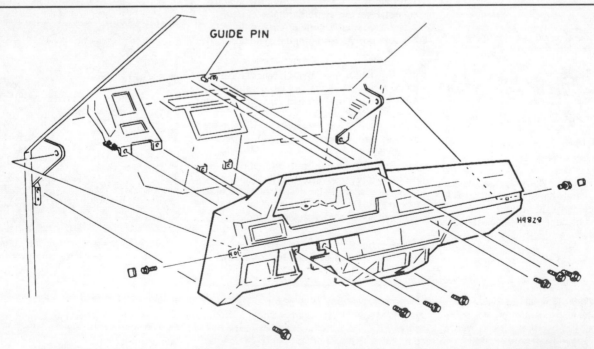

GUIDE PIN

14.8 After removing the bolts, support the instrument panel and pull it off the guide pin (1984 and 1985 models)

16 Power window system - description and check

The power window system operates the electric motors mounted in the doors which lower and raise the windows. The system consists of the control switches, the motors (regulators), glass mechanisms and associated wiring.

Because of the complexity of the power window system and the special tools and techniques required for diagnosis, repair should be left to a dealer service department or a repair shop. However, it is possible for the home mechanic to make simple checks of the wiring connections and motors for minor faults which can be easily repaired. These include:

a) *Inspect the power window actuating switches for broken wires and loose connections.*

b) *Check the power window fuse and/or circuit breaker.*

c) *Remove the door panel(s) and check the power window motor wires to see if they're loose or damaged. Inspect the glass mechanisms for damage which could cause binding.*

17 Cruise control system - description and check

The cruise control system maintains vehicle speed with a vacuum actuated servo motor located in the engine compartment, which is connected to the throttle linkage by a cable. The system consists of the servo motor, clutch switch, brake switch, control switches, a relay and associated vacuum hoses.

Because of the complexity of the cruise control system and the special tools and techniques required for diagnosis, repair should be left to a dealer service department or a repair shop. However, it is possible for the home mechanic to make simple checks of the wiring and vacuum connections for minor faults which can be easily repaired. These include:

a) *Inspect the cruise control actuating switches for broken wires and loose connections.*

b) *Check the cruise control fuse.*

c) *The cruise control system is operated by vacuum so it's critical that all vacuum switches, hoses and connections are secure. Check the hoses in the engine compartment for tight connections, cracks and obvious vacuum leaks.*

18 Wiring diagrams - general information

Since it isn't possible to include all wiring diagrams for every year covered by this manual, the following diagrams are those that are typical and most commonly needed.

Prior to troubleshooting any circuits, check the fuse and circuit breakers (if equipped) to make sure they're in good condition. Make sure the battery is properly charged and check the cable connections (Chapter 1).

When checking a circuit, make sure that all connectors are clean, with no broken or loose terminals. When unplugging a connector, do not pull on the wires. Pull only on the connector housings themselves.

Refer to the accompanying table for the wire color codes applicable to your vehicle.

Bl	**Black**
Y	**Yellow**
Bu	**Blue**
G	**Green**
R	**Red**
W	**White**
Br	**Brown**
0	**Orange**
Lb	**Light blue**
Lg	**Light green**
P	**Pink**
Gr	**Grey**

Wiring diagram color codes

12

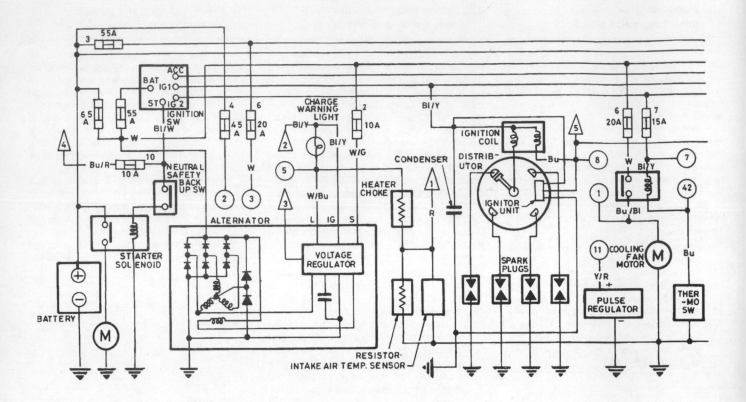

Typical engine compartment wiring diagram (carbureted vehicles) (US models)

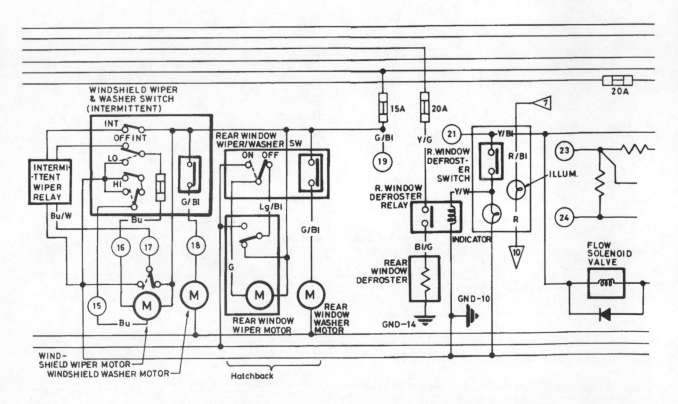

Typical instrument panel wiring diagram (carbureted vehicles) (US models) (1 of 6)

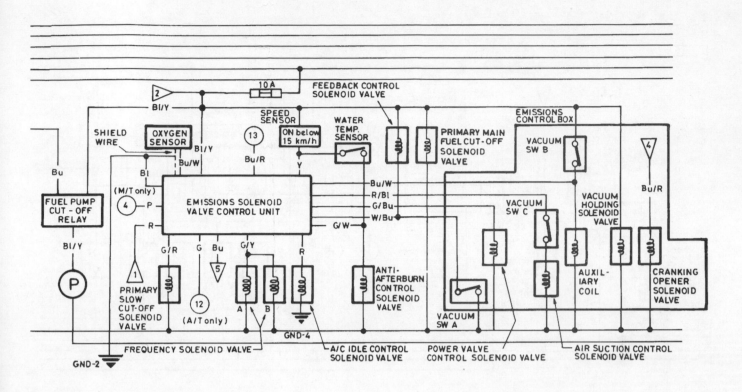

Typical engine compartment wiring diagram (carbureted vehicles) (US models) (continued))

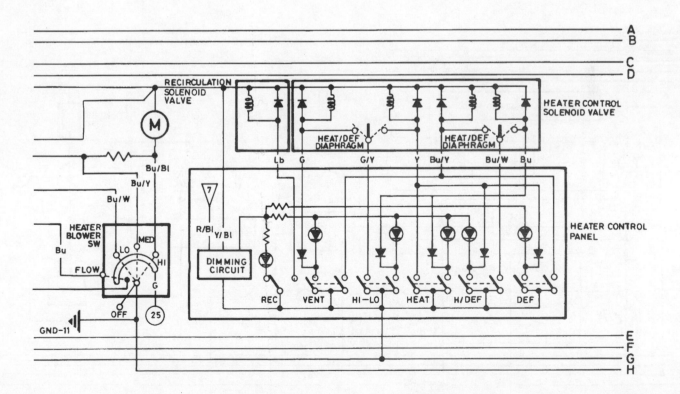

Typical instrument panel wiring diagram (carbureted vehicles) (US models) (2 of 6)

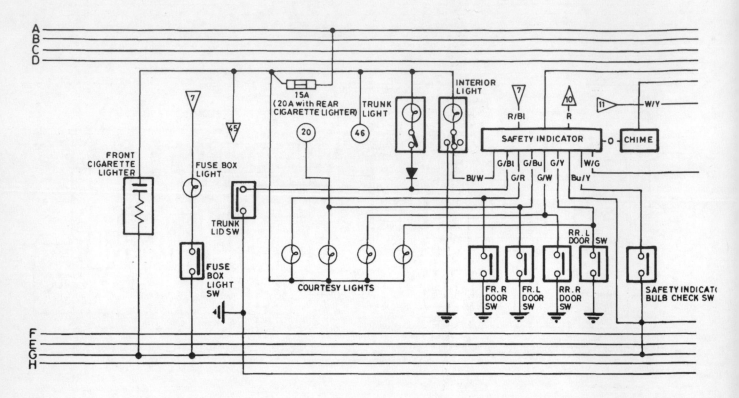

Typical instrument panel wiring diagram (carbureted vehicles) (US models) (3 of 6)

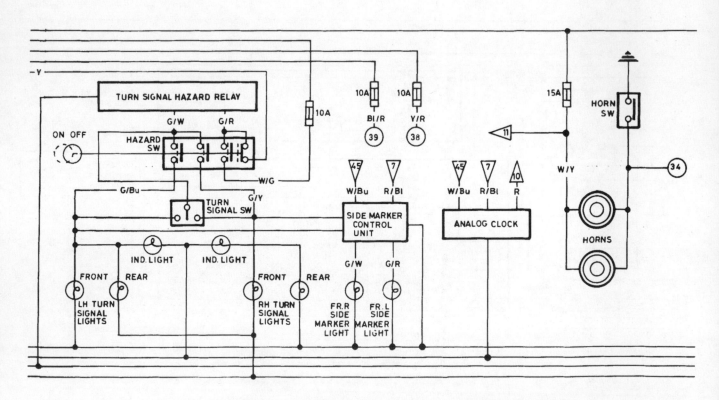

Typical instrument panel wiring diagram (carbureted vehicles) (US models) (5 of 6)

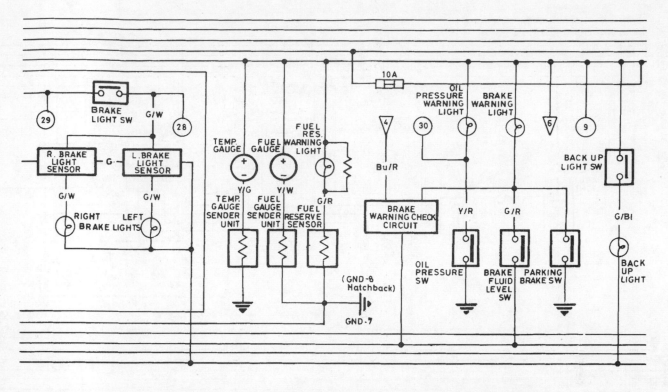

Typical instrument panel wiring diagram (carbureted vehicles) (US models) (4 of 6)

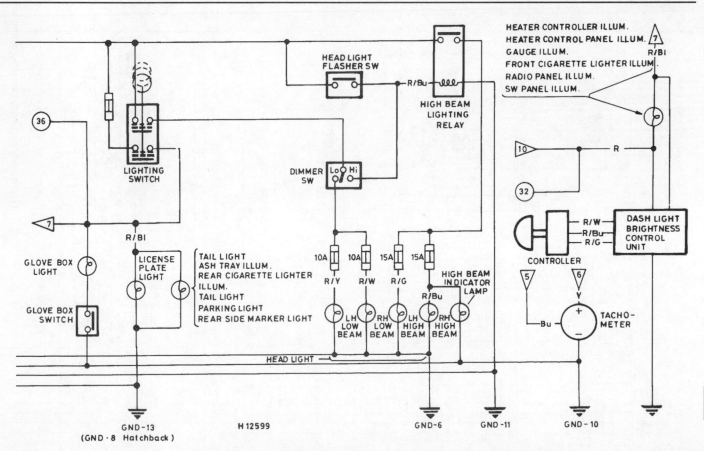

Typical instrument panel wiring diagram (carbureted vehicles) (US models) (6 of 6)

12

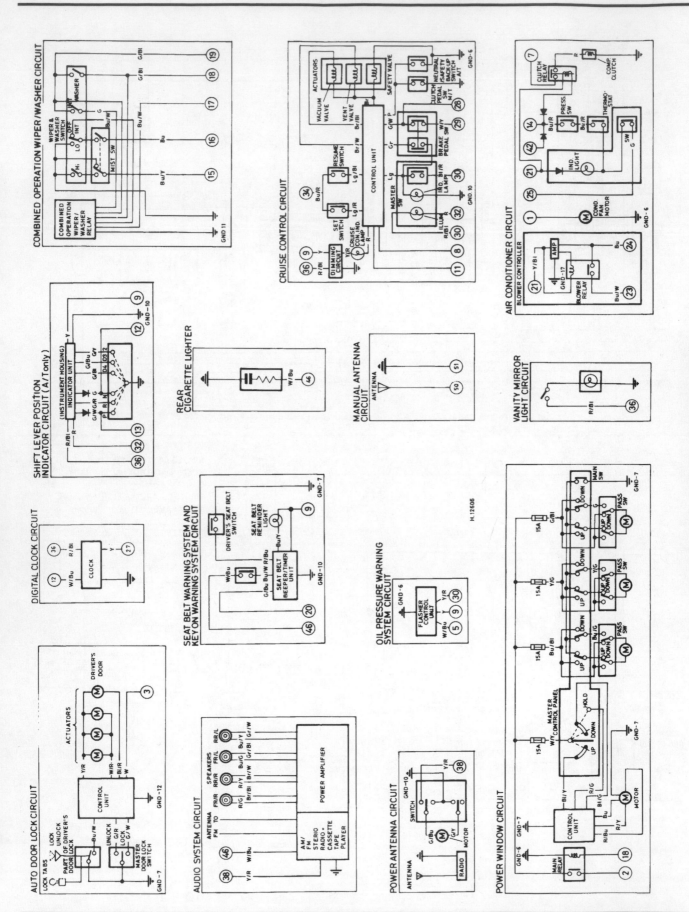

Typical sub-system wiring diagrams (carbureted vehicles) (US models)

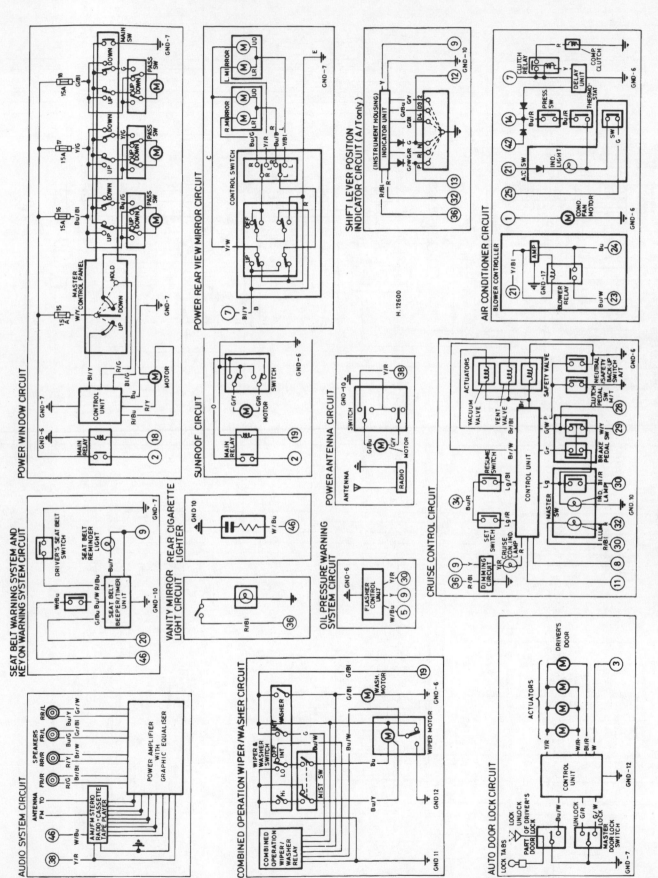

Typical sub-system wiring diagrams (fuel injected vehicles) (US models)

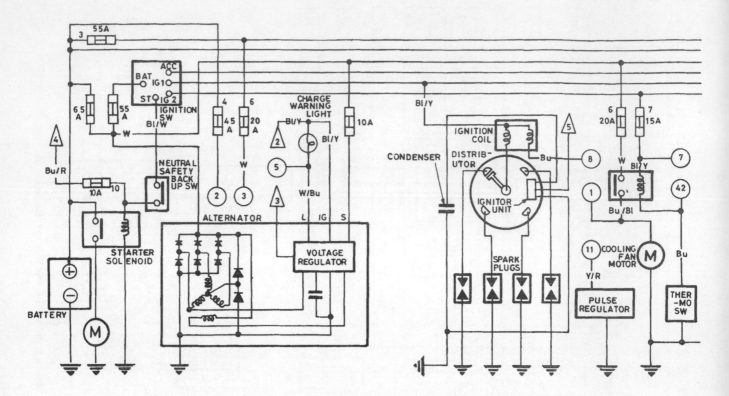

Typical engine compartment wiring diagram (fuel injected vehicles) (US models) (1 of 3)

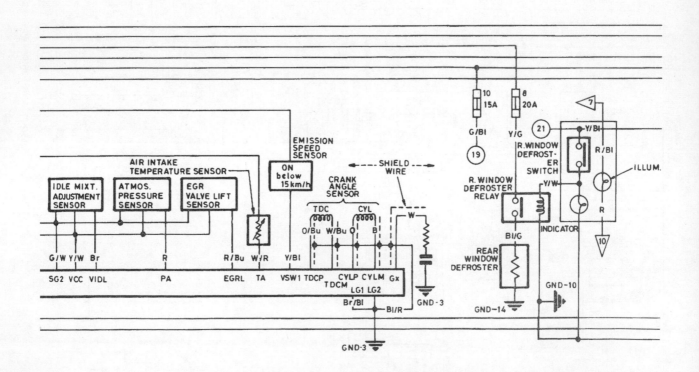

Typical engine compartment wiring diagram (fuel injected vehicles) (US models) (3 of 3)

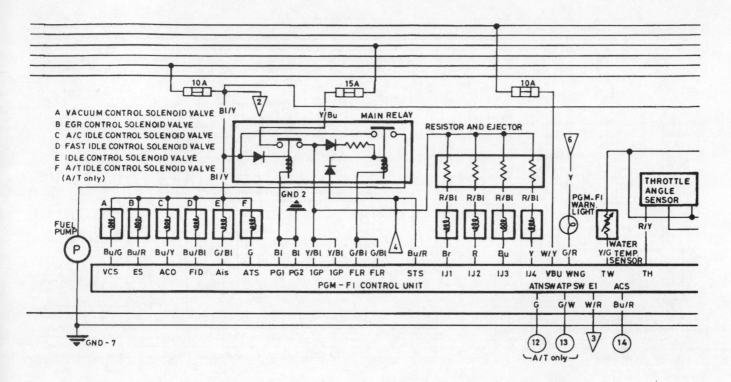

Typical engine compartment wiring diagram (fuel injected vehicles) (US models) (2 of 3)

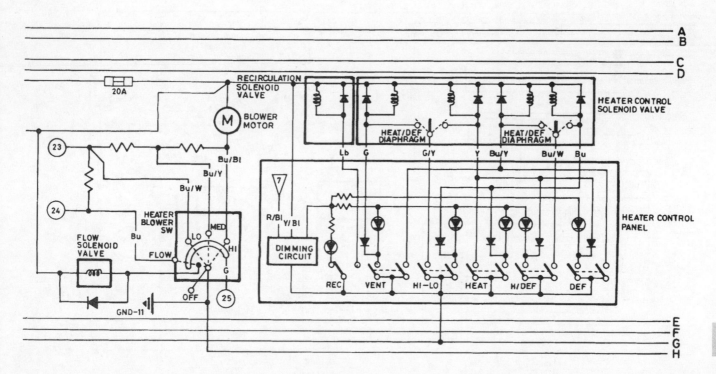

Typical instrument panel wiring diagram (fuel injected vehicles) (US models) (1 of 5)

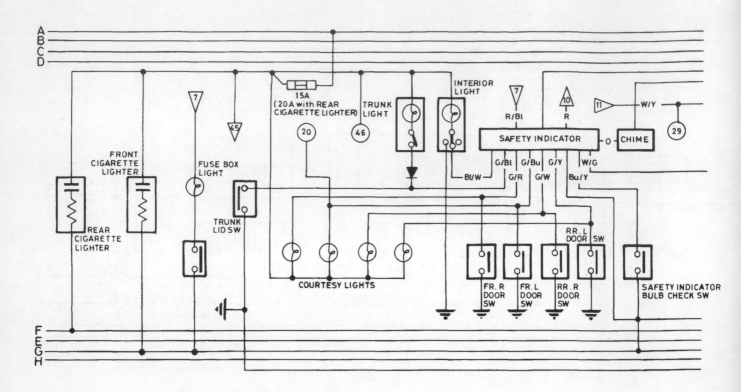

Typical instrument panel wiring diagram (fuel injected vehicles) (US models) (2 of 5)

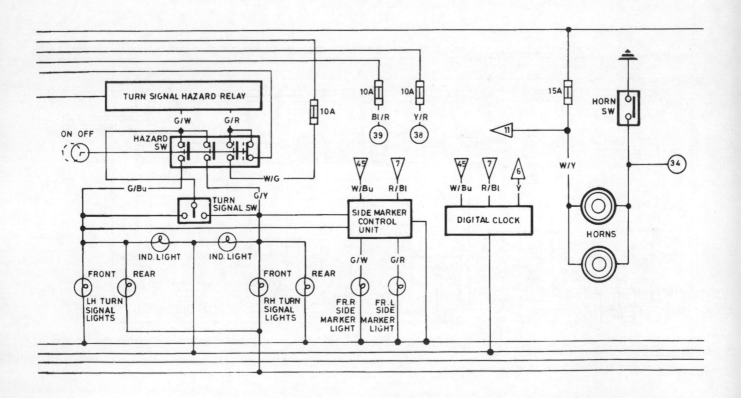

Typical instrument panel wiring diagram (fuel injected vehicles) (US models) (4 of 5)

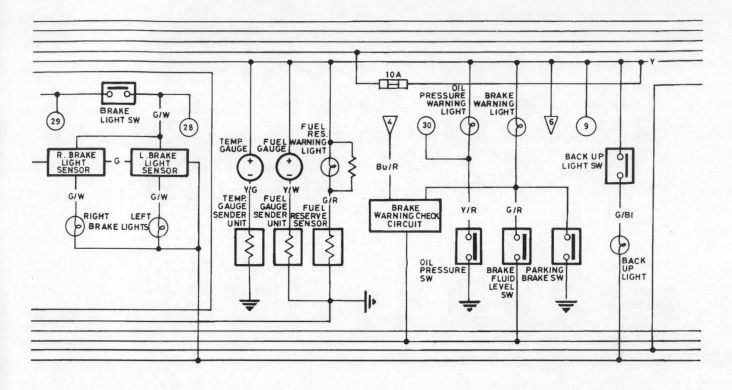

Typical instrument panel wiring diagram (fuel injected vehicles) (US models) (3 of 5)

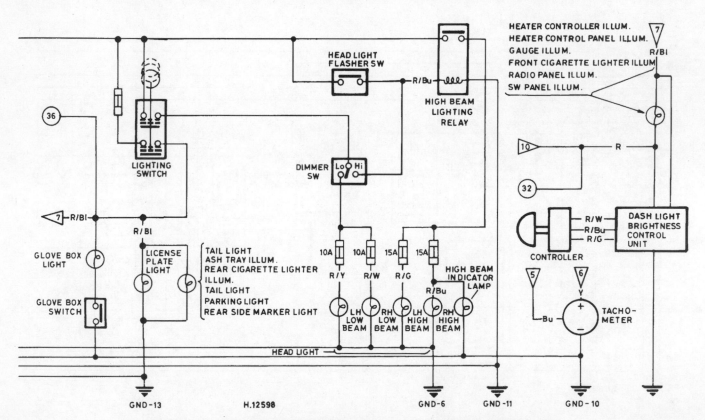

Typical sub-system wiring diagrams (fuel injected vehicles) (US models) (5 of 5)

12

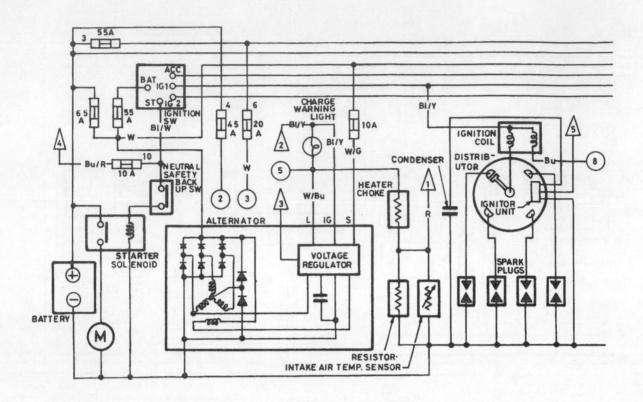

Typical engine compartment wiring diagram (Canadian models)

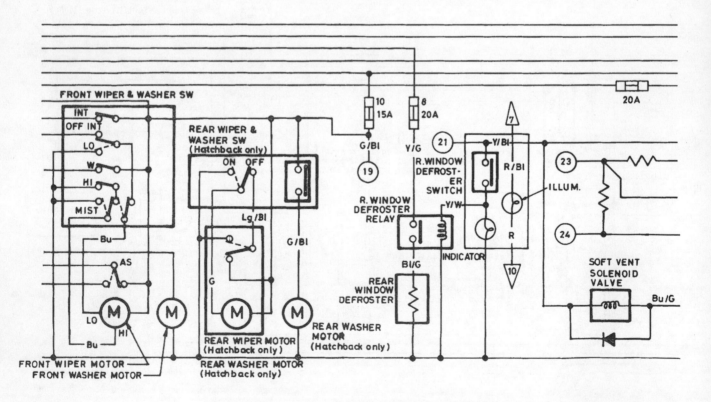

Typical instrument wiring diagram (Canadian models) (1 of 6)

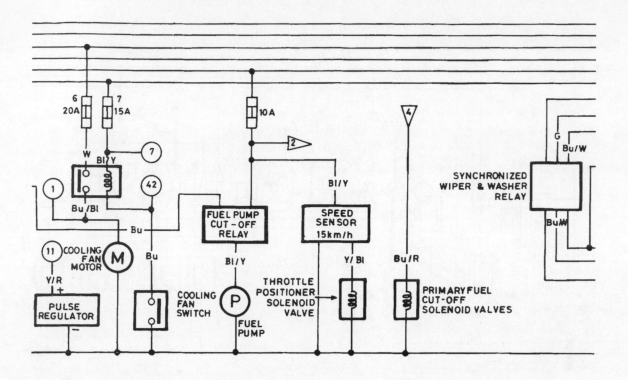

Typical engine compartment wiring diagram (Canadian models) (continued)

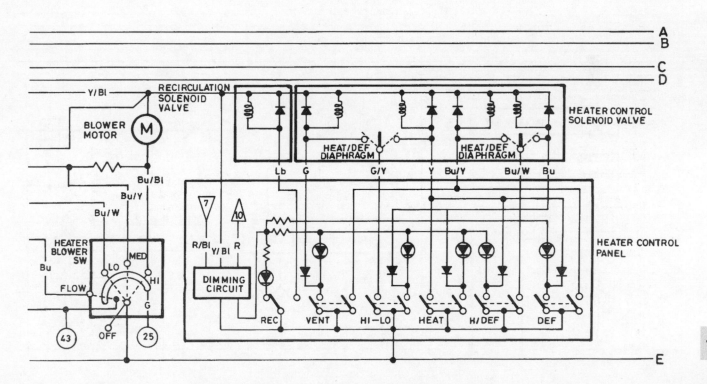

Typical instrument panel wiring diagram (Canadian models) (2 of 6)

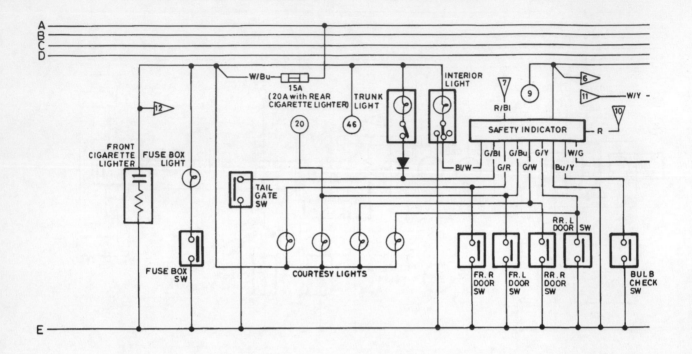

Typical instrument panel wiring diagram (Canadian models) (3 of 6)

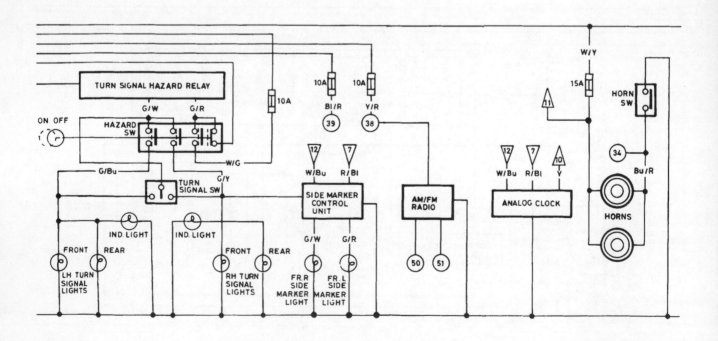

Typical instrument panel wiring diagram (Canadian models) (5 of 6)

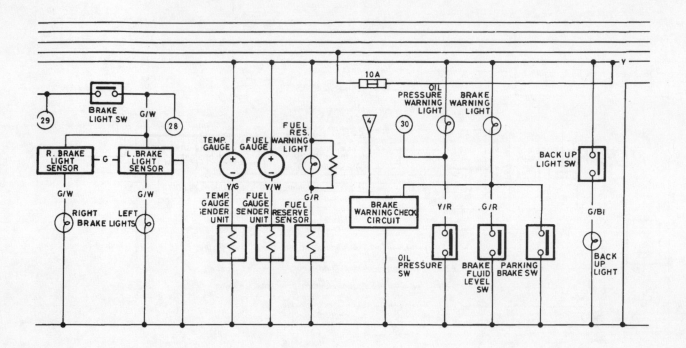

Typical instrument panel wiring diagram (Canadian models) (4 of 6)

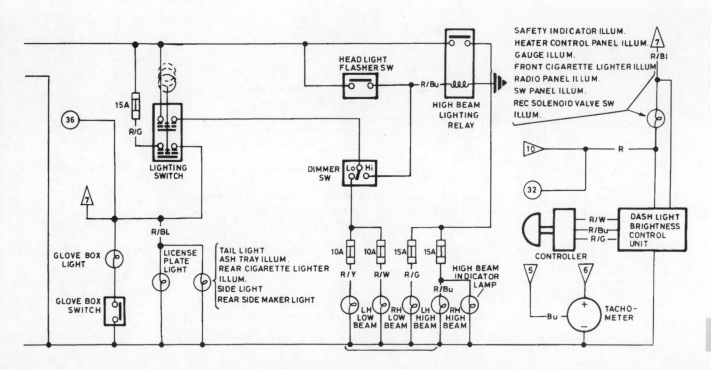

Typical instrument panel wiring diagram (Canadian models) (6 of 6)

12

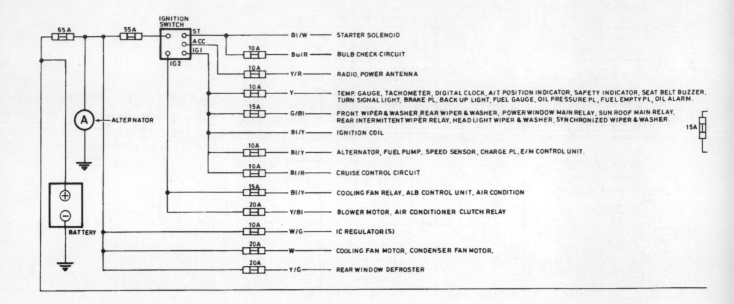

Typical instrument panel fuse circuit wiring diagram (Canadian models)

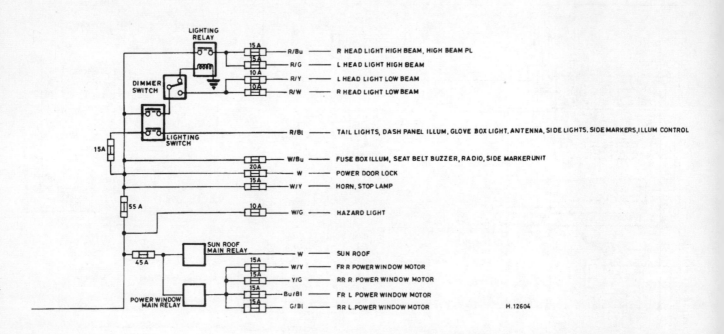

Typical interior lighting wiring diagram (Canadian models)

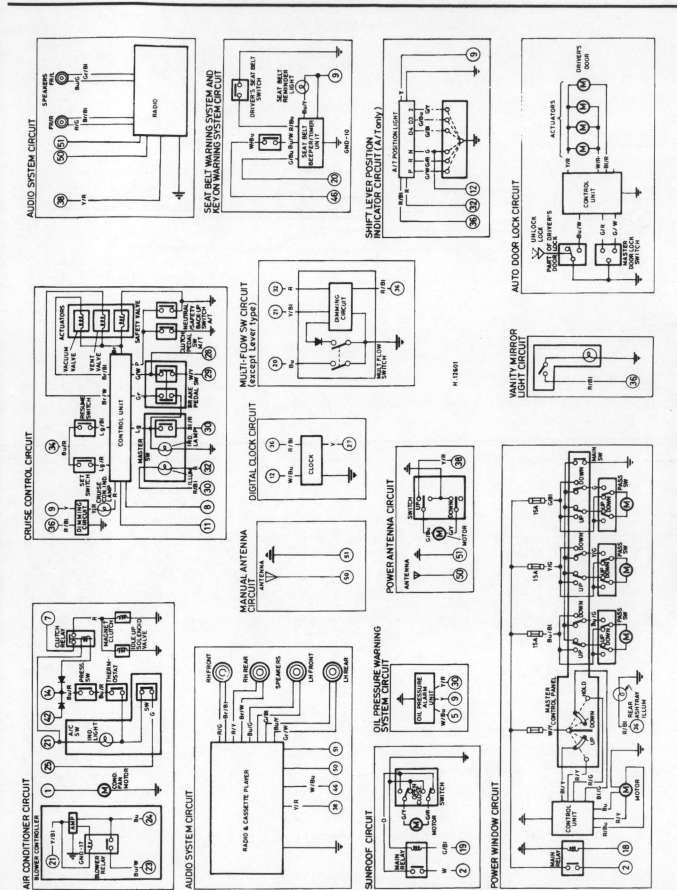

Typical sub-system wiring diagrams (Canadian models)

12

Notes

Index

A

B

Haynes Automotive Manuals

NOTE: New manuals are added to this list on a periodic basis. If you do not see a listing for your vehicle, consult your local Haynes dealer for the latest product information.

ACURA
*12020 Integra '86 thru '89 & **Legend** '86 thru '90

AMC
　　　 Jeep CJ - *see JEEP (50020)*
14020 Mid-size models, Concord, Hornet, Gremlin & Spirit '70 thru '83
14025 (Renault) Alliance & Encore '83 thru '87

AUDI
15020 4000 all models '80 thru '87
15025 5000 all models '77 thru '83
15026 5000 all models '84 thru '88

AUSTIN-HEALEY
　　　 Sprite - *see MG Midget (66015)*

BMW
*18020 3/5 Series not including diesel or all-wheel drive models '82 thru '92
*18021 3 Series except 325iX models '92 thru '97
18025 320i all 4 cyl models '75 thru '83
18035 528i & 530i all models '75 thru '80
18050 1500 thru 2002 except Turbo '59 thru '77

BUICK
　　　 Century (front wheel drive) - *see GM (829)*
*19020 **Buick, Oldsmobile & Pontiac Full-size (Front wheel drive)** all models '85 thru '98
　　　 Buick Electra, LeSabre and Park Avenue;
　　　 Oldsmobile Delta 88 Royale, Ninety Eight and Regency; **Pontiac** Bonneville
19025 **Buick Oldsmobile & Pontiac Full-size (Rear wheel drive)**
　　　 Buick Estate '70 thru '90, Electra '70 thru '84, LeSabre '70 thru '85, Limited '74 thru '79
　　　 Oldsmobile Custom Cruiser '70 thru '90, Delta 88 '70 thru '85, Ninety-eight '70 thru '84
　　　 Pontiac Bonneville '70 thru '81, Catalina '70 thru '81, Grandville '70 thru '75, Parisienne '83 thru '86
19030 **Mid-size Regal & Century** all rear-drive models with V6, V8 and Turbo '74 thru '87
　　　 Regal - *see GENERAL MOTORS (38010)*
　　　 Riviera - *see GENERAL MOTORS (38030)*
　　　 Roadmaster - *see CHEVROLET (24046)*
　　　 Skyhawk - *see GENERAL MOTORS (38015)*
　　　 Skylark '80 thru '85 - *see GM (38020)*
　　　 Skylark '86 on - *see GM (38025)*
　　　 Somerset - *see GENERAL MOTORS (38025)*

CADILLAC
*21030 **Cadillac Rear Wheel Drive** all gasoline models '70 thru '93
　　　 Cimarron - *see GENERAL MOTORS (38015)*
　　　 Eldorado - *see GENERAL MOTORS (38030)*
　　　 Seville '80 thru '85 - *see GM (38030)*

CHEVROLET
*24010 Astro & GMC Safari Mini-vans '85 thru '93
24015 Camaro V8 all models '70 thru '81
24016 Camaro all models '82 thru '92
　　　 Cavalier - *see GENERAL MOTORS (38015)*
　　　 Celebrity - *see GENERAL MOTORS (38005)*
24017 Camaro & Firebird '93 thru '97
24020 Chevelle, Malibu & El Camino '69 thru '87
24024 Chevette & Pontiac T1000 '76 thru '87
　　　 Citation - *see GENERAL MOTORS (38020)*
*24032 Corsica/Beretta all models '87 thru '96
24040 Corvette all V8 models '68 thru '82
*24041 Corvette all models '84 thru '96
10305 Chevrolet Engine Overhaul Manual
24045 Full-size Sedans Caprice, Impala, Biscayne, Bel Air & Wagons '69 thru '90
24046 Impala SS & Caprice and Buick Roadmaster '91 thru '96
　　　 Lumina - *see GENERAL MOTORS (38010)*

24048 Lumina & Monte Carlo '95 thru '98
　　　 Lumina APV - *see GM (38035)*
24050 Luv Pick-up all 2WD & 4WD '72 thru '82
*24055 Monte Carlo all models '70 thru '88
　　　 Monte Carlo '95 thru '98 - *see LUMINA (24048)*
24059 Nova all V8 models '69 thru '79
*24060 Nova and Geo Prizm '85 thru '92
24064 Pick-ups '67 thru '87 - Chevrolet & GMC, all V8 & in-line 6 cyl, 2WD & 4WD '67 thru '87; Suburbans, Blazers & Jimmys '67 thru '91
*24065 Pick-ups '88 thru '98 - Chevrolet & GMC, all full-size pick-ups, '88 thru '98; Blazer & Jimmy '92 thru '94; Suburban '92 thru '98; Tahoe & Yukon '98
24070 S-10 & S-15 Pick-ups '82 thru '93, Blazer & Jimmy '83 thru '94,
*24071 S-10 & S-15 Pick-ups '94 thru '96 Blazer & Jimmy '95 thru '96
*24075 Sprint & Geo Metro '85 thru '94
*24080 Vans - Chevrolet & GMC, V8 & in-line 6 cylinder models '68 thru '96

CHRYSLER
25015 **Chrysler Cirrus, Dodge Stratus, Plymouth Breeze** '95 thru '98
25025 **Chrysler Concorde, New Yorker & LHS, Dodge Intrepid, Eagle Vision,** '93 thru '97
10310 **Chrysler Engine Overhaul Manual**
*25020 Full-size Front-Wheel Drive '88 thru '93
　　　 K-Cars - *see DODGE Aries (30008)*
　　　 Laser - *see DODGE Daytona (30030)*
*25030 **Chrysler & Plymouth Mid-size** front wheel drive '82 thru '95
　　　 Rear-wheel Drive - *see Dodge (30050)*

DATSUN
28005 200SX all models '80 thru '83
28007 B-210 all models '73 thru '78
28009 210 all models '79 thru '82
28012 240Z, 260Z & 280Z Coupe '70 thru '78
28014 280ZX Coupe & 2+2 '79 thru '83
　　　 300ZX - *see NISSAN (72010)*
28016 310 all models '78 thru '82
28018 510 & PL521 Pick-up '68 thru '73
28020 510 all models '78 thru '81
28022 620 Series Pick-up all models '73 thru '79
　　　 720 Series Pick-up - *see NISSAN (72030)*
28025 810/Maxima all gasoline models, '77 thru '84

DODGE
　　　 400 & 600 - *see CHRYSLER (25030)*
*30008 Aries & Plymouth Reliant '81 thru '89
30010 Caravan & Plymouth Voyager Mini-Vans all models '84 thru '95
*30011 Caravan & Plymouth Voyager Mini-Vans all models '96 thru '98
30012 Challenger/Plymouth Saporro '78 thru '83
30016 Colt & Plymouth Champ (front wheel drive) all models '78 thru '87
*30020 Dakota Pick-ups all models '87 thru '96
30025 Dart, Demon, Plymouth Barracuda, Duster & Valiant 6 cyl models '67 thru '76
*30030 Daytona & Chrysler Laser '84 thru '89
　　　 Intrepid - *see CHRYSLER (25025)*
*30034 Neon all models '95 thru '97
*30035 Omni & Plymouth Horizon '78 thru '90
*30040 Pick-ups all full-size models '74 thru '93
*30041 Pick-ups all full-size models '94 thru '98
*30045 Ram 50/D50 Pick-ups & Raider and Plymouth Arrow Pick-ups '79 thru '93
30050 Dodge/Plymouth/Chrysler rear wheel drive '71 thru '89
*30055 Shadow & Plymouth Sundance '87 thru '94
*30060 Spirit & Plymouth Acclaim '89 thru '95
*30065 Vans - Dodge & Plymouth '71 thru '96

EAGLE
　　　 Talon - *see Mitsubishi Eclipse (68030)*
　　　 Vision - *see CHRYSLER (25025)*

FIAT
34010 124 Sport Coupe & Spider '68 thru '78
34025 X1/9 all models '74 thru '80

FORD
10355 **Ford Automatic Transmission Overhaul**
*36004 Aerostar Mini-vans all models '86 thru '96
*36006 Contour & Mercury Mystique '95 thru '98
36008 Courier Pick-up all models '72 thru '82
36012 Crown Victoria & Mercury Grand Marquis '88 thru '96
10320 Ford Engine Overhaul Manual
36016 Escort/Mercury Lynx all models '81 thru '90
*36020 Escort/Mercury Tracer '91 thru '96
*36024 Explorer & Mazda Navajo '91 thru '95
36028 Fairmont & Mercury Zephyr '78 thru '83
36030 Festiva & Aspire '88 thru '97
36032 Fiesta all models '77 thru '80
36036 Ford & Mercury Full-size, Ford LTD & Mercury Marquis ('75 thru '82); Ford Custom 500,Country Squire, Crown Victoria & Mercury Colony Park ('75 thru '87); Ford LTD Crown Victoria & Mercury Gran Marquis ('83 thru '87)
36040 Granada & Mercury Monarch '75 thru '80
36044 Ford & Mercury Mid-size, Ford Thunderbird & Mercury Cougar ('75 thru '82); Ford LTD & Mercury Marquis ('83 thru '86); Ford Torino,Gran Torino, Elite, Ranchero pick-up, LTD II, Mercury Montego, Comet, XR-7 & Lincoln Versailles ('75 thru '86)
36048 Mustang V8 all models '64-1/2 thru '73
36049 Mustang II 4 cyl, V6 & V8 models '74 thru '78
36050 Mustang & Mercury Capri all models Mustang, '79 thru '93; Capri, '79 thru '86
*36051 Mustang all models '94 thru '97
36054 Pick-ups & Bronco '73 thru '79
36058 Pick-ups & Bronco '80 thru '96
36059 Pick-ups, Expedition & Mercury Navigator '97 thru '98
36062 Pinto & Mercury Bobcat '75 thru '80
36066 Probe all models '89 thru '92
36070 Ranger/Bronco II gasoline models '83 thru '92
*36071 Ranger '93 thru '97 & Mazda Pick-ups '94 thru '97
36074 Taurus & Mercury Sable '86 thru '95
*36075 Taurus & Mercury Sable '96 thru '98
*36078 Tempo & Mercury Topaz '84 thru '94
36082 Thunderbird/Mercury Cougar '83 thru '88
*36086 Thunderbird/Mercury Cougar '89 and '97
36090 Vans all V8 Econoline models '69 thru '91
*36094 Vans full size '92-'95
*36097 Windstar Mini-van '95-'98

GENERAL MOTORS
*10360 **GM Automatic Transmission Overhaul**
*38005 **Buick Century, Chevrolet Celebrity, Oldsmobile Cutlass Ciera & Pontiac 6000** all models '82 thru '96
*38010 **Buick Regal, Chevrolet Lumina, Oldsmobile Cutlass Supreme & Pontiac Grand Prix** front-wheel drive models '88 thru '95
*38015 **Buick Skyhawk, Cadillac Cimarron, Chevrolet Cavalier, Oldsmobile Firenza & Pontiac J-2000 & Sunbird** '82 thru '94
*38016 **Chevrolet Cavalier & Pontiac Sunfire** '95 thru '98
38020 **Buick Skylark, Chevrolet Citation, Olds Omega, Pontiac Phoenix** '80 thru '85
38025 **Buick Skylark & Somerset, Oldsmobile Achieva & Calais and Pontiac Grand Am** all models '85 thru '95
38030 **Cadillac Eldorado** '71 thru '85, **Seville** '80 thru '85, **Oldsmobile Toronado** '71 thru '85 & **Buick Riviera** '79 thru '85
*38035 **Chevrolet Lumina APV, Olds Silhouette & Pontiac Trans Sport** all models '90 thru '95
　　　 General Motors Full-size Rear-wheel Drive - *see BUICK (19025)*

(Continued on other side)

---

* Listings shown with an asterisk (*) indicate model coverage as of this printing. These titles will be periodically updated to include later model years - consult your Haynes dealer for more information.

Haynes North America, Inc., 861 Lawrence Drive, Newbury Park, CA 91320-1514 • (805) 498-6703

Haynes Automotive Manuals (continued)

NOTE: New manuals are added to this list on a periodic basis. If you do not see a listing for your vehicle, consult your local Haynes dealer for the latest product information.

GEO

	Metro - see CHEVROLET Sprint (24075)
	Prizm - '85 thru '92 see CHEVY (24060), '93 thru '96 see TOYOTA Corolla (92036)
*40030	Storm all models '90 thru '93
	Tracker - see SUZUKI Samurai (90010)

GMC

	Safari - see CHEVROLET ASTRO (24010)
	Vans & Pick-ups - see CHEVROLET

HONDA

42010	Accord CVCC all models '76 thru '83
42011	Accord all models '84 thru '89
42012	Accord all models '90 thru '93
42013	Accord all models '94 thru '95
42020	Civic 1200 all models '73 thru '79
42021	Civic 1300 & 1500 CVCC '80 thru '83
42022	Civic 1500 CVCC all models '75 thru '79
42023	Civic all models '84 thru '91
*42024	Civic & del Sol '92 thru '95
*42040	Prelude CVCC all models '79 thru '89

HYUNDAI

*43015	Excel all models '86 thru '94

ISUZU

	Hombre - see CHEVROLET S-10 (24071)
*47017	Rodeo '91 thru '97; Amigo '89 thru '94; Honda Passport '95 thru '97
*47020	Trooper & Pick-up, all gasoline models Pick-up, '81 thru '93; Trooper, '84 thru '91

JAGUAR

*49010	XJ6 all 6 cyl models '68 thru '86
*49011	XJ6 all models '88 thru '94
*49015	XJ12 & XJS all 12 cyl models '72 thru '85

JEEP

*50010	Cherokee, Comanche & Wagoneer Limited all models '84 thru '96
50020	CJ all models '49 thru '86
*50025	Grand Cherokee all models '93 thru '98
50029	Grand Wagoneer & Pick-up '72 thru '91 Grand Wagoneer '84 thru '91, Cherokee & Wagoneer '72 thru '83, Pick-up '72 thru '88
*50030	Wrangler all models '87 thru '95

LINCOLN

	Navigator - see FORD Pick-up (36059)
59010	Rear Wheel Drive all models '70 thru '96

MAZDA

61010	GLC Hatchback (rear wheel drive) '77 thru '83
61011	GLC (front wheel drive) '81 thru '85
*61015	323 & Protegé '90 thru '97
*61016	MX-5 Miata '90 thru '97
*61020	MPV all models '89 thru '94
	Navajo - see Ford Explorer (36024)
61030	Pick-ups '72 thru '93
	Pick-ups '94 thru '96 - see Ford Ranger (36071)
*61035	RX-7 all models '79 thru '85
*61036	RX-7 all models '86 thru '91
61040	626 (rear wheel drive) all models '79 thru '82
*61041	626/MX-6 (front wheel drive) '83 thru '91

MERCEDES-BENZ

63012	123 Series Diesel '76 thru '85
*63015	190 Series four-cyl gas models, '84 thru '88
63020	230/250/280 6 cyl sohc models '68 thru '72
63025	280 123 Series gasoline models '77 thru '81
63030	350 & 450 all models '71 thru '80

MERCURY

	See FORD Listing.

MG

66010	MGB Roadster & GT Coupe '62 thru '80
66015	MG Midget, Austin Healey Sprite '58 thru '80

MITSUBISHI

*68020	Cordia, Tredia, Galant, Precis & Mirage '83 thru '93
*68030	Eclipse, Eagle Talon & Ply. Laser '90 thru '94
*68040	Pick-up '83 thru '96 & Montero '83 thru '93

NISSAN

72010	300ZX all models including Turbo '84 thru '89
*72015	Altima all models '93 thru '97
*72020	Maxima all models '85 thru '91
72030	Pick-ups '80 thru '96 Pathfinder '87 thru '95
72040	Pulsar all models '83 thru '86
*72050	Sentra all models '82 thru '94
*72051	Sentra & 200SX all models '95 thru '98
*72060	Stanza all models '82 thru '90

OLDSMOBILE

*73015	Cutlass V6 & V8 gas models '74 thru '88
	For other OLDSMOBILE titles, see BUICK, CHEVROLET or GENERAL MOTORS listing.

PLYMOUTH

	For PLYMOUTH titles, see DODGE listing.

PONTIAC

79008	Fiero all models '84 thru '88
79018	Firebird V8 models except Turbo '70 thru '81
79019	Firebird all models '82 thru '92
	For other PONTIAC titles, see BUICK, CHEVROLET or GENERAL MOTORS listing.

PORSCHE

*80020	911 except Turbo & Carrera 4 '65 thru '89
80025	914 all 4 cyl models '69 thru '76
80030	924 all models including Turbo '76 thru '82
*80035	944 all models including Turbo '83 thru '89

RENAULT

	Alliance & Encore - see AMC (14020)

SAAB

*84010	900 all models including Turbo '79 thru '88

SATURN

87010	Saturn all models '91 thru '96

SUBARU

89002	1100, 1300, 1400 & 1600 '71 thru '79
*89003	1600 & 1800 2WD & 4WD '80 thru '94

SUZUKI

*90010	Samurai/Sidekick & Geo Tracker '86 thru '96

TOYOTA

92005	Camry all models '83 thru '91
92006	Camry all models '92 thru '96
92015	Celica Rear Wheel Drive '71 thru '85
*92020	Celica Front Wheel Drive '86 thru '93
92025	Celica Supra all models '79 thru '92
92030	Corolla all models '75 thru '79
92032	Corolla all rear wheel drive models '80 thru '87
92035	Corolla all front wheel drive models '84 thru '92
*92036	Corolla & Geo Prizm '93 thru '97
92040	Corolla Tercel all models '80 thru '82
92045	Corona all models '74 thru '82
92050	Cressida all models '78 thru '82
92055	Land Cruiser FJ40, 43, 45, 55 '68 thru '82
92056	Land Cruiser FJ60, 62, 80, FZJ80 '80 thru '96
*92065	MR2 all models '85 thru '87
92070	Pick-up all models '69 thru '78
*92075	Pick-up all models '79 thru '95
*92076	Tacoma '95 thru '98, 4Runner '96 thru '98, & T100 '93 thru '98
*92080	Previa all models '91 thru '95
92085	Tercel all models '87 thru '94

TRIUMPH

94007	Spitfire all models '62 thru '81
94010	TR7 all models '75 thru '81

VW

96008	Beetle & Karmann Ghia '54 thru '79
96012	Dasher all gasoline models '74 thru '81
*96016	Rabbit, Jetta, Scirocco, & Pick-up gas models '74 thru '91 & Convertible '80 thru '92
96017	Golf & Jetta all models '93 thru '97
96020	Rabbit, Jetta & Pick-up diesel '77 thru '84
96030	Transporter 1600 all models '68 thru '79
96035	Transporter 1700, 1800 & 2000 '72 thru '79
96040	Type 3 1500 & 1600 all models '63 thru '73
96045	Vanagon all air-cooled models '80 thru '83

VOLVO

97010	120, 130 Series & 1800 Sports '61 thru '73
97015	140 Series all models '66 thru '74
*97020	240 Series all models '76 thru '93
97025	260 Series all models '75 thru '82
*97040	740 & 760 Series all models '82 thru '88

TECHBOOK MANUALS

10205	Automotive Computer Codes
10210	Automotive Emissions Control Manual
10215	Fuel Injection Manual, 1978 thru 1985
10220	Fuel Injection Manual, 1986 thru 1996
10225	Holley Carburetor Manual
10230	Rochester Carburetor Manual
10240	Weber/Zenith/Stromberg/SU Carburetors
10305	Chevrolet Engine Overhaul Manual
10310	Chrysler Engine Overhaul Manual
10320	Ford Engine Overhaul Manual
10330	GM and Ford Diesel Engine Repair Manual
10340	Small Engine Repair Manual
10345	Suspension, Steering & Driveline Manual
10355	Ford Automatic Transmission Overhaul
10360	GM Automatic Transmission Overhaul
10405	Automotive Body Repair & Painting
10410	Automotive Brake Manual
10415	Automotive Detailing Manual
10420	Automotive Eelectrical Manual
10425	Automotive Heating & Air Conditioning
10430	Automotive Reference Manual & Dictionary
10435	Automotive Tools Manual
10440	Used Car Buying Guide
10445	Welding Manual
10450	ATV Basics

SPANISH MANUALS

98903	Reparación de Carrocería & Pintura
98905	Códigos Automotrices de la Computadora
98910	Frenos Automotriz
98915	Inyección de Combustible 1986 al 1994
99040	Chevrolet & GMC Camionetas '67 al '87 Incluye Suburban, Blazer & Jimmy '67 al '91
99041	Chevrolet & GMC Camionetas '88 al '95 Incluye Suburban '92 al '95, Blazer & Jimmy '92 al '94, Tahoe y Yukon '95
99042	Chevrolet & GMC Camionetas Cerradas '68 al '95
99055	Dodge Caravan & Plymouth Voyager '84 al '95
99075	Ford Camionetas y Bronco '80 al '94
99077	Ford Camionetas Cerradas '69 al '91
99083	Ford Modelos de Tamaño Grande '75 al '87
99088	Ford Modelos de Tamaño Mediano '75 al '86
99091	Ford Taurus & Mercury Sable '86 al '95
99095	GM Modelos de Tamaño Grande '70 al '90
99100	GM Modelos de Tamaño Mediano '70 al '88
99110	Nissan Camionetas '80 al '96, Pathfinder '87 al '95
99118	Nissan Sentra '82 al '94
99125	Toyota Camionetas y 4Runner '79 al '95

* Listings shown with an asterisk (*) indicate model coverage as of this printing. These titles will be periodically updated to include later model years - consult your Haynes dealer for more information.

Over 100 Haynes motorcycle manuals also available

5-98

Haynes North America, Inc., 861 Lawrence Drive, Newbury Park, CA 91320-1514 • (805) 498-6703